P9-BJL-626

Longman
Dictionary of
Applied
Linguistics

Jack Richards
John Platt
Heidi Weber

Consultants
Professor C.N. Candlin
Professor John Oller Jr

Longman Dictionary of Applied Linguistics

Longman

Editorial
Adrian Stenton
Sue Lambert

Diagrams
Jerry Collins

Longman Group Limited
Longman House, Burnt Mill, Harlow,
Essex CM20 2JE, England
and associated companies throughout the world.

© Longman Group Limited 1985
All rights reserved; no part of this publication
may be reproduced, stored in a retrieval system,
or transmitted in any form or by any means, electronic,
mechanical, photocopying, recording, or otherwise,
without the prior written permission of the Publishers.

First published 1985
ISBN 0 582 55708 9

Set in Linotron 202 Times with Univers Bold

Printed in Great Britain by
Richard Clay (The Chaucer Press) Ltd,
Bungay, Suffolk

Pronunciation table

CONSONANTS		VOWELS	
SYMBOL	KEY WORD	SYMBOL	KEY WORD
b	back	æ	bad
d	day	ɑ	farm *American English*
ð	then	ɑː	calm
dʒ	jump	ɒ	pot *British English*
f	few	aɪ	bite
g	gay	aʊ	now
h	hot	aɪə	tire
j	yet	aʊə	tower
k	key	ɔ	form *American English*
l	led	ɔː	caught
m	sum	ɔɪ	boy
n	sun	ɔɪə	employer
ŋ	sung	e	bed
p	pen	eə	there
r	red	eɪ	make
s	soon	eɪə	player
ʃ	fishing	ə	about
t	tea	əʊ	note
tʃ	cheer	əʊə	lower
θ	thing	ɜ	bird *American English*
v	view	ɜː	bird
w	wet	i	pretty
z	zero	iː	sheep
ʒ	pleasure	ɪ	ship
		ɪə	here
		o	port *American English*
		uː	boot
		ʊ	put
		ʊə	poor
		ʌ	cut

‖   separates British and American pronunciations: British on the left, American on the right

/ˈ/   shows main stress

/ˌ/   shows secondary stress

/ʳ/   at the end of a word means that /r/ is usually pronounced in American English and is pronounced in British English when the next word begins with a vowel sound

/ə̍/   means that some speakers use /ɪ/ and others use /ə/

/i/   means many American speakers use /iː/ but many British speakers use /ɪ/

/ə/   means that /ə/ may or may not be used

iii

Guide to the dictionary

pronunciation (see table on p iii)

related word

aphasia /əˈfeɪʒə/ *n* **aphasic** /əˈfeɪzɪk/ *adj* — part of speech

less common alternative

also **dysphasia** *n*

loss of the ability to use and understand language, usually caused by damage to the brain. The loss may be total or partial, and may affect spoken and/or written language ability.

There are different types of aphasia: **agraphia** is difficulty in writing; **alexia** is difficulty in reading; **anomia** is difficulty in using proper nouns; and **agrammatism** is difficulty in using grammatical words like prepositions, articles, etc.

Aphasia can be studied in order to discover how the brain processes language.

terms explained within entry

see also BRAIN, NEUROLINGUISTICS

other related entries it may be useful to look up

[*Further reading*: Dalton & Hardcastle 1977]

abbreviation for term

contrastive analysis /ˌkən'traːstɪv əˈnæləsəs ‖ -'træ-/ *n*

also **CA**

pronunciation, with American form after the ‖ (see table on p iii)

the comparison of the linguistic systems of two languages, for example the sound system or the grammatical system. Contrastive analysis was developed and practised in the 1950s and 1960s, as an application of STRUCTURAL LINGUISTICS to language teaching, and is based on the following assumptions:

term explained at its own alphabetical entry

(a) the main difficulties in learning a new language are caused by interference from the first language (see LANGUAGE TRANSFER).

(b) these difficulties can be predicted by contrastive analysis.

(c) teaching materials can make use of contrastive analysis to reduce the effects of interference.

Contrastive analysis was more successful in PHONOLOGY than in other areas of language, and declined in the 1970s as interference was replaced by other explanations of learning difficulties (see ERROR ANALYSIS, INTERLANGUAGE). In recent years contrastive analysis has been applied to other areas of language, for example the discourse systems (see DISCOURSE ANALYSIS). This is called **contrastive discourse analysis**.

see also COMPARATIVE LINGUISTICS

[*Further reading*: Lado 1957; James 1980]

books where further information/ discussion will be found (see p 315)

entry for a less common alternative

dysphasia /dɪsˈfeɪʒə/ *n*
another term for APHASIA

entry for an abbreviation

CA /ˌsiː ˈeɪ/ *n*
an abbreviation for CONTRASTIVE ANALYSIS

entry for a word explained elsewhere

agrammatism /əˈɡræmətɪzəm/ *n*
see under APHASIA

Introduction

Who is this dictionary for?

This dictionary is intended for:

- students taking undergraduate or graduate courses in applied linguistics, language teaching and language arts, particularly those planning to take up a career in the teaching of English as a Second or Foreign Language or in foreign language teaching
- language teachers doing in-service or pre-service courses, such as the RSA Certificate for Overseas Teachers of English, Diplomas in Applied Linguistics, TESL/TEFL and similar programmes
- students doing introductory courses in linguistics and related areas
- teachers and others interested in the practical applications of language study

Why this dictionary?

In teaching courses in applied linguistics in many parts of the world over the last 15 years, we have often had to sympathize with the bewilderment students experience when first encountering the literature in applied linguistics. It is, as one student put it, a terminological jungle. While this is of course no more true of applied linguistics than other disciplines, the rapid expansion of applied linguistics in recent years has led to the development of a field which is becoming increasingly rigorous and sophisticated in both its theory and its methodological applications and developments. One consequence of this expansion in research interests and practical developments has been a widespread introduction of new terms and concepts, many of which were quite unknown ten years ago.

The scope of the dictionary

The dictionary was written for those with little or no background in linguistics, whose mother tongue is English or who use English as a second or foreign language. We have given special attention to English, and the majority of the examples in the dictionary are from English. However, users who are interested in other languages should find the dictionary useful. Although the dictionary is not intended primarily for those who already have a specialized training in applied linguistics, they may find it useful as a reference book in areas with which they are less familiar. It should also be useful to general readers who need further information about the terms which occur in the field of applied linguistics.

A word of explanation is in order as to what we mean by *applied linguistics* in this dictionary. For the purposes of this book, "applied linguistics" refers to "the applied linguistics of language teaching", rather than to the broader applications of language study in such areas as medicine, law, stylistics, language planning or dictionary compilation. The term "applied linguistics" has at least three main uses today. It is used (1) to refer to the study of language teaching and learning; (2) to refer to the applications of language study in any area of practical concern; (3) to refer to the applications of the findings of theoretical linguistics. However, in general usage the term refers to the study of language teaching and learning. Many graduate and undergraduate training programmes in language teaching lead to certificates and degrees in "applied linguistics" and are taught in departments having that name. This is the sense in which we use the term and in which this is therefore a dictionary of applied linguistics.

The content and subject matter of the applied linguistics of language teaching and learning generally include the following areas of study, which are those covered in this dictionary:

- introductory linguistics, including phonology, phonetics, syntax, morphology and semantics
- English grammar (or the grammar of the language the student is specializing in)
- discourse analysis
- sociolinguistics, including the sociology of language and communicative competence
- psycholinguistics, including first and second language acquisition, contrastive analysis, error analysis and learning theories
- the teaching of listening, speaking, reading and writing
- the methodology of language teaching, including methods, course and syllabus design
- language testing and basic statistics

This dictionary therefore covers the terms students would most frequently encounter in introductory courses in these areas.

What the dictionary contains

This dictionary contains more than 1500 entries which define, in as simple and precise a way as possible, the most frequently occurring terms found in the eight areas listed above. Each term was selected on the basis of its importance within an area and reflects the fact that the term has a particular meaning when used within that area, a meaning unlikely to be listed in other dictionaries. Only words which are in common usage in applied linguistics have been included. Words used only by an individual scholar and which have not passed into more general usage have not been included.

In order to draw up the list of terms defined in the dictionary, an initial headword list was compiled, based on an analysis of the terms used in a wide sample of introductory textbooks in each area and through surveying the major journals in the field. This provisional headword list was then widely circulated to specialists in the field to provide further suggestions. Although the experts consulted were not always in agreement as to what constitutes the core lexicon of applied linguistics, we have tried to ensure that the dictionary contains a comprehensive sample of the terms students are most likely to encounter.

During the four years the dictionary was in preparation, definitions were written in consultation with experts in each field. Our aim has been to produce clear and simple definitions which communicate the basic and essential meanings of a term in non-technical language. Definitions are self-contained as far as possible, but cross references show links to other terms and concepts, and references provide information where a fuller discussion of a term or concept can be found.

Acknowledgements

The dictionary could not have been prepared without the support and encouragement of colleagues in many institutions around the world. We wish to thank:

■ Colleagues of the following institutions, in which the provisional headword lists were circulated for suggestions and additions:

Center for Applied Linguistics, Washington DC, USA

Chinese University, Hong Kong

Guangzhou Institute of Foreign Languages, China

Harvard University, Boston, USA

Hebrew University, Jerusalem, Israel

Monash University, Melbourne, Australia

Ontario Institute for Studies in Education, Toronto, Canada

Regional Language Centre, Singapore

University of California at Los Angeles, USA

University of Edinburgh, Scotland

University of Hawaii, USA

University of Hong Kong

University of Illinois at Urbana Champaign, USA

University of London, England

Victoria University of Wellington, New Zealand

■ The following, for reviewing the headword list and suggesting terms for inclusion or exclusion:

Brian Blomfield

H. Douglas Brown

Christopher Brumfit

Michael Clyne

Andrew Cohen

S. Pit Corder

Geoffrey Crewes

James Garton

Francisco Gomes de Matos

Gui Shih-chun

Frances Hinefotis

Nobuyuki Hino

Janet Holmes

Rodcrick Jacobs

Dora E. Johnson

Francis Johnson

R. Keith Johnson

Graeme Kennedy

Richard Noss

Michael Palmer

Terry Quinn

Wilga Rivers

Ted Rodgers

Gloria Sampson

John Schumann

Tom Scovel

H. H. Stern

Peter Strevens

Henry Widdowson

■ The following, for comments on entries:

Keith Allan

Janet Dangar

Alan Davies

Richard Day

Janet Gundel

Michael Halliday

Roderick Jacobs

Catherine Johns-Lewis

Elizabeth Kimmel

Paul La Forge

Charles Mason

Ted Plaister

Joan Rubin

Richard Schmidt

■ The following, for clerical, typing and research assistance:

Daniela Antas

Nobuyuki Hino

Ursula Kutschbach

Sunny Lam

David Li

■ Special thanks are due to:

Lyle Bachman, University of Illinois at Urbana Champaign, for detailed advice and suggestions on terms and definitions in the areas of testing and statistics

Danny Steinberg, Rikkyo University, Tokyo and Robert Ilson, Associate Director of the Survey of English Usage for detailed comments and suggestions on entries

John Oller, Jr and Christopher Candlin, who have been associated with the dictionary in an advisory capacity since its inception and who have given valuable advice on all aspects of the project

Della Summers and Adrian Stenton of the Longman ELT Dictionary and Reference Division, who struggled to teach us the principles of definition writing

Invitation to readers

With a developing discipline such as applied linguistics, a project such as this is never complete. We hope to revise and expand the range of terms covered based on feedback from readers. We invite you to write to us with suggestions for additional entries or improvements. Communications will be acknowledged and where possible made use of for the improvement of the next edition of the dictionary. Please send your suggestions to Jack Richards.

Jack C. Richards,
Dept of English as a Second Language,
University of Hawaii,
Honolulu, Hawaii 96822, USA

John Platt and Heidi Weber,
Dept of Linguistics,
Monash University,
Clayton, Victoria 3168,
Australia

A

abstract noun /'æbstrækt 'naʊn/ *n*
see under CONCRETE NOUN

accent[1] /'æksənt ‖ 'æksent/ *n*
greater emphasis on a syllable so that it stands out from the other syllables in a word.
For example, in English the noun *'import* has the accent on the first syllable *im-* while the verb *im'port* has the accent on the second syllable *-port*:
> *This car is a foreign import.*
> *We import all our coffee.*
see also PROMINENCE, STRESS
[*Further reading*: Gimson 1980; Wells 1982]

accent[2] *n*
In the written form of some languages, particularly in French, a mark which is placed over a vowel. An accent may show:
(a) a difference in pronunciation (see DIACRITIC). .
  For example, in the French word *prés* "meadows", the **acute accent** on the *e* indicates a different vowel sound from that in *près* "near" with a **grave accent**.
(b) a difference in meaning without any change in pronunciation, eg French *ou* "or" and *où* "where".

accent[3] *n*
a particular way of speaking which tells the listener something about the speaker's background.
A person's pronunciation may show:
(a) the region or country they come from, eg
  a northern accent
  an American accent
(b) what social class they belong to, eg
  a lower middle class accent
(c) whether or not the speaker is a native speaker of the language, eg *She speaks English with an accent/with a German accent.*
see also DIALECT, SOCIOLECT
[*Further reading*: Rivers 1981; Trudgill 1975]

acceptable alternative method /ək'septəbəl ɔːl'tɜːnətɪv 'meθəd ‖ ɔl'tɜr-, æl-/ *n*
see under CLOZE PROCEDURE

acceptable word method /ək'septəbəl 'wɜːd 'meθəd ‖ -ɜr-/ *n*
see under CLOZE PROCEDURE

accommodation /ə,kɒmə'deɪʃən ‖ ə,kɑ-/ *n*
when a person changes their way of speaking to make it sound more

like or less like the speech of the person they are talking to.
For example, a teacher may use simpler words and sentence
structures when he/she is talking to a class of young children. This is
called **convergence**.

A person may exaggerate their rural accent because they are
annoyed by the attitude of someone from the city. This is called
divergence.

see also ACCENT³

[*Further reading*: Giles & Powesland 1975]

acculturation /əˌkʌltʃəˈreɪʃən/ *n*

a process in which changes in the language, culture, and system of
values of a group happen through interaction with another group
with a different language, culture, and system of values.

For example, in second language learning, acculturation may affect
how well one group (eg a group of immigrants in a country) learn
the language of another (eg the dominant group).

see also ASSIMILATION², SOCIAL DISTANCE

[*Further reading*: Schumann 1978]

accuracy /ˈækjərəsi/ *n*

see under FLUENCY

accusative case /əˈkjuːzətɪv ˌkeɪs/ *n*

the form of a noun or noun phrase which usually shows that the
noun or noun phrase functions as the direct object of the verb in a
sentence.

see also CASE¹

[*Further reading*: Lyons 1968]

achievement test /əˈtʃiːvmənt ˌtest/ *n*

a test which measures how much of a language someone has learned
with reference to a particular course of study or programme of
instruction.

The difference between this and a more general type of test called a
PROFICIENCY TEST is that the latter is not linked to any particular
course of instruction.

For example, an achievement test might be a listening
comprehension test based on a particular set of dialogues in a
textbook. The test helps the teacher to judge the success of his or
her teaching and to identify the weaknesses of his or her students.
A proficiency test might use similar test items but would not be
linked to any particular textbook or language SYLLABUS.

Language achievement tests and language proficiency tests differ
mainly in the way they are prepared and interpreted.

[*Further reading*: Valette 1977]

acoustic filtering /əˈkuːstɪk ˈfɪltərɪŋ/ *n*

(in listening comprehension) When someone is able to hear and identify only some of the sounds that are being spoken, this is called acoustic filtering.

For example, when someone is learning a foreign language, the speech sounds of their native language may act as a filter, making it difficult for them to hear and identify new or unfamiliar sounds in the foreign language.

[*Further reading*: Rivers 1972]

acoustic phonetics /ə'kuːstɪk fə'netɪks/ *n*
see under PHONETICS

acquisition /ˌækwə'zɪʃən/ *n*
The process by which a person learns a language is sometimes called acquisition instead of learning, because some linguists believe that the development of a first language in a child is a special process.
For example, Chomsky believes that:
(a) children are born with special language learning abilities
(b) they do not have to be taught language or corrected for their mistakes
(c) they learn language by being exposed to it
(d) linguistic rules develop unconsciously
Children are said to **acquire** the rules of their mother tongue by being exposed to examples of the language, and by using the language for communication.
Language acquisition is studied by linguists, psychologists, and applied linguists to discover the nature of language and of the language learning process.
see also LANGUAGE ACQUISITION DEVICE, ORDER OF ACQUISITION, MONITOR HYPOTHESIS
[*Further reading*: Dale 1975; Elliot 1981]

acquisition order /ˌækwə'zɪʃən 'ɔːdər ‖ 'ɔr-/ *n*
another term for ORDER OF ACQUISITION

acrolect /'ækrəlekt/ *n* **acrolectal** /ækrə'lektəl/ *adj*
see under POST-CREOLE CONTINUUM

active/passive language knowledge /'æktɪv 'pæsɪv 'læŋgwɪdʒ 'nɒlɪdʒ ‖ 'nɑ-/ *n*
also **productive/receptive language knowledge**
The ability of a person to actively produce their own speech and writing is called their **active language knowledge**. This is compared to their ability to understand the speech and writing of other people, their **passive language knowledge**.
Native speakers of a language can understand many more words than they actively use. Some people have a **passive vocabulary** (ie words they understand) of up to 100,000 words, but an **active vocabulary** (ie words they use) of between 10,000 and 20,000 words.
In foreign language learning, an active vocabulary of about 3000 to

5000 words, and a passive vocabulary of about 5000 to 10,000 words is regarded as the intermediate to upper intermediate level of proficiency.
[*Further reading*: Watts 1944; Mackey 1965]

active vocabulary /ˈæktɪv vəˈkæbjʊləri, vəʊ- ‖ -bjələri/ *n*
see under ACTIVE/PASSIVE LANGUAGE KNOWLEDGE

active voice /ˈæktɪv ˈvɔɪs/ *n*
see under VOICE[1]

acute accent /əˈkjuːt ˈæksənt ‖ ˈæksent/ *n*
the accent ´, eg on French *prés* "meadows".
see also under ACCENT[2]

adaptation /ˌædəpˈteɪʃən/ *n*
When a teacher makes changes to published texts or materials to make them more suitable or appropriate for a particular group of learners or a particular teaching need, this is called adaptation.
[*Further reading*: Madsen & Bowen 1978]

additive bilingual education /ˌædətɪv baɪˈlɪŋgwəl ˌedʒʊˈkeɪʃən ‖ ˌedʒə-/ *n*
also **additive bilingualism** /ˈædətɪv baɪˈlɪŋgwəlɪzəm/
a form of BILINGUAL EDUCATION in which the language of instruction is not the mother tongue or home language of the children, and is not intended to replace it. In an additive bilingual education programme the first language is maintained and supported.
For example, the bilingual programmes in French for English-speaking Canadians are intended to give the children a second language, not to replace English with French.
When the language of instruction is likely to replace the children's first language, this is called **subtractive bilingualism**.
see also IMMERSION PROGRAMME
[*Further reading*: Swain 1978]

address form /əˈdres ˈfɔːm ‖ fɔrm/ *n*
also **form of address**
the word or words used to address somebody, in speech or writing. The way in which people address one another usually depends on their age, sex, social class, and personal relationship.
For example, many languages have different second person pronoun forms which are used according to whether the speaker wants to address someone politely or more informally, eg in German *Sie – du*, in French *vous – tu*, and in Spanish *ustéd – tu*.
If a language has only one second person pronoun form, eg English *you*, other address forms are used to show formality or informality, eg *sir, Mr Brown, Brown, Billy*.
The address forms of a language are arranged into a complex **address system** with its own rules which need to be learned if a person wants to communicate effectively.

see also COMMUNICATIVE COMPETENCE

[*Further reading*: Brown & Gilman 1972; Ervin-Tripp 1972]

address system /əˈdres ˈsɪstəm/ *n*

see under ADDRESS FORM

adjacency pair /əˈdʒeɪsənsi ˌpeər/ *n*

a sequence of two related utterances by two different speakers. The second utterance is always a response to the first.

In the following example, speaker A makes a complaint, and speaker B replies with a denial:

A: *You left the light on.*
B: *It wasn't me!*

The sequence of Complaint – Denial is an adjacency pair. Other examples of adjacency pairs are Greeting – Greeting, Question – Answer, Invitation – Acceptance/Refusal, Offer – Decline, Complaint – Apology.

Adjacency pairs are part of the structure of conversation and are studied in CONVERSATIONAL ANALYSIS.

[*Further reading*: Coulthard 1985]

adjectival noun /ˌædʒɪkˈtaɪvəl ˈnaʊn/ *n*

an adjective used as a noun, eg *the poor, the rich, the sick, the old.*

see also SUBSTANTIVE

adjective /ˈædʒɪktɪv/ *n*

a word that describes the thing, quality, state, or action which a noun refers to. For example *black* in *a black hat* is an adjective.

In English, adjectives usually have the following properties:

(a) they can be used before a noun, eg *a heavy bag*
(b) they can be used after *be, become, seem*, etc as complements, eg *the bag is heavy*
(c) they can be used after a noun as a complement, eg *these books make the bag heavy*
(d) they can be modified by an adverb, eg *a very heavy bag*
(e) they can be used in a comparative or superlative form, eg *the bag seems heavier now*

see also COMPLEMENT, COMPARATIVE, ATTRIBUTIVE ADJECTIVE

[*Further reading*: Quirk et al 1985]

adjective complement /ˈædʒɪktɪv ˈkɒmpləmənt ‖ ˈkɑm-/ *n*

see under COMPLEMENT

adjunct /ˈædʒʌŋkt/ *n*

ADVERBIALS may be classified as adjuncts, conjuncts, or disjuncts.

An **adjunct** is part of the basic structure of the clause or sentence in which it occurs, and modifies the verb. Adverbs of time, place, frequency, degree, and manner, are examples of adjuncts.

He died in England.
I have almost finished.

Conjuncts are not part of the basic structure of a clause or sentence.

They show how what is said in the sentence containing the conjunct connects with what is said in another sentence or sentences.

Altogether, it was a happy week.

However the weather was not good.

Disjuncts (also called **sentential adverbs**) are adverbs which show the speaker's attitude to or evaluation of what is said in the rest of the sentence.

<u>Naturally</u>, I paid for my own meal.

I had to pay for my own meal, <u>unfortunately</u>.

see also ADVERB

[*Further reading*: Quirk et al 1985]

adnominal /əd'nɒmənl ‖ æd'nɑ-/ *n, adj*
a word or phrase which occurs next to a noun and which gives further information about it.

For example, an adnominal may be:

(a) an adjective,

eg *blue* in *the blue sea*

(b) another noun,

eg *jade* in *the jade statue*

(c) a phrase,

eg *at the corner* in *the shop at the corner*

An adnominal is a type of MODIFIER.

adverb /'ædvɜːb ‖ -ɜrb/ *n*
a word that describes or adds to the meaning of a verb, an adjective, another adverb, or a sentence, and which answers such questions as *how?*, *where?*, or *when?*. In English many adverbs have an *-ly* ending.

For example, **adverbs of manner** eg *carefully*, *slowly*, **adverbs of place** eg *here*, *there*, *locally*, and **adverbs of time** eg *now*, *hourly*, *yesterday*.

A phrase or clause which functions as an adverb is called an **adverb phrase/adverb clause**.

see also ADVERBIAL, ADVERB PARTICLE, ADVERBIAL CLAUSE, ADJUNCT

adverbial /əd'vɜːbɪəl ‖ -ɜr-/ *adj*
any word, phrase, or clause that functions like an ADVERB. An adverb is a single-word adverbial.

adverbial clause /əd'vɜːbɪəl 'klɔːz ‖ -ɜr-/ *n*
a clause which functions as an adverb.

For example:

<u>When I arrived</u> I went straight to my room. (adverbial clause of time)

<u>Wherever we looked</u> there was dust. (adverbial clause of place)

We painted the walls yellow <u>to brighten the room</u>. (adverbial clause of purpose)

see also ADVERB, PREPOSITION

[*Further reading*: Quirk et al 1985]

adverb particle /'ædvɜːb 'pɑːtɪkəl ‖ 'ædvɜrb 'pɑrtɪkəl/ *n*
also **prepositional adverb**
a word such as *in, on, back,* when it modifies a verb rather than a
noun. Words like *in, out, up, down, on,* may belong grammatically
with both nouns (eg *in the box, on the wall*) and verbs (eg *come in,
eat up, wake up, die away*). When they are linked with nouns they
are known as PREPOSITIONS and when they are linked with verbs they
are known as adverb particles. The combination of verb+adverb
particle is known as a PHRASAL VERB.
[*Further reading:* Close 1975]

affected object /ə'fektəd 'ɒbdʒɪkt ‖ 'ɑb-/ *n*
see under OBJECT OF RESULT

affective filtering /'æfektɪv 'fɪltərɪŋ/ *n*
When someone selects one variety of speech as a model for learning
the language, this is called affective filtering.
For example, learners will hear English spoken by many different
groups (eg parents, teachers, different social and ethnic groups) but
will often model their own speech on only one of these, such as the
speech of their friends of the same group (= their PEER GROUP).
[*Further reading:* Dulay, Burt, & Krashen 1982]

affective meaning /ə'fektɪv 'miːnɪŋ/ *n*
another term for CONNOTATION

affective variable /'æfektɪv 'veərɪəbəl/ *n*
see under COGNITIVE VARIABLE

affix /'æfɪks/ *n*
a letter or sound, or group of letters or sounds, (= a MORPHEME)
which is added to a word, and which changes the meaning or
function of the word.
Affixes are BOUND FORMS that can be added:
(a) to the beginning of a word (= a **prefix**), eg English *un-* which
    usually changes the meaning of a word to its opposite: *kind –
    unkind*
(b) to the end of a word (= a **suffix**), eg English *-ness* which usually
    changes an adjective into a noun: *kind – kindness*
(c) within a word (= an **infix**), eg Tagalog *-um-* which shows that a
    verb is in the past tense: *sulat* "to write" – *sumulat* "wrote"
see also COMBINING FORM
[*Further reading:* Lyons 1981]

affricate /'æfrɪkət/ *n* **affricated** /'æfrɪˌkeɪtəd/ *adj*
a speech sound (a CONSONANT) which is produced by stopping the
airstream from the lungs, and then slowly releasing it with friction.
The first part of an affricate is similar to a STOP, the second part is
similar to a FRICATIVE.
For example, in English the /tʃ/ in /tʃaɪld/ *child*, and the /dʒ/ in

agent

/dʒæm/ *jam* are affricates.

see also MANNER OF ARTICULATION, PLACE OF ARTICULATION
[*Further reading*: Gimson 1980]

agent /ˈeɪdʒənt/ *n*
(in some grammars) the noun or noun phrase which refers to the person or animal which performs the action of the verb.
For example, in the English sentences:
Anthea cut the grass.
The grass was cut by Anthea.
Anthea is the agent.
The term agent is sometimes used only for the noun or noun phrase which follows *by* in passive sentences, even if it does not refer to the performer of an action, eg *everyone* in *She was admired by everyone.*
see also SUBJECT, AGENTIVE CASE, AGENTIVE OBJECT
[*Further reading*: Brown & Miller 1980]

agentive case /ˈeɪdʒəntɪv ˌkeɪs/ *n*
In CASE GRAMMAR the noun or noun phrase that refers to the person or animal who performs or initiates the action of the verb is in the agentive case.
For example, in:
Tom pruned the roses.
Tom is in the agentive case.
But the subject of the verb is not necessarily always in the agentive case. In the sentence:
Tom loves roses.
Tom does not perform an action, but his attitude to roses is mentioned. *Tom* in this sentence is therefore not agentive but dative (see DATIVE CASE[2]).
see also CASE GRAMMAR
[*Further reading*: Fillmore 1968]

agentive object /ˈeɪdʒəntɪv ˈɒbdʒɪkt ‖ ˈɑb-/ *n*
the object of a verb which itself performs the action of the verb.
For example, in the sentence:
Fred galloped the horse.
Fred initiates the action, but it is *the horse* which actually gallops.
see also AGENT, AGENTIVE CASE
[*Further reading*: Lyons 1968]

agglutinating language /əˈɡluːtəneɪtɪŋ ˈlæŋɡwɪdʒ/ *n*
also **agglutinative language** /əˈɡluːtənətɪv ˈlæŋɡwɪdʒ ‖ -neɪtɪv/
a language in which various AFFIXes may be added to the stem of a word to add to its meaning or to show its grammatical function.
For example, in Swahili *wametulipa* "they have paid us" consists of:

| wa | me | tu | lipa |
| they + | perfective marker + | us + | pay |

Languages which are highly agglutinating include Finnish, Hungarian, Swahili, and Turkish, although there is no clear-cut distinction between agglutinating languages, INFLECTING LANGUAGES, and ISOLATING LANGUAGES.

Sometimes agglutinating languages and inflecting languages are called **synthetic languages**.

[*Further reading*: Lyons 1968]

agrammatism /əˈgræmətɪzəm/ *n*
see under APHASIA

agraphia /eɪˈgræfɪə/ *n*
see under APHASIA

agreement /əˈgriːmənt/ *n*
another term for CONCORD

AI /ˌeɪ ˈaɪ/ *n*
an abbreviation for ARTIFICIAL INTELLIGENCE

aim /eɪm/ *n*
see under OBJECTIVE

alexia /eɪˈleksɪə/ *n*
see under APHASIA

alienable possession /ˈeɪlɪənəbəl pəˈzeʃən/ *n*
see under INALIENABLE POSSESSION

allomorph /ˈæləmɔːf ‖ -mɔrf/ *n*
any of the different forms of a MORPHEME.

For example, in English the plural morpheme is often shown in writing by adding -*s* to the end of a word, eg *cat*/kæt/ – *cats*/kæts/. Sometimes this plural morpheme is pronounced /z/, eg *dog* /dɒg/ – *dogs* /dɒgz/, and sometimes it is pronounced /ɪz/, eg *class* /klɑːs/ – *classes* /klɑːsɪz/.

/s/, /z/, and /ɪz/ all have the same grammatical function in these examples, they all show plural; they are all allomorphs of the plural morpheme.

[*Further reading*: Aitchison 1978]

allophone /ˈæləfəʊn/ *n* **allophonic** /ˌæləˈfɒnɪk ‖ -ˈfɑ-/ *adj*
any of the different forms of a PHONEME.

For example, in English the phoneme /p/ is used in words like *span*/spæn/ and *spare*/speər/.

When /p/ occurs at the beginning of words like *put* /pʊt/ and *pair* /peər/, it is said with a little puff of air (see ASPIRATION).

Both the unaspirated /p/ (or [p]) in *span*, and the aspirated /p/ (or [pʰ]) in *put* have the same phonemic function, ie they are both heard and identified as /p/ and not eg as /b/; they are both allophones of the phoneme /p/.

[*Further reading*: Gimson 1980]

alphabet /ˈælfəbet/ *n* **alphabetic** /ˌælfəˈbetɪk/ *adj*
a set of letters which are used to write a language.

The English alphabet uses roman script and consists of 26 letters – a, b, c, etc.

The Russian alphabet uses cyrillic script and consists of 31 letters – а, б, в, etc.

The Arabic alphabet uses arabic script and consists of 29 letters – ا , ب, ت , etc.

see also ALPHABETIC WRITING
[*Further reading*: Gelb 1963]

alphabetic method /ˌælfə'betɪk 'meθəd/ *n*
a method of teaching children to read. It is used in teaching reading in the mother tongue.
Children are taught the names of the letters of the alphabet – *a* "ay", *b* "bee", *c* "see", etc – and when they see a new or unfamiliar word, eg *bag,* they repeat the letter names – "bee ay gee". It is thought that this "spelling" of the word helps the child to recognize it.
see also PHONICS
[*Further reading*: Goodacre 1978]

alphabetic writing /ˌælfə'betɪk 'raɪtɪŋ/ *n*
a writing system made up of separate letters which represent sounds (see under ALPHABET).
Some examples of alphabetic writing systems are
(a) Roman (or Latin) script, used for many European languages including English. It has also been adopted for many non-European languages, eg Swahili, Indonesian and Turkish.
(b) Arabic script, used for Arabic and languages such as Persian, Urdu and Malay, which also uses Roman script.
(c) Cyrillic script, used for Russian and languages such as Ukrainian and Bulgarian.
see also IDIOGRAPHIC WRITING, SYLLABIC WRITING
[*Further reading*: Gelb 1963]

alternate form reliability /ɔːl'tɜːnət fɔːm rɪˌlaɪə'bɪləti ‖ 'ɔltɜr-, 'æl-fɔrm rɪˌlaɪə'bɪləti/ *n*
also **parallel form reliability, equivalent form reliability**
(in testing) an estimate of the RELIABILITY of a test, usually employing a correlation between two or more forms of a test which are equivalent in content and difficulty.
see also CORRELATION
[*Further reading*: Ebel 1972]

alternate forms /ɔːl'tɜːnət fɔːmz ‖ ɔltɜr-, æl- fɔrmz/ *n*
another term for PARALLEL FORMS

alternate response item /ɔːl'tɜːnət rɪ'spɒns 'aɪtəm ‖ 'ɔltɜr-, 'æl--'spɑns/ *n*
see under TEST ITEM

alternation /ˌɔːltə'neɪʃən ‖ ˌɔltər-, ˌæltər-/ *n* **alternant**
/ɔːl'tɜːnənt ‖ ɔl'tɜr-, æl-/ *n*
The relationship between the different forms of a linguistic unit is
called alternation. The term is used especially in MORPHOLOGY and in
PHONOLOGY.
For example, the related vowels /iː/ and /e/ in:
   deceive /dɪ'siːv/ *deception* /dɪ'sepʃən/
   receive /rɪ'siːv/ *reception* /rɪ'sepʃən/
are in alternation.
The ALLOPHONES of a PHONEME and the ALLOMORPHS of a MORPHEME are
also in alternation, or alternants.
[*Further reading*: Hyman 1975]

alternation rules /ˌɔːltə'neɪʃən ruːlz ‖ ˌɔltər-, æl-/ *n*
see under SPEECH STYLES

alternative /ɔːl'tɜːnətɪv ‖ ɔl'tɜr-, æl-/ *n*
see under MULTIPLE-CHOICE ITEM

alveolar /ˌælvi'əʊləʳ, æl'vɪələʳ/ *adj*
describes a speech sound (a CONSONANT) which is produced by the
front of the tongue touching or nearly touching the gum ridge
behind the upper teeth (the **alveolar ridge**).
For example, in English the /t/ in /tɪn/ *tin*, and the /d/ in /dɪn/ *din*
are alveolar STOPS.
In English alveolar stops are made with the tip of the tongue, but
alveolar FRICATIVES – the /s/ in /sɪp/ *sip*, and the /z/ in /zuː/ *zoo* – are
made with the part of the tongue which is just behind the tip, the
blade.
see also LAMINAL, PLACE OF ARTICULATION, MANNER OF ARTICULATION
[*Further reading*: Gimson 1980]

alveolar ridge /ˌælvi'əʊləʳ 'rɪdʒ, æl'vɪələʳ/ *n*
also **alveolum** /ˌælvi'əʊləm, æl'vɪələm/
see under PLACE OF ARTICULATION

ambiguous /æm'bɪgjʊəs/ *adj* **ambiguity** /ˌæmbɪ'gjuːəti/ *n*
A word, phrase, or sentence which has more than one meaning is
said to be ambiguous.
An example of **grammatical ambiguity** is the sentence:
   The lamb is too hot to eat.
which can mean either:
(a) the lamb is so hot that it cannot eat anything
or:
(b) the cooked lamb is too hot for someone to eat it
There are several types of **lexical ambiguity**:
(a) a word can have several meanings, eg *face* meaning "human
    face", "face of a clock", "cliff face" (see also POLYSEMY)
(b) two or more words can sound the same but have different

meanings, eg *bank* in *to put money in a bank*, *the bank of a river* (see also HOMONYMS[3])

Usually, additional information either from the speaker or writer or from the situation indicates which meaning is intended.

Ambiguity is used extensively in creative writing, especially in poetry.

see also DISAMBIGUATION

[*Further reading*: Fromkin & Rodman 1983; Lyons 1981]

Ameslan /'æməˈzlæn/ *n*
an acronym for American Sign Language
see under SIGN LANGUAGE

analogy /əˈnælədʒi/ *n*
another term for OVERGENERALIZATION

analysis of covariance /əˈnæləsəs əv ˌkəʊˈveərɪəns/ *n*
also **ancova**
(in statistics) a procedure similar to ANALYSIS OF VARIANCE, used to statistically equate groups in order to control the effects of one or more variables. For example if we were comparing the effect of a teaching method on three groups of subjects, and one group had a higher MEAN IQ than the others, analysis of covariance could be used to make the groups equivalent by adjusting the effects of IQ.
[*Further reading*: Hardyck & Petrinovich 1976]

analysis of variance /əˈnæləsəs əv ˈveərɪəns/ *n*
also **anova**
(in statistics) a procedure for testing whether the difference among the MEANs of two or more groups is significant, for example to compare the effectiveness of a teaching method on three different age groups.
see also ANALYSIS OF COVARIANCE
[*Further reading*: Hardyck & Petrinovich 1976]

analytic approach /ˌænəˈlɪtɪk əˈprəʊtʃ/ *n*
see under SYNTHETIC APPROACH

analytic language /ˌænəˈlɪtɪk ˈlæŋgwɪdʒ/ *n*
another term for ISOLATING LANGUAGE

analytic style /ˌænəˈlɪtɪk ˈstaɪl/ *n*
see under GLOBAL LEARNING

anaphora /əˈnæfərə/ *n* **anaphoric** /ˌænəˈfɒrɪk ‖ -ˈfɔ-/ *adj*
The use of a word or phrase which refers back to another word or phrase which was used earlier in a text or conversation is called anaphora.
For example, in the sentence:
Tom likes ice cream but Bill can't eat it.
the word *it* refers back to *ice cream*: *it* is a substitute for *ice cream*, and *ice cream* is the **antecedent** of *it*.

Some verbs may be anaphoric, especially the English verb *do*. In the sentence:

Mary works hard and so does Doris.

does is anaphoric and is a substitute for *works*.

see also CATAPHORA

[*Further reading*: Lyons 1968]

ancova /æŋˈkəʊvə/ *n*

another term for ANALYSIS OF COVARIANCE

animate noun /ˈænəmət ˈnaʊn/ *n*

a noun which refers to a living being, for example persons, animals, fish, etc.

For example, the English nouns *woman* and *fish* are animate nouns. Nouns like *stone* and *water* are called **inanimate nouns**.

see also SEMANTIC FEATURES

[*Further reading*: Lyons 1968]

anomia /eɪˈnəʊmɪə/ *n*

see under APHASIA

anomie /ˈænəmi/ *n*

also **anomy**

feelings of social uncertainty or dissatisfaction which people who do not have strong attachments to a particular social group may have. Anomie has been studied as an affective variable (see under COGNITIVE VARIABLE) in second/foreign language learning. In learning a new language people may begin to move away from their own language and culture, and have feelings of insecurity. At the same time they may not be sure about their feelings towards the new language group. Feelings of anomie may be highest when a high level of language ability is reached. This may lead a person to look for chances to speak their own language as a relief.

[*Further reading*: Lambert 1967]

anova /ˈænəʊvə/ *n*

another term for ANALYSIS OF VARIANCE

antecedent /ˌæntəˈsiːdənt/ *n*

see under ANAPHORA

anthropological linguistics /ˌænθrəpəˈlɒdʒɪkəl lɪŋˈgwɪstɪks ‖ -ˈlɑ-/ *n*

a branch of linguistics which studies the relationship between language and culture in a community, eg its traditions, beliefs, and family structure.

For example, anthropological linguists have studied the ways in which relationships within the family are expressed in different cultures (kinship terminology), and they have studied how people communicate with one another at certain social and cultural events, eg ceremonies, rituals, and meetings, and then related this to the overall structure of the particular community.

Some areas of anthropological linguistics are closely related to areas of SOCIOLINGUISTICS and the ETHNOGRAPHY OF COMMUNICATION.
[*Further reading*: Ardener 1971]

anticipation error /æn͵tɪsə'peɪʃən ͵ərər/ *n*
see under SPEECH ERRORS

anticipatory subject /æn͵tɪsə'peɪtəri 'sʌbdʒɪkt ‖ æn'tɪsəpeɪtəri, -əpətori/ *n*
see under EXTRAPOSITION

antonym /'æntənɪm/ *n* **antonymy** /æn'tɒnəmi ‖ -tɑ-/ *n*
a word which is opposite in meaning to another word.
For example, in English *male* and *female*, and *big* and *small* are antonyms.
A distinction is sometimes made between pairs like *male* and *female*, and pairs like *big* and *small*, according to whether or not the words are gradable (see under GRADABLE).
A person who is not *male* must be *female*, but something which is not *big* is not necessarily *small*, it may be somewhere between the two sizes.
male and *female* are called **complementaries** (or ungradable antonyms); *big* and *small* are called gradable antonyms or a **gradable pair**.
Some linguists use the term antonym to mean only gradable pairs.
see also SYNONYM
[*Further reading*: Fromkin & Rodman 1983; Lyons 1981]

apex /'eɪpeks/ *n*
the tip of the tongue
see also under APICAL, PLACE OF ARTICULATION

aphasia /ə'feɪʒə/ *n* **aphasic** /ə'feɪzɪk/ *adj*
also **dysphasia** *n*
loss of the ability to use and understand language, usually caused by damage to the brain. The loss may be total or partial, and may affect spoken and/or written language ability.
There are different types of aphasia: **agraphia** is difficulty in writing; **alexia** is difficulty in reading; **anomia** is difficulty in using proper nouns; and **agrammatism** is difficulty in using grammatical words like prepositions, articles, etc.
Aphasia can be studied in order to discover how the brain processes language.
see also BRAIN, NEUROLINGUISTICS
[*Further reading*: Dalton & Hardcastle 1977]

apical /'eɪpɪkəl/ *adj*
describes a speech sound (a CONSONANT) which is produced by the tip of the tongue (the **apex**) touching some part of the mouth.
For example, in English the /t/ in /tɪn/ *tin* is an apical STOP.

If the tongue touches the upper teeth, the sounds are sometimes called **apico-dental**, eg French and German /t/ and /d/.

If the tongue touches the gum ridge behind the upper teeth (the **alveolar ridge**), the sounds are sometimes called **apico-alveolar**, eg English /t/ and /d/.

see also PLACE OF ARTICULATION, MANNER OF ARTICULATION

[*Further reading*: Gimson 1980]

a posteriori syllabus /ˌeɪ pɒstɪəriˈɔːraɪ ˈsɪləbəs, ˌɑː pɒstɪəriˈɔːriː ‖ pɑ-/ *n*
see under A PRIORI SYLLABUS

applied linguistics /əˈplaɪd lɪŋˈgwɪstɪks/ *n*
(1) the study of second and foreign language learning and teaching.
(2) the study of language and linguistics in relation to practical problems, such as LEXICOGRAPHY, TRANSLATION, SPEECH PATHOLOGY, etc. Applied linguistics uses information from sociology, psychology, anthropology, and INFORMATION THEORY as well as from linguistics in order to develop its own theoretical models of language and language use, and then uses this information and theory in practical areas such as syllabus design, SPEECH THERAPY, LANGUAGE PLANNING, STYLISTICS, etc.
see also ETHNOGRAPHY OF COMMUNICATION

[*Further reading*: Corder 1973; Kaplan 1980]

apposition /ˌæpəˈzɪʃən/ *n* **appositive** /əˈpɒzətɪv ‖ -ˈpɑ-/ *n, adj*
When two words, phrases, or clauses in a sentence have the same REFERENCE, they are said to be in apposition.
For example, in the sentence:
My sister, Helen Wilson, will travel with me.
My sister and *Helen Wilson* refer to the same person, and are called appositives.
The sentence can be rewritten with either of the two appositives missing, and still make sense:
My sister will travel with me.
Helen Wilson will travel with me.
[*Further reading*: Quirk et al 1985]

appreciative comprehension /əˈpriːʃjətɪv ˌkɒmprɪˈhenʃən ‖ ˌkɑm-/ *n*
see under READING

approach /əˈprəʊtʃ/ *n*
Language teaching is sometimes discussed in terms of three related aspects: approach, METHOD, and **technique**.
Different theories about the nature of language and how languages are learned (the approach) imply different ways of teaching language (the method), and different methods make use of different kinds of classroom activity (the technique).
Examples of different approaches are the aural-oral approach (see AUDIOLINGUAL METHOD), the COGNITIVE CODE APPROACH, the COMMUNICATIVE APPROACH, etc. Examples of different methods which

are based on a particular approach are the AUDIOLINGUAL METHOD, the DIRECT METHOD, etc. Examples of techniques used in particular methods are DRILLS, DIALOGUES, ROLE-PLAYS, sentence completion, etc.
[*Further reading*: Anthony 1963]

appropriateness /ə'prəʊprɪ-ətnəs/ *n* **appropriate** /ə'prəʊprɪ-ət/ *adj*
When producing an utterance, a speaker needs to know that it is grammatical, and also that it is suitable (appropriate) for the particular situation.
For example:
Give me a glass of water!
is grammatical, but it would not be appropriate if the speaker wanted to be polite. A request such as:
May I have a glass of water, please?
would be more appropriate.
see also GRAMMATICAL[1,2], CORRECT, COMMUNICATIVE COMPETENCE
[*Further reading*: Hymes 1974]

appropriate word method /ə'prəʊprɪ-ət 'wɜːd 'meθəd ‖ 'wɜrd/ *n*
see under CLOZE PROCEDURE

approximative system /ə'prɒksəmətɪv 'sɪstəm ‖ ə'prɑk-/ *n*
see under INTERLANGUAGE

a priori syllabus /ˌeɪ praɪ'ɔːraɪ 'sɪləbəs, ˌɑː pri'ɔːriː/ *n*
In language teaching, a distinction is sometimes made between two kinds of syllabuses. A syllabus prepared in advance of a course, and used as a basis for developing classroom activities, may be referred to as an a priori syllabus. This may be contrasted with a syllabus which is not developed in advance but which is prepared after a course is taught, as a "record" of the language and activities used in the course (an **a posteriori syllabus**). An a posteriori syllabus is sometimes called a **retrospective syllabus.**
see also SYLLABUS

aptitude /'æptətjuːd ‖ -tuːd/ *n*
see LANGUAGE APTITUDE

aptitude test /'æptətjuːd 'test ‖ -tuːd/ *n*
see LANGUAGE APTITUDE TEST

areal linguistics /'eərɪəl lɪŋ'gwɪstɪks/ *n*
the study of the languages or dialects which are spoken in a particular area.
An example is a study of two neighbouring languages to see how they influence each other in terms of grammar, vocabulary, pronunciation, etc.
see also DIALECTOLOGY

argument /'ɑːgjʊmənt ‖ 'ɑrgjə-/ *n*
see under PROPOSITION

article /ˈɑːtɪkəl ‖ ˈɑr-/ n

a word which is used with a noun, and which shows whether the noun refers to something definite or something indefinite.

For example, English has two articles: the **definite article** *the*, and the **indefinite article** *a* or *an*.

The main use of the definite article in English is to show that the noun refers to a particular example of something, eg:

(a) by referring to something which is known to both the speaker and the hearer:
  She is in the garden.
  He is at the post office.

(b) by referring backwards to something already mentioned:
  There is a man waiting outside. Who, the man in the brown coat?

(c) by referring forward to something:
  The chair in the living room is broken.

(d) by referring to something as a group or class:
  The lion is a dangerous animal.

The main use of the indefinite article in English is to show that the noun refers to something general or to something which has not been identified by the speaker, eg:

(a) by referring to one example of a group or class:
  Pass me a pencil, please.

(b) by referring to something as an example of a group or class:
  A dog is a friendly animal.

When nouns are used without an article in English, this is sometimes called **zero article**. For example:
  Cats like sleeping.
  Silver is a precious metal.

see also DETERMINER

[*Further reading*: Close 1975]

articulation /ɑːˌtɪkjʊˈleɪʃən ‖ ɑrˌtɪkjə-/ n **articulate** /ɑːˈtɪkjʊleɪt ‖ ɑrˈtɪkjə-/ v

the production of speech sounds in the mouth and throat (see VOCAL TRACT). In describing and analysing speech sounds a distinction is made between the MANNER OF ARTICULATION and the PLACE OF ARTICULATION.

[*Further reading*: Gimson 1980]

articulator /ɑːˈtɪkjʊleɪtəʳ ‖ ɑrˈtɪkjə-/ n

a part of the mouth, nose, or throat which is used in producing speech, eg the tongue, lips, alveolar ridge, etc.

see also PLACE OF ARTICULATION

articulatory phonetics /ɑːˈtɪkjʊlətəri fəˈnetɪks ‖ ɑrˌtɪkjə-/ n

see under PHONETICS

artificial intelligence /ˌɑːtəˈfɪʃəl ɪnˈtelədʒəns ‖ ˌɑr-/ n

also **AI**

the study of computer models of intelligent behaviour to learn about human intelligence. For example, workers in artificial intelligence construct computer models of language, memory, reasoning, creativity, etc, to learn how human beings speak, remember, think, act creatively, etc.

[*Further reading*: Dehn & Schank 1982]

artificial language /ˌɑɪtə̇'fɪʃəl 'læŋgwɪdʒ ‖ ˌɑr-/ *n*
also **auxiliary language**

a language which has been invented for a particular purpose, and which has no NATIVE SPEAKER*s*.

For example, Esperanto was invented by L. L. Zamenhof and was intended to be learned as a second language and used for international communication.

Artificial languages are also invented for experiments on aspects of natural language use.

see also NATURAL LANGUAGE

aspect /'æspekt/ *n*

a grammatical category which deals with how the event described by a verb is viewed, such as whether it is in progress, habitual, repeated, momentary, etc. Aspect may be indicated by PREFIX*es*, SUFFIX*es* or other changes to the verb, or by AUXILIARY VERB*s*, as in English. English has two aspects: PROGRESSIVE and PERFECT.

see also TENSE[1]

[*Further reading*: Comrie 1976]

Aspects Model /'æspekts 'mɒdl ‖ 'mɑ-/ *n*

see under GENERATIVE TRANSFORMATIONAL GRAMMAR

aspiration /ˌæspə̇'reɪʃən/ *n* **aspirate** /'æspə̇reɪt/ *v* **aspirated**
/'æspə̇reɪtə̇d/ *adj*

the little puff of air that sometimes follows a speech sound.

For example, in English the /p/ is aspirated at the beginning of the word /pæn/ *pan*, but when it is preceded by an /s/, eg in /spæn/ *span* there is no puff of air. The /p/ in *span* in **unaspirated**.

In phonetic notation, aspiration is shown by the symbol [ʰ] or ['], eg [pʰɪn] or [p'ɪn] *pin*.

Aspiration increases when a word or syllable is stressed, eg:
   Ouch! I stepped on a PIN.

[*Further reading*: Gimson 1980]

assessment /ə'sesmənt/ *n* **assess** /ə'ses/ *v*

the measurement of the ability of a person or the quality or success of a teaching course, etc.

Assessment may be by test, interview, questionnaire, observation, etc.

For example, assessment of the comprehension of an immigrant child may be necessary to discover if the child is able to follow a course of study in a school, or whether extra language teaching is needed.

Students may be tested at the beginning and again at the end of a

course of study to assess the quality of the teaching on the course.
[*Further reading*: Ebel 1972]

assimilation[1] /ə,sɪmə'leɪʃən/ *n* **assimilate** /ə'sɪməleɪt/ *v*
When a speech sound changes, and becomes more like another
sound which follows it or precedes it, this is called assimilation.
For example, in English the negative PREFIX appears as *im-* before
words such as *possible*: *impossible*. As *possible* starts with a BILABIAL
sound, the prefix *im-* ends in a bilabial sound. Before words like
tolerant, however, the prefix is *in-*: *intolerant*. As *tolerant* starts with
an ALVEOLAR sound, the prefix *in-* ends in an alveolar sound. As the
following sounds bring about the change, this process is called
regressive assimilation.
On the other hand, the difference between the /s/ in the English
word *cats* and the /z/ in the English word *dogs* is an example of
progressive assimilation because the preceding sounds bring about
the change.
[*Further reading*: Gimson 1980]

assimilation[2] *n*
a process in which a group gradually gives up its own language,
culture, and system of values and takes on those of another group
with a different language, culture, and system of values, through a
period of interaction.
see also ACCULTURATION, SOCIAL DISTANCE
[*Further reading*: Schumann 1978]

associative learning /ə'səʊʃiətɪv 'lɜːnɪŋ, -ʃətɪv ‖ 'lɜr-/ *n*
learning which happens when a connection or association is made,
usually between two things.
For example:
(a) When someone hears the word *table*, they may think of the
    word *food*, because this word is often used with or near *table*.
    This is called **association by contiguity**.
(b) When someone hears the word *delicate*, they may think of the
    word *fragile*, because it has a similar meaning. This is called
    association by similarity.
(c) When someone hears the word *happy*, they may think of the
    word *sad*, because it has the opposite meaning. This is called
    association by contrast.
Associative learning theory has been used in studies of memory,
learning, and verbal learning.
see also VERBAL LEARNING, WORD ASSOCIATION, PAIRED-ASSOCIATE LEARNING
[*Further reading*: Gagné 1970]

associative meaning /ə'səʊʃiətɪv 'miːnɪŋ, -ʃətɪv/ *n*
The associative meaning of a word is the total of all the meanings a
person thinks of when they hear the word.

For example, in a word association test a person might be given a word (a **stimulus**) and then asked to list all the things they think of (the **response**).

For example:

stimulus	response
puppy	*warm*
	young
	furry
	lively
	kitten

warm, *young*, *furry*, *lively*, *kitten* make up the associative meaning of *puppy* for that person.

Associative meaning has been used in studies of memory and thought.

see also WORD ASSOCIATION, STIMULUS-RESPONSE THEORY

[*Further reading*: Deese 1965]

asyllabic /ˌeɪsəˈlæbɪk/ *adj*
see under SYLLABLE

atomistic approach /ˌætəˈmɪstɪk əˈprəʊtʃ/ *n*
see under GESTALT PSYCHOLOGY

attention /əˈtenʃən/ *n*
the ability a person has to concentrate on something, or part of something, while ignoring other things. The length of time a person can attend to a single event or activity is sometimes called the **attention span**. In learning theory the attention phase is regarded as the first stage in learning.

[*Further reading*: Gagné 1970]

attitude /ˈætətjuːd ‖ -tuːd/ *n*
see LANGUAGE ATTITUDE

attitude scale /ˈætətjuːd ˌskeɪl ‖ -tuːd/ *n*
a technique for measuring a person's reaction to something.

A common scale is the **Likert Scale**. With this a statement of belief or attitude is shown to someone, and they are asked to show how strongly they agree or disagree with the statement by marking a scale like the one shown below:

Foreign languages are important for all educated adults.

1	2	3	4	5	6	7
strongly disagree		disagree		agree		strongly agree

Attitude scales have been used to study MOTIVATION in second and foreign language learning.

[*Further reading*: Oller 1979]

attributive adjective /əˈtrɪbjʊtɪv ˈædʒəktɪv ‖ -bjə-/ *n*
an adjective which is used before a noun.
For example, *good* in *a good book* is an attributive adjective.
An adjective which is used after a verb, especially after the verbs
be, *become*, *seem*, etc is called a **predicative adjective**. For example,
good in *The book was very good*.
Many adjectives in English are like *good*, and can be used both
attributively and predicatively, but some, like *main* and *utter*, can
only be used attributively, eg *a busy main road, an utter fool*, and
some, like *afraid* and *asleep*, can only be used predicatively eg *The boy
was asleep, The dog seems afraid*.
Many nouns in English can also be used attributively, eg *paper* in *a
paper cup*.
see also ADJECTIVE
[*Further reading*: Close 1975]

audiolingual method /ˌɔːdi-əʊˈlɪŋgwəl ˈmeθəd/ *n*
also **aural-oral method, mim-mem method**
a method of foreign or second language teaching which (a)
emphasizes the teaching of speaking and listening before reading
and writing (b) uses DIALOGUEs and DRILLs (c) discourages use of the
mother tongue in the classroom (d) often makes use of CONTRASTIVE
ANALYSIS. The audiolingual method was prominent in the 1950s and
1960s, especially in the United States, and has been widely used in
many other parts of the world.
The theory behind the audiolingual method is the **aural-oral
approach** to language teaching, which contains the following beliefs
about language and language learning: (a) speaking and listening are
the most basic language skills (b) each language has its own unique
structure and rule system (c) a language is learned through forming
habits. These ideas were based partly on the theory of STRUCTURAL
LINGUISTICS and partly on BEHAVIOURISM.
Criticism of the audiolingual method is based on criticism of its theory
and its techniques (see COGNITIVE CODE APPROACH, COMMUNICATIVE
APPROACH).
see also APPROACH, MIM-MEM METHOD
[*Further reading*: Rivers 1964, 1981; Richards & Rogers 1986]

audio-visual aid /ˌɔːdi-əʊˈvɪʒuəl ˈeɪd/ *n*
an audio or visual device used by a teacher to help learning. For
example, pictures, charts, and flashcards are visual aids; radio,
records, and tape-recorders are auditory aids. Film, television, and
video are audio-visual aids.

audio-visual method /ˌɔːdi-əʊˈvɪʒuəl ˈmeθəd/ *n*
also **structural global method**
a method of foreign language teaching which (a) teaches speaking
and listening before reading and writing (b) does not use the mother
tongue in the classroom (c) uses recorded dialogues with film-strip

picture sequences to present language items (d) uses drills to teach basic grammar and vocabulary.

The audio-visual method was developed in France in the 1950s, and is based on the belief that (a) language is learned through communication (b) translation can be avoided if new language items are taught in situations (c) choice of items for teaching should be based on a careful analysis of the language being taught.

see also AUDIOLINGUAL METHOD

[*Further reading*: Gougenheim et al 1964]

auditory /'ɔːdə́təri ‖ -tori/ *adj*
of or related to hearing

auditory discrimination /'ɔːdə́təri dɪˌskrɪmə́'neɪʃən ‖ -tori/ *n*
the ability to hear and recognize the different sounds in a language. In particular the ability to recognize the different PHONEMEs, and the different STRESS and INTONATION patterns.

see also PERCEPTION

auditory feedback /'ɔːdə́təri 'fiːdbæk ‖ -tori/ *n*
When a person speaks, they can hear what they are saying, and can use this information to MONITOR their speech and to correct any mistakes. This is called auditory feedback.

For example, in the following utterance the speaker uses auditory feedback to correct his/her pronunciation:

Would you like a cup of cea or toffee – I mean tea or coffee?

see also FEEDBACK, DELAYED AUDITORY FEEDBACK

[*Further reading*: Dalton & Hardcastle 1977]

auditory perception /'ɔːdə́təri pə'sepʃən ‖ -tori pər-/ *n*
see under PERCEPTION

auditory phonetics /'ɔːdə́təri fə'netɪks ‖ -tori/ *n*
see under PHONETICS

aural-oral approach /ˌaʊrəl 'ɔːrəl ə'prəʊtʃ ‖ 'o-/ *n*
see under AUDIOLINGUAL METHOD

aural-oral method /ˌaʊrəl 'ɔːrəl 'meθəd ‖ 'o-/ *n*
another term for AUDIOLINGUAL METHOD

authenticity /ˌɔːθen'tɪsə́ti/ *n* **authentic** /ɔː'θentɪk/ *adj*
the degree to which language teaching materials have the qualities of natural speech or writing.

Texts which are taken from newspapers, magazines, etc, and tapes of natural speech taken from ordinary radio or television programmes, etc, are called authentic materials.

When a teacher prepares texts or tapes for use in the classroom, he/she often has to use simplified examples.

automatic translation /ˌɔːtəmætɪk trænz'leɪʃən/ *n*
see under COMPUTATIONAL LINGUISTICS

auxiliary /ɔːgˈzɪljeri/ n
another term for AUXILIARY VERB

auxiliary language /ɔːgˈzɪljəri ˈlæŋgwɪdʒ, ɔːk- ‖ ɔgˈzɪljəri, -ˈzɪləri/ n
another term for LINGUA FRANCA and ARTIFICIAL LANGUAGE

auxiliary verb /ɔːgˈzɪljəri ˈvɜːb, ɔːk- ‖ ɔgˈzɪljəri, -ˈzɪləri ˈvɜrb/ n
also **auxiliary**
a verb which is used with another verb in a sentence, and which shows grammatical functions such as ASPECT, VOICE[1], MOOD, TENSE[1], and PERSON.
In English *be*, *do*, and *have* and the MODAL verbs like *may*, *can*, and *will* are all auxiliaries. For example:
She is working.
He didn't come.
They have finished.
You may go now.
Can you manage?
They will arrive tomorrow.
The verbs *working*, *come*, *finished*, *go*, *manage*, and *arrive* in these sentences are called **lexical verbs**, or **full verbs**. Lexical verbs can be used as the only verb in a sentence, eg *She works at the factory.*
be, *do*, and *have* can also be used as lexical verbs, eg *He is happy*, *She does computer studies at university*, and *They have three children*.
[*Further reading*: Quirk et al 1985]

availability /əˌveɪləˈbɪləti/ n **available** /əˈveɪləbəl/ adj
When students are asked to think of the words that can be used to talk about a particular topic, they will be able to think of some words immediately. Those words which they remember first and most easily are said to have a high availability.
For example, when a group of secondary school children were asked to list words for *parts of the body*, they included *leg*, *hand*, *eye*, *nose*, and *ears*. These were the five most available words.
Available words are not always the most frequently occurring words in a language. Lists of available words have been used to choose vocabulary for language teaching.
[*Further reading*: Savard & Richards 1969]

avoidance strategy /əˈvɔɪdəns ˈstrætədʒi/ n
When speaking or writing a second/foreign language, a speaker will often try to avoid using a difficult word or structure, and will use a simpler word or structure instead. This is called an avoidance strategy. For example, a student who is not sure of the use of the relative clause in English may avoid using it and use two simpler sentences instead. eg:
That's my building. I live there.
instead of:
That's the building where I live.
[*Further reading*: Faerch & Kasper 1983; Schachter 1974]

B

babbling /ˈbæblɪŋ/ n
speech-like sounds produced by very young children.
Babies begin to produce babbling sounds like /dæ/, /mæ/, /næ/, /bæ/, at the age of about three or four months. At around 9–12 months, real words begin to be produced.
[*Further reading*: de Villiers & de Villiers 1978]

baby talk /ˈbeɪbi ˌtɔːk/ n
another term for CARETAKER SPEECH

backchaining /ˈbækˌtʃeɪnɪŋ/ n
another term for BACKWARD BUILD-UP

back channel cue /ˈbæk ˈtʃænl ˈkjuː/ n
see under FEEDBACK

back formation /ˈbæk fɔːˌmeɪʃən ‖ fɔr-/ n
When a new word is made by the removal of an AFFIX from an existing word, this is called back formation.
For example, the verb *televise* was formed from the noun *television*, and the verb *peddle* was formed from the noun *peddler*.
New words are usually formed by adding affixes to existing words (see DERIVATION).

background /ˈbækɡraʊnd/ n
see under FUNCTIONAL SENTENCE PERSPECTIVE

background information /ˈbækɡraʊnd ˌɪnfəˈmeɪʃən ‖ ˌɪnfər-/ n
see under GROUNDING

back-shift /ˈbækʃɪft/ n
see under DIRECT SPEECH

back vowel /ˈbæk ˈvaʊəl/ n
see under VOWEL

backward build-up /ˈbækwəd ˈbɪldʌp ‖ -ərd/ n
also **backchaining**
a language teaching technique in which an utterance is divided into parts, and then the students are taught to say it by repeating the last part, and then the last two parts, etc, until they can repeat the whole utterance.
For example:

Teacher	Students
some letters	*some letters*
to post some letters	*to post some letters*
to the post office to post some letters	*to the post office to post some letters*
I'm going to the post office to post some letters.	*I'm going to the post office to post some letters.*

[*Further reading*: Rivers 1981]

balanced bilingual /ˈbælənst baɪˈlɪŋgwəl/ *n*
see under BILINGUAL

bare infinitive /ˈbeəʳ ɪnˈfɪnə̆tɪv/ *n*
see under INFINITIVE

basal /ˈbeɪsəl/ *adj*
When a course to teach reading has a number of graded parts, the first or most basic part is called the **basal reading programme**, and uses basic reading textbooks called **basal readers**.

base component /ˈbeɪs kəmˈpəʊnənt/ *n*
also **phrase structure component**
(In GENERATIVE TRANSFORMATIONAL GRAMMAR) the part dealing with syntax is divided into two components: the base component and the TRANSFORMATIONAL COMPONENT. The base component generates the basic sentence patterns of a language; the transformational component transforms these into sentences.
The base component consists of a set of rules and a vocabulary list (**lexicon**) which contains morphemes and idioms (see under LEXICAL ENTRY). The main rules are called **phrase structure rules** or **rewrite rules**.
For example, the rule
   S → NP + VP
means that a sentence (S) can be analysed (rewritten) as consisting of a noun phrase (NP) and a verb phrase (VP).
The rule
   VP → V (+NP)
means that a verb phrase can be further rewritten as simply a verb or as a verb and a noun phrase.
The lexicon gives information about the class that a word belongs to, eg N for nouns, V for verbs, and information about the grammatical structures with which the word may occur. For example, the English verb *sleep* cannot have an object after it. The simplified table below shows the rules and lexicon which are necessary to form the basic sentence structure for *the baby slept*.

Phrase Structure Rules	Lexicon
1. S → NP + VP 2. NP → DET(erminer) + N(oun) 3. VP → T(ense) + V(erb) 4. T(ense) → PAST	baby: N sleep: V – Object the: DET

A diagram, called a **tree diagram**, may show the way the rules are applied and how the words from the lexicon are fitted in for a particular sentence.
This simplified diagram shows the basic DEEP STRUCTURE for the sentence *The baby slept.*

base form

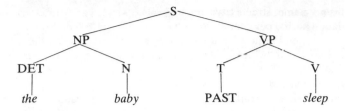

The rules of the transformational component change the above structure into the sentence *The baby slept* (**surface structure**).
see also PHRASE MARKER, PHRASE, STRUCTURE GRAMMAR,
TRANSFORMATIONAL COMPONENT
[*Further reading*: Aitchison 1978; Chomsky 1965]

base form /ˈbeɪs ˌfɔːm ‖ ˌfɔrm/ *n*
another term for ROOT or STEM[1].
For example, the English word *helpful* has the base form *help*.

Basic English /ˈbeɪsɪk ˈɪŋglɪʃ/ *n*
Basic English is a simplified type of English developed by C. K.
Ogden and I. A. Richards in 1929. It was intended to be used as a
second language for international communication.
Basic English uses only 850 words and fewer grammatical rules than
normal English, but it is claimed that anything that can be said in
ordinary English can also be said in Basic English.
see also LINGUA FRANCA
[*Further reading*: Ogden 1930]

basilect /ˈbeɪsəlekt/ *n*
see under POST-CREOLE CONTINUUM

battery of tests /ˈbætəri əv ˈtests/ *n*
also **test battery**
a group of tests which are given together to a student or group of
students.

behavioural objective /bɪˈheɪvɪərəl əbˈdʒektɪv/ *n*
also **performance objective**, **instructional objective**
(in developing a CURRICULUM) a statement of what a learner is expected
to know or be able to do after completing all or part of an educational
programme. A behavioural objective has three characteristics:
(a) it clearly describes the goals of learning in terms of observable
   behaviour
(b) it describes the conditions under which the behaviour will be
   expected to occur
(c) it states an acceptable standard of performance (the **criterion**).
For example one of the behavioural objectives for a conversation
course might be.
   "Given an oral request, the learner will say his/her name, address
   and telephone number to a native speaker of English and spell

his/her name, street, city, so that an interviewer can write down the data with 100 per cent accuracy."

"Given an oral request" and "to a native speaker" describe the conditions, and "with 100 per cent accuracy" describes the criterion, in this objective.

see also OBJECTIVE

[*Further reading*: Pratt 1980]

behaviourism /bɪ'heɪvɪərɪzəm/ *n*
also **behaviourist theory, behaviourist psychology**
a theory of psychology which states that human and animal behaviour can and should be studied in terms of physical processes only. It led to theories of learning which explained how an external event (a **stimulus**) caused a change in the behaviour of an individual (a **response**) without using concepts like "mind" or "ideas", or any kind of mental behaviour.

Behaviourism was an important influence on psychology, education, and language teaching, especially in the United States, and was used by psychologists like Skinner, Osgood, and Staats to explain first language learning.

see also STIMULUS-RESPONSE THEORY, COGNITIVE PSYCHOLOGY

[*Further reading*: Skinner 1957]

behaviourist psychology /bɪ'heɪvɪərɪst saɪ'kɒlədʒi ‖ -'kɑ-/ *n*
another term for BEHAVIOURISM

behaviourist theory /bɪ'heɪvɪərɪst 'θɪəri/ *n*
another term for BEHAVIOURISM

benefactive case /benə'fæktɪv 'keɪs/ *n*
(In CASE GRAMMAR) the noun or noun phrase that refers to the person or animal who benefits, or is meant to benefit, from the action of the verb is in the benefactive case.

For example, in the sentences:
Joan baked a cake for Louise.
Joan baked Louise a cake.
Louise is in the benefactive case.

[*Further reading*: Fillmore 1968]

BEV /ˌbiː iː 'viː/ *n*
an abbreviation for BLACK ENGLISH VERNACULAR

bicultural /baɪ'kʌltʃərəl/ *adj* **biculturalism** /baɪ'kʌltʃərəlɪzəm/ *n*
A person who knows the social habits, beliefs, customs, etc of two different social groups can be described as bicultural.

A distinction is made between biculturalism and BILINGUALISM. For example, a person may be able to speak two languages, but may not know how to act according to the social patterns of the second or foreign language community. This person can be described as bilingual, but not as bicultural.

bidialectal /ˌbaɪdaɪəˈlektəl/ *adj* **bidialectalism** /ˌbaɪdaɪəˈlektəlɪzəm/ *n*
A person who knows and can use two different DIALECTS can be described as bidialectal. The two dialects are often a prestige dialect, which may be used at school or at work and is often the STANDARD VARIETY, and a non-prestige dialect, which may be used only at home or with friends.
see also BILINGUAL, BILINGUAL EDUCATION, DIGLOSSIA

bidialectal education /ˌbaɪdaɪəˈlektəl ˌedjʊˈkeɪʃən ‖ ˌedʒə-/ *n*
see under BILINGUAL EDUCATION

bilabial /ˌbaɪˈleɪbɪəl/ *adj*
describes a speech sound (a CONSONANT) which is produced by the two lips.
For example, in English the /p/ in /pɪn/ *pin*, and the /b/ in /bɪn/ *bin* are bilabial STOPS.
see also PLACE OF ARTICULATION, MANNER OF ARTICULATION
[*Further reading*: Gimson 1980]

bilingual /baɪˈlɪŋgwəl/ *n, adj*
a person who knows and uses two languages.
In everyday use the word bilingual usually means a person who speaks, reads, or understands two languages equally well (a **balanced bilingual**), but a bilingual person usually has a better knowledge of one language than of the other.
For example, he/she may:
(a) be able to read and write in only one language
(b) use each language in different types of situation (DOMAINS), eg one language at home and the other at work
(c) use each language for different communicative purposes, eg one language for talking about school life and the other for talking about personal feelings
see also BILINGUALISM, DIGLOSSIA, MULTILINGUAL
[*Further reading*: Fishman 1971; Haugen 1969]

bilingual education /baɪˈlɪŋgwəl ˌedjʊˈkeɪʃən ‖ ˌedʒə-/ *n*
the use of a second or foreign language in school for the teaching of content subjects.
Bilingual education programmes may be of different types and include:
(a) the use of a single school language which is not the child's home language. This is sometimes called an IMMERSION PROGRAMME.
(b) the use of the child's home language when the child enters school but later a gradual change to the use of the school language for teaching some subjects and the home language for teaching others. This is sometimes called **maintenance bilingual education**.
(c) the partial or total use of the child's home language when the child enters school, and a later change to the use of the school

language only. This is sometimes called **transitional bilingual education**.

When the school language is a STANDARD DIALECT and the child's home language a different dialect (eg Hawaiian Creole, Black English) this is sometimes called **bidialectal** or **biloquial education**.

see also BILINGUALISM, ADDITIVE BILINGUAL EDUCATION

[*Further reading*: Swain 1978; Parker 1977; Trudgill 1975]

bilingualism /baɪˈlɪŋgwəlɪzəm/ *n*

the use of at least two languages either by an individual (see BILINGUAL) or by a group of speakers, such as the inhabitants of a particular region or a nation.

Bilingualism is common in, for example, the Province of Quebec in Canada where both English and French are spoken, and parts of Wales, where both Welsh and English are spoken.

see also COMPOUND BILINGUALISM, DIGLOSSIA, MULTILINGUALISM

[*Further reading*: Fishman 1971; Haugen 1969]

bilingual syntax measure /baɪˈlɪŋgwəl ˈsɪntæks ˈmeʒər/ *n*

a published language test which measures a child's use of grammatical structures.

In the test, the child is shown a colourful picture or set of pictures by an examiner, and is then asked questions about them. The pictures and questions are designed to make the child respond with a certain kind of grammatical structure.

[*Further reading*: Burt, Dulay, & Hernández-Chávez 1975]

biliterate /baɪˈlɪtərət/ *n*

see under LITERACY

biloquial education /baɪˈləʊkwɪəl edjʊˈkeɪʃən ‖ edʒə-/ *n*

see under BILINGUAL EDUCATION

bimodal distribution /baɪˈməʊdl ˌdɪstrəˈbjuːʃən/ *n*

see under MODE

binary digit /ˈbaɪnəri ˈdɪdʒət/ *n*

another term for BIT

binary feature /ˈbaɪnəri ˈfiːtʃər/ *n*

a property of a phoneme or a word which can be used to describe the phoneme or word.

A binary feature is either present or absent.

For example, in English a /t/ sounds different from a /d/ because a /d/ is pronounced with the vocal cords vibrating (is voiced), and a /t/ is pronounced with the vocal cords not vibrating (is voiceless). VOICE is therefore one of the features which describe /d/ and /t/. This is usually shown like this:

/d/ [+voice]   (= voice present)
/t/ [−voice]   (= voice absent)

When a binary feature can be used to distinguish between two phonemes, like voice with /d/ and /t/, the phonemes are in **binary opposition** (see also DISTINCTIVE FEATURE.)

Binary features are also used to describe the semantic properties of words (see also SEMANTIC FEATURES).

[*Further reading*: Hyman 1975; Jakobson, Fant, & Halle 1952]

binary opposition /'baɪnəri ˌɒpə'zɪʃən ‖ ˌɑ-/ *n*
  see under BINARY FEATURE

bi-polar adjective /baɪ'pəʊləʳ 'ædʒəktɪv/ *n*
  see under SEMANTIC DIFFERENTIAL

bit /bɪt/ *n*
also **binary digit** /'baɪnəri 'dɪdʒət/
  (in INFORMATION THEORY) a unit of information.
  A bit is the amount of information given by a choice between two alternatives, eg on or off. Computers and other electronic systems measure information in bits.
  [*Further reading*: Lyons 1968]

black English vernacular /'blæk 'ɪŋglɪʃ və'nækjʊləʳ ‖ vər'nækjələr/ *n*
also **BEV**
  the type of English spoken by some Black Americans in the United States.
  Since the 1960s this variety of English has been studied by a number of American linguists.
  Some features of BEV are:
  (a) final consonants are sometimes deleted, eg:
    /hæn/ *hand*
  (b) the verb *to be* is not always used, eg:
    We on tape
  (c) the verb is not always marked for third person singular, eg:
    He know something
  see also VERNACULAR, VARIABLE[1]
  [*Further reading*: Labov 1972b]

body language /'bɒdi 'læŋgwɪdʒ ‖ 'bɑdi/ *n*
  the use of facial expressions, body movements, etc to communicate meaning from one person to another.
  In linguistics, this type of meaning is studied in PARALINGUISTICS.
  see also PROXEMICS

borrowing /'bɒrəʊɪŋ ‖ 'bɑ-,'bɔ-/ *n* **borrow** /'bɒrəʊ ‖ 'bɑ-,'bɔ-/ *v*
  a word or phrase which has been taken from one language and used in another language.
  For example, English has taken *coup d'état* (the sudden seizure of government power) from French, *al fresco* (in the open air) from Italian and *moccasin* (a type of shoe) from an American Indian language.
  When a borrowing is a single word, it is called a **loan word**.

Sometimes, speakers try to pronounce borrowings as they are pronounced in the original language. However, if a borrowed word or phrase is widely used, most speakers will pronounce it according to the sound system of their own language.

For example, French /garaʒ/ *garage* has become in British English /ˈgærɑːʒ/ or /ˈgærɪdʒ/, though American English keeps something like the French pronunciation.

bottom-up process /ˌbɒtəm ˈʌp ˈprəʊses ‖ ˈprɑ-/ *n*
see under TOP-DOWN PROCESS

boundaries /ˈbaʊndəriz/ *n*
divisions between linguistic units. There are different types of boundaries.
For example, boundaries may be
(a) between words, eg *the##child*
(b) between the parts of a word such as STEM[1] and AFFIX, eg *kind#ness*
(c) between SYLLABLE*s*, eg /beɪ +bi/ *baby*
see also JUNCTURE
[*Further reading*: Hyman 1975]

bound form /ˈbaʊnd ˌfɔːm ‖ fɔrm/ *n*
also **bound morpheme**
a linguistic form (a MORPHEME) which is never used alone but must be used with another morpheme, eg as an AFFIX or COMBINING FORM.
For example, the English suffix *-ing* must be used with a verb stem, eg *writing, loving, driving.*
A form which can be used on its own is called a **free form**, eg *Betty, horse, red, write, love, drive.*
[*Further reading*: Fromkin & Rodman 1983; Bloomfield 1933]

bound morpheme /ˈbaʊnd ˈmɔːfiːm ‖ ˈmɔr-/ *n*
another term for BOUND FORM

brain /breɪn/ *n*
the organ of the body, in the upper part of the head, which controls thought and feeling.

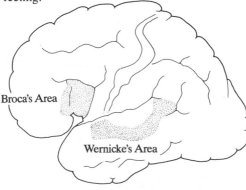

The brain consists of two main parts, the **left hemisphere** and the **right hemisphere**. As the brain develops, it is thought that different bodily functions (eg speech, hearing, sensations, actions) are gradually brought under the control of different areas of the brain. The development of control over different functions in different parts of the brain is known as **cerebral dominance** or **lateralization**. Those parts of the brain which control language are usually in the left hemisphere. One area in the left hemisphere is known as **Broca's area**, or the speech centre, because it is an important area involved in speech. Damage to this area of the brain leads to different types of APHASIA. Another area called **Wernicke's area** is thought to be involved in understanding language. The exact role of these two areas in language is not yet fully understood however.

[*Further reading*: Lenneberg 1967; Penfield & Lamar Roberts 1959]

branching programme /ˈbrɑːntʃɪŋ ˌprəʊgræm ‖ ˈbræn-/ *n*
see under PROGRAMMED LEARNING

breath group /ˈbreθ ˌgruːp/ *n*
a stretch of speech which is uttered during one period of breathing out.
see also SPEECH RHYTHM

broad notation /ˈbrɔːd nəʊˈteɪʃən/ *n*
also **broad transcription** /ˈbrɔːd trænˈskrɪpʃən/ *n*
see under NOTATION

Broca's area /ˈbrəʊkəz ˈeərɪə/ *n*
see under BRAIN

CA /ˌsiː ˈeɪ/ *n*
an abbreviation for CONTRASTIVE ANALYSIS

CAI /ˌsiː ˌeɪ ˈaɪ/ *n*
an abbreviation for COMPUTER ASSISTED INSTRUCTION

call-word /ˈkɔːl ˌwɜːd ‖ ˌwɜrd/ *n*
see under DRILL

calque /kælk/ *n*
also **loan translation**
a type of BORROWING, in which each morpheme or word is translated into the equivalent morpheme or word in another language. For example, the English word *almighty* is a calque from the Latin *omnipotens*:

    omni + *potens*
    "all"   "mighty"
    all + *mighty* = *almighty*

A calque may be a word, a phrase, or even a short sentence.

canonical form /kəˈnɒnɪkəl ˈfɔːm ‖ kəˈnɑ- ˈfɔrm/ *n*
the form of a linguistic item which is usually shown as the standard form.
For example, the plural morpheme in English is usually shown as *-s*, even though it may appear as *-s, -es, -en*, etc. *-s* is the canonical form.

cardinal number /ˈkɑːdənəl ˈnʌmbər ‖ ˈkɑr-/ *n*
also **cardinal**
see under NUMBER[2]

cardinal vowel /ˈkɑːdənəl ˈvaʊəl ‖ ˈkɑr-/ *n*
any of the VOWELs in the cardinal vowel system. The cardinal vowel system was invented by Daniel Jones as a means of describing the vowels in any language. The cardinal vowels themselves do not belong to any particular language, but are possible vowels to be used as a reference point.
The cardinal vowel [i] is made with the front of the tongue as high as possible in the mouth without touching the roof of the mouth. It is a **front vowel**. By gradually lowering the tongue, three more front vowels were established: [e], [ɛ] and [a]. The difference in tongue position for [i] and [e], for [e] and [ɛ] and for [ɛ] and [a] is approximately equal and the difference in sound between each vowel and the next one is also similar. All these front vowels are made with fairly spread lips.
Cardinal vowel [ɑ] is made with the back of the tongue as low as possible in the mouth. It is a **back vowel**. By gradually raising the

back of the tongue from the [ɑ] position, three other cardinal vowels were established: [ɔ], [o] and [u]. These three are made with the lips gradually more rounded.

These eight vowels are known as the **primary cardinal vowels**. The five vowels: [i], [e], [ɛ], [a] and [ɑ] are **unrounded vowels** and [ɔ], [o] and [u] are **rounded vowels**.

With the tongue in these eight positions, a secondary series of cardinal vowels was established. Where the primary cardinal vowels are unrounded, the **secondary cardinal vowels** are rounded. Where the primary cardinal vowels are rounded, the secondary cardinal vowels are unrounded.

	unrounded	rounded
primary	i e ɛ a ɑ	ɔ o u

	rounded	unrounded
secondary	y ø œ Œ ɒ	ʌ ɣ ɯ

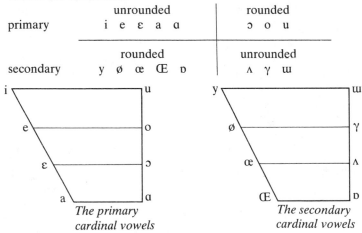

The primary cardinal vowels

The secondary cardinal vowels

[*Further reading*: Gimson 1980]

caretaker speech /ˈkeə,teɪkəʳ spiːtʃ ‖ ˈkeər-/ *n*
also **motherese, mother talk, baby talk**
the simple speech used by mothers, fathers, babysitters, etc when they talk to young children who are learning to talk.
Caretaker speech usually has:
(a) shorter utterances than speech to other adults
(b) grammatically simple utterances
(c) few abstract or difficult words, with a lot of repetition
(d) clearer pronunciation, sometimes with exaggerated INTONATION patterns
Caretaker speech is easier for children to understand, and many people believe that it helps children to learn language.
see also FOREIGNER TALK
[*Further reading*: Snow & Ferguson 1977]

case[1] /keɪs/ *n*
(in some languages) a grammatical category that shows the function of a noun or noun phrase in a sentence. The form of the noun or noun phrase changes (by INFLECTION) to show the different functions or cases.

For example, in the German sentence:

Ursula kaufte einen neuen Tisch.

Ursula bought a new table.

in the noun phrase *einen neuen Tisch*, the article *ein* and the adjective *neu* have the inflectional ending *-en* to show that the noun phrase is in the ACCUSATIVE CASE because it is the direct object of the verb.

In the sentence:

Der Tisch ist sehr groß.

The table is very big.

in the noun phrase *der Tisch*, the article has the inflectional ending *-er* to show that the noun phrase is in the NOMINATIVE CASE because it is the subject of the verb.

German has four cases; accusative, nominative, DATIVE[1], and GENITIVE. Some languages have more or fewer, and some have none at all. In these languages the functions shown by case may be shown by WORD ORDER or by PREPOSITIONS.

[*Further reading*: Lyons 1968]

case[2]

see under CASE GRAMMAR

case grammar /'keɪs ˌɡræmərʳ/ n

an approach to grammar which stresses the semantic relationships in a sentence.

Case grammar is a type of GENERATIVE GRAMMAR developed by Fillmore.

In case grammar, the verb is regarded as the most important part of the sentence, and has a number of semantic relationships with various noun phrases. These relationships are called **cases**.

For example, in the sentences:

Smith killed the policeman with a revolver.

This revolver killed the policeman.

with a revolver and *This revolver* have different syntactic functions, but their semantic relationship with the verb *kill* is the same in both sentences. The revolver is the instrument with which the action of the verb is performed. *with a revolver* and *This revolver* are said to be in the INSTRUMENTAL CASE.

The instrumental case is just one of the cases associated with the verb *kill*. Other cases are AGENTIVE (the performer of the action – *Smith*), and DATIVE (the receiver of the action – *the policeman*).

As the examples show, case relationships can be shown in different syntactic structures. Case grammar is thus DEEP STRUCTURE.

Case grammar has been used for the grammatical description of languages, and also for the description of child language acquisition.

see also AGENTIVE CASE, BENEFACTIVE CASE, DATIVE CASE[2], FACTITIVE CASE, INSTRUMENTAL CASE, LOCATIVE CASE, OBJECTIVE CASE

[*Further reading*: Brown & Miller 1980; Fillmore 1968]

case study /'keɪs ˌstʌdi/ *n*
the study of the speech, writing, or language use of one person, either at one point in time or over a period of time, eg the language acquisition of a child over a period of one year.

cataphora /ˌkə'tæfərə/ *n* **cataphoric** /ˌkætə'fɒrɪk ‖ -'farɪk/ *adj*
The use of a word or phrase which refers forward to another word or phrase which will be used later in the text or conversation is called cataphora.
For example, in the sentence:
When I met her, Mary looked ill.
the word *her* refers forward to *Mary*.
Examples of cataphoric sentences are:
My reasons are as follows: One, I don't . . .
Here is the news. The Prime Minister . . .
see also ANAPHORA

categorize /'kætəgəraɪz/ *v* **categorization** /ˌkætəgəraɪ'zeɪʃən, ˌkætəgərə-/ *n*
to put items into groups (**categories**) according to their nature or use.
For example:
(a) nouns may be categorized into ANIMATE and inanimate nouns.
(b) verbs may be categorized into TRANSITIVE and intransitive verbs.

category /'kætəgəri ‖ -gori/ *n*
see GRAMMATICAL CATEGORY

category symbol /'kætəgəri ˌsɪmbəl ‖ -gori/ *n*
see under GRAMMATICAL CATEGORY[2]

catenation /ˌkætə'neɪʃən/ *n* **catenate** /'kætəˌneɪt/ *v*
the linking of sounds together in speech, such as the grouping of phonemes into SYLLABLE*s*, and the the grouping of syllables and words through ASSIMILATION[1], ELISION, and JUNCTURE. Languages differ in the way they combine sounds. Two languages may share many sounds, but combine them in different ways. Spanish learners of English for example may pronounce *steak* as [estek], because although Spanish has the combination /-st/ after a stressed vowel it does not have it before one.

causative verb /'kɔːzətɪv 'vɜːb ‖ 'vɜrb/ *n*
a verb which shows that someone or something brings about or casues an action or a state.
For example, in:
Peter killed the rabbit.
killed is a causative verb, but in:
The rabbit died.
died is not.
Some languages often form causative verbs from non-causative verbs by adding affixes, eg in Malay:

Gelas itu jatuh ke lantai
glass the fall to floor
"The glass fell to the floor."
Dia menjatuhkan gelas itu
He cause to fall glass the
"He dropped the glass."

Causative verbs are always TRANSITIVE.

see also INCHOATIVE VERB

central nervous system /ˈsentrəl ˈnɜːvəs ˈsɪstəm ‖ ˈnɜr-/ *n*
the part of the nervous system which consists of the brain and the spinal cord.

central tendency /ˈsentrəl ˈtendənsi/ *n*
(in statistics) any estimate of the central point around which scores tend to cluster. The most common measures of central tendency are the MODE, the MEDIAN, and the MEAN.

central vowel /ˈsentrəl ˈvaʊəl/ *n*
see under VOWEL

cerebral dominance /ˈserəbrəl ˈdɒmənəns ‖ səˈriː-, ˈserə- ˈdɑ-/ *n*
see under BRAIN

channel /ˈtʃænl/ *n*
(1) (in SOCIOLINGUISTICS) the way in which a MESSAGE is conveyed from one person to another.
The two most common channels of communication are speech and writing. Other examples are the use of drum beats, smoke signals, or flags.
(2) (in INFORMATION THEORY) the path along which information is sent.
In telephone communication, for example, the message is changed into electrical signals by the telephone and the channel of communication is the telephone wire.
[*Further reading*: Hymes 1974]

child language /ˈtʃaɪld ˈlæŋgwɪdʒ/ *n*
the type of language spoken by young children who are still learning their mother tongue.
Child language is different from adult language in many ways. For example:
(a) different sentence structures, eg *Why not you coming?* instead of *Why aren't you coming?*
(b) different word forms, eg *goed* instead of *went, mouses* instead of *mice*
Differences like these show that children have their own set of rules, and do not learn language by simply imitating adults.
see also ACQUISITION
[*Further reading*: Fletcher & Garman 1979]

Chi-square /'kaɪ 'skweəʳ/ n
also χ^2

(in statistics) a procedure which is used to determine whether the
relationship between two or more different variables is independent.
For example if we wanted to find out if there is a relationship
between ability to write and belonging to a particular social or
economic group, Chi-square could be used. It measures whether a
particular distribution of observed values is sufficiently different
from an expected distribution to indicate that it cannot be explained
as a chance occurrence.
[*Further reading*: Ebel 1972]

choral repetition /'kɔːrəl ˌrepə'tɪʃən ‖ 'ko-/ n
also **chorus repetition** /'kɔːrəs ˌrepə'tɪʃən ‖ 'ko-/

When a teacher asks a whole group or class of students to repeat an
example together, this is called choral repetition.

chunking /'tʃʌŋkɪŋ/ n

the division of utterances into parts, as part of the process of
learning or comprehension. The different parts of the utterance are
called **chunks**.
For example, the sentence:

It was because of the rain that I was late.

might be divided into two parts – *It was because of the rain* and *that
I was late* – and then the meaning of each part worked out
separately.
These chunks are sometimes called **constituents**, and the process of
chunking is sometimes called **constituent identification**.
In sentence production, chunks are sometimes called ROUTINE*s*.
[*Further reading*: Clark & Clark 1977]

class /klɑːs ‖ klæs/ n **classify** /'klæsəfaɪ/ v

(in linguistics) a group of items which have something in common.
For example, in English words can be grouped (classified) into WORD
CLASSes according to how they combine with other words to form
phrases and sentences, how they change their form, etc. So *horse,
child, tree* belong to the word class noun, and *beautiful, noisy, hard*
belong to the word class adjective.
see also FORM CLASS, OPEN CLASS, TAXONOMIC

classifier[1] /'klæsəfaɪəʳ/ n

a word or affix used with a noun, which shows the sub-class to
which the noun belongs.
For example, in Malay *ekor* "tail" is a classifier for animals and is
used with numerals:

lima ekor lembu
five   ox   "five oxen"

Some languages such as Malay, Chinese, and various African
languages have an extensive system of classifiers. In English, a few
classifiers are still used, eg *head of* in:

five head of cattle
In languages such as Swahili, the affix classifying a noun is also added to its MODIFIER*s*, PREDICATE, etc.

classifier[2] *n*

(in SYSTEMIC LINGUISTICS) a word in a NOUN PHRASE[1] which shows the sub-class to which a person or thing belongs.
For example, nouns and adjectives can function as classifiers:

classifier	noun classified
electric	*trains*
steam	*trains*

see also MODIFIER, HEAD
[*Further reading*: Halliday 1982]

classroom interaction /ˈklɑːsruːm ɪntəˈrækʃən, -rʊm ‖ ˈklæs-/ *n*

the patterns of verbal and non-verbal communication and the types of social relationships which occur within classrooms. The study of classroom interaction may be a part of studies of classroom DISCOURSE, TEACHER TALK, and SECOND LANGUAGE ACQUISITION.
see also INTERACTION ANALYSIS

classroom management /ˈklɑːsruːm ˈmænədʒmənt, -rʊm ‖ ˈklæs-/ *n*

(in language teaching) the ways in which student behaviour, movement, interaction, etc during a class is organized and controlled by the teacher (or sometimes by the learners themselves) to enable teaching to take place most effectively. Classroom management includes procedures for grouping students for different types of classroom activities, use of LESSON PLAN*s*, handling of equipment, aids, etc, and the direction and management of student behaviour and activity.

clause /klɔːz/ *n*

a group of words which form a grammatical unit and which contain a subject and a FINITE VERB. A clause forms a sentence or part of a sentence and often functions as a noun, adjective, or adverb.
For example:
I hurried home.
Because I was late, they went without me.
Clauses are classified as DEPENDENT or independent, eg:

I hurried	*because I was late*.
independent clause	dependent clause

A clause is different from a **phrase**.
A phrase is a group of words which form a grammatical unit. A phrase does not contain a finite verb and does not have a subject-predicate structure:
For example:
I liked her expensive new car.
George hates working in the garden.

Phrases are usually classified according to their central word or HEAD, eg NOUN PHRASE[1], VERB PHRASE, etc.

see also RELATIVE CLAUSE

[*Further reading*: Quirk et al 1985]

cleft sentence /'kleft 'sentəns/ *n*

a sentence which has been divided into two parts, each with its own verb, to emphasize a particular piece of information.

Cleft sentences usually begin with *It* plus a form of the verb *be*, followed by the element which is being emphasized.

For example, the sentence *Mrs Smith gave Mary a dress.* can be turned into the following cleft sentences:

   It was Mrs Smith who gave Mary a dress.

   It was Mary that Mrs Smith gave the dress to.

   It was a dress that Mrs Smith gave to Mary.

In English a sentence with a *wh-clause* (eg *what I want*) as subject or complement is known as a **pseudo-cleft sentence**. For example:

   A good holiday is what I need.

   What I need is a good holiday.

[*Further reading*: Quirk et al 1985]

CLL /,si: el 'el/ *n*

an abbreviation for COMMUNITY LANGUAGE LEARNING

closed class /'kləʊzd 'klɑːs ‖ 'klæs/ *n*

see under OPEN CLASS

closed-ended response /'kləʊzd ,endəd rɪ'spɒns ‖ -'spɑns/ *n*

see under TEST ITEM

closed set /'kləʊzd 'set/ *n*

see under OPEN CLASS

closed syllable /'kləʊzd 'sɪləbəl/ *n*

see under SYLLABLE

close vowel /'kləʊs 'vaʊəl/ *n*

also **high vowel**

see under VOWEL

clozentropy /,kləʊ'zentrəpi/ *n*

a method of scoring cloze tests, based on the acceptable word method.

A cloze test is first given to a group of native speakers, and their responses are listed in frequency order.

When the test is given to non-native speakers, someone who responds with a high frequency word scores more than someone who responds with a low frequency word.

see also CLOZE PROCEDURE

cloze passage /'kləʊz 'pæsɪdʒ/ *n*

see under CLOZE PROCEDURE

cloze procedure /ˈkləʊz prəˈsiːdʒəʳ/ *n*

a technique for measuring reading comprehension. In a **cloze test**, words are removed from a reading passage at regular intervals, leaving blanks. For example every fifth word may be removed. The reader must then read the passage and try to guess the missing words.

For example, a **cloze passage** looks like this:

A passage used in _____ cloze test is a _____ of written material in _____ words have been regularly _____. The subjects must then _____ to reconstruct the passage _____ filling in the missing _____.

Here, the reader has to guess *a*, *passage*, *which*, *removed*, *try*, *by*, *words*.

The cloze procedure can also be used to judge the difficulty of reading materials.

If the cloze procedure is being used for language testing, the reader is given a score according to how well the words guessed matched the original words, or whether or not they made sense. Two types of scoring procedure are used:

(a) the reader must guess the exact word which was used in the original (as in the example above). This is called the **exact word method**.

(b) the reader can guess any word that is appropriate or acceptable in the context. This is called the **acceptable word method** (also the **appropriate word method**, the **acceptable alternative method**, and the **contextually appropriate method**).

see also CLOZENTROPY

[*Further reading*: Oller 1979]

cloze test /ˈkləʊz ˈtest/ *n*

see under CLOZE PROCEDURE

cluster /ˈklʌstəʳ/ *n*

see CONSONANT CLUSTER

cluster reduction /ˈklʌstəʳ rɪˌdʌkʃən/ *n*

When a speaker leaves out one or more of the CONSONANTS in a group of consonants (CONSONANT CLUSTER), this is called cluster reduction. This can occur at the beginning, the middle or the end of a word and is found in the speech of both native speakers and language learners.

For example, a learner of English whose native language has no final consonant clusters may reduce the cluster /nts/ to /ns/ or /n/, and pronounce *wants* as /wɒns/ or /wɒn/.

coda /ˈkəʊdə/ *n*

see under SYLLABLE

codability /ˌkəʊdəˈbɪləti/ *n*

Languages differ in the degree to which they provide words for the

description or naming of particular things, events, experiences, and states. For example, English makes a distinction between *blue* and *green* whereas some languages have a single word for this colour range. The degree to which an aspect of experience can be described by the vocabulary of a language is called codability.
[*Further reading*: Miller & Johnson-Laird 1976]

code¹ /kəʊd/ *n*
A term which is used instead of LANGUAGE, SPEECH VARIETY, or DIALECT. It is sometimes considered to be a more neutral term than the others. People also use "code" when they want to stress the uses of a language or language variety in a particular community. For example, a Puerto Rican in New York City may have two codes: English and Spanish. He or she may use one code (English) at work and the other code (Spanish) at home or when talking to neighbours.
see also CODE SELECTION, CODE SWITCHING
[*Further reading*: Hudson 1981; Hymes 1974]

code² *n*
a term used by the British educational sociologist Bernstein for different ways of conveying meaning in a social context. Bernstein distinguished between **elaborated code** and **restricted code**.
The restricted code is said to have a more reduced vocabulary range, to use more question tags, to use PRONOUNS like *he* and *she* instead of nouns and to use gestures such as hand movements to help give meaning to what is said. It is claimed that speakers using a restricted code assume that their addressees share a great many of their attitudes and expectations.
On the other hand, persons using an elaborated code are said to make greater use of adjectives, more complicated sentence structures and the pronoun *I*. The elaborated code is claimed to be more explicit and speakers using it do not assume the same degree of shared attitudes and expectations on the part of the addressee. It has been claimed that while middle-class children have access to both codes, working-class children have access only to the restricted code.
There has been a great deal of controversy over Bernstein's codes as they have been linked to theories which relate language learning to social class and educational policies.
see also DEFICIT HYPOTHESIS
[*Further reading*: Bernstein 1971]

code³ *n*
any system of signals which can be used for sending a MESSAGE. A natural language is an example of a code, as are Morse code, braille, and SIGN LANGUAGE.
The medium through which the signals are sent (eg by telephone, in writing) is called the CHANNEL (b).

code selection /ˈkəʊd sə̩ˌlekʃən/ n

the selection of a particular language or language variety for a given situation.

If someone uses more than one code when communicating with others, they usually select one code for certain purposes, in certain places, and with certain people and use another code for other purposes in other places, and with other people. This code selection is often quite regular and its patterns can be investigated.

For example, a Chinese in Singapore may use Hokkien (a Southern Chinese dialect) at home, Singapore English at work, and Bazaar Malay to Indian or Malay stallholders at the market.

The code a person selects may often depend on the ethnic background, sex, age, and level of education of the speaker and of the person with whom he/she is speaking.

see also CODE SWITCHING, DIGLOSSIA, DOMAIN

[*Further reading*: Fishman 1971; Platt & Weber 1980]

code switching /ˈkəʊd ˌswɪtʃɪŋ/ n

a change by a speaker (or writer) from one language or language variety to another one. Code switching can take place in a conversation when one speaker uses one language and the other speaker answers in a different language. A person may start speaking one language and then change to another one in the middle of their speech, or sometimes even in the middle of a sentence.

For example, from the speech of a German immigrant in Australia:
Das handelt von einem secondhand dealer and his son.
"That is about a . . ." [from Clyne 1972]

see also CODE SELECTION

[*Further reading*: Clyne 1972; Fishman 1971]

coefficient of determination /ˌkəʊə̩ˈfɪʃənt əv dɪˌtɜːmə̩ˈneɪʃən ‖ -ɜr-/ n

also **r^2**

a measure of the amount of variability shared or predicted by two VARIABLES. It is equal to the square of r (r = coefficient of CORRELATION). For example a correlation coefficient of +.70 indicates that 49% (ie +.70^2) of the variability is shared by the two variables, ie, 51% of the variability is not shared or predicted by the variables.

[*Further reading*: Hardyck & Petrinovich 1976]

cognate /ˈkɒɡneɪt ‖ ˈkɑɡ-/ n, adj

a word in one language which is similar in form and meaning to a word in another language because both languages are related. For example English *brother* and German *Bruder*.

Sometimes words in two languages are similar in form and meaning but are BORROWINGs and not cognate forms.

For example, *kampuni* in the African language Swahili, is a borrowing from English *company*.

see also FALSE COGNATE

cognition /kɒgˈnɪʃən ‖ kɑg-/ *n* **cognitive** /ˈkɒgnətɪv ‖ ˈkɑg-/ *adj*
the various mental processes used in thinking, remembering, perceiving, recognizing, classifying, etc.
see also COGNITIVE PSYCHOLOGY

cognitive code approach /ˈkɒgnətɪv ˈkəʊd əˌprəʊtʃ ‖ ˈkɑg-/ *n*
an approach to second and foreign language teaching which is based on the belief that language learning is a process which involves active mental processes and not simply the forming of habits. It gives importance to the learner's active part in the process of using and learning language, particularly in the learning of grammatical rules. Although it has not led to any particular method of language teaching, the COMMUNICATIVE APPROACH makes some use of cognitive code principles.
[*Further reading*: Rivers 1981]

cognitive meaning /ˈkɒgnətɪv ˈmiːnɪŋ ‖ ˈkɑg-/ *n*
another term for DENOTATION

cognitive process /ˈkɒgnətɪv ˈprəʊses ‖ ˈkɑg-, ˈprɑ-/ *n*
also **cognitive strategy**
any mental process which learners make use of in language learning, such as INFERENCING, GENERALIZATION, DEDUCTIVE LEARNING, MONITORING, and MEMORIZING.

cognitive psychology /ˈkɒgnətɪv saɪˈkɒlədʒi ‖ˈkɑg- saɪˈkɑ-/ *n*
a branch of psychology which deals with the study of the nature and learning of systems of knowledge, particularly those processes involved in thought, perception, comprehension, memory, and learning.
In recent years cognitive psychology has been related to mentalistic approaches to linguistics, especially Chomsky's GENERATIVE TRANSFORMATIONAL GRAMMAR, which links language structure to the nature of human cognitive processes.
see also BEHAVIOURISM
[*Further reading*: Neisser 1967]

cognitive science /ˈkɒgnətɪv ˈsaɪəns ‖ ˈkɑg-/ *n*
a discipline which draws on research in LINGUISTICS, PSYCHOLINGUISTICS, COGNITIVE PSYCHOLOGY and ARTIFICIAL INTELLIGENCE. Cognitive science deals with the scientific study of thinking, reasoning and the intellectual processes of the mind; it is concerned with how knowledge is represented in the mind, how language is understood, how images are understood, and with what the mental processes underlying INFERENCING, learning, problem solving, and planning, are.
[*Further reading*: Johnson-Laird & Wason 1977]

cognitive strategy /ˈkɒgnətɪv ˈstrætədʒi ‖ˈkɑg-/ *n*
another term for COGNITIVE PROCESS and COGNITIVE STYLE

cognitive style /ˈkɒɡnətɪv ˈstaɪl ‖ ˈkɑɡ-/ *n*
also **cognitive strategy, learning style**

the particular way in which a learner tries to learn something.
In second or foreign language learning, different learners may prefer different solutions to learning problems. For example, some may want explanations for grammatical rules; others may not need explanations. Some may feel writing down words or sentences helps them to remember them. Others may find they remember things better if they are associated with pictures. These are called differences of cognitive style.

see also FIELD DEPENDENCE, GLOBAL LEARNING
[*Further reading*: Brown 1980]

cognitive variable /ˈkɒɡnətɪv ˈveərɪəbəl ‖ ˈkɑɡ-/ *n*

When a person tries to learn something, his/her success is partly governed by intelligence, memory, and the ability to analyse and evaluate. These are called cognitive variables.
But attitudes, emotions, motivation, personality, etc may also influence learning. These are called **affective variables**.
For example, the attitude a learner has towards a foreign language may affect his/her success in learning it.
One technique for measuring this aspect of learning is the SEMANTIC DIFFERENTIAL.

see also EMPATHY, LANGUAGE ATTITUDES, MOTIVATION
[*Further reading*: Brown 1980; Jakobovits 1970]

coherence /kəʊˈhɪərəns/ *n* **coherent** /kəʊˈhɪərənt/ *adj*

the relationships which link the meanings of UTTERANCEs in a DISCOURSE or of the sentences in a text.
These links may be based on the speakers' shared knowledge. For example:

    A: *Could you give me a lift home?*
    B: *Sorry, I'm visiting my sister.*

There is no grammatical or lexical link between A's question and B's reply (see COHESION) but the exchange has coherence because both A and B know that B's sister lives in the opposite direction to A's home.
Generally a PARAGRAPH has coherence if it is a series of sentences that develop a main idea (ie with a TOPIC SENTENCE and supporting sentences which relate to it).

see also SCHEME, TEXT LINGUISTICS, CONVERSATIONAL MAXIM
[*Further reading*: Coulthard 1985]

cohesion /kəʊˈhiːʒən/ *n*

the grammatical and/or lexical relationships between the different elements of a text. This may be the relationship between different sentences or between different parts of a sentence. For example:

(a) A: *Is Jenny coming to the party?*
     B: *Yes, she is.*

cohort

There is a link between *Jenny* and *she* and also between *is* . . .
coming and *is*.
(b) In the sentence:
> *If you are going to London, I can give you the address of a good*
> *hotel there.*

the link is between *London* and *there* (see ANAPHORA).
see also COHERENCE
[*Further reading*: Halliday & Hasan 1976]

cohort /'kəʊhɔːt ‖ -hɔrt/ *n*
(in experimental research) a group of people who have some feature
in common (eg age, IQ, or number of months they have studied a
foreign language).

collective noun /kə'lektɪv 'naʊn/ *n*
a noun which refers to a collection of people, animals, or things as a
group. For example *school*, *family*, *government* are collective nouns.
When collective nouns are used in the singular, they may be used
with either a singular verb or a plural verb. For example:
> *The government is going to look into this matter.*
> *The government are looking into this matter.*

The use of the plural verb suggests that the noun refers to
something which is seen as a group of individuals, whereas the use
of the singular verb suggests something seen as a single whole.
see also NOUN
[*Further reading*: Quirk et al 1985]

collocation /ˌkɒlə'keɪʃən ‖ ˌkɑ-/ *n* **collocate** /'kɒləkeɪt ‖ 'kɑ-/ *v*
the way in which words are used together regularly.
Collocation refers to the restrictions on how words can be used
together, for example which prepositions are used with particular
verbs, or which verbs and nouns are used together.
For example, in English the verb *perform* is used with *operation*,
but not with *discussion*:
> *The doctor performed the operation.*
> **The committee performed a discussion.*

instead we say:
> *The committee held/had a discussion.*

perform is used with (collocates with) *operation*, and *hold* and *have*
collocate with *discussion*.
high collocates with *probability*, but not with *chance*:
> *a high probability*   but   *a good chance*

do collocates with *damage*, *duty*, and *wrong*, but not with *trouble*,
noise, and *excuse*:
> *do a lot of damage   do one's duty   do wrong*
> *make trouble   make a lot of noise   make an excuse*

see also IDIOM
[*Further reading*: Bolinger 1975]

colloquial speech /kəˈləʊkwɪəl ˈspiːtʃ/ n
also **informal speech**

the type of speech used in everyday, informal situations when the speaker is not paying particular attention to pronunciation, choice of words, or sentence structure. Colloquial speech is not necessarily non-prestige speech and should not be considered as SUB-STANDARD. Educated native speakers of a language normally use colloquial speech in informal situations with friends, fellow workers, and members of the family.

For example, they might say:

Why don't you come around this evening?

rather than the more formal

We should be delighted if you would pay us a visit this evening.

It is often difficult for language learners to realize that in certain situations colloquial speech is more appropriate than extremely formal speech.

see also STYLE

combining form /kəmˈbaɪnɪŋ ˌfɔːm ‖ ˌfɔrm/ n

a BOUND FORM that can form a new word by combining with another combining form, a word, or sometimes an AFFIX. For example, the combining form *astr(o)*-, 'star', can form the word *astrology* with the combining form *-(o)logy*, the word *astrophysics* with the word *physics*, and the word *astral* with the suffix *-al*. Groups of MORPHEMEs like the *-blooded* of *warm-blooded* or the *-making* of *trouble-making* are also sometimes regarded as combining forms.

see also WORD FORMATION

comment /ˈkɒment ‖ ˈkɑ-/ n

see under TOPIC²

comment clause /ˈkɒment ˌklɔːz ‖ ˈkɑ-/ n

a clause which comments on another clause in a sentence. For example:

She is, I believe, a New Zealander.

Coming from you, that sounds surprising.

Comment clauses function as ADJUNCTs or disjuncts, and are optional in the sentence structure.

[*Further reading*: Quirk et al 1985]

commissive /kəˈmɪsɪv/ n

see under SPEECH ACT CLASSIFICATION

common core /ˈkɒmən ˈkɔːʳ ‖ ˈkɑmən ˈkɔr/ n

(in language teaching) those basic aspects of a language (eg vocabulary and grammar) which a learner needs to know whatever his or her purpose is in learning the language. When designing a language SYLLABUS a teacher must decide how much of the language content of the course must be common core and how much must be directed to the learner's particular needs, eg for science or business.

see also ENGLISH FOR SPECIAL PURPOSES

common noun /ˈkɒmən ˈnaʊn ‖ ˈkɑ-/ n
see under PROPER NOUN

communication /kəˌmjuːnɪˈkeɪʃən/ n **communicate** /kəˈmjuːnɪkeɪt/ v
the exchange of ideas, information, etc between two or more
persons. In an act of communication there is usually at least one
speaker or **sender**, a MESSAGE which is transmitted, and a person or
persons for whom this message is intended (the **receiver**). The study
of communication is central to SOCIOLINGUISTICS, PSYCHOLINGUISTICS,
and INFORMATION THEORY.
see also COMMUNICATIVE COMPETENCE, SPEECH EVENT
[*Further reading*: Coulthard 1985; Hymes 1974]

communication strategy /kəˌmjuːnɪˈkeɪʃən ˈstrætədʒi/ n
a way used to express a meaning in a second or foreign language,
by a learner who has a limited command of the language. In trying
to communicate, a learner may have to make up for a lack of
knowledge of grammar or vocabulary.
For example the learner may not be able to say *It's against the law
to park here* and so he/she may say *This place, cannot park*. For
handkerchief a learner could say *a cloth for my nose*, and for
apartment complex the learner could say *building*. The use of
PARAPHRASE and other communication strategies (eg gesture and
mime) characterize the INTERLANGUAGE of some language learners.
see also ACCOMMODATION, FOREIGNER TALK
[*Further reading*: Faerch & Kasper 1983; Tarone 1977]

communication theory /kəˌmjuːnɪˈkeɪʃən ˈθɪəri/ n
another term for INFORMATION THEORY

communicative approach /kəˈmjuːnɪkətɪv əˈprəʊtʃ/ n
also **communicative language teaching**
an APPROACH to foreign or second language teaching which
emphasizes that the goal of language learning is COMMUNICATIVE
COMPETENCE.
The communicative approach has been developed particularly by
British applied linguists as a reaction away from grammar-based
approaches such as the aural-oral approach (see under AUDIOLINGUAL
METHOD). Teaching materials used with a communicative approach
often
(a) teach the language needed to express and understand different
    kinds of functions, such as requesting, describing, expressing likes
    and dislikes, etc
(b) are based on a NOTIONAL SYLLABUS or some other communicatively
    organized syllabus
(c) emphasize the processes of communication, such as using
    language appropriately in different types of situations; using
    language to perform different kinds of tasks, eg to solve puzzles,
    to get information, etc; using language for social interaction with
    other people.
[*Further reading*: Littlewood 1981; Richards & Rogers 1986]

communicative competence /kə'mju:nə̀kətɪv 'kɒmpə̀təns ‖ 'kʌm-/ *n*
the ability not only to apply the grammatical rules of a language in
order to form grammatically correct sentences but also to know
when and where to use these sentences and to whom.
Communicative competence includes:

(a) knowledge of the grammar and vocabulary of the LANGUAGE[2]
(see COMPETENCE)

(b) knowledge of RULES OF SPEAKING (eg knowing how to begin and
end conversations, knowing what topics may be talked about in
different types of SPEECH EVENTS, knowing which ADDRESS FORMS
should be used with different persons one speaks to and in
different situations

(c) knowing how to use and respond to different types of SPEECH
ACTS, such as requests, apologies, thanks, and invitations

(d) knowing how to use language appropriately (see
APPROPRIATENESS)

For example when someone wishes to communicate with others,
they must recognize the social setting, their relationship to the other
person(s) (see ROLE RELATIONSHIP), and the types of language that can
be used for a particular occasion. They must also be able to
interpret written or spoken sentences within the total context in
which they are used.
For example, the English statement *It's rather cold in here* could be
a request, particularly to someone in a lower role relationship, to
close a window or door or to turn on the heating.
see also STYLE, PRAGMATICS
[*Further reading*: Coulthard 1985; Hymes 1974]

communicative drill /kə'mju:nə̀kətɪv 'drɪl/ *n*
see under MEANINGFUL DRILL

communicative function /kə'mju:nə̀kətɪv 'fʌŋkʃən/ *n*
the extent to which a language is used in a community. Some
languages may be used for very specific purposes, such as the
language called *Pali*, which is used only for religious purposes in
Buddhism. Other languages are used for almost all the
communicative needs of a community, eg Japanese in Japan.

communicative interference /kə'mju:nə̀kətɪv ˌɪntə'fɪərəns ‖ -tər-/ *n*
interference (see LANGUAGE TRANSFER) which is caused by the use of
RULES OF SPEAKING (eg greetings, ways of opening or closing
conversations, ADDRESS SYSTEMS) from one language when speaking
another. For example, conversations in English often open with a
health question (*How are you*?) but in other languages, such as
Malay, open with a food question (*Have you eaten yet*?). A Malay-
speaking student learning English who opened a conversation in
English with *Have you eaten yet*? would be speaking with
communicative interference from Malay to English.

communicative language teaching

communicative language teaching /kə'mjuːnə̀kətɪv 'læŋgwɪdʒ
'tiːtʃɪŋ/ *n*
another term for COMMUNICATIVE APPROACH

community language /kə'mjuːnə̀ti ˌlæŋgwɪdʒ/ *n*
a language used within a particular community, including languages
spoken by ethnic minority groups.
For example, in Australia, apart from English, languages such as
Italian, Greek, Polish, Arabic, and Australian Aboriginal languages
are community languages.
Community language should not be confused with COMMUNITY
LANGUAGE LEARNING.

Community Language Learning /kə'mjuːnə̀ti 'læŋgwɪdʒ 'lɜːnɪŋ ‖
'lɜr-/ *n*
also **CLL**
a METHOD of second and foreign language teaching developed by
Charles Curran. Community Language Learning is an application of
counselling learning to second and foreign language teaching and
learning. It uses techniques developed in group counselling to help
people with psychological and emotional problems. The method
makes use of group learning in small or large groups. These groups
are the "community". The method places emphasis on the learners'
personal feelings and their reactions to language learning. Learners
say things which they want to talk about, in their native language.
The teacher (known as "Counselor") translates the learner's
sentences into the foreign language, and the learner then repeats
this to other members of the group.
[*Further reading*: Curran 1976; Richards & Rogers 1986]

comparative /kəm'pærətɪv/ *n*
also **comparative degree**
the form of an adjective or adverb which is used to show
comparison between two things. In English, the comparative is
formed with the suffix *-er*, or with *more*:

This is   better
           more useful   than that.

The **superlative** is the form of an adjective or adverb which shows the
most or the least in quality, quantity, or intensity. In English, the
superlative is formed with the suffix *-est* or with *most*:

She is   the tallest
          the most beautiful   in the class.

comparative clause /kəm'pærətɪv 'klɔːz/ *n*
also **comparative sentence**
a clause which contains a standard with which someone or
something referred to in an INDEPENDENT CLAUSE is compared. In
English, comparative clauses are often introduced with *than* or *as*:

> *Tom is much taller <u>than John is</u>.*
> *Jane doesn't write <u>as neatly as Fiona does</u>.*

[*Further reading*: Quirk et al 1985]

comparative degree /kəmˈpærətɪv dɪˈgriː/ *n*
another term for COMPARATIVE

comparative historical linguistics /kəmˈpærətɪv hɪˈstɒrɪkəl lɪŋˈgwɪstɪks ‖ -ˈstɔ-, -ˈstɑ-/ *n*
also **comparative philology, philology, historical linguistics**
a branch of linguistics which studies language change and language relationships. By comparing earlier and later forms of a language and by comparing different languages, it has been possible to show that certain languages are related, eg the INDO-EUROPEAN LANGUAGES. It has also been possible to reconstruct forms which are believed to have occurred in a particular language before written records were available.
For example **p* in an ancestor language to all the Indo-European languages is said to be related to /p/ in Sanskrit as in *pita* "father" and /f/ in English as in *father*.
see also DIACHRONIC LINGUISTICS
[*Further reading*: Aitchison 1981; Lehmann 1973]

comparative linguistics /kəmˈpærətɪv lɪŋˈgwɪstɪks/ *n*
a branch of linguistics which studies two or more languages in order to compare their structures and to show whether they are similar or different. Comparative linguistics is used in the study of language types (see TYPOLOGY) and in COMPARATIVE HISTORICAL LINGUISTICS. It is also used by some applied linguists for establishing differences between the learner's native language and the TARGET LANGUAGE[1] in the areas of syntax, vocabulary, and sound systems.
see also CONTRASTIVE ANALYSIS
[*Further reading*: Bolinger 1975]

comparative philology /kəmˈpærətɪv fəˈlɒlədʒi ‖ -ˈlɑ-/ *n*
another term for COMPARATIVE HISTORICAL LINGUISTICS

comparative sentence /kəmˈpærətɪv ˈsentəns/
another term for COMPARATIVE CLAUSE

compensatory instruction /kəmˈpensətəri ɪnˈstrʌkʃən, kɒmpənˈseɪ- ‖ kəmˈpensətori/ *n*
also **compensatory education** /kəmˈpensətəri ˌedjʊˈkeɪʃən, kɒmpənˈseɪ- ‖ kəmˈpensətori ˌedʒə-/
a special education programme for children whose home background is said to lack certain kinds of language experience. For example, children who are not read to at home or who do not have story books at home.
see also CULTURAL DEPRIVATION

competence /'kɒmpǝ̇tǝns ‖ 'kɑm-/ *n*

(in GENERATIVE TRANSFORMATIONAL GRAMMAR) a person's internalized grammar of a language. This means a person's ability to create and understand sentences, including sentences they have never heard before. It also includes a person's knowledge of what are and what are not sentences of a particular language.

For example, a speaker of English would recognize *I want to go home* as an English sentence but would not accept a sentence such as *I want going home* even though all the words in it are English words.

Competence often refers to the **ideal speaker/hearer**, that is an idealized but not a real person who would have a complete knowledge of the whole language. A distinction is made between competence and PERFORMANCE, which is the actual use of the language by individuals in speech and writing.

see also COMMUNICATIVE COMPETENCE

[*Further reading*: Aitchison 1978; Chomsky 1965]

complement /'kɒmplǝ̇mǝnt ‖ 'kɑm-/ *n* **complementation**
/ˌkɒmplǝmǝn'teɪʃǝn ‖ ˌkɑm-/ *n*

(in grammar) that part of the sentence which follows the verb and which thus *completes* the sentence. The commonest complements are:

(a) **subject complement**: the complement linked to a subject by *be* or a linking verb:
She is a doctor.

(b) **object complement**: the complement linked to an object:
We made her the chairperson.

(c) **adjective complement**: the complement linked to an adjective:
I am glad that you can come.

(d) **prepositional complement**: the complement linked to a preposition:
They argued about what to do.

While ADJUNCTs are optional parts of sentences, complements are often obligatory parts of the sentences in which they occur.

A clause which functions as a complement is called a **complement(ary) clause**. For example:
The question is why you did it.

[*Further reading*: Quirk et al 1985]

complement(ary) clause /ˌkɒmplǝ̇'mentǝri 'klɔːz ‖ ˌkɑm-/ *n*
see under COMPLEMENT

complementaries /ˌkɒmplǝ̇'mentǝriz ‖ ˌkɑm-/ *n*
see under ANTONYM

complex sentence /'kɒmpleks 'sentǝns ‖ 'kɑm-/ *n*
a sentence which contains one or more DEPENDENT CLAUSEs, in addition to its independent, or main, clause. For example:

When it rained, we went inside.
(dep cl)   (ind cl)

A sentence which contains two or more independent clauses which are joined by co-ordination is called a **compound sentence**. For example:

He is a small boy but he is very strong.
(ind cl)   (ind cl)

I'll either phone you or I will send you a note.
(ind cl)   (ind cl)

A sentence which contains only one PREDICATE is called a **simple sentence**. For example:

I like milk.
   (pred)

complex transitive verb /ˈkɒmpleks ˈtrænsətɪv ˈvɜːb ‖ ˈkɑm- ˈvɜrb/ *n*
see under TRANSITIVE VERB

componential analysis /ˌkɒmpəˈnenʃəl əˈnæləsəs/ *n*
(1) (in semantics) an approach to the study of meaning which analyses a word into a set of meaning **components** or semantic features. For example, the meaning of the English word *boy* may be shown as:
   <+human> <+male> <−adult>
Usually, componential analysis is applied to a group of related words which may differ from one another only by one or two components.
This approach was developed in ANTHROPOLOGICAL LINGUISTICS for the study of kinship and other terms in various languages.
(2) any approach to linguistics which analyses linguistic units, usually words or sounds, into smaller parts or components. This approach has been used in phonology and semantics.
see also DISTINCTIVE FEATURE, SEMANTIC FEATURES
[*Further reading*: Lyons 1981]

components /kəmˈpəʊnənts/ *n*
see under COMPONENTIAL ANALYSIS

composition /ˌkɒmpəˈzɪʃən ‖ ˌkɑm-/ *n*
(in language teaching) writing practice which deals with texts longer than a single sentence, such as paragraphs, essays, and reports.
Two types of composition are commonly used: (a) **free composition**, in which the student's writing is not controlled or limited in any way, such as essay questions, or writing about a particular topic.
(b) **controlled composition**, in which the student's writing is controlled by various means, such as by providing questions to be answered, sentences to be completed, or words or pictures to follow.

compound adjective /ˈkɒmpaʊnd ˈædʒəktɪv ‖ ˈkɑm-/ *n*
see under COMPOUND WORD

compound bilingualism /ˈkɒmpaʊnd baɪˈlɪŋgwəlɪzəm ‖ ˈkɑm-/ *n*
There is a theory that a bilingual person relates words to their meanings in one of two ways.
Compound bilingualism means that the bilingual has one system of word meanings, which is used for both the first and the second language. For a French/English bilingual, the French word *pain* ("bread") and the English word *bread* have the same meaning.
Co-ordinate bilingualism means that the bilingual has two systems of meanings for words; one system is for the words the person knows in the first language and the other is for the words he or she knows in the second language.
For a French/English bilingual the French word *pain* and the English word *bread* would not have exactly the same meanings.
This theory was an attempt to show how the different conditions under which people become bilingual could lead to different systems of meaning. The distinction between compound and co-ordinate bilingualism has been used in studies of vocabulary learning, but has not been found useful as a general model of bilingualism.
[*Further reading*: Ervin & Osgood 1954]

compound noun /ˈkɒmpaʊnd ˈnaʊn ‖ ˈkɑm-/ *n*
see under COMPOUND WORD

compound sentence /ˈkɒmpaʊnd ˈsentəns ‖ ˈkɑm-/ *n*
see under COMPLEX SENTENCE

compound word /ˈkɒmpaʊnd ˈwɜːd ‖ ˈkɑm- ˈwɜrd/ *n*
a combination of two or more words which functions as a single word.
For example *self-made* (a **compound adjective**) as in *He was a self-made man* and *flower shop* (a **compound noun**) as in *They went to the flower shop*. Compound words are written either as a single word (eg *headache*), as hyphenated words (eg *self-government*), or as two words (eg *police station*).
see also PHRASAL VERB

comprehensible input /ˌkɒmprɪˈhensəbəl ˈɪnpʊt ‖ ˌkɑm-/ *n*
INPUT language which contains linguistic items that are slightly beyond the learner's present linguistic COMPETENCE.
see also INPUT HYPOTHESIS
[*Further reading*: Krashen 1985]

comprehension /ˌkɒmprɪˈhenʃən ‖ ˌkɑm-/ *n*
the process by which a person understands the meaning of written or spoken language. The measurement of listening and reading comprehension abilities is an important part of the assessment of a person's proficiency in a second or foreign language.
see also INFORMATION PROCESSING, READING, DECODING
[*Further reading*: Heaton 1975]

comprehension approach /ˌkɒmprɪˈhenʃən əˈprəʊtʃ ‖ ˌkɑm-/ *n*
(in language teaching) an APPROACH to second and foreign language
teaching which emphasizes that:
(a) before learners are taught speaking, there should be a period of
    training in listening comprehension
(b) comprehension should be taught by teaching learners to
    understand meaning in the TARGET LANGUAGE[1]
(c) the learners' level of comprehension should always exceed their
    ability to produce language
(d) productive language skills will emerge more naturally when
    learners have well developed comprehension skills
(e) such an approach reflects how children learn their first language.
Although this approach has not led to a specific METHOD of language
teaching, similar principles are found in the TOTAL PHYSICAL RESPONSE
METHOD and the NATURAL APPROACH (2).
[*Further reading*: Winitz 1981]

computational linguistics /ˌkɒmpjʊˈteɪʃənəl lɪŋˈgwɪstɪks ‖ ˌkɑm-/ *n*
an approach to linguistics which uses mathematical techniques, often
with the aid of a computer. Computational linguistics includes the
analysis of language data, eg in order to establish the order in which
learners acquire various grammatical rules or the frequency of
occurrence of some particular item. It also includes research on
automatic translation, electronic production of artificial speech
(**speech synthesis**) and the automatic recognition of human speech.

computer assisted instruction /kəmˈpjuːtər əˈsɪstəd ɪnˈstrʌkʃən/ *n*
also **CAI, computer assisted language learning (CALL)** /kəmˈpjuːtər
əˈsɪstəd ˈlæŋgwɪdʒ ˌlɜːnɪŋ ‖ ˌlɜr-/, **computer based instruction**
/kəmˈpjuːtəʳ beɪst inˈstrʌkʃən/
the use of a computer in a teaching programme. This may include:
(a) a teaching programme which is presented by a computer in a
    sequence. The student responds on the computer, and the
    computer indicates whether the responses are correct or
    incorrect (see PROGRAMMED LEARNING).
(b) the use of computers to monitor student progress, to direct
    students into appropriate lessons, material, etc. This is also
    called **computer-managed instruction**.
see also INTERACTIVE

concept /ˈkɒnsept ‖ ˈkɑn-/ *n*
the general idea or meaning which is associated with a word or
symbol in a person's mind. Concepts are the abstract meanings
which words and other linguistic items represent. Linguists believe
all languages can express the same concepts, although some
languages may have fewer names for some concepts than are found
in other languages, or may distinguish between concepts differently.
The forming of concepts is closely related to language ACQUISITION,
and the use of concepts to form PROPOSITIONs is basic to human
thought and communication.

conceptual meaning

concept formation /ˈkɒnsept fɔːˈmeɪʃən ‖ ˌkɑn- fɔr-/ *n*
(in child development) the process of forming CONCEPTS, and an
important part of the development of thought.

conceptual meaning /kənˈseptʃuəl ˈmiːnɪŋ/ *n*
another term for DENOTATION

concord /ˈkɒŋkɔːd ‖ ˈkɑŋkɔrd/ *n*
also **agreement**
a type of grammatical relationship between two or more elements in
a sentence, in which both or all elements show a particular feature.
For example, in English a third person singular subject occurs with a
singular verb, and a plural subject occurs with a plural verb (**number
concord**):
   He walks   They walk
Concord may affect CASE, GENDER, NUMBER, and PERSON.
see also GOVERNMENT

concrete noun /ˈkɒŋkriːt ‖ ˈkɑŋ-/ *n*
a noun which refers to a physical thing, rather than a quality, state,
or action. For example *book, house*, and *machine* are concrete nouns.
A noun which refers to a quality, state, or action is called an
abstract noun. For example *happiness, idea*, and *punishment* are
abstract nouns.
see also NOUN

concrete operational stage /ˈkɒŋkriːt ɒpəˈreɪʃənəl ˈsteɪdʒ ‖ ˈkɑŋ- ɑpə-/ *n*
see under GENETIC EPISTEMOLOGY

concurrent validity /kənˈkʌrənt vəˈlɪdəti ‖ -ˈkɜr-/ *n*
the degree to which a test correlates with some other test which is
aimed at measuring the same skill, or with some other comparable
measure of the skill being tested. For example to determine the
concurrent validity of a listening comprehension test one could
determine the correlation between scores of a group of learners on
this test with their scores on an existing valid and reliable test of
listening comprehension. The resulting COEFFICIENT OF CORRELATION
would provide a measure of the concurrent VALIDITY of the test.
[*Further reading*: Oller 1979]

conditional /kənˈdɪʃənəl/ *n*
a grammatical MOOD which describes an imaginary or hypothetical
situation or event. In some languages it is expressed by adding an
AFFIX to the verb, eg *je donnerais* ("I would give") in French, where
ais is the conditional affix added to the verb infinitive *donner* ("to
give"). In English, *should* and *would* are also sometimes described
as the conditional in sentences such as:
   We should like to meet her.   I would go if I could.

conditional clause /kənˈdɪʃənəl klɔːz/ *n*
(in English) ADVERBIAL CLAUSES beginning with *if*, *unless* or

56

conjunctions with similar meanings, where a state or situation in one clause is dependent on something that may or will happen, and which is described in another clause. For example:

If it rains, we will go home.
If you worked harder, you would succeed.
You won't be able to drive unless you have a licence.

[*Further reading*: Close 1975]

conditioned response /kən'dɪʃənd rɪ'spɒns ‖ -'spɑns/ *n*
(in behaviourist psychology (see BEHAVIOURISM)) a response which is not a normal or automatic response to a STIMULUS but which has been learned through the formation of a chain of associations (see STIMULUS-RESPONSE THEORY). For example, the Russian psychologist Pavlov noted that dogs produce saliva in the mouth when they see or smell food. This is an unconditioned response to a stimulus, the food. By ringing a bell as the dog sees the food, it is possible to train the dog to salivate when it hears the bell, even when food is absent. The salivation is now a conditioned response. Behavioural psychologists believe that people are conditioned to learn many forms of behaviour, including language, through the process of training or **conditioning**, and that learning consists of stimulus-response connections.

see also OPERANT CONDITIONING

[*Further reading*: Gagné 1970]

conditioning /kən'dɪʃənɪŋ/ *n*
see under CONDITIONED RESPONSE

conjoining /kən'dʒɔɪnɪŋ/ *n* **conjoin** /kən'dʒɔɪn/ *v*
(in GENERATIVE TRANSFORMATIONAL GRAMMAR), a term used for the linking together of words, phrases, or clauses, etc which are of equal status. For example:

John likes apples and pears.
Betty went to the butcher's and to the supermarket.

see also CONJUNCTION, EMBEDDING

conjugation[1] /ˌkɒndʒʊ'geɪʃən ‖ ˌkɑndʒə-/ *n*
a class of verbs which follow the same pattern for changes in TENSE, PERSON, or NUMBER. For example, in French there are four regular conjugations as well as irregular verbs. The verbs *donner* "to give", *parler* "to speak", *chercher* "to look for", etc are described as belonging to the *-er* (or 1st) conjugation.

conjugation[2] *n* **conjugate** /'kɒndʒʊgət ‖ 'kɑndʒə-/ *v*
the way in which a particular verb changes (conjugates) for TENSE, PERSON, or NUMBER. For example, the French verb *donner* "to give": *je donne* "I give", *nous donnons* "we give", *je donnerai* "I shall give", *j'ai donné* "I have given, I gave".

conjunct /'kɒndʒʌŋkt ‖ 'kɑn-/ *n*
see under ADJUNCT

conjunction /kənˈdʒʌŋkʃən/ n
also **connective**

(1) a word which joins words, phrases, or clauses together, such as
but, and, when:

John *and* Mary went.
She sings *but* I don't.

Units larger than single words which function as conjunctions are
sometimes known as **conjunctives**, for example *so that, as long as,
as if*:

She ran fast *so that* she could catch the bus.

Adverbs which are used to introduce or connect clauses are
sometimes known as **conjunctive adverbs**, for example *however,
nevertheless*:

She is 86, *nevertheless* she enjoys good health.

(2) the process by which such joining takes place.

There are two types of conjunction:

(a) **Co-ordination**, through the use of **co-ordinating conjunctions**
(also known as **co-ordinators**) such as *and, or, but*. These join
linguistic units which are equivalent or of the same rank.
For example:

It rained, *but* I went for a walk anyway.
Shall we go home *or* go to see a movie.

The two clauses are **co-ordinate clauses**.

(b) **Subordination**, through the use of **subordinating conjunctions**
(also known as **subordinators**) such as *because, when, unless,
that*. These join an INDEPENDENT CLAUSE and a DEPENDENT CLAUSE
For example:

I knew *that* he was lying.
Unless it rains, we'll play tennis at 4.

conjunctive /kənˈdʒʌŋktɪv/ n
see under CONJUNCTION

conjunctive adverb /kənˈdʒʌŋktɪv ˈædvɜːb ‖ -vɜrb/ n
see under CONJUNCTION

connective /kəˈnektɪv/ n
another term for CONJUNCTION

connotation /ˌkɒnəˈteɪʃən ‖ ˌkɑ-/ n **connotative** /ˈkɒnəteɪtɪv,
kəˈnəʊtətɪv ‖ ˈkɑnə-/ adj

the additional meanings that a word or phrase has beyond its central
meaning (see DENOTATION). These meanings show people's emotions
and attitudes towards what the word or phrase refers to.

For example, *child* could be defined as a *young human being* but
there are many other characteristics which different people associate
with *child*, eg *affectionate, amusing, lovable, sweet, mischievous,
noisy, irritating, grubby*.

Some connotations may be shared by a group of people of the same
cultural or social background, sex, or age; others may be restricted

to one or several individuals and depend on their personal experience.

In a meaning system, that part of the meaning which is covered by connotation is sometimes referred to as **affective meaning**, **connotative meaning**, or **emotive meaning**.
[*Further reading*: Leech 1981; Lyons 1977]

connotative meaning /ˈkɒnəteɪtɪv ˈmiːnɪŋ, kəˈnəʊtətɪv ‖ ˈkɑnə-/ *n*
another term for CONNOTATION

consecutive interpretation /kənˈsekjʊtɪv ɪnˌtɜːprəˈteɪʃən ‖ -ˌtɜr-/ *n*
see under INTERPRETATION

consonant /ˈkɒnsənənt ‖ ˈkɑn-/ *n*
a speech sound where the airstream from the lungs is either completely blocked (STOP), partially blocked (LATERAL) or where the opening is so narrow that the air escapes with audible friction (FRICATIVE). With some consonants (NASALS) the airstream is blocked in the mouth but allowed to escape through the nose.

With the other group of speech sounds, the VOWELs, the air from the lungs is not blocked.

There are a number of cases where the distinction is not clear-cut, such as the /j/ at the beginning of the English word *yes* where there is only very slight friction, and linguists have sometimes called these **semi-vowels** or **semi-consonants**.

see also MANNER OF ARTICULATION, PLACE OF ARTICULATION
[*Further reading*: Gimson 1980]

consonant cluster /ˈkɒnsənənt ˈklʌstəʳ ‖ ˈkɑn-/ *n*
a sequence of two or more consonants. Consonant clusters may occur at the beginning of a word (an **initial cluster**), at the end of a word (a **final cluster**), or within a word (a **medial cluster**). For example, in English:

initial cluster: /spl/ in /splæʃ/ *splash*
final cluster: /st/ in /test/ *test*
medial cluster: /str/ in /ˈpeɪstri/ *pastry*

Languages differ greatly in the ways in which consonants can form clusters, and in which positions in the word the clusters can occur. For example, in Serbo-Croatian, there are many three-consonant clusters in initial position which do not occur in English, eg /smr/, /zdr/, /zgr/, /zdv/. Other languages, for example Polynesian languages, do not have any consonant clusters at all.

see also CLUSTER REDUCTION

consonant system /ˈkɒnsənənt ˈsɪstəm ‖ ˈkɑn-/ *n*
The CONSONANTs of a language form systems. For example, English has, among other consonants, two parallel series of STOPs:

	BILABIAL	ALVEOLAR	VELAR
VOICELESS	p	t	k
VOICED	b	d	g

Maori, a Polynesian language, has only one series: /p/, /t/, /k/ with no voiceless/voiced contrast (see VOICE²).

constative /'kɒnstətɪv ‖ 'kɑn-/ *n*
see under PERFORMATIVE

constituent /kən'stɪtʃʊənt/ *n*
a linguistic unit which is part of a larger construction (see CONSTITUENT STRUCTURE).
see also under DISCONTINUOUS CONSTITUENT, CHUNKING

constituent identification /kən'stɪtʃʊənt aɪ,dentəfə'keɪʃən/ *n*
see under CHUNKING

constituent structure /kən'stɪtʃʊənt ,strʌktʃəʳ/ *n*
the arrangement of linguistic units (CONSTITUENTs) in a phrase, clause, sentence, etc, in order to show their relationship to one another. A constituent structure can be represented in various ways. A popular way is to use a **tree diagram**.
For example, the constituent structure of the sentence *The penguin swallowed the fish* can be shown as:

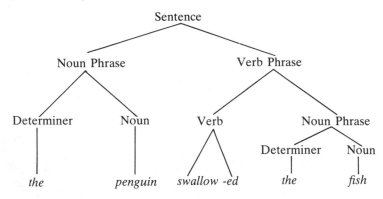

see also PHRASE STRUCTURE GRAMMAR
[*Further reading*: Aitchison 1978]

constriction /kən'strɪkʃən/ *n* **constricted** /kən'strɪktəd/ *adj*
(in the production of speech sounds) the narrowing of any part of the mouth or the throat (the VOCAL TRACT) to restrict the passage of the airstream from the lungs.
see also MANNER OF ARTICULATION

construct validity /ˈkɒnstrʌkt vəˈlɪdəti ‖ ˈkɑn-/ *n*
(in testing) a form of VALIDITY which is based on the degree to which
the items in a test reflect the essential aspects of the theory on
which the test is based (the **construct**). For example, the greater the
relationship which can be demonstrated between a test of
COMMUNICATIVE COMPETENCE in a language and the theory of
communicative competence, the greater the construct validity of the
test.
[*Further reading*: Oller 1979; Ebel 1972]

contact language /ˈkɒntækt ˈlæŋgwɪdʒ ‖ ˈkɑn-/ *n*
see under PIDGIN

content validity /ˈkɒntent vəˈlɪdəti ‖ ˈkɑn-/ *n*
(in testing) a form of VALIDITY which is based on the degree to which
a test adequately and sufficiently measures the particular skills or
behaviour it sets out to measure. For example, a test of
pronunciation skills in a language would have low content validity if
it tested only some of the skills which are required for accurate
pronunciation, such as a test which tested the ability to pronounce
isolated sounds, but not STRESS, INTONATION, or the pronunciation of
sounds within words. Content validity is of particular importance in
CRITERION REFERENCED TESTS, where the test content must represent
the content of what has been taught in a course.
[*Further reading*: Oller 1979; Ebel 1972]

content word /ˈkɒntent ˌwɜːd ‖ ˈkɑn-ˌwɛrd/ *n*
Words can be divided into two classes: **content words** and **function
words**.
Content words are words which refer to a thing, quality, state, or
action and which have meaning (**lexical meaning**) when the words
are used alone. Content words are mainly nouns, verbs, adjectives,
and adverbs, eg *book, run, musical, quickly*.
Function words are words which have little meaning on their own,
but which show grammatical relationships in and between sentences
(**grammatical meaning**). Conjunctions, prepositions, articles, eg *and,
to, the*, are function words.
Function words are also called **form words, empty words, functors,
grammatical words, structural words, structure words**. Content
words are also called **full words, lexical words**.
see also WORD CLASS

context /ˈkɒntekst ‖ ˈkɑn-/ *n* **contextual** /kənˈtɛkstʃuəl/ *adj*
that which occurs before and/or after a word, a PHRASE or even a
longer UTTERANCE or a TEXT. The context often helps in
understanding the particular meaning of the word, phrase, etc. For
example, the word *loud* in *loud music* is usually understood as
meaning "noisy" whereas in *a tie with a loud pattern* it is understood as
"unpleasantly colourful". The context may also be the broader social
situation in which a linguistic item is used. For example, in ordinary

usage, *spinster* refers to an older unmarried woman but in a legal context it refers to *any* unmarried woman.

see also CONTEXTUAL MEANING

contextually appropriate method /kən'tekstʃʊəli ə'prəʊprɪ-ət 'meθəd/ *n*

see under CLOZE PROCEDURE

contextual meaning /ˌkən'tekstʃʊəl 'miːnɪŋ/ *n*

the meaning a linguistic item has in context, for example the meaning a word has within a particular sentence, or a sentence has in a particular paragraph. The question *Do you know the meaning of war?* for example, may have two different contextual meanings:

(a) it may mean *Do you know the meaning of the word war?*, when said by a language teacher to a class of students.

(b) it may mean *War produces death, injury, and suffering*, when said by an injured soldier to a politician who favours war.

contingency table /ˌkən'tɪndʒənsi 'teɪbəl/ *n*

a table which displays data concerning two VARIABLES[2]. For example, if we wanted to determine the relationship between the scores students obtained on a grammar test and the number of hours spent in preparation for the test, a contingency table could be used to show the number of students obtaining different test scores according to the amount of time they spent in preparation. The CHI-SQUARE test can be used to test the STATISTICAL SIGNIFICANCE of the relationship between the two variables (ie between the scores and the preparation time).

	Test scores			
	0→10	11→20	21→30	total
hours spent in preparation	10	6	4	20
	2	5	9	16
total	12	11	13	36

a contingency table

continuous /kən'tɪnjʊəs/ *n*

another term for PROGRESSIVE

continuum /kən'tɪnjʊəm/ *n*

see under SPEECH CONTINUUM

contraction /kən'trækʃən/ *n*

the reduction of a linguistic form and often its combination with another form. For example:

I shall into *I'll*
they are into *they're*
did not into *didn't*

contrastive analysis /ˌkən'trɑːstɪv ə'næləsəs ‖ -'træ-/ *n*
also **CA**

the comparison of the linguistic systems of two languages, for example the sound system or the grammatical system. Contrastive analysis was developed and practised in the 1950s and 1960s, as an application of STRUCTURAL LINGUISTICS to language teaching, and is based on the following assumptions:
(a) the main difficulties in learning a new language are caused by interference from the first language (see LANGUAGE TRANSFER).
(b) these difficulties can be predicted by contrastive analysis.
(c) teaching materials can make use of contrastive analysis to reduce the effects of interference.

Contrastive analysis was more successful in PHONOLOGY than in other areas of language, and declined in the 1970s as interference was replaced by other explanations of learning difficulties (see ERROR ANALYSIS, INTERLANGUAGE). In recent years contrastive analysis has been applied to other areas of language, for example the discourse systems (see DISCOURSE ANALYSIS). This is called **contrastive discourse analysis.**

see also COMPARATIVE LINGUISTICS
[*Further reading*: Lado 1957; James 1980]

contrastive discourse analysis /kən'trɑːstɪv 'dɪskɔːs ə'næləsəs ‖ -'træ- -ɔrs/ *n*
see under CONTRASTIVE ANALYSIS

contrastive stress /kən'trɑːstɪv 'stres ‖ -'træ-/ *n*
stronger emphasis (STRESS) on a word in order to contrast it with another word or phrase. For example:
Q: *Did you speak to Mr Brown?*
A: *No, I spoke to Mrs Brown.*
where the stress is on *Mrs*.
Sometimes, contrastive stress is used because the speaker wants to emphasize a particular point. For example:
Joan is studying French and German.
as a reply to the question:
Is Joan studying French or German?

control group /kən'trəʊl ˌgruːp/ *n*
one of two groups used in certain kinds of experimental research, the other being the **experimental group**. For example if we wanted to study the effectiveness of a new teaching method, one group (the experimental group) may be taught using the new method, and another group, the control group, by using the usual teaching method. The control group is chosen because of its equivalence to the experimental group (eg by assigning students to the two groups

at random). In studying the effects of the new method, the experimental group is compared with the control group.

controlled composition /kənˈtrəʊld kɒmpəˈzɪʃən ‖ kɑm-/ *n*
see under COMPOSITION

conventionalized speech /kənˈvenʃənəlaɪzd ˈspiːtʃ/ *n*
another term for ROUTINE

convergence[1] /kənˈvɜːdʒəns ‖ -ɜr-/ *n*
the process of two or more languages or language varieties becoming more similar to one another. For example:
(a) if one language variety gains status, then the speakers of another variety may change their pronunciation to be more like it, and use words and grammatical structures from it.
(b) if speakers of two language varieties mix together, by moving to the same area for example, both varieties may change to become more like each other.
see also DIVERGENCE[1]

convergence[2] *n*
see under ACCOMMODATION

conversational analysis /ˌkɒnvəˈseɪʃənəl əˈnæləsəs ‖ ˌkɑnvər-/ *n*
the analysis of natural conversation in order to discover what the linguistic characteristics of conversation are and how conversation is used in ordinary life.
Conversational analysis includes the study of:
(a) how speakers decide when to speak during a conversation (ie rules of TURN-TAKING)
(b) how the sentences of two or more speakers are related (see ADJACENCY PAIR, CONVERSATIONAL MAXIM)
(c) the different functions that conversation is used for (for example to establish ROLES, and to communicate politeness or intimacy)
see also DISCOURSE ANALYSIS, ETHNOMETHODOLOGY, SPEECH ACT
[*Further reading*: Coulthard 1985]

conversational implicature /ˌkɒnvəˈseɪʃənəl ˈɪmplɪkətʃʊəʳ ‖ ˌkɑnvər--tʃər/ *n*
see under CONVERSATIONAL MAXIM

conversational maxim /ˌkɒnvəˈseɪʃənəl ˈmæksəm ‖ ˌkɑnvər-/ *n*
an unwritten rule about conversation which people know and which influences the form of conversational exchanges. For example in the following exchange
   A: *Let's go to the movies.*
   B: *I have an examination in the morning.*
B's reply might appear not to be connected to A's remark. However, since A has made an invitation and since a reply to an invitation is usually either an acceptance or a refusal, B's reply is here understood as an excuse for not accepting the invitation (ie a

refusal). B has used the "maxim" that speakers normally give
replies which are relevant to the question that has been asked.
The philosopher Grice has suggested that there are four
conversational maxims:
(a) The maxim of quantity: give as much information as is needed.
(b) The maxim of quality: speak truthfully.
(c) The maxim of relevance: say things that are relevant.
(d) The maxim of manner: say things clearly and briefly.
The use of conversational maxims to imply meaning during
conversation is called **conversational implicature**, and the "co-
operation" between speakers in using the maxims is sometimes
called the **co-operative principle**.
see also ADJACENCY PAIR, COHERENCE, REALITY PRINCIPLE
[*Further reading*: Grice 1967; Clark & Clark 1977]

conversational routine /ˌkɒnvəˈseɪʃənəl ruːˈtiːn ‖ ˌkɑnvər-/ *n*
see under ROUTINE

co-occurrence rule /ˈkəʊəˈkʌrəns ˌruːl ‖ -əˈkɜ-/ *n*
see under SPEECH STYLES

co-operative principle /kəʊˈɒpərətɪv ˈprɪnsəpəl ‖ -ˈɑp-/ *n*
see under CONVERSATIONAL MAXIM

co-ordinate bilingualism /kəʊˈɔːdənət baɪˈlɪŋgwəlɪzəm ‖ -ˈɔr-/ *n*
see under COMPOUND BILINGUALISM

co-ordinate clause /kəʊˈɔːdənət ˈklɔːz ‖ -ˈɔr-/ *n*
see under CONJUNCTION

co-ordinating conjunction /kəʊˈɔːdəneɪtɪŋ kənˈdʒʌŋkʃən ‖ -ˈɔr-/ *n*
see under CONJUNCTION

co-ordination /kəʊˌɔːdəˈneɪʃən ‖ -ˈɔr-/ *n*
see under CONJUNCTION

co-ordinator /kəʊˈɔːdəneɪtər ‖ -ˈɔr-/ *n*
see under CONJUNCTION

copula /ˈkɒpjʊlə ‖ ˈkɑpjələ/ *n* **copulative** /ˈkɒpjʊlətɪv ‖ ˈkɑpjəleɪ-/ *adj*
also **linking verb**
a verb that links a SUBJECT to a COMPLEMENT. For example:
He is sick. She looked afraid.
The verb *be* is sometimes known as **the copula** since this is its main
function in English. The following are copulative verbs, ie they can
be used copulatively: *feel, look, prove, remain, resemble, sound,
stay, become, grow, turn, smell, taste.*
see also TRANSITIVE VERB
[*Further reading*: Quirk et al 1985]

correct /kəˈrekt/ *adj* **correctness** /kəˈrektnəs/ *n*
a term which is used to state that particular language usage, eg the
pronunciation of a word is *right* as opposed to *wrong*. For example:

This is the correct pronunciation.

The term often expresses a particular attitude to language usage (see PRESCRIPTIVE GRAMMAR). It has become more common to abandon absolute judgments of *right* and *wrong* and to consider a usage as being more or less APPROPRIATE in a particular social setting.

see also ERROR

[*Further reading*: Hughes & Trudgill 1979]

correlation /ˌkɒrə'leɪʃən ‖ ˌkɔ-, ˌkɑ-/ *n*

a measure of the strength of the relationship between two sets of data. For example we may wish to determine the **relationship** between the scores of a group of students on a mathematics test and on a language test. A common coefficient of correlation used is known as *Pearson Product Moment Coefficient* symbolized by *r*. Its value varies from -1.00 to $+1.00$, with the value of zero indicating the absence of any correlation and either a minus or plus one indicating perfect correspondence of scores. For example if students received quite similar scores on two tests their scores would have a high positive correlation. If their scores on one test were the reverse of their scores on the other, their scores would have a high negative correlation. If their scores on the two tests were not related in any predictable way their scores would have a zero correlation.

[*Further reading*: Hardyck & Petrinovich 1976]

counselling learning /'kaʊnsəlɪŋ 'lɜːnɪŋ ‖ 'lɜr-/ *n*

see under COMMUNITY LANGUAGE LEARNING

countable noun /'kaʊntəbəl 'naʊn/ *n*

also **count noun** /'kaʊnt ˌnaʊn/

a noun which has both singular and plural forms. For example:

word – words, machine – machines, bridge – bridges

A noun which does not usually occur in the plural is called an **uncountable noun** or a **mass noun**. For example:

education, homework, harm.

see also NOUN

course density /'kɔːs 'densəti ‖ 'kors/ *n*

(in course design and syllabus design (see COURSE DESIGN)) the rate at which new teaching points are introduced and reintroduced in a course or syllabus in order to achieve a satisfactory rate of learning. In language courses where the main emphasis is on grammar and vocabulary, learners can generally learn four or five items per hour for active use and another four or five for passive use. Targets of 2000 items for active use and a further 2000 for passive recognition are commonly set for a 400 hour course of instruction.

[*Further reading*: Sager, Dungworth, & McDonald 1980]

course design /'kɔːs dɪ'zaɪn ‖ 'kors/ *n*

also **language programme design, programme design**

(in language teaching) the development of a language programme or set of teaching materials. Whereas **syllabus design** generally refers to procedures for deciding what will be taught in a language programme, course design includes how a syllabus will be carried out. For example:

(a) what teaching METHOD and materials will be needed to achieve the OBJECTIVES

(b) how much time will be required

(c) how classroom activities will be sequenced and organized

(d) what sort of PLACEMENT TESTS, ACHIEVEMENT TESTS and other sorts of tests will be used

(e) how the programme will be evaluated (see EVALUATION)

Course design is part of the broader process of CURRICULUM DEVELOPMENT.

see also COURSE DENSITY

[*Further reading*: Howatt 1974]

coverage /ˈkʌvərɪdʒ/ *n*

the degree to which words and structures can be used to replace other words and structures, because they have a similar meaning. For example *seat* includes the meanings of *chair*, *bench*, and *stool*, and *What time is it please?* can replace *Could you kindly tell me the time?* Coverage is a principle used to help select language items for language teaching, since items with a high degree of coverage are likely to be most useful to language learners.

see also SELECTION

[*Further reading*: Mackey 1965; West 1953]

creative construction hypothesis /kriˈeɪtɪv kənˈstrʌkʃən haɪˈpɒθəsəs ‖ -ˈpɑ-/ *n*

a theory about how second and foreign language learners work out language rules. The theory was proposed by Dulay and Burt, who claim that learners work out the rules of their TARGET LANGUAGE[1] by:

(a) using natural mental processes, such as GENERALIZATION

(b) using similar processes to first language learners

(c) not relying very much on the rules of the first language

(d) using processes which lead to the creation of new forms and structures which are not found in the target language. For example:

She goed to school. (instead of *She went to school*)

What you are doing? (instead of *What are you doing?*)

[*Further reading*: Dulay & Burt 1974; Dulay, Burt, & Krashen 1982]

creole /ˈkriːəʊl/ *n*

a PIDGIN language which has become the native language of a group of speakers, being used for all or many of their daily communicative needs. Usually, the sentence structures and vocabulary range of a creole are far more complex than those of a pidgin language. Creoles are usually classified according to the language from which most of their vocabulary comes, eg English-based, French-based, Portuguese-based, and Swahili-based creoles.

Examples of English-based creoles are Jamaican Creole, Hawaiian Creole and Krio in Sierra Leone, West Africa.

see also CREOLIZATION, POST-CREOLE CONTINUUM

[*Further reading*: Todd 1984]

creolization /ˌkriːəʊlaɪˈzeɪʃən/ *n*
the process by which a PIDGIN becomes a CREOLE.
Creolization involves the expansion of the vocabulary and the grammatical system.

criterion /kraɪˈtɪərɪən/ *n*
see under BEHAVIOURAL OBJECTIVE

criterion measure /kraɪˈtɪərɪən ˈmeʒəʳ/ *n*
(in testing) a standard against which a test can be compared as a measure of its VALIDITY. A criterion measure may be another test which is known to be valid, or another valid indicator of performance.
see also CRITERION-RELATED VALIDITY

[*Further reading*: Valette 1977]

criterion referenced test /kraɪˈtɪərɪən ˈrefərənst ˈtest/ *n*
a test which measures a student's performance according to a particular standard or criterion which has been agreed upon. The student must reach this level of performance to pass the test, and a student's score is therefore interpreted with reference to the criterion score, rather than to the scores of other students. This may be contrasted with a **norm referenced test.** This is a test which is designed to measure how the performance of a particular student or group of students compares with the performance of another student or group of students whose scores are given as the norm. A student's score is therefore interpreted with reference to the scores of other students or groups of students, rather than to an agreed criterion score.

[*Further reading*: Ebel 1972]

criterion-related validity /kraɪˈtɪərɪən rɪˈleɪtəd vəˈlɪdəti/ *n*
(in testing) a form of VALIDITY in which a test is compared or correlated with an outside CRITERION MEASURE.

critical comprehension /ˈkrɪtɪkəl ˌkɒmprɪˈhenʃən ‖ ˌkɑm-/ *n*
see under READING

critical period hypothesis /ˈkrɪtɪkəl ˈpɪərɪəd haɪˈpɒθəsəs ‖ -ˈpɑ-/ *n*
the theory that in child development there is a period during which language can be acquired more easily than at any other time. According to the biologist Lenneberg, the critical period lasts until puberty (around age 12 or 13 years), and is due to biological development. Lenneberg suggested that language learning may be

more difficult after puberty because the brain lacks the ability for adaptation. This, he believed, was because the language functions of the brain have already been established in a particular part of the brain; that is, because **lateralization** (see BRAIN) has already occurred by this time.

[*Further reading*: Lenneberg 1967]

cross-section(al) method /krɒs 'sekʃənəl 'meθəd ‖ krɔs/ *n*
also **cross-section(al) study** /krɒs 'sekʃənəl 'stʌdi ‖ krɔs/
a study of a group of different individuals or subjects at a single point in time, in order to measure or study a particular topic or aspect of language (for example use of the tense system of a language). This can be contrasted with a **longitudinal method** or **longitudinal study**, in which an individual or group is studied over a period of time (for example, to study how the use of the tense system changes and develops with age). This approach has been used to study first language learning.

cue /kjuː/ *n*
(in language teaching) a signal given by the teacher in order to produce a **response** by the students. For example in practising questions:

cue	response
time	*What time is it?*
day	*What day is it?*

Cues may be words, signals, actions, etc.
see also DRILL

cultural deprivation /'kʌltʃərəl ˌdeprə'veɪʃn/ *n*
also **cultural disadvantage** /'kʌltʃərəl ˌdɪsəd'vaːntɪdʒ ‖ -'væn-/
the theory that some children, particularly those from lower social and economic backgrounds, lack certain home experiences and that this may lead to learning difficulties in school. For example, children from homes which lack books or educational games and activities to stimulate thought and language development may not perform well in school. Since many other factors could explain why some children do not perform well in school, this theory is an insufficient explanation for differences in children's learning abilities.
see also COMPENSATORY INSTRUCTION, CULTURAL RELATIVISM
[*Further reading*: Edwards 1979]

cultural pluralism /'kʌltʃərəl 'plʊərəlɪzəm/ *n*
a situation in which an individual or group has more than one set of cultural beliefs, values, and attitudes. The teaching of a foreign language or programmes in BILINGUAL EDUCATION are sometimes said to encourage cultural pluralism. An educational programme which aims to develop cultural pluralism is sometimes referred to as **multicultural education**, for example a programme designed to teach about different ethnic groups in a country.

cultural relativism /'kʌltʃərəl 'relətɪvɪzəm/ *n*
the theory that a culture can only be understood on its own terms.
This means that standards, attitudes, and beliefs from one culture
should not be used in the study or description of another culture.
According to this theory there are no universal cultural beliefs or
values, or these are not regarded as important. Cultural relativism
has been part of the discussions of LINGUISTIC RELATIVITY and
CULTURAL DEPRIVATION.
[*Further reading*: Hymes 1964]

culture /'kʌltʃər/ *n*
the total set of beliefs, attitudes, customs, behaviour, social habits,
etc of the members of a particular society.
see also BICULTURAL

culture fair /'kʌltʃər 'feər/ *adj*
also **culture free** /'kʌltʃər 'friː/
(in language testing) A test which does not favour members of a
particular cultural group, because it is based on assumptions, beliefs,
and knowledge which are common to all the groups being tested, is
called culture fair. For example, the following test item is not
culture fair:
    Bananas are _____ (a) *brown*, (b) *green*, (c) *yellow*.
The item is culturally biased because for some people bananas are
thought of as yellow, but for others green bananas are eaten, and
cooked bananas are brown. If only one of these answers is marked
as correct, the test favours a particular cultural group.

culture shock /'kʌltʃər ˌʃɒk ‖ ˌʃak/ *n*
strong feelings of discomfort, fear, or insecurity which a person may
have when they enter another culture. For example, when a person
moves to live in a foreign country, they may have a period of
culture shock until they become familiar with the new culture.

curriculum[1] /kə'rɪkjʊləm ‖ -kjə-/ *n*
an educational programme which states:
(a) the educational purpose of the programme (the **ends**)
(b) the content, teaching procedures and learning experiences which
    will be necessary to achieve this purpose (the **means**)
(c) some means for assessing whether or not the educational ends
    have been achieved.
see also EVALUATION
[*Further reading*: Pratt 1980]

curriculum[2]
another term for SYLLABUS

curriculum development /kə'rɪkjʊləm dɪ'veləpmənt ‖ -kje-/ *n*
also **curriculum design** /kə'rɪkjʊləm dɪ'zaɪn ‖ -kje-/
the study and development of the goals, content, implementation, and

evaluation of an educational system. In language teaching, curriculum development (also called **syllabus design**) includes:

(a) the study of the purposes for which a learner needs a language (NEEDS ANALYSIS)

(b) the setting of OBJECTIVES, and the development of a SYLLABUS, teaching METHODS, and materials

(c) the EVALUATION of the effects of these procedures on the learner's language ability.

[*Further reading*: Pratt 1980]

cyclical approach /ˈsaɪklɪkəl əˈprəʊtʃ/ *n*
another term for SPIRAL APPROACH

dative case[1] /'deɪtɪv ˌkeɪs/ *n*

the form of a noun or noun phrase which usually shows that the
noun or noun phrase functions as the INDIRECT OBJECT of a verb.
For example, in the German sentence:

Sie	gab	der	Katze	eine	Schale	Milch.
She	gave	the	cat	a	dish (of)	milk

in the noun phrase *der Katze*, the article has the inflectional ending
-er to show that the noun phrase is in the dative case because it is
the indirect object of the verb.
see also CASE[1]
[*Further reading*: Lyons 1968]

dative case[2] *n*

(In CASE GRAMMAR) the noun or noun phrase which refers to the
person or animal affected by the state or action of the verb is in the
dative case.
For example, in the sentences:

Gregory was frightened by the storm.

I persuaded Tom to go.

Gregory and *Tom* are in the dative case. Both Gregory and Tom are
affected by something: Gregory is frightened and Tom experiences
persuasion.
The dative case is sometimes called the **experiencer case**.
[*Further reading*: Fillmore 1968]

declarative /dɪ'kleərətɪv/ *n*

see under SPEECH ACT CLASSIFICATION

declarative sentence /dɪ'kleərətɪv 'sentəns/ *n*

a sentence which is in the form of a STATEMENT. For example:

I'm leaving now.

Declarative sentences may or may not have the function of a statement.
For example:

I suppose you're coming this evening.

often functions as a question.

I'd like you to leave immediately.

often functions as an order or request.

declension /dɪ'klenʃən/ *n* **decline** /dɪ'klaɪn/ *v*

a list of the case forms (see CASE[1]) of a noun phrase in a particular
language.
For example, in German:

nominative case:	*der Mann*	"the man"
accusative case:	*den Mann*	"the man"
dative case:	*dem Mann*	"to the man"
genitive case:	*des Mannes*	"of the man"

decoding /ˌdiː'kəʊdɪŋ/ *n* **decode** /ˌdiː'kəʊd/ *v*

the process of trying to understand the meaning of a word, phrase, or sentence.

When decoding a speech UTTERANCE, the listener must:

(a) hold the utterance in short term memory (see MEMORY)

(b) analyse the utterance into segments (see CHUNKING) and identify clauses, phrases, and other linguistic units

(c) identify the underlying propositions and illocutionary meaning (see SPEECH ACT).

Decoding is also used to mean the interpretation of any set of symbols which carry a meaning, for example a secret code or a Morse signal.

see also ENCODING, MESSAGE, INFORMATION PROCESSING, INFORMATION THEORY

[*Further reading*: Leeson 1975; Clark & Clark 1977]

decreolization /diːˌkriːəʊlaɪ'zeɪʃən/ *n*

the process by which a CREOLE becomes more like the standard language from which most of its vocabulary comes. For example, an English-based creole may become more like Standard English. If educational opportunities increase in a region where a creole is spoken and the standard language is taught, then there will be a range from the creole spoken by those with little or no education to the standard language spoken by those with high levels of education. This has been happening in countries like Jamaica and Guyana where there is a range from an English-based creole to a variety close to standard educated English.

see also POST-CREOLE CONTINUUM

[*Further reading*: Bickerton 1975]

deductive learning /dɪ'dʌktɪv 'lɜːnɪŋ ‖ 'lɜr-/ *n*
also **learning by deduction**

an approach to language teaching in which learners are taught rules and given specific information about a language. They then apply these rules when they use the language. Language teaching methods which emphasize the study of the grammatical rules of a language (for example the GRAMMAR TRANSLATION METHOD) make use of the principle of deductive learning.

This may be contrasted with **inductive learning** or **learning by induction**, in which learners are not taught grammatical or other types of rules directly but are left to discover or induce rules from their experience of using the language. Language teaching methods which emphasize use of the language rather than presentation of information about the language (for example the DIRECT METHOD, COMMUNICATIVE APPROACH, and COUNSELLING LEARNING) make use of the principle of inductive learning.

[*Further reading*: Kelly 1969; Steinberg 1982]

deep structure /'diːp ˌstrʌktʃərˈ/ n
also **underlying structure**

(in generative transformational grammar) each sentence is considered to have two levels of structure: the deep structure and the **surface structure**. The surface structure is generally the syntactic structure of the sentence which a person speaks, hears, reads or writes, eg the passive (see VOICE[1]) sentence:

The newspaper was not delivered today.

The deep structure is much more abstract and is considered to be in the speaker's, writer's, hearer's or reader's mind. The deep structure for the above sentence would be something like:

(NEGATIVE) *someone* (PAST TENSE) *deliver the newspaper today* (PASSIVE)

The items in brackets are not lexical items but grammatical concepts which shape the final form of the sentence. Rules which describe deep structure are in the first part of the grammar (BASE COMPONENT). Rules which transform these structures ("transformational rules") are in the second part of the grammar (TRANSFORMATIONAL COMPONENT).

see also under BASE COMPONENT

[*Further reading*: Aitchison 1978; Chomsky 1965]

deficit hypothesis /'defəsət haɪˈpɒθəsəs ‖ -'pɑ-/ n
also **verbal deficit hypothesis**

the theory that the language of some children may be lacking in vocabulary, grammar, or the means of expressing complex ideas, and may therefore be inadequate as a basis for success in school. Linguists have criticized this hypothesis and contrasted it with the **difference hypothesis**. This states that although the language of some children (eg children from certain social and ethnic groups) may be different from that of middle-class children, all DIALECTs are equally complex and children can use them to express complex ideas and to form a basis for school learning.

see also CULTURAL DEPRIVATION

[*Further reading*: Williams 1970]

defining relative clause /dɪˈfaɪnɪŋ ˈrelətɪv ˌklɔːz/ n
also **restrictive relative clause**

a CLAUSE which gives additional information about a noun or noun phrase in a sentence. A defining relative clause restricts or helps to define the meaning of the noun. It usually begins with *who, which, whom, whose*, or *that*, and in written English is not separated from the noun by a comma:

The man whom you met is my uncle.
The woman that you want to speak to has left.

This may be contrasted with a **non-defining relative clause** (also called a **non-restrictive relative clause**), which gives additional information but which does not restrict or define the noun or noun phrase. In writing, it is separated by a comma:

My uncle, who is 64, still plays football.

defining vocabulary /dɪ'faɪnɪŋ və'kæbjʊləri, vəʊ- ‖ -bjəleri/ n
a basic list of words with which other words can be explained or defined. Defining vocabularies are used to write definitions in dictionaries for children and for people studying foreign languages. They are based on research into WORD FREQUENCY. In the *Longman Dictionary of Contemporary English*, all definitions are written using a 2000 word defining vocabulary, so that anyone who knows the meaning of those 2000 words will be able to understand all the definitions in the dictionary.

definite article /'defənət 'ɑːtɪkəl ‖ 'ɑr-/ n
see under ARTICLE

deictic /'daɪktɪk, deɪ'ɪktɪk/ *adj* **deixis** /'daɪksəs/ n
a term for a word or phrase which directly relates an utterance to a time, place, or person(s).
Examples of deictic expressions in English are:
(a) *here* and *there*, which refer to a place in relation to the speaker:
   The letter is here. (near the speaker)
   The letter is over there. (farther away from the speaker)
(b) *I* which refers to the speaker or writer.
   you which refers to the person or persons addressed.
   he/she/they which refer to some other person or persons.
[*Further reading*: Lyons 1977]

delayed auditory feedback /dɪ'leɪd 'ɔːdətəri 'fiːdbæk ‖ -tori/ n
a technique which shows how speakers depend on AUDITORY FEEDBACK (ie hearing what they have just said) when speaking. In studies of delayed auditory feedback, speakers wear earphones through which they hear what they have just said, but after a short delay. The effect of this on speakers is that it is very difficult for them to speak normally.
[*Further reading*: Foss & Hakes 1978]

deletion /dɪ'liːʃən/ n **delete** /dɪ'liːt/ v
When a speaker leaves out a sound, morpheme, or word from what he/she is saying, this is called deletion. For example, in casual or rapid speech, speakers of English often delete the final consonant in some unstressed words, so *a friend of mine* becomes *a friend o' mine*.

demonstrative /dɪ'mɒnstrətɪv ‖ dɪ'mɑn-/ n
a word (a PRONOUN or a DETERMINER) which refers to something in terms of whether it is near to or distant from the speaker.
The demonstratives in English are: *this, that, these, those.*
For example:
   You take these books (here) *and I'll take those* (there).
[*Further reading*: Quirk et al 1985]

denotation /ˌdiːnəʊˈteɪʃən/ *n* **denotative** /dɪˈnəʊtətɪv ‖ ˈdiːnəʊˌteɪtɪv, dɪˈnəʊtə-/ *adj*

that part of the meaning of a word or phrase that relates it to phenomena in the real world or in a fictional or possible world. For example, the denotation of the English word *bird* is a two-legged, winged, egg-laying, warm-blooded creature with a beak.

In a meaning system, **denotative meaning** may be regarded as the "central" meaning or "core" meaning of a lexical item. It is often equated with referential meaning (see REFERENCE) and with **cognitive meaning** and **conceptual meaning** although some linguists and philosophers make a distinction between these concepts.

see also CONNOTATION

[*Further reading*: Leech 1981; Lyons 1977]

denotative meaning /dɪˈnəʊtətɪv ˈmiːnɪŋ ‖ ˈdiːnəʊˌteɪtɪv, dɪˈnəʊtə-/ *n*

see under DENOTATION

dental /ˈdentl/ *adj*

describes a speech sound (a CONSONANT) produced by the front of the tongue touching the back of the upper front teeth.

For example, in French the /t/ in /tɛr/ *terre* "earth" and the /d/ in /du/ *doux* "sweet" are dental STOPS.

In English, /t/ and /d/ are usually ALVEOLAR stops. The use of dental in place of alveolar sounds by non-native speakers of English helps to create a "foreign accent".

see also PLACE OF ARTICULATION, MANNER OF ARTICULATION

[*Further reading*: Gimson 1980]

dependency grammar /dɪˈpendənsi ˌɡræməʳ/ *n*

a grammatical theory in which the verb is considered to be the central and most important unit. Verbs are classified according to the number of noun phrases they require to complete a sentence. This number is called the **valency** of the verb. The English verb *blush*, for instance, would have a valency of one:

The verb *give*, as in *The salesgirl gave Jane the parcel* would have a valency of three:

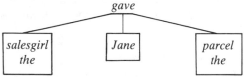

This type of grammar has been developed mainly in France and Germany and is different from many other grammars because of its verb-centred approach.

see also CASE GRAMMAR

[*Further reading*: Lyons 1977]

dependent clause /dɪ'pendənt 'klɔːz/ *n*
also **subordinate clause**

a clause which must be used with another clause to form a complete grammatical construction. It depends on the other clause and is subordinate to it.

A clause which can be used on its own is called an **independent clause**.

For example:

When it rains, please bring in the washing.
dependent   independent
clause   clause
She told me   that she was going abroad.
independent   dependent
clause   clause

Dependent or subordinate clauses are often linked to independent clauses by a subordinating CONJUNCTION like *when, that*, etc, or by a relative pronoun like *who, whose*, etc.

An independent clause (also called a **main clause** or a **principal clause**) does not depend on another clause, although it may be linked to another independent clause, or to a dependent clause. For example:

I will put the money in the bank or I will spend it.
independent   independent
clause   clause
I am going straight home after I've seen the movie.
independent   dependent
clause   clause

[*Further reading*: Quirk et al 1985]

dependent variable /dɪ'pendənt 'veərɪəbəl/ *n*

(in research) a VARIABLE[2] which changes or is influenced according to changes in one or more **independent variables**. In empirical studies, one variable (the independent variable) may be studied as a cause or predictor, and another variable (the dependent variable) as the effect or result of the independent variable. For example, we may wish to study the effects of attitudes and motivation on language proficiency. Attitudes and motivation would be the independent variables, while language proficiency would be the dependent variable.

[*Further reading*: Ebel 1972]

derivation /ˌderə'veɪʃən/ *n* **derive** /dɪ'raɪv/ *v*

(in MORPHOLOGY and WORD FORMATION) the formation of new words by adding AFFIX*es* to other words or morphemes.

For example, the noun *insanity* is derived from the adjective *sane* by the addition of the negative prefix *in-* and the noun-forming suffix *-ity*.

see also BACK FORMATION, INFLECTION

derived score /dɪˈraɪvd ˈskɔːʳ ‖ ˈskɔr/ *n*
(in statistics) any type of score other than a RAW SCORE. A derived score is calculated by converting a raw score or scores into units of another scale. For example the number of correct responses in a test (the raw score) may be converted into grades from A to F (a derived score).
see also STANDARD SCORE

descriptive function /dɪˈskrɪptɪv ˌfʌŋkʃən/ *n*
see under FUNCTIONS OF LANGUAGE[1]

descriptive grammar /dɪˈskrɪptɪv ˌɡræməʳ/ *n*
a grammar which describes how a language is actually spoken and/or written, and does not state or prescribe how it ought to be spoken or written.
If a descriptive grammar of a non-prestige variety of English were written, it might show, for example, that speakers of this variety sometimes said:

I seen 'im.	instead of	*I saw him.*
'im 'n me done it.	instead of	*He and I did it.*

see also PRESCRIPTIVE GRAMMAR

determiner /dɪˈtɜːmɪnəʳ ‖ -ɜr-/ *n*
a word which is used with a noun, and which limits the meaning of the noun in some way. For example, in English the following words can be used as determiners:
(a) ARTICLES, eg *a pencil, the garden*
(b) DEMONSTRATIVES, eg *this box, that car*
(c) POSSESSIVES, eg *her house, my bicycle*
(d) QUANTIFIERS, eg *some milk, many people*
(e) NUMERALS, eg *the first day, three chairs*
[*Further reading*: Close 1975]

developmental error /dɪˌveləpˈmentl ˈerəʳ/ *n*
an ERROR in the language use of a first or second language learner which is the result of a normal pattern of development, and which is common among language learners. For example, in learning English, first and second language learners often produce verb forms such as *comed, goed*, and *breaked* instead of *came, went*, and *broke*. This is thought to be because they have learned the rule for regular past tense formation and then apply it to all verbs. Later such errors disappear as the learner's language ability increases. These OVERGENERALIZATIONS are a natural or developmental stage in language learning.
see also INTERLANGUAGE, ERROR ANALYSIS
[*Further reading*: Dulay, Burt, & Krashen 1982]

developmental functions of language /dɪˌveləpˈmentl ˌfʌŋkʃənz əv ˈlæŋɡwɪdʒ/ *n*
According to Halliday, a young child in the early stages of language development is able to master a number of elementary functions of

language. Each of these functions has a choice of meanings attached to it. He distinguishes seven initial functions:

(a) **Instrumental** ("I want"): used for satisfying material needs
(b) **Regulatory** ("do as I tell you"): used for controlling the behaviour of others
(c) **Interactional** ("me and you"): used for getting along with other people
(d) **Personal** ("here I come"): used for identifying and expressing the self
(e) **Heuristic** ("tell me why"): used for exploring the world around and inside one
(f) **Imaginative** ("let's pretend"): used for creating a world of one's own
(g) **Informative** ("I've got something to tell you"): used for communicating new information.

At about 18 months, the child is beginning to master the adult's system of communication, including grammar, vocabulary and meaning components (see FUNCTIONS OF LANGUAGE[2]).
[*Further reading*: Halliday 1978]

developmental interdependence hypothesis /dɪveləp'mentl ɪntədɪ'pendəns haɪ'pɒθəsəs ‖ ˌɪntər- haɪ'pɑ-/ *n*
see under THRESHOLD HYPOTHESIS

developmental psychology /dɪveləp'mentl saɪ'kɒləʤi ‖ -'kɑ-/ *n*
a branch of psychology which deals with the development of mental, emotional, psychological, and social processes and behaviour in individuals, particularly from birth to early childhood.
see also GENETIC EPISTEMOLOGY
[*Further reading*: Ausubel 1977]

deviant /'diːvɪənt/ *adj*
This term is used to describe any pronunciation, word, or sentence structure which does not conform to a NORM[1]. The norm could be that of the STANDARD VARIETY or it could be based on the language spoken by a high status social group.
An example of a sentence which would be deviant in Standard English is *I seen him* instead of *I saw him*.
[*Further reading*: Bailey & Görlach 1982; Pride 1982]

devoicing /ˌdiː'vɔɪsɪŋ/ *n*
see under VOICE[2]

diachronic linguistics /daɪə'krɒnɪk lɪŋ'gwɪstɪks ‖ -'krɑ-/ *n*
an approach to linguistics which studies how a language changes over a period of time, for example the change in the sound system of English from Early English to Modern British English.
Diachronic linguistics has been contrasted with **synchronic linguistics** which is the study of a language system at one particular point in time, for example the sound system of Modern British English.

time 1	description of the sound system of Early English	synchronic study
	description of changes between the two systems	diachronic study
time 2	description of the sound system of Modern British English	synchronic study

The need for diachronic and synchronic descriptions to be kept apart was emphasized by the Swiss linguist Saussure. Not all approaches to linguistic analysis make this distinction (see GENERATIVE PHONOLOGY).

see also COMPARATIVE HISTORICAL LINGUISTICS

[*Further reading*: Aitchison 1981; Saussure 1966]

diacritic /ˌdaɪəˈkrɪtɪk/ *n*

a mark placed over, under, or through a letter to show that it has a sound value different from that of the same letter without the mark. For example, in Spanish the sign ~ over *n* as in *mañana* "tomorrow" shows that the first *n* represents [nj] whereas the second *n* represents [n].

Diacritics are also used in phonetic script (see NOTATION). For example, [d̪] shows that it is a DENTAL STOP, made with the tongue against the front teeth.

see also ACCENT[2]

diagnostic test /ˌdaɪəgˈnɒstɪk ˈtest ‖ -ˈnɑ-/ *n*

a test which is designed to show what skills or knowledge a learner knows and doesn't know. For example a diagnostic pronunciation test may be used to measure the learner's pronunciation of English sounds. It would show which sounds a student is and is not able to pronounce. Diagnostic tests may be used to find out how much a learner knows before beginning a language course.

[*Further reading*: Valette 1977]

dialect /ˈdaɪəlekt/ *n* **dialectal** /ˌdaɪəˈlektl/ *adj*

a variety of a language, spoken in one part of a country (**regional dialect**), or by people belonging to a particular social class (social dialect or SOCIOLECT), which is different in some words, grammar, and/or pronunciation from other forms of the same language.

A dialect is often associated with a particular ACCENT[3]. Sometimes a dialect gains status and becomes the STANDARD VARIETY of a country.

see also SPEECH VARIETY

[*Further reading*: Hughes & Trudgill 1979]

dialectology /ˌdaɪəlekˈtɒlədʒi ‖ -ˈtɑ-/ *n*

the study of the regional variations of a language (see DIALECT).

Usually, studies in dialectology have concentrated on different words used in various dialects for the same object or on different pronunciations of the same word in different dialects.
see also AREAL LINGUISTICS

dialogue /'daɪəlɒg ‖ -lɑg/ *n*
(in language teaching) a model conversation, used to practise speaking. Dialogues are often specially written to practise language items, contain simplified grammar and vocabulary, and so may be rather different from real-life conversation.

dichotic listening /daɪ'kɒtɪk 'lɪsənɪŋ ‖ -'kɑ-/ *n*
a technique which has been used to study how the brain controls hearing and language. Subjects wear earphones and receive different sounds in the right and left ear. They are then asked to repeat what they hear. Subjects find it easier to repeat what they heard in one ear than in the other, and this is thought to indicate which brain hemisphere controls language for them (see BRAIN). The ability to perceive language better in the right ear than the left ear is called a **right-ear advantage**, and the ability to perceive language better in the left ear is called **left-ear advantage**.
[*Further reading*: Foss & Hakes 1977]

dictation /dɪk'teɪʃən/ *n*
a technique used in both language teaching and language testing in which a passage is read aloud to students, with pauses during which they must try to write down what they heard as accurately as possible.
[*Further reading*: Rivers & Temperley 1978]

dicto-comp /'dɪktəʊkɒmp ‖ -kɑmp/ *n*
a technique for practising composition in language classes. A passage is read to a class, and then the students must write out what they understand and remember from the passage, keeping as closely to the original as possible but using their own words where necessary.
see also DICTATION

difference hypothesis /'dɪfərəns haɪ'pɒθəsəs ‖ -'pɑ-/ *n*
see under DEFICIT HYPOTHESIS

diglossia /daɪ'glɒsɪə ‖ -'glɔ-,-'glɑ-/ *n*
When two languages or language varieties exist side by side in a community and each one is used for different purposes, this is called diglossia. Usually, one is a more standard variety called the **High variety** or **H-variety**, which is used in government, the media, education, and for religious services. The other one is usually a non-prestige variety called the **Low-variety** or **L-variety**, which is used in the family, with friends, when shopping, etc.
An example of diglossia can be found in the German speaking part of Switzerland, where the H(igh) variety is a form of standard

German (Hochdeutsch) and the L(ow) variety is called
Schwyzertüütsch, which is a range of regional Swiss dialects. Other
countries where diglossia exists are, for example, Haiti and the Arab
nations.

see also BILINGUALISM, MULTILINGUALISM, CODE SELECTION

[*Further reading*: Ferguson 1959]

diminutive /dɪ̩'mɪnjʊtɪv ‖ -njə-/ *n, adj*
(in MORPHOLOGY) a form which has an AFFIX with the meaning of
"little", "small", etc.
For example, in English, *-let* as in *piglet* and *starlet*, and *-ling* as in
duckling.

diphthong /'dɪfθɒŋ, 'dɪp- ‖ -θɒŋ/ *n* **diphthongal** /dɪf'θɒŋɡəl, dɪp- ‖
-'θɒŋ-/ *adj* **diphthongize** /'dɪfθɒŋɡaɪz, 'dɪp- ‖ -θɒŋ-/ *v*
a speech sound which is usually considered as one distinctive vowel
of a particular language but really involves two vowels, with one
vowel gliding to the other.
For example, the diphthong /aɪ/ in the English word *my*/maɪ/, which
consists of the vowel /a/ gliding into the vowel /ɪ/.

see also GLIDE

[*Further reading*: Gimson 1980]

directive /dɪ̩'rektɪv, daɪ-/ *n*
see under SPEECH ACT CLASSIFICATION

direct method /dɪ̩'rekt 'meθəd, daɪ-/ *n*
a method of foreign or second language teaching which has the
following features:
(a) only the target language should be used in class
(b) meanings should be communicated "directly" (hence the name
    of the method) by associating speech forms with actions,
    objects, mime, gestures, and situations
(c) reading and writing should be taught only after speaking
(d) grammar should only be taught inductively (see DEDUCTIVE
    LEARNING); ie grammar rules should not be taught to the learners
The direct method was developed in the late 19th century as a
reaction against the GRAMMAR TRANSLATION METHOD.

[*Further reading*: Titone 1968]

direct object /'daɪrekt 'ɒbdʒɪ̩kt ‖ 'ɑb-/ *n*
see under OBJECT[1]

direct speech /dɪ̩'rekt 'spiːtʃ, daɪ-/ *n*
the style used in writing to report what a speaker actually said,
without introducing any grammatical changes. In English the
speaker's words may be written between quotation marks. For
example:
    actual utterance: "*You are a thief.*"
    direct speech: *He said "You are a thief.*"
This may be contrasted with **indirect speech** also called **reported**

speech, in which the speaker's words are not reported as they were actually said but are reported, for example, in the form of a *that*-clause. For example:

indirect speech: *He said that you were a thief.*

In English, several grammatical changes occur in indirect speech, including a change of tense that is called **back-shift**. For example:

direct speech	indirect speech
She said "I am tired."	*She said that she was tired.*
He said "The school opened a year ago."	*He said the school had opened a year ago.*

A question as it is reported in indirect speech is called an **indirect question**. For example:

question	indirect question
I asked "Is that your sister?"	*I asked if that was your sister.*
"When are you coming?" he asked.	*He asked when I was coming.*

[*Further reading*: Quirk et al 1985]

disambiguation /ˌdɪsæmbɪgjʊ'eɪʃən/ *n* **disambiguate** /ˌdɪsæm'bɪgjʊeɪt/ *v*

the use of linguistic analysis to show the different structures of an ambiguous sentence. For example:

The lamb is too hot to eat.

can be analysed as:

(a) The lamb is so hot that it cannot eat anything

or:

(b) The cooked lamb is too hot for someone to eat it.

see also AMBIGUOUS

discontinuous constituent /ˌdɪskən'tɪnjʊəs kən'stɪtʃʊənt/ *n*

Parts of a sentence which belong to the same CONSTITUENT but which are separated by other constituents are called a discontinuous constituent. For example:

(a) in French, the negative of the verb is formed with the discontinuous constituent *ne . . .pas* as in:
Paul ne mange pas beaucoup. "Paul doesn't eat much"

(b) in English; the phrasal verb *pick up* in
The player picked the ball up.
is a discontinuous constituent.

[*Further reading*: Quirk et al 1985]

discourse /'dɪskɔːs ‖ -ors/ *n*

a general term for examples of language use, ie language which has been produced as the result of an act of communication.

Whereas grammar refers to the rules a language uses to form grammatical units such as CLAUSE, PHRASE, and SENTENCE, discourse refers to larger units of language such as paragraphs, conversations, and interviews.

Sometimes the study of both written and spoken discourse is known as DISCOURSE ANALYSIS; some researchers however use discourse analysis to refer to the study of spoken discourse and TEXT LINGUISTICS to refer to the study of written discourse.

discourse analysis /'dɪskɔːs ə,næləsəs ‖ -ɔrs/ n
the study of how sentences in spoken and written language form larger meaningful units such as paragraphs, conversations, interviews, etc (see DISCOURSE).
For example, discourse analysis deals with:
(a) how the choice of articles, pronouns, and tenses affects the structure of the discourse (see ADDRESS FORMS, COHESION)
(b) the relationship between utterances in a discourse (see ADJACENCY PAIRS, COHERENCE)
(c) the MOVES made by speakers to introduce a new topic, change the topic, or assert a higher ROLE RELATIONSHIP to the other participants
Analysis of spoken discourse is sometimes called CONVERSATIONAL ANALYSIS. Some linguists use the term TEXT LINGUISTICS for the study of written discourse.
Recent analyses have been carried out on discourse in the classroom. Such analyses can be useful in finding out about the effectiveness of teaching methods and the types of teacher-student relationships.
see also SPEECH EVENT
[*Further reading*: Coulthard 1985; Sinclair & Coulthard 1975]

discourse structure /'dɪskɔːs ,strʌktʃər ‖ -ɔrs/ n
another term for SCHEME

discrete /dɪ'skriːt/ adj **discreteness** /dɪ'skriːtnəs/ n
(of a linguistic unit) having clearly defined boundaries.
In PHONOLOGY, the distinctive sound units of a language (the PHONEMES) are considered to be discrete units. For example, the English word *pin* would consist of three such units: /p/, /ɪ/, and /n/.

discrete-point test /dɪ,skriːt 'pɔɪnt ,test/ n
a language test which measures knowledge of individual language items, such as a grammar test which has different sections on tenses, adverbs, and prepositions. Discrete point tests are based on the theory that language consists of different parts (eg grammar, sounds, vocabulary) and different skills (eg listening, speaking, reading, and writing) and these are made up of elements that can be tested separately. Tests consisting of MULTIPLE-CHOICE ITEMS are usually discrete point tests. Discrete point tests can be contrasted with **integrative tests**.
An integrative test is one which requires a learner to use several language skills at the same time, such as a dictation test, because it requires the learner to use knowledge of grammar, vocabulary, and listening comprehension.
[*Further reading*: Oller 1979]

discrimination[1] /dɪˌskrɪmə̇'neɪʃən/ *n*
see under STIMULUS-RESPONSE THEORY

discrimination[2] *n*
also **discrimination power**
(in testing) the degree to which a test or an item in a test
distinguishes among better and weaker students who take the test.
For example, if all the students who took a test scored around 85%,
yet the students were known to be of different degrees of ability,
the test would fail to discriminate.
In ITEM ANALYSIS, the CORRELATION between the answers to an
individual item and the scores on the whole test is often used as an
estimate of discrimination.
A measure of the discrimination of a test is known as a
discrimination index.
see also ITEM DISCRIMINATION
[*Further reading*: Ebel 1972]

discrimination index /dɪˌskrɪmə̇'neɪʃən 'ɪndeks/ *n*
see under DISCRIMINATION[2]

discrimination power /dɪˌskrɪmə̇'neɪʃən 'paʊəʳ/ *n*
another term for DISCRIMINATION[2]

disjunct /'dɪsdʒʌŋkt/ *n*
also **sentential adverb**
see under ADJUNCT

dispersion /dɪ'spɜːʃən ‖ dɪ'spɜrʒən/ *n*
(in testing) the amount of spread among the scores in a group. For
example if the scores of students on a test were widely spread from
low, middle to high, the scores would be said to have a large
dispersion. Some common statistical measures of dispersion are
VARIANCE, STANDARD DEVIATION, and RANGE.
[*Further reading*: Ebel 1972; Hardyck & Petrinovich 1976]

distinctive feature /dɪˌstɪŋktɪv 'fiːtʃəʳ/ *n*
(in PHONOLOGY) a particular characteristic which distinguishes one
distinctive sound of a language (see PHONEME) from another or one
group of sounds from another group.
For example, in the English sound system, one distinctive feature
which distinguishes the /p/ in *pin* from the /b/ in *bin* is VOICE[2]. The
/b/ is a voiced STOP whereas the /p/ is a voiceless stop (see VOICE[2]).
In GENERATIVE PHONOLOGY, distinctive features play an important part
in the writing of phonological rules. The features are generally
shown in the form of a binary opposition, that is the feature is
either present [+] or absent [−].
For example, vowels and sounds such as /l/, /n/, and /m/, where the
air passes relatively freely through the mouth or nose, have the
feature [+ sonorant] whereas sounds such as /p/, /k/, and /s/, where

the air is stopped either completely or partially, have the feature [– sonorant].

see also BINARY FEATURE

[*Further reading*: Hyman 1975]

distractor /dɪ'stræktər/ *n*
see under TEST ITEM, MULTIPLE CHOICE ITEM

distribution[1] /ˌdɪstrə'bjuːʃən/ *n*
(in statistics) the pattern of scores or measures in a group. For example the distribution of scores in a test may be displayed in a table:

Test scores	Frequency
10	1
20	1
30	3
40	7
50	10
60	6
70	5
80	2
90	2
100	0

distribution[2] *n*
The range of positions in which a particular unit of a language, eg a PHONEME or a word, can occur is called its distribution.
For example, in English, the phoneme /ŋ/, usually written *ng*, cannot occur at the beginning of a word but it can occur in final position, as in *sing*. In other languages, /ŋ/ may occur word initially, as in Cantonese *ngoh* "I".

disyllabic /ˌdɪsə'læbɪk, ˌdaɪ-/ *adj*
consisting of two SYLLABLES, eg the English word *garden* /'gɑː‖ 'gɑr/ + /dən/.
see also MONOSYLLABIC

ditransitive verb /daɪ'trænsətɪv 'vɜːb ‖ 'vɜrb/ *n*
see under TRANSITIVE VERB

divergence[1] /daɪ'vɜːdʒəns, də-‖ -ɜr-/ *n*
the process of two or more languages or language varieties becoming less like each other. For example, if speakers of a language migrate to another area, the variety of language spoken by them may become less similar to the variety spoken by those who did not migrate, ie there will be divergence. This has been the case with English spoken in the United Kingdom compared with the varieties of English spoken in the USA, Canada, Australia, and New Zealand.
see also CONVERGENCE[1]

divergence[2] *n*

see under ACCOMMODATION

domain /dəˈmeɪn, dəʊ-/ *n*

an area of human activity in which one particular speech variety or a combination of several speech varieties is regularly used. A domain can be considered as a group of related **speech situations** (see SPEECH EVENT). For instance situations in which the persons talking to one another are members of the family, eg mother and children, father and mother, elder sister and younger sister, would all belong to the Family Domain. In BILINGUAL and MULTILINGUAL communities, one language may be used in some domains and another language in other domains. For example, Puerto Ricans in the USA may use Spanish in the Family Domain and English in the Employment Domain.

see also DIGLOSSIA, SPEECH EVENT

[*Further reading*: Fishman 1971]

dominant language /ˈdɒmənənt ˈlæŋgwɪdʒ ‖ ˈdɑ-/ *n*
also **dominant dialect** /ˈdɒmənənt ˈdaɪəlekt ‖ ˈdɑ-/

see under LANGUAGE DOMINANCE

dominate /ˈdɒməneɪt ‖ ˈdɑ-/ *v*

see under NODE

dorsal /ˈdɔːsəl ‖ ˈdɔr-/ *n, adj*

see under VELAR

dorsum /ˈdɔːsəm ‖ ˈdɔr-/ *n*

see under PLACE OF ARTICULATION

double negative /ˌdʌbəl ˈnegətɪv/ *n*

a construction in which two negative words are used.
For example, in NONSTANDARD English

I never seen nothing.

instead of

I haven't seen anything.

A double negative does not become a positive. It is used for emphasis. In some languages, eg Serbo-Croatian, double negatives are quite usual and are not considered as nonstandard.

drill /drɪl/ *n*

a technique commonly used in language teaching for practising sounds or sentence patterns in a language, based on guided repetition or practice. A drill which practises some aspect of grammar or sentence formation is often known as **pattern practice**. There are usually two parts to a drill.

(a) The teacher provides a word or sentence as a stimulus (the **call-word** or CUE).

(b) Students make various types of responses based on repetition, substitution, or transformation. For example:

type of drill	teacher's cue	student
substitution drill	*We bought a book.* *pencil*	*We bought a pencil.*
repetition drill	*We bought a book.* *We bought a pencil.*	*We bought a book.* *We bought a pencil.*
transformation drill	*I bought a book.*	*Did you buy a book?* *What did you buy?*

see also FOUR PHASE DRILL
[*Further reading*: Rivers & Temperley 1978]

dual /'djuːəl ‖ 'duːəl/ *adj, n*
see under LANGUAGE UNIVERSAL

dyad /'daɪ-æd, -əd/ *n*
two people in communication with each other. A dyad can be considered as the smallest part of a larger communication network. For example, in describing language use within a family, some dyads would be mother-child, grandmother-child, elder sister-younger sister.

dynamic verb /daɪ'næmɪk 'vɜːb ‖ daɪ'næmɪk, də- 'vɜrb/ *n*
see under STATIVE VERB

dysfluency /dɪs'fluːənsi/ *n* **dysfluent** /dɪs'fluənt/ *adj*
see under FLUENCY

dyslexia /dɪs'leksɪə/ *n* **dyslexic** /dɪs'leksɪk/ *adj*
also **word blindness**
a general term sometimes used to describe any continuing problem in learning to read, such as difficulty in distinguishing letter shapes and words. Reading specialists do not agree on the nature or causes of such reading problems however, and both medical and psychological explanations have been made. Because of the very general way in which the term is often used, many reading specialists prefer not to use the term, and describe reading problems in terms of specific reading difficulties.
[*Further reading*: Money 1962]

dysphasia /dɪs'feɪʒə/ *n*
another term for APHASIA

EAP /ˌiː eɪ ˈpiː/ *n*

an abbreviation for English for Academic Purposes (see under
ENGLISH FOR SPECIAL PURPOSES)

echolalia/ˌekəʊˈleɪlɪə/ *n*

a type of speech disorder or APHASIA in which all or most of a
speaker's utterances consist of the simple repetition or echoing of
words or phrases which the speaker hears.

eclectic method /ɪˈklektɪk ˈmeθəd/ *n*

a term sometimes used for the practice of using features of several
different METHODs in language teaching, for example, by using both
audiolingual and communicative language teaching techniques.
see also AUDIOLINGUAL METHOD, COMMUNICATIVE APPROACH

educational linguistics /edjʊˈkeɪʃənəl lɪŋˈgwɪstɪks ‖ edʒə-/ *n*

a term sometimes used in the USA to refer to a branch of APPLIED
LINGUISTICS (2) which deals with the relationship between language
and education.
[*Further reading*: Spolsky 1978]

educational technology /edjʊˈkeɪʃənəl tekˈnɒlədʒi ‖ edʒə- tekˈnɑ-/ *n*

(1) the use of machines and educational equipment of different sorts
(eg language laboratories, tape recorders, video, etc) to assist
teachers and learners.
(2) a system of instruction which contains (a) an analysis of what
learners need to know and be able to do (b) a description of these
needs as BEHAVIOURAL OBJECTIVEs and (c) (1) above.

effected object /ɪˈfektəd ˈɒbdʒɪkt ‖ ˈɑb-/ *n*

another term for OBJECT OF RESULT

EFL /ˌiː ef ˈel/ *n*

an abbreviation for ENGLISH AS A FOREIGN LANGUAGE

egocentric speech /ˌegəʊˈsentrɪk ˈspiːtʃ, ˌiːgəʊ-/ *n*

speech which is not addressed to other people. This is one of two
types of speech which Piaget observed in the speech of children
learning a first language. Egocentric speech serves the purpose of
giving pleasure to the child and of expressing the child's thoughts,
and provides an opportunity for the child to experiment or play with
speech. It may be contrasted with **socialized speech**, or speech which
is addressed to other people and which is used for communication.
[*Further reading*: Piaget 1955; Vygotsky 1962]

EGP /ˌiː dʒiː ˈpiː/ *n*

an abbreviation for English for General Purposes (see under ENGLISH
FOR SPECIAL PURPOSES)

egressive /eɪˈgresɪv/ *adj*
of speech sounds which are produced with air from the lungs moving out through the mouth and/or nose. Most speech sounds in most languages are egressive.

elaborated code /ɪˈlæbəreɪtəd ˈkəʊd/ *n*
see under CODE²

elicitation /ɪˌlɪsəˈteɪʃən/ *n*
(in language teaching) techniques or procedures which a teacher uses to get learners to actively produce speech or writing.

elicitation procedure /ɪˌlɪsəˈteɪʃən prəˌsiːdʒəʳ/ *n*
also **elicitation technique** /ɪˌlɪsəˈteɪʃən tekˌniːk/
(in linguistics or SECOND LANGUAGE ACQUISITION research) a technique used to obtain information about how someone uses a particular language item. The subject may be asked to describe a picture, tell a story, or finish an incomplete sentence. These procedures are used to get a fuller understanding of linguistic knowledge than the study of naturally occurring speech or writing can provide.
[*Further reading*: Quirk & Greenbaum 1970]

elicited imitation /ɪˈlɪsətəd ɪmɪˈteɪʃən/ *n*
an ELICITATION PROCEDURE in which a person has to repeat a sentence which he or she sees or hears. When people are asked to repeat a sentence which uses linguistic rules which they themselves cannot or do not use, they often make changes in the sentence so that it is more like their own speech. Elicited imitation can be used to study a person's knowledge of a language. For example:

stimulus sentence	elicited imitation
Why can't the man climb over the fence?	*Why the man can't climb over the fence?*

[*Further reading*: Swain, Dumas, & Naiman 1974]

elision /ɪˈlɪʒən/ *n* **elide** /ɪˈlaɪd/ *v*
the leaving out of a sound or sounds in speech. For example, in rapid informal speech in English, *suppose* is often pronounced as [spəʊz], *factory* as [ˈfæktri] and *mostly* as [ˈməʊsli].
see also ELLIPSIS, EPENTHESIS
[*Further reading*: Gimson 1980]

ellipsis /ɪˈlɪpsəs/ *n* **elliptical** /ɪˈlɪptɪkəl/ *adj*
the leaving out of words or phrases from sentences where they are unnecessary because they have already been referred to or mentioned. For example, when the subject of the verb in two co-ordinated clauses is the same, it may be omitted to avoid repetition:
The man went to the door and (he) opened it. (subject ellipsis)
Mary ate an apple and Jane (ate) a pear. (verb ellipsis)
see also ELISION
[*Further reading*: Quirk et al 1985]

ELT /ˌi: el 'ti:/ *n*

an abbreviation for English Language Teaching. It is used especially in Britain to refer to the teaching of ENGLISH AS A SECOND LANGUAGE or ENGLISH AS A FOREIGN LANGUAGE. In north American usage this is often referred to as TESOL.

embedded sentence /ɪm'bedɪd 'sentəns/ *n*

see under EMBEDDING

embedding /ɪm'bedɪŋ/ *n* **embed** /ɪm'bed/ *v*

(in GENERATIVE TRANSFORMATIONAL GRAMMAR) the occurrence of a sentence within another sentence.
For example, in:
The news that he had got married surprised his friends.

(1) The news ↑ surprised his friends.
  (2) (that) he had got married

sentence (2) is embedded in sentence (1) and is therefore an **embedded sentence**.
[*Further reading*: Aitchison 1978; Bach 1974]

emotive meaning /ɪ'məʊtɪv ˌmi:nɪŋ/ *n*

another term for CONNOTATION

empathy /'empəθi/ *n* **empathize** /'empəθaɪz/ *v*

the quality of being able to imagine and share the thoughts, feelings, and point of view of other people. Empathy is thought to contribute to the attitudes we have towards a person or group with a different language and culture from our own, and it may contribute to the degree of success with which a person learns another language.
[*Further reading*: Brown 1980; Gardner & Lambert 1972]

emphatic pronoun /ɪm'fætɪk 'prəʊnaʊn/ *n*

a pronoun which gives additional emphasis to a noun phrase or which draws attention to it. In English these are formed in the same way as REFLEXIVE PRONOUNs, by adding *-self, -selves* to the pronouns.
For example:
I myself cooked the dinner.
We spoke to the President herself.

empirical investigation /ɪm'pɪrəkəl ɪnˌvestə'geɪʃən/ *n*

see under FIELD WORK

empirical validity /ɪmˌpɪrəkəl və'lɪdəti/ *n*

a measure of the VALIDITY of a test, arrived at by comparing the test with one or more CRITERION MEASUREs. Such comparisons could be with:
(a) other valid tests or other independent measures obtained at the

empiricism

same time (eg an assessment made by the teacher) (CONCURRENT VALIDITY)

(b) other valid tests or other performance criteria obtained at a later time (PREDICTIVE VALIDITY).

see also CONSTRUCT VALIDITY

[*Further reading*: Ebel 1972]

empiricism /ɪmˈpɪrəsɪzəm/ n **empiricist** /ɪmˈpɪrəsɪst/ n
an approach to psychology which states that the development of theory must be related to observable facts and experiments (see BEHAVIOURISM), or which states that all human knowledge comes from experience. Empiricism contrasts with the view that many forms of human knowledge are in-born or innate (see INNATIST HYPOTHESIS).

[*Further reading*: Steinberg 1982]

empty word /ˈempti ˈwɜːd ‖ ˈwɜrd/ n
see under CONTENT WORD

enabling skills /ɪˈneɪblɪŋ ˈskɪlz/ n
another term for MICRO-SKILLS

encoding /ɪnˈkəʊdɪŋ/ n **encode** /ɪnˈkəʊd/ v
the process of turning a message into a set of symbols, as part of the act of communication.

In encoding speech, the speaker must:

(a) select a meaning to be communicated

(b) turn it into linguistic form using semantic systems (eg concepts, PROPOSITIONS), grammatical systems (eg words, phrases, clauses), and phonological systems (eg PHONEMES, SYLLABLES).

Different systems of communication make use of different types of symbols to encode messages (eg pictorial representation, morse code, drum beats).

see also DECODING

[*Further reading*: Clark & Clark 1977]

endoglossic /ˌendəʊˈɡlɒsɪk ‖ -ˈɡlɔ-,-ˈɡlɑ-/ adj
When a language is the NATIVE LANGUAGE of all or most of the population of a region, it is called endoglossic. For example, English is endoglossic for the United Kingdom, Australia, and the USA, but not for nations such as Ghana or Singapore, even though it is an important language and medium of education in these countries.

see also EXOGLOSSIC

endonormative /ˌendəʊˈnɔːmətɪv ‖ -ˈnɔr-/ adj
When a language has a NORM[1] within the area where it is spoken, it is called endonormative. In England and the USA, for example, English is endonormative. This is not the case for English in a country where it is a SECOND LANGUAGE, such as Malaysia, Nigeria, or Hong Kong.

see also EXONORMATIVE

English as a Foreign Language *n*
also **EFL**

the role of English in countries where it is taught as a subject in schools but not used as a medium of instruction in education nor as a language of communication (eg in government, business, or industry) within the country.

see also ENGLISH AS A SECOND LANGUAGE

English as an International Language *n*

the role of English as a language of international communication, for example, when a Brazilian and a Japanese businessman use English to negotiate a business contract. The type of English used on such occasions need not necessarily be based on native speaker varieties of English (eg American English or British English) but will vary according to the mother tongue of the people speaking it and the purposes for which it is being used.

see also NON-NATIVE VARIETIES OF ENGLISH

[*Further reading*: Smith 1981]

English as a Second Dialect *n*
also **ESD**

the role of standard English (see STANDARD VARIETY) for those who speak other dialects of English.

see also BIDIALECTAL, BILINGUAL EDUCATION

English as a Second Language *n*
also **ESL**

(1) the role of English for immigrant and other minority groups in English-speaking countries. These people may use their mother tongue at home or among friends, but use English at school and at work. This is sometimes called **English for Speakers of other Languages**, or **ESOL**.

(2) the role of English in countries where it is widely used within the country (eg as a language of instruction at school, as a language of business and government, and of everyday communication by some people) but is not the first language of the population (eg in Singapore, the Philippines, India, and Nigeria).

(3) in US usage, the role of English in countries where it is not a first language (eg Germany and Japan). In British usage, this is called ENGLISH AS A FOREIGN LANGUAGE.

see also ENGLISH AS A FOREIGN LANGUAGE

English as a second language programme *n*
also **ESL/ESOL programme**

a programme for teaching English to speakers of other languages in English-speaking countries. ESL programmes are generally based on particular language teaching methods and teach language skills (speaking, understanding, reading, and writing). They may be school programmes for immigrant and other non-English-speaking children, used together with BILINGUAL EDUCATION or with regular school programmes, or community programmes for adults.

English for Academic Purposes *n*
also **EAP**
see under ENGLISH FOR SPECIAL PURPOSES

English for General Purposes *n*
also **EGP**
see under ENGLISH FOR SPECIAL PURPOSES

English for Science and Technology *n*
also **EST**
see under ENGLISH FOR SPECIAL PURPOSES

English for Speakers of Other Languages *n*
also **ESOL**
see under ENGLISH AS A SECOND LANGUAGE (1)

English for Special Purposes *n*
also **English for Specific Purposes, ESP**
the role of English in a language course or programme of instruction in which the content and aims of the course are fixed by the specific needs of a particular group of learners. For example courses in **English for Academic Purposes, English for Science and Technology**, and English for Nursing. These courses may be compared with those which aim to teach general language proficiency, **English for General Purposes**.
see also LANGUAGES FOR SPECIAL PURPOSES
[*Further reading*: Robinson 1980]

English medium school /ˈɪŋglɪʃ ˌmiːdɪəm ˈskuːl/ *n*
a school in which English is used as the major medium of instruction. This term is usually used in countries where English is a SECOND LANGUAGE.

epenthesis /ɪˈpenθəsəs/ *n* **epenthetic** /ˌepənˈθetɪk/ *adj*
the addition of a vowel or consonant at the beginning of a word or between sounds. This often happens in language learning when the language which is being learned has different combinations of vowels or consonants from the learner's first language. For example, Spanish learners of English often say [espiːk] *espeak* for *speak*, as Spanish does not have words starting with the CONSONANT CLUSTER /sp/. Many speakers of other languages do not use combinations like the /lm/ or /lp/ of English and add an epenthetic vowel, for example [fɪləm] *filem* for *film*, and [heləp] *helep* for *help*.
see also ELISION, INTRUSION

episodic memory /epəˈsɒdɪk ˈmeməri ‖ -ˈsɑ-/ *n*
that part of the MEMORY which is organized in terms of personal experiences and episodes.
For example, if a subject was asked the question "What were you

doing on Friday night at 7 pm?" he or she may think of all the things that happened from 5 pm up to 7 pm. The person builds up a sequence of events or episodes to help find the wanted information. Episodic memory may be contrasted with **semantic memory**. Semantic memory is that part of the memory in which words are organized according to semantic groups or classes. Words are believed to be stored in long term memory according to their semantic properties. Thus *canary* is linked in memory to *bird*, and *rose* is linked to *flower*. These links are a part of semantic memory.
[*Further reading*: Glucksberg & Danks 1975]

equational /ɪˈkweɪʒ ənəl/ *adj*
another term for EQUATIVE

equative /ɪˈkweɪtɪv/ *adj*
also **equational**
A sentence in which the SUBJECT and COMPLEMENT refer to the same person or thing is called an equative sentence.
For example, the English sentence:
 Susan is the girl I was talking about.
 subject complement

equivalent form reliability /ɪˈkwɪvələnt fɔːm rɪˌlaɪəˈbɪləti ‖ fɔrm/ *n*
another term for ALTERNATE FORM RELIABILITY

equivalent forms /ɪˈkwɪvələnt ˈfɔːmz ‖ ˈfɔrmz/ *n*
another term for PARALLEL FORMS

error /ˈerər/ *n*
(1) (in the speech or writing of a second or foreign language learner), the use of a linguistic item (eg a word, a grammatical item, a SPEECH ACT, etc) in a way which a fluent or native speaker of the language regards as showing faulty or incomplete learning.
A distinction is sometimes made between an error, which results from incomplete knowledge, and a **mistake** made by a learner when writing or speaking and which is caused by lack of attention, fatigue, carelessness, or some other aspect of PERFORMANCE.
Errors are sometimes classified according to vocabulary (**lexical error**), pronunciation (**phonological error**), grammar, (**syntactic error**), misunderstanding of a speaker's intention or meaning (**interpretive error**), production of the wrong communicative effect eg through the faulty use of a speech act or one of the RULES OF SPEAKING (**pragmatic error**).
In the study of second and foreign language learning, errors have been studied to discover the processes learners make use of in learning and using a language (see ERROR ANALYSIS).
(2) see under SPEECH ERROR.
see also DEVELOPMENTAL ERROR, GLOBAL ERROR
[*Further reading*: Richards 1974]

error analysis /ˈerər əˈnæləsəs/ *n*

the study and analysis of the ERRORS made by second and foreign language learners. Error analysis may be carried out in order to:

(a) find out how well someone knows a language
(b) find out how a person learns a language
(c) obtain information on common difficulties in language learning, as an aid in teaching or in the preparation of teaching materials.

Error analysis may be used as well as or instead of CONTRASTIVE ANALYSIS.

see also ERROR GRAVITY, GLOBAL ERROR

[*Further reading*: Richards 1974]

error gravity /ˈerər ˈgrævəti/ *n*

a measure of the effect that errors made by people speaking a second or foreign language have on communication or on other speakers of the language. The degree of error gravity of different kinds of errors (eg errors of pronunciation, grammar, vocabulary, etc) varies; some errors have little effect, some cause irritation, while others may cause communication difficulties.

For example, in the sentences below, (a) causes greater interference with communication than (b) and shows a greater degree of error gravity.

(a) *Since the harvest was good, was rain a lot last year.*
(b) *The harvest was good last year, because plenty of rain.*

[*Further reading*: Svartvik 1973; Burt & Kiparsky 1972]

ESD /ˌiː es ˈdiː/ *n*

an abbreviation for ENGLISH AS A SECOND DIALECT

ESL /ˌiː es ˈel/ *n*

an abbreviation for ENGLISH AS A SECOND LANGUAGE

ESOL /ˌiː es əʊ ˈel, ˈiːsɒl/ *n*

an abbreviation for English tor Speakers of Other Languages (see ENGLISH AS A SECOND LANGUAGE (1))

ESP /ˌiː es ˈpiː/ *n*

an abbreviation for ENGLISH FOR SPECIAL PURPOSES

essay test /ˈeseɪ ˌtest/ *n*

a SUBJECTIVE TEST in which a person is required to write an extended piece of text on a set topic.

EST /ˌiː es ˈtiː/ *n*

an abbreviation for English for Science and Technology (see under ENGLISH FOR SPECIAL PURPOSES)

ethnographic research /ˌeθnəˈgræfɪk rɪˈsɜːtʃ ‖ rɪˈsɜrtʃ, ˈriːsɜrtʃ/ *n*

see under ETHNOGRAPHY

ethnography /eθˈnɒgrəfi ‖ -ˈnɑ-/ *n*

the study of the life and culture of a society or ethnic group, especially by personal observation. The related field of **ethnology** studies the comparison of the cultures of different societies or ethnic groups.

In studies of language learning or in descriptions of how a language is used, the term **ethnographic research** is sometimes used to refer to the observation and description of naturally occurring language (eg between mother and child, between teacher and students, etc).
see also ETHNOGRAPHY OF COMMUNICATION

ethnography of communication /eθ'nɑgrəfi əv kə,mju:nə'keɪʃən ‖ eθ'nɑ-/ n
the study of the place of language in culture and society. Language is not studied in isolation but within a social and/or cultural setting. Ethnography of communication studies, for example, how people in a particular group or community communicate with each other and how the social relationships between these people affect the type of language they use.

The concept of an ethnography of communication was advocated by the American social anthropologist and linguist Hymes and this approach is important in SOCIOLINGUISTICS and APPLIED LINGUISTICS.
see also COMMUNICATIVE COMPETENCE, ETHNOMETHODOLOGY, ROLE RELATIONSHIP, SPEECH EVENT
[*Further reading*: Hymes 1974; Saville-Troike 1982]

ethnology /eθ'nɒlədʒi ‖ -'nɑ-/ n
see under ETHNOGRAPHY

ethnomethodology /,eθnəʊmeθə'dɒlədʒi ‖ -'dɑ-/ n
ethnomethodologist /eθnəʊmeθə'dɒlədʒəst ‖ -'dɑ-/ n
a branch of sociology which studies how people organize and understand the activities of ordinary life. It studies people's relations with each other and how social interaction takes place between people. Ethnomethodologists have studied such things as relationships between children and adults, interviews, telephone conversation, and TURN TAKING in conversation. Language is not the main interest of ethnomethodologists, but their observations on how language is used in everyday activities such as conversation are of interest to linguists and sociolinguists.
see also ETHNOGRAPHY OF COMMUNICATION
[*Further reading*: Garfinkel 1967; Turner 1970]

etymology /etə'mɒlədʒi ‖ -'mɑ-/ n **etymological** /,etəmə'lɒdʒɪkəl ‖ -'lɑ-/ adj
the study of the origin of words, and of their history and changes in their meaning.

For example, the etymology of the modern English noun *fish* can be traced back to Old English *fisc*.

In some cases there is a change in meaning. For example the word *meat*, which now normally means "animal flesh used as food", is from the Old English word *mete* which meant "food in general".

evaluation /ɪˌvæljuˈeɪʃən/ n

in general, the systematic gathering of information for purposes of decision making. Evaluation uses both quantitative methods (eg tests), qualitative methods (eg observations, ratings (see RATING SCALE)) and value judgments. In LANGUAGE PLANNING, evaluation frequently involves gathering information on patterns of language use, language ability, and attitudes towards language. In language teaching programmes, evaluation is related to decisions to be made about the quality of the programme itself, and decisions about individuals in the programmes. The evaluation of programmes may involve the study of CURRICULUM², OBJECTIVES, materials, and tests or grading systems. The evaluation of individuals involves decisions about entrance to programmes, placement, progress, and achievement. In evaluating both programmes and individuals, tests and other measures are frequently used.

see also FORMATIVE EVALUATION

[*Further reading*: Popham 1975]

evaluative comprehension /ɪˈvæljuətɪv ˌkɒmprəˈhenʃən ‖ ˌkɑm-/ n

see under READING

exact word method /ɪgˌzækt ˈwɜːd ˌmeθəd ‖ ˈwɜrd-/ n

see under CLOZE PROCEDURE

exclamation¹ /ˌekskləˈmeɪʃən/ n

an utterance, which may not have the structure of a full sentence, and which shows strong emotion. For example: *Good God!* or *Damn!*

see also INTERJECTION

exclamation² n

also **exclamatory sentence** /ɪkˈsklæmətəri ˈsentəns ‖ -tori/

an utterance which shows the speaker's or writer's feelings. Exclamations begin with a phrase using *what* or *how*, but they do not reverse the order of the subject and the auxiliary verb:

> *How clever she is!*
> *What a good dog!*

see also STATEMENT, QUESTION

[*Further reading*: Quirk et al 1985]

exclusive (first person) pronoun /ɪkˈskluːsɪv ˈprəʊnaʊn/ n

a first person pronoun which does not include the person being spoken or written to.

In some languages there is a distinction between first person plural pronouns which include the persons who are addressed (**inclusive pronouns**) and those which do not (exclusive pronouns). For example, in Malay:

exclusive	inclusive
kami	*kita*
"we"	"we"

The lack of this distinction in English occasionally causes problems. For example, *We really must see that film next week* can be ambiguous unless it is clear from the context whether the person addressed is included or not.

see also PERSONAL PRONOUNS

existential /ˌegzɪ'stenʃəl/ *adj*

(in linguistics) describes a particular type of sentence structure which often expresses the existence or location of persons, animals, things, or ideas.

In English, a common existential sentence structure is:

There + a form of the verb *be*

For example:

There are four bedrooms in this house.

Another frequently used existential structure uses the verb *to have*.

For example:

This house has four bedrooms.

[*Further reading*: Lyons 1968]

exoglossic /ˌeksəʊ'glɒsɪk ‖ -'glɔ-, -'glɑ-/ *adj*

when a language is not the NATIVE LANGUAGE of all or most of the population of a region it is called exoglossic.

For example, English is exoglossic in Ghana and Singapore where it is not a native language for many people although it is a medium of education.

see also ENDOGLOSSIC

exonormative /ˌeksəʊ'nɔːmətɪv ‖ -'nɔr-/ *adj*

When a language has its NORM[1] outside the area where it is spoken or taught, it is called exonormative.

For example, English is exonormative in countries where it is not the NATIVE LANGUAGE but where it is, for instance, a SECOND LANGUAGE, eg in Hong Kong.

In some countries such as Australia, there has been a change from an external to an internal norm, ie from a British to a local Australian standard.

see also ENDONORMATIVE

expansion /ɪk'spænʃən/ *n*

see under MODELLING

expectancy theory /ɪk'spektənsi ˌθɪəri/ *n*

the theory that knowledge of a language includes knowing whether a word or utterance is likely to occur in a particular context or situation. For example, in the sentence below, "expected" words in (1) and (2) are *dress* and *change*:

When the girl fell into the water she wet the pretty (1) she was wearing and had to go home and (2) it.

Knowledge of the expectancies of occurrence of language items is made use of in the comprehension of language.

see also PRAGMATICS

[*Further reading*: Oller 1979]

experiencer case /ɪk'spɪərɪənsər ˌkeɪs/ n

see under DATIVE CASE[2]

experimental design /ɪksperə'mentl dɪ'zaɪn/ n

see under EXPERIMENTAL METHOD

experimental group /ɪksperə'mentl ˌgruːp/ n

see under CONTROL GROUP

experimental method /ɪksperə'mentl ˌmeθəd/ n

an approach to educational research in which an idea or HYPOTHESIS is tested or verified by setting up situations in which the relationship between different subjects or variables can be determined (see DEPENDENT VARIABLE). The description of the purposes of the research, its plan, the statistical procedures used, etc, in an experimental study is called the **experimental design**.

[*Further reading*: Bailey 1982]

explicit performative /ɪk'splɪsɪt pə'fɔːmətɪv ‖ -'fɔr-/ n

see under PERFORMATIVE

exponent /ɪk'spəʊnənt/ n

see under FUNCTIONAL SYLLABUS

expressive /ɪk'spresɪv/ n

see under SPEECH ACT CLASSIFICATION

expressive function /ɪkˌspresɪv 'fʌŋkʃən/ n

see under FUNCTIONS OF LANGUAGE[1]

Extended Standard Theory /ɪkˌstendəd 'stændəd ˌθɪəri ‖ -ərd/ n

see under GENERATIVE TRANSFORMATIONAL GRAMMAR

extensive reading /ɪk'stensɪv 'riːdɪŋ/ n

In language teaching, reading activities are sometimes classified as extensive and intensive.

Extensive reading means reading in quantity and in order to gain a general understanding of what is read. It is intended to develop good reading habits, to build up knowledge of vocabulary and structure, and to encourage a liking for reading.

Intensive reading is generally at a slower speed, and requires a higher degree of understanding than extensive reading.

[*Further reading*: Mackay et al 1979]

external speech /ɪk'stɜːnəl 'spiːtʃ ‖ -ɜr-/ n

see under INNER SPEECH

extinction /ɪk'stɪŋkʃən/ n

see under STIMULUS-RESPONSE THEORY

extralinguistic /ˌekstrə lɪŋˈgwɪstɪk/ *adj*

describes those features in communication which are not directly a part of verbal language but which either contribute in conveying a MESSAGE, eg hand movements, facial expressions, etc, or have an influence on language use, eg signalling a speaker's age, sex, or social class.

see also PARALINGUISTICS, SIGŃ LANGUAGE

extraposition/ˌekstrəpəˈzɪʃən/ *n*

the process of moving a word, phrase, or clause to a position in a sentence which is different from the position it usually has.

For example, the subject of some sentences can be moved to the end of the sentence:

subject

(a) *Trying to get tickets was difficult.*
(b) *It was difficult trying to get tickets.*

In sentence (b) *It* is called the **anticipatory subject**, and *trying to get tickets* is called the **postponed subject**.

[*Further reading*: Quirk et al 1985]

face /feɪs/ *n*

In communication between two or more persons, the positive image or impression of oneself that one shows or intends to show to the other PARTICIPANTS is called face. In any social meeting between people, the participants attempt to communicate a positive image of themselves which reflects the values and beliefs of the participants. For example Mr Smith's "face" during a particular meeting might be that of "a sophisticated, intelligent, witty, and educated person". If this image is not accepted by the other participants, feelings may be hurt and there is a consequent "loss of face". Social contacts between people thus involve what the sociologist of language, Goffman, called **face-work**, that is, efforts by the participants to communicate a positive face and to prevent loss of face. The study of face and face-work is important in considering how languages express POLITENESS.

[*Further reading*: Goffman 1959, 1967; Levinson 1983]

face to face interaction /'feɪs tə 'feɪs ɪntə'rækʃən/ *n*
also **face to face communication** /'feɪs tə 'feɪs kəmjuːnəˈkeɪʃən/
communication between people in which the PARTICIPANTS are physically present. In contrast there are some situations where speaker and hearer may be in different locations, such as a telephone conversation.

face validity /'feɪs vəˈlɪdəti/ *n*

(in testing) the degree to which a test appears to measure the knowledge or abilities it claims to measure, based on the subjective judgment of an observer.

For example, if a test of reading comprehension contains many dialect words which might be unknown to the students the test may be said to lack face validity.

see also VALIDITY

[*Further reading*: Heaton 1975]

face-work /'feɪswɜːk ‖ -ɜr-/ *n*
see under FACE

facility value /fəˈsɪləti 'væljuː/ *n*
another term for ITEM FACILITY

factitive case /'fæktətɪv ˌkeɪs/ *n*

In CASE GRAMMAR, the noun or noun phrase which refers to something which is made or created by the action of the verb is in the factitive case.

For example, in the sentence:
Tony built the shed.
the shed is in the factitive case.

However, in the sentence:

Tony repaired the shed.

the shed is not in the factitive case as it already existed when the repair work was done. In this sentence, *the shed* is in the OBJECTIVE CASE.

The factitive case is sometimes called the **result** (or **resultative**) **case.**

[*Further reading*: Fillmore 1968]

factive verb /ˌfæktɪv ˈvɜːb ‖ ˈvɜrb/ *n*

a verb followed by a clause which the speaker or writer considers to express a fact. For example, in:

I regret that we were not able to come to your party.

regret is a factive verb.

Other factive verbs in English include *remember* and *deplore*.

[*Further reading*: Kiparsky & Kiparsky 1971]

factor analysis /ˈfæktər əˈnæləsəs/ *n*

in statistics, a technique which is used to determine what underlying VARIABLES[2] account for the CORRELATIONS among different observed variables. For example if we give a group of students tests in geometry, algebra, arithmetic, reading and writing, we can find out what factors are common to all the tests, using factor analysis. A factor analysis might show that there are two factors in the tests; one related to mathematics and the other related to language proficiency. These factors may be interpreted as abilities or traits which these tests measure to differing degrees.

[*Further reading*: Ebel 1972]

false beginner /ˈfɔːls bɪˈɡɪnəʳ/ *n*

(in language teaching) a learner who has had a limited amount of previous instruction in a language, but who because of extremely limited language proficiency is classified as at the beginning level of language instruction. A false beginner is sometimes contrasted with a **true beginner**, ie someone who has no knowledge of the language.

false cognate /ˈfɔːls ˈkɒɡneɪt ‖ ˈkɑɡ-/ *n*

also **faux amis, false friend** /ˈfɔːls ˈfrend/

a word which has the same or very similar form in two languages, but which has a different meaning in each. The similarity may cause a second language learner to use the word wrongly. For example the French word *expérience* means "experiment", and not "experience". French learners of English might thus write or say: *Yesterday we performed an interesting experience in the laboratory.*

False cognates may be identified by CONTRASTIVE ANALYSIS.

familiarity /fəˌmɪliˈærəti/ *n*

a measure of how frequently a linguistic item is thought to be used, or the degree to which it is known. This may be measured by asking people to show on a RATING SCALE whether they think they use a given word or structure *never, sometimes,* or *often.* Word familiarity has been used within the study of learning and memory, and has also been made use of as a way of selecting vocabulary for language teaching.

[*Further reading*: Richards 1970]

faux amis /ˌfəʊzæˈmiː/ *n*
another term for FALSE COGNATE

feature /ˈfiːtʃəʳ/ *n*
see DISTINCTIVE FEATURE, SEMANTIC FEATURES

feedback /ˈfiːdbæk/ *n*
any information which provides a report on the result of behaviour. For example, verbal or facial signals which listeners give to speakers to indicate that they understand what the speaker is saying. In DISCOURSE ANALYSIS, feedback given while someone is speaking is sometimes called **back channel cues**, for example comments such as *uh, yeah, really*, smiles, headshakes, and grunts which indicate success or failure in communication.
see also AUDITORY FEEDBACK, DELAYED AUDITORY FEEDBACK

felicity conditions /fəˈlɪsəti kənˈdɪʃənz/ *n*
(in SPEECH ACT theory) the conditions which must be fulfilled for a speech act to be satisfactorily performed or realized. For example, the sentence *I promise the sun will set today* cannot be considered as a true promise, because we can only make promises about future acts which are under our control. The felicity conditions necessary for promises are:
(a) A sentence is used which states a future act of the speaker.
(b) The speaker has the ability to do the act.
(c) The hearer prefers the speaker to do the act rather than not to do it.
(d) The speaker would not otherwise usually do the act.
(e) The speaker intends to do the act.
[*Further reading*: Searle 1981]

field /fiːld/ *n*
see FIELD THEORY, LEXICAL FIELD

field dependence /ˈfiːld dɪˈpendəns/ *n* **field dependent** /ˈfiːld dɪˈpendənt/ *adj*
a learning style in which a learner tends to look at the whole of a learning task which contains many items. The learner has difficulty in studying a particular item when it occurs within a "field" of other items.
A **field independent** learning style is one in which a learner is able to identify or focus on particular items and is not distracted by other items in the background or context.
Field dependence and independence have been studied as a difference of COGNITIVE STYLE in language learning.
[*Further reading*: Naiman et al 1975]

field independence /'fiːld ɪndɪ'pendəns/ *n*
see under FIELD DEPENDENCE

field methods /'fiːld 'meθədz/ *n*
see under FIELD WORK

field of discourse /ˌfiːld əv 'dɪskɔːs ‖ -ɔrs/ *n*
see under SOCIAL CONTEXT

field theory /'fiːld 'θɪəri/ *n*
also **theory of semantic fields**
(in semantics) the theory that the vocabulary of a language is organized into groups of words that refer to an area of meaning (such as colours, items of furniture, types of vehicle, etc). When a word changes in meaning or if a new word is coined, the meaning of the other words in the group must change in meaning or disappear. For example, in 18th century German, the word *braun* "brown" covered the meaning of the two English words *brown* and *violet*. Later on, when *violett* entered the German language from French, the meaning of *braun* changed to cover only the meaning of the English word *brown*.
see also LEXICAL FIELD

field work /'fiːld ˌwɜːk ‖ ˌwɜrk/ *n*
(in linguistics) the collection of data for analysis from the speakers' and/or writers of a particular language or dialect. Different procedures (called **field methods**) are used to obtain data.
For example:
(a) the recording of speakers to obtain speech samples for analysis of sounds, sentence structures, and lexical use. The people recorded may be native speakers of a particular language or speakers for whom it is a SECOND LANGUAGE.
(b) questionnaires or interviews, eg in bilingual or multilingual communities, to obtain information on attitudes to language and/or language choice.
(c) written or oral tests to obtain samples of the language use of second or foreign language learners.
The collection and the use of data (**empirical investigation**) plays an important part in the research work of many sociolinguists and applied linguists.

figure of speech /ˌfɪgər əv 'spiːtʃ ‖ ˌfɪgjər/ *n*
a word or phrase which is used for special effect, and which does not have its usual or literal meaning. The two most common figures of speech are the **simile** and the **metaphor** but there are many other less common ones.
A simile is an expression in which something is compared to something else by the use of a FUNCTION WORD such as *like* or *as*. In *Tom eats like a horse*, Tom's appetite is compared to that of a horse. *My hands are as cold as ice* means that my hands are very cold.

In a metaphor, no function words are used. Something is described by stating another thing with which it can be compared.

In *His words stabbed at her heart*, the words did not actually stab, but their effect is compared to the stabbing of a knife.

filled pause /ˈfɪld ˈpɔːz/ *n*
see under PAUSING

filler /ˈfɪləʳ/ *n*
see under TAGMEMICS

final /ˈfaɪnəl/ *adj*
occurring at the end of a linguistic unit, eg word final, clause final. For example, a group of consonants at the end of a word such as *st* in the English word *list* is called a final CONSONANT CLUSTER.
see also INITIAL, MEDIAL

finite verb /ˈfaɪnaɪt ˈvɜːb ‖ ˈvɜrb/ *n*
a form of a verb which is marked to show that it is related to a subject in PERSON and/or NUMBER, and which shows TENSE[1]. A **non-finite verb** form is not marked according to differences in the person or number of the subject, and has no tense. The INFINITIVE and the PARTICIPLES are non-finite forms of verbs in English. For example:

We	*want*	*to leave.*
She	*wants*	
I	*wanted*	
	finite verb forms	non-finite form

[*Further reading*: Quirk et al 1985]

first language /ˈfɜːst ˈlæŋgwɪdʒ ‖ ˈfɜrst/ *n*
(generally) a person's mother tongue or the language acquired first. In multilingual communities, however, where a child may gradually shift from the main use of one language to the main use of another (eg because of the influence of a school language), first language may refer to the language the child feels most comfortable using. Often this term is used synonymously with NATIVE LANGUAGE.
First language is also known as **L1**.

Firthian linguistics /ˈfɜːθɪən lɪŋˈgwɪstɪks ‖ -ɜr-/ *n*
an approach to linguistics which is based on the ideas developed by the British linguist J.R. Firth (1890–1969) and which had a considerable influence on linguists in Britain.
It suggests that different systems of analysis may be needed for describing one particular level of linguistic structure. For example, when analysing sentences, one system of analysis may be used for investigating the structure of sentences and another for the intonation patterns that are related to spoken sentences.
Another idea related to Firthian linguistics is that the meaning of

sentences must be looked at in context and that there is a definite relationship between an utterance and the situation in which it is said (see SOCIAL CONTEXT).

Firthian linguistics has been further developed by a number of British linguists, the most well-known of whom is M.A.K. Halliday.
see also FUNCTIONS OF LANGUAGE[2], SYSTEMIC GRAMMAR
[*Further reading*: Robins 1980]

fixed response item /ˈfɪkst rɪˈspɒns ˈaɪtəm ‖ -ˈspɑns/ *n*
see under TEST ITEM

fixed stress /ˈfɪkst ˈstres/ *n*
STRESS which occurs regularly on the same syllable in a word in a particular language.
Languages which rigidly follow a fixed stress pattern are rare. There are always exceptions to the rule but Hungarian, for instance, usually stresses the first syllable of a word, and Polish usually stresses the second syllable from the end of a word (the penultimate syllable).
see also FREE STRESS
[*Further reading*: Hyman 1975]

flap /flæp/ *n*
also **tap**
a speech sound (a CONSONANT) which is produced by making a single tap, usually by the tongue against a firm surface in the mouth.
For example, for some speakers of English the r-sound in words like *very, sorry*, and *Mary* may be an ALVEOLAR flap, produced by a slight tap with the tip of the tongue against the alveolar ridge, the gum ridge behind the upper front teeth.
see also FRICTIONLESS CONTINUANT, MANNER OF ARTICULATION, PLACE OF ARTICULATION, ROLL
[*Further reading*: Gimson 1980]

flashcard /ˈflæʃkɑːd ‖ -ɑr-/ *n*
(in language teaching) a card with words, sentences, or pictures on it, used as an aid or CUE in a language lesson.

FLES /ˌef el iː ˈes/ *n*
an abbreviation for FOREIGN LANGUAGES IN THE ELEMENTARY SCHOOL

fluency /ˈfluːənsi/ *n* **fluent** /ˈfluːənt/ *adj*
the features which give speech the qualities of being natural and normal, including native-like use of PAUSING, RHYTHM, INTONATION, STRESS, rate of speaking, and use of interjections and interruptions.
If speech disorders cause a breakdown in normal speech (eg as with APHASIA or stuttering), the resulting speech may be referred to as **dysfluent**, or as an example of **dysfluency**.
In second and foreign language teaching, fluency describes a level of proficiency in communication, which includes:
(a) the ability to produce written and/or spoken language with ease

(b) the ability to speak with a good but not necessarily perfect command of intonation, vocabulary, and grammar

(c) the ability to communicate ideas effectively

(d) the ability to produce continuous speech without causing comprehension difficulties or a breakdown of communication.

It is sometimes contrasted with **accuracy**, which refers to the ability to produce grammatically correct sentences but may not include the ability to speak or write fluently.

[*Further reading*: Dalton & Hardcastle 1977]

focus /'fəʊkəs/ n
see under FUNCTIONAL SENTENCE PERSPECTIVE

foreground(ed) information /'fɔːgraʊndɪd ˌɪnfə'meɪʃən ‖ 'for- ˌɪnfər-/ n
see under GROUNDING

foreigner talk /'fɒrənər ˌtɔːk ‖ 'fɔ-, 'fɑ-/ n
the type of speech often used by native speakers of a language when speaking to foreigners who are not proficient in the language. Some of the characteristics of foreigner talk are:

(a) it is slower and louder than normal speech, often with exaggerated pronunciation

(b) it uses simpler vocabulary and grammar. For example, articles, function words, and INFLECTIONS may be omitted, and complex verb forms are replaced by simpler ones.

(c) topics are sometimes repeated or moved to the front of sentences, for example: *Your bag? Where you leave your bag?*

Native speakers often feel that this type of speech is easier for foreigners to understand.

see also ACCOMMODATION, CARETAKER SPEECH, PIDGIN, INTERLANGUAGE

[*Further reading*: Ferguson 1971]

foreign language /'fɒrən 'læŋgwɪdʒ ‖ 'fɔ-,'fɑ-/ n
(1) a language which is not a NATIVE LANGUAGE in a country. A foreign language is usually studied either for communication with foreigners who speak the language, or for reading printed materials in the language.

In North American applied linguistics usage, "foreign language" and "**second language**" are often used to mean the same in this sense.

(2) In British usage, a distinction is often made between foreign language and **second language**.

(a) a foreign language is a language which is taught as a school subject but which is not used as a medium of instruction in schools nor as a language of communication within a country (eg in government, business, or industry). English is described as a foreign language in France, Japan, China, etc.

(b) a second language is a language which is not a native language in a country but which is widely used as a medium of communication (eg in education and in government) and which is usually used alongside another language or languages. English is described as a second language in countries such as Fiji, Singapore, and Nigeria.

In *both* Britain and North America, the term "second language" would describe a native language in a country as learnt by people living there who have another FIRST LANGUAGE. English in the UK would be called the second language of immigrants and people whose first language is Welsh.

Foreign Languages in the Elementary School *n*
also **FLES**

(1) the teaching of foreign languages in elementary schools.

(2) the name of a movement which aims to increase the amount of foreign language teaching in elementary schools in the USA.

Foreign Service Institute Oral Interview *n*
also **FSI**

a technique for testing the spoken language proficiency of adult foreign language learners. The technique was developed by the United States Foreign Service Institute. It consists of a set of RATING SCALES which are used to judge pronunciation, grammar, vocabulary, and fluency during a 30 minute interview between the learner and, usually, two interviewers.

[*Further reading*: Oller 1979]

form /fɔːm ‖ fɔrm/ *n*

the means by which an element of language is expressed in speech or writing. Forms can be shown by the standard writing system for a language or by phonetic or phonemic symbols. For example, in English:

written form	spoken form
house	/haʊs/

Often a distinction is made between the spoken or written form of a linguistic unit and its meaning or function.

For example, in English the written form -*s* and the spoken forms /s/ and /z/ have a common function. They show the plural of nouns:

/kæts/ *cats* /dɒgz ‖ dɔgz/ *dogs*

formal operational stage /'fɔːməl ɒpə'reɪʃənəl 'steɪdʒ ‖ 'fɔr- ɑpə-/ *n*
see under GENETIC EPISTEMOLOGY

formal speech /'fɔːməl 'spiːtʃ ‖ 'fɔr-/ *n*

the type of speech used in situations when the speaker is very careful about pronunciation and choice of words and sentence structure. This type of speech may be used, for example, at official functions, and in debates and ceremonies. The English sentence

Ladies and gentlemen, it gives me great pleasure to be present here tonight.

is an example of formal speech.

see also STYLE, COLLOQUIAL SPEECH, STYLISTIC VARIATION

formal universal /'fɔːməl juːnə̀'vɜːsəl ‖ 'fɔr- -'vɜr-/ *n*
see under LANGUAGE UNIVERSAL

formative /'fɔːmətɪv ‖ 'fɔr-/ *n*
(in GENERATIVE TRANSFORMATIONAL GRAMMAR) the minimum
grammatical unit in a language. For example, in:
The drivers started the engines.
the formatives would be:
the + drive + er + s + start + ed + the + engine + s
see also MORPHEME

formative evaluation /'fɔːmətɪv ɪvæljʊ'eɪʃən ‖ 'fɔr-/ *n*
the process of providing information to curriculum developers during
the development of a curriculum or programme, in order to improve
it. Formative evaluation is also used in syllabus design and the
development of language teaching programmes and materials.
Summative evaluation is the process of providing information to
decision makers, after the programme is completed, about whether
or not the programme was effective and successful.
see also EVALUATION
[*Further reading*: Scriven 1967]

formative test /'fɔːmətɪv 'test ‖ 'fɔr-/ *n*
a test which is given during a course of instruction and which
informs both the student and the teacher how well the student is
doing. A formative test includes only topics which have been taught,
and shows whether the student needs extra work or attention. It is
usually a pass or fail test. If a student fails he or she is able to do
more study and take the test again.
A **summative test** is one given at the end of a course of instruction,
and which measures or "sums up" how much a student has learned
from the course. A summative test is usually a graded test, ie it is
marked according to a scale or set of grades.
[*Further reading*: Valette 1977]

form class /'fɔːm ˌklɑːs ‖ 'fɔrm ˌklæs/ *n*
(in linguistics) a group of items which can be used in similar
positions in a structure.
For example, in the sentence:
The . . . is here.
the words *dog, book, evidence*, etc could be used. They all belong to
the same form class of nouns.
see also WORD CLASS, ÒPEN CLASS

form of address /'fɔːm əv ə'dres ‖ 'fɔrm əv ə'dres, 'ædres/ *n*
another term for ADDRESS FORM

formula /'fɔːmjələ ‖ -ɔr-/ *n* (plural **formulae** /'fɔːmjəliː, -laɪ ‖ -ɔr-/ or
formulas)
another term for ROUTINE

formulaic speech /ˌfɔːmjəˈleɪ-ɪk ˈspiːtʃ ‖ -ɔr-/ *n*
also **formulaic expression** /ˌfɔːmjəˈleɪ-ɪk ɪkˈspreʃən ‖ -ɔr-/, **formulaic language** /ˌfɔːmjəˈleɪ-ɪk ˈlæŋgwɪdʒ ‖ -ɔr-/
  another term for ROUTINE

form word /ˈfɔːm ˌwɜːd ‖ ˈfɔrm, wɜrd/ *n*
  see under CONTENT WORD

fortis /ˈfɔːtə̇s ‖ -ɔr-/ *adj*
  describes a CONSONANT which is produced with a relatively greater amount of muscular force and breath, eg in English /p/, /t/, and /k/. The opposite to fortis is **lenis**, which describes consonants which are produced with less muscular effort and little or no ASPIRATION, eg in English /b/, /d/, and /g/.
  see MANNER OF ARTICULATION, VOICE[2]
  [*Further reading*: Gimson 1980]

fossilization /ˌfɒsə̇laɪˈzeɪʃən ‖ ˌfɑ-/ *n* **fossilized** *adj*
  (in second or foreign language learning) a process which sometimes occurs in which incorrect linguistic features become a permanent part of the way a person speaks or writes a language. Aspects of pronunciation, vocabulary usage, and grammar may become fixed or fossilized in second or foreign language learning. Fossilized features of pronunciation contribute to a person's foreign accent.
  see also INTERLANGUAGE
  [*Further reading*: Selinker 1972]

four phase drill /ˈfɔːʳ ˈfeɪz ˈdrɪl ‖ ˈfor/ *n*
  a type of DRILL used in language teaching materials in a LANGUAGE LABORATORY. A four phase drill has four parts as follows:
  (a) a stimulus on the tape
  (b) a space for the student's response
  (c) the correct response
  (d) a space for the student to repeat the correct response.

frame /freɪm/ *n*
  another term for SCRIPT

free composition /ˈfriː kɒmpəˈzɪʃən ‖ kɑm-/ *n*
  see under COMPOSITION

free form /ˈfriː ˌfɔːm ‖ ˌfɔrm/ *n*
also **free morpheme** /ˈfriː ˈmɔːfiːm ‖ ˈmɔr-/
  see under BOUND FORM

free practice /ˈfriː ˈpræktə̇s/ *n*
  another term for **production stage**
  see under STAGE

free response item /ˈfriː rɪˈspɒns ˈaɪtəm ‖ -ˈspɑns/ *n*
  see under TEST ITEM

free stress /'friː 'stres/ n

> STRESS which does not occur regularly on the same syllable in words in a particular language.
>
> For example, English has free stress. The main stress may occur:
>> on the first syllable: eg 'interval
>> on the second syllable: in'terrogate
>> on the third syllable: eg inter'ference
>
> see also FIXED STRESS
>
> [*Further reading*: Hyman 1975]

free translation /'friː trænz'leɪʃən,træns-/ n

> see under TRANSLATION

free variation /ˌfriː veəri'eɪʃən/ n

> When two or more linguistic items occur in the same position without any apparent change of meaning they are said to be in free variation.
>
> For example, *who* and *whom* in the English sentence:
>
> *The man* $\begin{cases} who \\ whom \end{cases}$ *we saw.*
>
> Such variations are now often considered as social variations or stylistic variations.
>
> see also VARIABLE[1], VARIATION

frequency[1] /'friːkwənsi/ n

> see under SOUND WAVE

frequency[2] n

> the number of occurrences of a linguistic item in a text or CORPUS. Different linguistic items have different frequencies of occurrence in speech and writing. In English, FUNCTION WORDS (eg *a*, *the*, *to*, etc) occur more frequently than verbs, nouns, adjectives, or adverbs. **Word frequency counts** arc used to select vocabulary for language teaching, in lexicography, in the study of literary style in STYLISTICS, and in TEXT LINGUISTICS.
>
> The twenty most frequently occurring words in a corpus of over one million words in a study of written American English by Kučera and Francis were:
>> *the, of, and, to, a, in, that, is, was, he, for, it,*
>> *with, as, his, on, be, at, by, I.*
>
> [*Further reading:* Kučera & Francis 1967]

frequency count /'friːkwensi ˌkəʊnt/ n

> a count of the total number of occurrences of linguistic items (eg syllables, phonemes, words, etc) in a corpus of language, such as a written text or a sample of spoken language. The study of the frequency of occurrence of linguistic items is known as language statistics and is a part of COMPUTATIONAL and MATHEMATICAL LINGUISTICS. A frequency count of the vocabulary occurring in a text or opus is known as a **word frequency count** or **word frequency list**.

fricative /'frɪkətɪv/ *n*

a speech sound (a CONSONANT) which is produced by allowing the airstream from the lungs to escape with friction. This is caused by bringing the two ARTICULATORS eg the upper teeth and the lower lip, close together but not close enough to stop the airstream completely.

For example, in English the /f/ in /fɪʃ/ *fish* is a fricative.

Some American linguists call a fricative a **spirant**.

see also MANNER OF ARTICULATION, PLACE OF ARTICULATION, SIBILANT, STOP

[*Further reading:* Gimson 1980]

frictionless continuant /'frɪkʃənləs kən'tɪnjʊənt/ *n*

a speech sound (a CONSONANT) which is produced by allowing the airstream from the lungs to move through the mouth and/or nose without friction.

For example, for some speakers of English the /r/ in /rəʊz/ *rose* is a frictionless continuant.

In terms of their articulation, frictionless continuants are very like vowels, but they function as consonants.

see also NASAL, LATERAL, FRICATIVE, STOP

[*Further reading:* Gimson 1980]

front vowel /'frʌnt ˌvaʊəl/ *n*

see under VOWEL

FSI /ˌef es 'aɪ/ *n*

an abbreviation for FOREIGN SERVICE INSTITUTE ORAL INTERVIEW

FSP /ˌef es 'piː/ *n*

an abbreviation for FUNCTIONAL SENTENCE PERSPECTIVE

full verb /'fʊl 'vɜːb ‖ 'vɜrb/ *n*

see under AUXILIARY VERB

full word /'fʊl 'wɜːd ‖ 'wɜrd/ *n*

see under CONTENT WORD

function /'fʌŋkʃən/ *n*

the purpose for which an utterance or unit of language is used. In language teaching, language functions are often described as categories of behaviour; eg requests, apologies, complaints, offers, compliments. The functional uses of language cannot be determined simply by studying the grammatical structure of sentences. For example, sentences in the imperative form (see MOOD) may perform a variety of different functions:

Give me that book. (Order)
Pass the jam. (Request)
Turn right at the corner. (Instruction)
Try the smoked salmon. (Suggestion)
Come round on Sunday. (Invitation)

In linguistics, the functional uses of language are studied in SPEECH ACT theory, SOCIOLINGUISTICS, and PRAGMATICS. In the COMMUNICATIVE APPROACH to language teaching, a SYLLABUS is often organized in terms of the different language functions the learner needs to express or understand.

Scc also FUNCTIONS OF LANGUAGE[1,2], FUNCTIONAL SYLLABUS, NOTIONAL SYLLABUS, SPEECH ACT, SPEECH ACT CLASSIFICATION

[*Further reading*: Wilkins 1976]

functional illiteracy /'fʌŋkʃənəl ɪ'lɪtərəsi/ *n*
see under LITERACY

functional linguistics /'fʌŋkʃənəl lɪŋ'gwɪstɪks/ *n*
an approach to linguistics which is concerned with language as an instrument of social interaction rather than as a system that is viewed in isolation. It considers the individual as a social being and investigates the way in which he or she acquires language and uses it in order to communicate with others in his or her social environment.
see also PRAGMATICS, SOCIAL CONTEXT, SPEECH EVENT
[*Further reading:* Halliday 1978]

functional literacy /'fʌŋkʃənəl 'lɪtərəsi/ *n*
see under LITERACY

functional load /'fʌŋkʃənəl 'ləʊd/ *n*
the relative importance of linguistic contrasts in a language. Not all the distinctions or contrasts within the structure of a language are of the same importance. For example the contrast between /p/ and /b/ at the beginning of words in English serves to distinguish many words, such as *pig – big*; *pack – back*; *pad – bad*, etc. The distinction /p/ – /b/ is thus said to have high functional load. But other contrasts such as the contrast between /ð/ and /θ/ in words like *wreathe – wreath* are not used to distinguish many words in English and are said to have low functional load.
[*Further reading:* Lyons 1968]

functional sentence perspective /'fʌŋkʃənəl 'sentəns pə'spektɪv ‖ pər-/ *n*
also **FSP**
a type of linguistic analysis associated with the PRAGUE SCHOOL which describes how information is distributed in sentences. FSP deals particularly with the effect of the distribution of known (or given) information and new information in DISCOURSE. The known information (known as **theme**, in FSP), refers to information that is not new to the reader or listener. The **rheme** refers to information that is new.
FSP differs from the traditional grammatical analysis of sentences because the distinction between subject – predicate is not always the

same as the theme – rheme contrast. For example we may compare the two sentences below:

1 *John* *sat in the front seat.* 2 *In the front seat sat John.*

Subject	Predicate	Predicate	Subject
Theme	Rheme	Theme	Rheme

John is the grammatical subject in both sentences, but Theme in 1 and Rheme in 2.

Other terms used to refer to the Theme – Rheme distinction are topic – comment (see TOPIC[2]), **Background – Focus, given – new information.**

[*Further reading*: Vachek 1964]

functional syllabus /ˈfʌŋkʃənəl ˈsɪləbəs/ *n*

(in language teaching) a SYLLABUS in which the language content is arranged in terms of functions or SPEECH ACTS together with the language items needed for them. For example, the functions might be identifying, describing, inviting, offering, etc in different types of DISCOURSE (ie speech or writing). The language skills involved might be listening, speaking, reading, or writing. The language items needed for these functions are called **exponents** or realizations. For example:

Type of discourse	Skill	Function	Exponents	
			Vocabulary	Structures
spoken	speaking listening	asking for directions	*bank harbour museum*	*Can you tell me where X is? Where is X?*

Often this term is used to refer to a certain type of NOTIONAL SYLLABUS.

see also COMMUNICATIVE APPROACH

[*Further reading:* Van Ek & Alexander 1975; Wilkins 1976]

functions of language[1] /ˈfʌŋkʃənz əv ˈlæŋgwɪdʒ/ *n*
also **language functions**

Language is often described as having three main functions: **descriptive**, **expressive**, and **social**. The descriptive function of language is to convey factual information. This is the type of information which can be stated or denied and in some cases even tested, for example:

It must be well below ten degrees outside.

The expressive function of language is to supply information about the speaker, his or her feelings, preferences, prejudices, and past experiences.

For example, the utterance:

I'm not inviting the Sandersons again.

may, with appropriate intonation, show that the speaker did not like the Sandersons and that this is the reason for not inviting them again.

The social function of language serves to establish and maintain social relations between people.

For example, the utterance:

Will that be all, Sir?

used by a waiter in a restaurant signals a particular social relationship between the waiter and the guest. The waiter puts the guest in a higher ROLE RELATIONSHIP.

Naturally, these functions overlap at times, particularly the expressive and the social functions.

[*Further reading:* Lyons 1977, 1981]

functions of language[2]
also **language functions**

The British linguist Halliday considers language as having three main functions:

(a) the **ideational function** is to organize the speaker's or writer's experience of the real or imaginary world, ie language refers to real or imagined persons, things, actions, events, states, etc.

(b) the **interpersonal function** is to indicate, establish, or maintain social relationships between people. It includes forms of address, speech function, MODALITY, etc.

(c) the **textual function** is to create written or spoken TEXTS which cohere within themselves and which fit the particular situation in which they are used.

see also DEVELOPMENTAL FUNCTIONS OF LANGUAGE, SOCIAL CONTEXT

[*Further reading*: Halliday 1978; de Joia & Stenton 1980]

function word /'fʌŋkʃən ˌwɜːd ‖ ˌwɜrd/ *n*
see under CONTENT WORD

functor /'fʌŋktər/ *n*
see under CONTENT WORD

fundamental frequency /ˌfʌndəˌmentl 'friːkwənsi/ *n*
see under SOUND WAVE

fusional language /'fjuːʒənəl 'læŋgwɪdʒ/ *n*
another term for INFLECTING LANGUAGE

future perfect /'fjuːtʃər 'pɜːfɪkt ‖ -ɜr-/ *n*
see under PERFECT

future tense /'fjuːtʃər 'tens/ *n*
a tense form used to indicate that the event described by a verb will take place at a future time. For example in the French sentence:

Je	partirai	demain.
I	leave+future	tomorrow.

the future tense ending -*ai* has been added to the verb infinitive *partir* (=leave). English has no future tense but uses a variety of different verb forms to express future time (eg *I leave tomorrow*; *I am leaving tomorrow*; *I will leave tomorrow*; *I am going to leave tomorrow*). *Will* in English is sometimes used to indicate future time (eg *Tomorrow will be Thursday*) but has many other functions, and is usually described as a MODAL verb.

fuzzy /ˈfʌzi/ *adj*

a term used by some linguists to describe a linguistic unit which has no clearly defined boundary. These units have "fuzzy borders", eg the English words *hill* and *mountain*. Another term used for a gradual transition from one linguistic unit to another is **gradience**.

gambit /ˈgæmbət/ *n*

(in CONVERSATIONAL ANALYSIS) sometimes used to describe a word or phrase in conversation which signals the function of the speaker's next turn in the conversation (see TURN-TAKING). Gambits may be used to show whether the speaker's contribution adds new information, develops something said by a previous speaker, expresses an opinion, agreement, etc. For example, gambits which signal that the speaker is going to express an opinion include:

The way I look at it . . .
To my mind . . .
In my opinion . . .

These examples can also be considered conversational ROUTINE*s*.
[*Further reading*: Coulmas 1981]

game /geɪm/ *n*

(in language teaching) an organized activity that usually has the following properties:
(a) a particular task or objective
(b) a set of rules
(c) competition between players
(d) communication between players by spoken or written language.

gender /ˈdʒendər/ *n*

(in some languages) a grammatical distinction in which words such as nouns, articles, adjectives, and pronouns are marked according to a distinction between masculine, feminine, and sometimes neuter. For example, in French, nouns are either masculine or feminine.
Masculine nouns are used with the articles *un* "a", and *le* "the", and feminine nouns are used with *une* and *la*:

une/la table "a/the table" (feminine)
un/le cheval "a/the horse" (masculine)

generalization /ˌdʒenərəlaɪˈzeɪʃən/ *n* **generalize** /ˈdʒenərəlaɪz/ *v*

(1) (in linguistics) a rule or principle which explains observed linguistic data.
(2) (in learning theory) a process common to all types of learning, which consists of the formation of a general rule or principle from the observation of particular examples. For example a child who sees the English words *book – books*, and *dog – dogs* may generalize that the concept of plural in English is formed by adding *s* to words.
see also OVERGENERALIZATION
[*Further reading*: Gagné 1970; Brown 1980]

generate /ˈdʒenəreɪt/ *v*

see under GENERATIVE GRAMMAR, RULE[2]

generative grammar /ˌdʒenərətɪv ˈgræməʳ/ *n*

a type of grammar which attempts to define and describe by a set of rules all the GRAMMATICAL sentences of a language and no ungrammatical ones. This type of grammar is said to **generate**, or produce, grammatical sentences.

The most important grammar of this type is GENERATIVE TRANSFORMATIONAL GRAMMAR.

[*Further reading*: Chomsky 1957]

generative phonology /ˌdʒenərətɪv fəˈnɒlədʒi ‖ -ˈnɑ-/ *n*

an approach to phonology which aims to describe the knowledge (COMPETENCE) which a native speaker must have to be able to produce and understand the sound system of his or her language. In generative phonology, the distinctive sounds of a language (the PHONEME*s*) are shown as groups of sound features (see DISTINCTIVE FEATURE*s*). Each sound is shown as a different set of features. For example, the phoneme /e/ could be shown by the features

$$\begin{bmatrix} \text{-high} \\ \text{-low} \\ \text{+tense} \end{bmatrix}$$

Phonological rules explain how these abstract units combine and vary when they are used in speech.

see also GENERATIVE TRANSFORMATIONAL GRAMMAR, SYSTEMATIC PHONEMICS

[*Further reading*: Hyman 1975; Chomsky & Halle 1968]

generative semantics/ˌdʒenərətɪv səˈmæntɪks/ *n*

an approach to linguistic theory which grew as a reaction to Chomsky's syntactic-based GENERATIVE TRANSFORMATIONAL GRAMMAR. It considers that all sentences are generated from a semantic structure. This semantic structure is often expressed in the form of a proposition which is similar to logical propositions in philosophy. Linguists working within this theory have, for instance, suggested that there is a semantic relationship between such sentences as

This dog strikes me as being like his master.

and

This dog reminds me of his master.

because they both have the semantic structure of

X perceives that Y is similar to Z.

see also INTERPRETIVE SEMANTICS

[*Further reading*: Aitchison 1978; Lakoff 1971]

generative transformational grammar /ˌdʒenərətɪv trænsfəˈmeɪʃənel ˈgræməʳ ‖ trænsfər-/ *n*

also **transformational grammar, TG grammar, generative transformational theory**

a theory of grammar which was proposed by the American linguist Chomsky in 1957. It has since been developed by him and many other linguists. Chomsky attempted to provide a model for the description of all languages. A generative transformational grammar tries to show, with a system of rules, the knowledge which a native speaker of a language uses in forming grammatical sentences (see COMPETENCE).

Chomsky has changed his theory over the years. The most well-known version was published in his book *Aspects of the Theory of Syntax* in 1965. It is often referred to as the **Aspects Model** or **Standard Theory**. This model consists of four main parts:

(a) the BASE COMPONENT, which produces or generates basic syntactic structures called DEEP STRUCTURES.

(b) the TRANSFORMATIONAL COMPONENT, which changes or transforms these basic structures into sentences called **surface structures.**

(c) the **phonological component**, which gives sentences a phonetic representation so that they can be pronounced (see GENERATIVE PHONOLOGY).

(d) the **semantic component**, which deals with the meaning of sentences (see INTERPRETATIVE SEMANTICS).

The relationship of the four components to one another can be seen in the simplified diagram below:

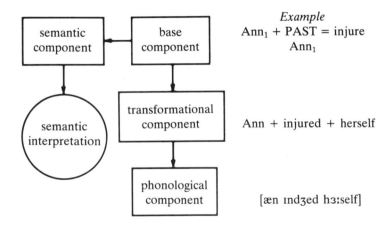

Example

Ann$_1$ + PAST = injure Ann$_1$

Ann + injured + herself

[æn ɪndʒed hɜːself]

Chomsky and others later modified the Aspects Model. They felt that not only the base component but also the transformational and phonological components had some effect on the semantic interpretation of a sentence (**Extended Standard Theory**).

see also PERFORMANCE

[*Further reading*: Aitchison 1978; Chomsky 1965]

generative transformational theory /ˌdʒenərətɪv trænsfə'meɪʃənəl 'θɪəri ‖ trænsfər-/ *n*

another term for GENERATIVE TRANSFORMATIONAL GRAMMAR

generic reference /dʒə'nerɪk 'refərəns/ *n*

a type of reference which is used to refer to a class of objects or things, rather than to a specific member of a class. For example in English:

specific reference	generic reference
The bird is sick.	*A tiger is a dangerous animal.*
The birds are sick.	*Tigers are dangerous animals.*
There is a bird in the cage.	*The tiger is a dangerous animal.*

[*Further reading*: Quirk et al 1985]

genetic epistemology /dʒəˈnetɪk ɪˌpɪstəˈmɒlədʒi ‖ -ˈmɑ-/ *n*
a term used to describe the theories of DEVELOPMENTAL PSYCHOLOGY of the Swiss psychologist Jean Piaget (1896–1980). Piaget listed several different stages which children pass through in mental development. The first stage is the **sensorimotor stage**, from birth to about 24 months, when children understand their environment mainly by acting on it. Through touch and sight children begin to understand basic relationships which affect them and objects in their experience. These include space, location of objects, and the relationships of cause and effect. But children cannot yet make use of abstract concepts. The next three stages are a movement towards more abstract processes. During the **pre-operational stage**, from around two to seven years, children develop the symbolic function, which includes such skills as language, mental imagery, and drawing. Children also begin to develop the mental ability to use CONCEPTS dealing with number, classification, order, and time, but use these concepts in a simple way. The **concrete operational stage** from about seven to eleven years is the period when children begin to use mental operations and acquire a number of concepts of conservation. During the formal operational stage (from around eleven onwards) children are able to deal with abstract concepts and PROPOSITIONS, and to make hypotheses, inferences, and deductions. Since the mental processes Piaget studied are important for language development, linguists and psycholinguists have made use of Piaget's ideas in studying how mental development and linguistic development are related.
[*Further reading*: Piaget 1952]

genitive case /ˈdʒenətɪv ˌkeɪs/ *n*
the form of a noun or noun phrase which usually shows that the noun or noun phrase is in a POSSESSIVE relation with another noun or noun phrase in a sentence.
For example, in the German sentence:
Dort drüben ist das Haus des Bürgermeisters.
Over there is   the house of the mayor.
                 the mayor's house.
in the noun phrase *des Bürgermeisters*, the article has the inflectional ending -*es* and the noun has the inflectional ending -*s* to show that they are in the genitive case because they refer to the owner of *das Haus*.

In the English sentence:

She took my father's car.

some linguists regard *my father's* as an example of the genitive case.

see also CASE[1]

[*Further reading*: Lyons 1968]

genre /'ʒɒnrə ‖ -ɑn-/ *n*

(in DISCOURSE ANALYSIS) a particular class of SPEECH EVENTs which are considered by the SPEECH COMMUNITY as being of the same type. Examples of genres are: prayers, sermons, conversations, songs, speeches, poems, letters, and novels. They have particular and distinctive characteristics. A group of several genres may be called a complex genre, for example a church service, which contains hymns, psalms, prayers, and a sermon.

see also SCHEME

[*Further reading*: Coulthard 1985; Saville-Troike 1982]

genre-scheme /'ʒɒnrə ˌskiːm ‖ -ɑn-/ *n*

another term for SCHEME

gerund /'dʒerənd/ *n*

also **gerundive** /dʒə'rʌndɪv/

a verb form which ends in *-ing*, but which is used in a sentence like a noun.

For example, in the English sentences:

Swimming is good for you.

I don't like smoking.

see also PARTICIPLE

gestalt psychology /gə'ʃtaːlt saɪ'kɒlədʒi ‖ -'kɑ-/ *n*

also **gestalt theory** /gə'ʃtaːlt θɪəri/

an approach to psychology in which behaviour is studied as undivided wholes or "gestalts". Gestalt psychologists believe that you cannot understand a person's response to a situation in terms of a combination of separate responses to a combination of separate stimuli, but that it should be studied as a whole response to the whole situation. Gestalt psychology is a **holistic approach**, in contrast with the **atomistic approach** of many experimental psychologists.

[*Further reading*: Miller 1962]

gestalt style /gə'ʃtaːlt 'staɪl/ *n*

another term for GLOBAL LEARNING

given – new information /'gɪvən ˌnjuː ˌɪnfə'meɪʃən ‖ ˌnuː -fər-/ *n*

see under FUNCTIONAL SENTENCE PERSPECTIVE

glide /glaɪd/ *n*

(in British linguistics) a vowel which is made by the tongue moving, or gliding, from one position to another one. This is the case with DIPHTHONGs, eg the English diphthong /aɪ/ as in *my*. Some American linguists use the term glide for the second element in a diphthong.

For these elements they use the phonetic symbols /w/, eg /bowt/ *boat* and /y/, eg /may/ *my*. They also refer to the /w/ in *will* and the /y/ in *yet* as glides, whereas in Britain they are referred to as SEMI-VOWELS.

see also CONSONANT

[*Further reading*: Gimson 1980]

global error /'gləʊbəl 'erə^r/ *n*

(in ERROR ANALYSIS) an error in the use of a major element of sentence structure, which makes a sentence or utterance difficult or impossible to understand. For example:

*I like take taxi but my friend said so not that we should be late for school.

This may be contrasted with a **local error**, which is an error in the use of an element of sentence structure, but which does not cause problems of comprehension. For example:

*If I heard from him I will let you know.

[*Further reading*: Burt & Kiparsky 1972]

global learning /'gləʊbəl 'lɜːnɪŋ ‖ 'lɜr-/ *n*
also **gestalt style**

a COGNITIVE STYLE in which the learner tries to remember something as a whole. For example, a learner may try to memorize complete sentences in a foreign language.

When a learner remembers something by separating it into parts, this is called an **analytic style**, or **part learning**. For example, a learner may divide a sentence into words, memorize the words, and then combine them again to make sentences.

see also GESTALT PSYCHOLOGY

global question /'gləʊbəl 'kwestʃən/ *n*

(in language teaching) a question used in a reading comprehension exercise. To answer a global question, a student needs a general understanding of the text or passage. A student's understanding of the details of a text can be tested with **specific questions**.

glottal stop /'glɒtl 'stɒp ‖ 'glɑtl 'stɑp/ *n*

a speech sound (a CONSONANT) which is produced by the rapid closing of the **glottis** (the space between the VOCAL CORDS), which traps the airstream from the lungs behind it, followed by a sudden release of the air as the glottis is opened.

In some varieties of British English, a glottal stop is used instead of a /t/ in words like ['bɒʔl] *bottle* and ['mæʔə^r] *matter*.

scc also STOP, PLACE OF ARTICULATION, MANNER OF ARTICULATION

[*Further reading*: Gimson 1980]

glottis /'glɒtə̣s ‖ 'glɑ-/ *n*

see under VOCAL CORDS

goal[1] /'gəʊl/ *n*

(in TRADITIONAL GRAMMAR) a term used by some linguists to refer to the person or thing which is affected by the action expressed by the verb. For example, in the English sentence:

Elizabeth smashed the vase.

vase is the goal.

goal² n

(in CASE GRAMMAR) the noun or noun phrase which refers to the place to which someone or something moves or is moved. For example in the sentences:

He loaded bricks on to the truck.
He loaded the truck with bricks.

the truck is the goal.

[*Further reading*: Fillmore 1971]

government /'gʌvənmənt, 'gʌvəmənt ‖ 'gʌvərn-/ n govern /'gʌvən ‖ -ərn/ v

a type of grammatical relationship between two or more elements in a sentence, in which the choice of one element causes the selection of a particular form of another element. In traditional grammar, the term government has typically been used to refer to the relationship between verbs and nouns or between prepositions and nouns. In German, for example, the preposition *mit* "with" governs, that is requires, the DATIVE CASE¹ of the noun that follows it:

Peter   kam   mit   seiner   Schwester.
Peter   came   with   his   sister.

Where *sein* "his" has the dative feminine case marker *er*.

see also CONCORD

[*Further reading*: Palmer 1971]

gradable /'greɪdəbəl/ adj gradability /ˌgreɪdə'bɪləti/ n

(of objects, people, ideas, etc) having a certain property to a greater or lesser degree. In English, this property is usually expressed by an adjective, eg *hot, cold, rich, poor*.

For example:

Was it really as cold last night as Thursday night?
Your plate is hotter than mine.

Usually, a comparison is implied, even if it is not expressed. *It's hot in here*, means "compared with outside" or "compared with the room temperature which suits me".

Adjectives which refer to something which can be described in degrees are known as **gradable adjectives**. The negation of a gradable adjective does not necessarily imply the opposite. For example, *not hot* does not necessarily mean *cold*, nor does *not rich* necessarily mean *poor*.

see also ANTONYM

[*Further reading*: Lyons 1977]

gradable adjective /'greɪdəbəl 'ædʒəktɪv/ n

see under GRADABLE

gradable pair /'greɪdəbəl 'peə^r/*n*
see under ANTONYM

gradation /ˌgrə'deɪʃən/ *n*
also **grading, sequencing**
the arrangement of the content of a language course or a textbook
so that it is presented in a helpful way. Gradation would affect the
order in which words, word meanings, tenses, structures, topics,
functions, skills, etc are presented. Gradation may be based on the
complexity of an item, its frequency in written or spoken English, or
its importance for the learner.
see also SELECTION
[*Further reading*: Mackey 1965]

graded reader /ˌgreɪdə́d 'riːdə^r/ *n*
also **simplified reader**
a text written for children learning their mother tongue, or for
second or foreign language learners, in which the language content
is based on a language grading scheme (see GRADATION). A graded
reader may use a restricted vocabulary or set of grammatical
structures.

gradience /'greɪdɪəns/ *n*
see under FUZZY

grading /'greɪdɪŋ/ *n*
another term for GRADATION

grammar[1] /'græmə^r/ *n*
a description of the structure of a language and the way in which
linguistic units such as words and phrases are combined to produce
sentences in the language. It usually takes into account the meanings
and functions these sentences have in the overall system of the
language. It may or may not include the description of the sounds of
a language (see PHONOLOGY, PHONEMICS).
see also MORPHOLOGY, SEMANTICS, SYNTAX

grammar[2] *n*
(in generative transformational theory) a set of rules and a lexicon
which describes the knowledge (COMPETENCE) which a speaker has of
his or her language.
see also GENERATIVE TRANSFORMATIONAL GRAMMAR

Grammar Translation Method /'græmə^r trænz'leɪʃən 'meθəd,
træns-/ *n*
a method of foreign or second language teaching which makes use
of translation and grammar study as the main teaching and learning
activities. The Grammar Translation Method was the traditional way
Latin and Greek were taught in Europe. In the 19th century it
began to be used to teach "modern" languages such as French,
German, and English, and it is still used in many countries today. A

grammatical¹

typical lesson would consist of the presentation of a grammatical rule, a study of lists of vocabulary, and a translation exercise. Because the Grammar Translation Method emphasizes reading rather than the ability to communicate in a language there was a reaction to it in the 19th century (see NATURAL APPROACH, DIRECT METHOD), and there was later a greater emphasis on the teaching of spoken language.
[*Further reading*: Howatt 1983; Kelly 1969]

grammatical¹ /grəˈmætəkəl/ *adj* **grammaticality** /grə,mætəˈkæləti/ *n*
A phrase, clause, or sentence which is acceptable because it follows the rules of a grammar (see GRAMMAR¹), is described as grammatical. For example, the English sentence:
They walk to school.
would be a grammatical sentence according to a grammar of Standard English, but the sentence:
They walks to school.
would be considered **ungrammatical** according to such a grammar.
[*Further reading*: Trudgill 1975]

grammatical² *adj* **grammaticalness** *n*
In GENERATIVE TRANSFORMATIONAL GRAMMAR, a sentence is grammatical if it follows the rules of a native speaker's COMPETENCE. For example:
The teacher who the man who the children saw pointed out is a cousin of Joan's.
would be a grammatical sentence because it can be generated by the rules of the grammar. However, it could be regarded as **unacceptable** because of its involved structure which makes it difficult for a listener to understand easily.

grammatical ambiguity /grə,mætəkəl æmbɪˈgjuːəti/ *n*
see under AMBIGUOUS

grammatical category¹ /grə,mætəkəl ˈkætəgəri ‖ -gori/ *n*
a class or group of items which fulfil the same or similar functions in a particular language. For example, CASE¹, PERSON, TENSE¹, and ASPECT are grammatical categories.
Some linguists also refer to related groups of words such as nouns, verbs, and adjectives as grammatical categories but these groups are usually referred to in TRADITIONAL GRAMMAR as PARTS OF SPEECH.

grammatical category² *n*
(in GENERATIVE TRANSFORMATIONAL GRAMMAR) a concept such as a SENTENCE, a NOUN PHRASE, a VERB. Grammatical categories are shown by **category symbols** such as S, NP, and V.

grammatical function /grə,mætəkəl ˈfʌŋkʃən/ *n*
the relationship that a CONSTITUENT in a sentence has with the other constituents. For example, in the English sentence:
Peter threw the ball.

Peter has the function of being the SUBJECT of the verb *throw*, and *the ball* has the function of being the OBJECT of the verb.

grammatical meaning /grə,mætəkəl 'miːnɪŋ/ *n*
see under CONTENT WORD

grammatical morpheme /grə,mætəkəl 'mɔːfiːm ‖ -ɔr-/ *n*
see under MORPHEME

grammatical word /grə'mætəkəl ,wɜːd ‖ ,wɜrd/ *n*
see under CONTENT WORD

grapheme /'græfiːm, 'grɑːfiːm ‖ 'græ-/ *n*
the smallest unit in a WRITING SYSTEM of a language. A grapheme usually has a relationship to the sound system of that language (see PHONEME). For example, the English word *box* consists of three graphemes, <b>, <o>, and <x>. The grapheme <b> refers to the phoneme /b/, the grapheme <o> to the phoneme /ɒ/ in many British English varieties but to the phoneme /ɑ/ in many American English varieties. The grapheme <x> refers to the phonemes /ks/. Sometimes a grapheme refers to a whole word, eg the grapheme <&> in English *Smith & Co.* refers to the word *and*.
[*Further reading*: Bolinger 1975]

grave accent /'grɑːv 'æksənt ‖ 'æksent/ *n*
the accent ` , eg on French *près* "near".
see also under ACCENT[2]

grounding /'graʊndɪŋ/ *n*
an aspect of the INFORMATION STRUCTURE of a sentence in which in an act of communication, speakers assume that some information is more important than other information. Information which is needed for the listener to understand new information is **background information**, and information which is new or considered more important is **foregrounded** or **foreground information**. For example, in the sentence *As I was coming to school this morning, I saw an accident*, *I saw an accident this morning* is foregrounded information and *As I was coming to school* is background information. The foregrounded information is contained in the main clause of the sentence, which comes after the clause containing background information.

group work /'gruːp ,wɜːk ‖ ,wɜrk/ *n*
(in language teaching) a learning activity which involves a small group of learners working together. The group may work on a single task, or on different parts of a larger task. Tasks for group members are often selected by the members of the group.
see also PAIR WORK

habit /ˈhæbət/ *n*

a pattern of behaviour that is regular and which has become almost automatic as a result of repetition. Linguists and psychologists disagree about how much habit formation is involved in language learning. The habit view of language learning is found in BEHAVIOURISM and contrasting views are found in COGNITIVE PSYCHOLOGY and in research in language ACQUISITION.

half-close vowel /ˈhɑːf kləʊs ˈvaʊəl ‖ ˈhæf/ *n*

see under VOWEL

half-open vowel /ˈhɑːf ˌəʊpən ˈvaʊəl ‖ ˈhæf/ *n*

see under VOWEL

halo effect /ˈheɪləʊ ɪˌfekt/ *n*

(in research) the effect of a feature which is not being tested, but which changes or influences the results. For example, a teacher who is rating a child according to "interest in learning English" may give the child a higher rating because he or she is well behaved in class.

hard palate /ˈhɑːd ˈpælət ‖ ˈhɑrd/ *n*

see under PLACE OF ARTICULATION

hardware /ˈhɑːdweər ‖ ˈhɑrd-/ *n*

the physical equipment which may be used in an educational system, such as a computer, video-cassette player, film projector, tape-recorder, cassette or record player.

The materials used in such equipment such as programs, tapes, and films are called **software**.

Hawthorn effect /ˈhɔːθɔːn ɪˌfekt ‖ -ɔrn/ *n*

(in research) the effect produced by the introduction of a new element into a learning situation. For example, if a new teaching method is used, there may be an improvement in learning which is due not to the method, but to the fact that it is new. Later on, the improvement may disappear.

head /hed/ *n*

the central part of a phrase. Other elements in the phrase are in some grammatical or semantic relationship to the head. For example, in the English noun phrase:

the fat lady in the floral dress

the noun *lady* is the head of the phrase.

see also MODIFIER, CLASSIFIER[2]

hemisphere /ˈheməˌsfɪər/ *n*

see under BRAIN

hesitation phenomena /ˌhezə'teɪʃən fə'nɒmənə ‖ -'nɑ-/ *n*
another term for PAUSING

heuristic /hjʊə'rɪstɪk/ *adj* **heuristics** *n*
(1) (in education) teaching procedures which encourage learners to learn through experience or by their own personal discoveries.
(2) (in learning) processes of conscious or unconscious inquiry or discovery. For example, in trying to discover the meanings of words in a foreign language, a learner may repeat aloud a sentence containing the word, several times, in an attempt to work out its meaning.
In FIRST-LANGUAGE learning these heuristic processes are sometimes known as **operating principles**, ie ways in which learners work out the meaning of utterances based on what they understand about the structure of the TARGET LANGUAGE¹. For example, among the operating principles a child may use are:
    a word which ends in *ing* is a verb.
    in a sequence of two nouns (eg Jane's doll) the first noun is the possessor and the second noun is the thing possessed.
[*Further reading*: Slobin 1973]

heuristic function /hjʊə'rɪstɪk ˌfʌŋkʃən/ *n*
see under DEVELOPMENTAL FUNCTIONS OF LANGUAGE

High variety /'haɪ və'raɪəti/ *n*
see under DIGLOSSIA

high vowel /'haɪ ˌvaʊəl/ *n*
another term for **close vowel**
see under VOWEL

historical linguistics /hɪ'stɒrəkəl lɪŋ'gwɪstɪks ‖ -'stɑ-/ *n*
another term for COMPARATIVE HISTORICAL LINGUISTICS

historic present /hɪ'stɒrɪk 'prezənt ‖ -'stɑ-/ *n*
a present tense used in a context where a past tense would normally be used, to create a more vivid effect, to show informality, or to show a sense of "friendliness" between speaker and hearer.
For example:
    Do you know what happened to me last night? I'm sitting in a restaurant when this guy comes up and pours water over me.

holistic approach /həʊ'lɪstɪk ə'prəʊtʃ/ *n*
see under GESTALT PSYCHOLOGY

holophrase /'hɒləfreɪz ‖ 'hɑ-/ *n* **holophrastic** /ˌhɒlə'fræstɪk ‖ ˌhɑ-/ *adj*
a single word which functions as a complex idea or sentence.
Holophrastic speech is one of the first stages in children's ACQUISITION of speech.

For example:

holophrases	intended meaning
Water!	*I want some water.*
More.	*Give me some more.*

[*Further reading*: Dale 1975]

home-school language switch /ˌhəʊm ˌskuːl ˈlæŋgwɪdʒ ˌswɪtʃ/ *n*
used in referring to the language used in a school setting to describe
the need to change ("switch") from one language spoken at home
to another used as the MEDIUM OF INSTRUCTION at school.
see also BILINGUAL EDUCATION, IMMERSION PROGRAMME

homographs /ˈhɒməgrɑːfs, ˈhəʊ- ‖ ˈhɑ-, ˈhəʊ-/ *n*
words which are written in the same way but which are pronounced
differently and which may have different meanings.
For example, the English words *lead* /liːd/ in *Does this road lead to
town?* and *lead* /led/ in *Lead is a heavy metal*, are homographs.
Homographs are sometimes called **homonyms**.
see also HOMOPHONES
[*Further reading*: Lyons 1968]

homonyms[1] /ˈhɒmənɪmz, ˈhəʊ- ‖ ˈhɑ-, ˈhəʊ-/ *n*
see under HOMOGRAPHS

homonyms[2] *n*
see under HOMOPHONES

homonyms[3] *n* **homonymy** /hɒˈmɒnəmi, həʊ- ‖ hɑˈmɑ-, həʊ-/ *n*
words which are written in the same way and sound alike but which
have different meanings.
For example, the English verbs *lie* in *You have to lie down* and *lie* in
Don't lie, tell the truth!
It is a well-known problem in SEMANTICS to tell the difference
between homonymy (several words with the same form but different
meanings) and POLYSEMY (a single word with more than one
meaning).
[*Further reading*: Lyons 1968]

homophones /ˈhɒməfəʊnz, ˈhəʊ- ‖ ˈhɑ-, ˈhəʊ-/ *n*
words which sound alike but are written differently and often have
different meanings.
For example, the English words *no* and *know* are both pronounced
/nəʊ/ in some varieties of British English.
Homophones are sometimes called **homonyms**.
see also HOMOGRAPHS
[*Further reading*: Lyons 1968]

homorganic /ˌhɒmɔːˈgænɪk ‖ ˌhɑmɔr-/ *adj*
describes speech sounds which have the same PLACE OF
ARTICULATION.

For example, the sounds /p/ and /m/ are both produced with the two lips (ie are BILABIAL), although one is a STOP and the other a NASAL.

see also ASSIMILATION, MANNER OF ARTICULATION

[*Further reading*: Gimson 1980]

honorifics /ˌɒnəˈrɪfɪks ‖ ˌɑnə-/ *n*

politeness formulas in a particular language which may be specific affixes, words, or sentence structures. Languages which have a complex system of honorifics are, for instance, Japanese, Madurese (a language of Eastern Java), and Hindi. Although English has no complex system of honorifics, expressions such as *would you . . .*, *may I . . .*, and polite ADDRESS FORMS fulfil similar functions.

[*Further reading*: Neustupny 1978]

humanistic approach /hjuːməˈnɪstɪk əˈprəʊtʃ/ *n*

(in language teaching) a term sometimes used for what underlies METHODS in which the following principles are considered important:

(a) the development of human values
(b) growth in self-awareness and in the understanding of others
(c) sensitivity to human feelings and emotions
(d) active student involvement in learning and in the way learning takes place (for this last reason such methods are also said to be STUDENT CENTRED).

The SILENT WAY and COMMUNITY LANGUAGE LEARNING are examples of "humanistic approaches".

see also APPROACH

[*Further reading*: Stevick 1980]

H-variety /ˈeɪtʃ vəˈraɪəti/ *n*

see under DIGLOSSIA

hypercorrection[1] /ˌhaɪpəkəˈrekʃən ‖ -pər-/ *n*

overgeneralization of a rule in language use. For example, the rule that an ADVERB modifies a VERB may be overextended and used in cases where an adjective would normally be used, as in *This meat smells freshly* instead of *This meat smells fresh*.

see also COPULA

hypercorrection[2] *n*

extreme care in speech or writing, especially in an attempt to speak or write in an educated manner.

For example, a speaker of a non-standard variety of English, when speaking formally, may practise more self-correction and use more formal vocabulary than speakers of a standard variety of English.

[*Further reading*: Labov 1972a]

hyponymy /haɪˈpɒnəmi, hɪ- ‖ -ˈpɑ-/ *n* **hyponym** /ˈhaɪpənɪm/ *n*

a relationship between two words, in which the meaning of one of the words includes the meaning of the other word.

For example, in English the words *animal* and *dog* are related in such a way that *dog* refers to a type of *animal*, and *animal* is a general term that includes *dog* and other types of animal.

The specific term, *dog*, is called a hyponym, and the general term, *animal*, is called a **superordinate**.

A superordinate term can have many hyponyms. For example:

superordinate: *vehicle*

hyponyms: *bus*   *car*   *lorry*   *van*

superordinate: *move*

hyponyms: *walk*   *run*   *swim*   *fly*

see also SYNONYM
[*Further reading*: Lyons 1968]

hypothesis /haɪˈpɒθəsəs ‖ -ˈpɑ-/ n

(in research using quantitative methods and statistical techniques for the analysis of data) a speculation concerning either observed or expected relationships among phenomena. For example, "Teaching method A is better than teaching method B". If for the purposes of research the speculation is translated into a statement which can be tested by quantitative methods, the statement is known as a **statistical hypothesis**.

The hypothesis that method A is better than method B can be regarded as a statistical hypothesis because it can be tested by studying the DISTRIBUTION[1] of test scores (obtained by giving a test to students taught by A and B) in a POPULATION (the students who take the test). For each statistical hypothesis that there is a relationship (eg a coefficient of CORRELATION) between two features (eg method A and good test scores), there is a corresponding, but often unstated, **null hypothesis** that there is no relationship between these two features. The statistical analysis of research results is frequently designed to determine whether this hypothesis of no relationship can be rejected, thus providing support for the preferred hypothesis.

Note that the plural of *hypothesis* is *hypotheses* /haɪˈpɒθəsiːz ‖ -ˈpɑ-/.
[*Further reading*: Ebel 1972]

hypothesis formation /haɪˈpɒθəsəs fɔːˈmeɪʃən ‖ -ˈpɑ- -ɔr-/ n

(in language learning) the formation of ideas ("hypotheses") about a language. These hypotheses may be conscious or unconscious. Most people would agree that at least some of these ideas come from the language we see and hear around us. But scholars (eg Chomsky) holding the INNATIST HYPOTHESIS have claimed that some of our most important and basic ideas about language in general are present at birth, and furthermore that this innate knowledge enables children learning their FIRST LANGUAGE to avoid forming ideas about it that could not possibly be true of any human language because such false ideas would violate LANGUAGE UNIVERSALS.

see also HYPOTHESIS TESTING

[*Further reading*: Elliot 1981]

hypothesis testing /haɪ'pɒθəsəs ˌtestɪŋ ‖ -'pɑ-/ *n*

(in language learning) the testing of ideas ("hypotheses") about a language to see whether they are right or wrong.

The most obvious way of doing this is to use the hypotheses to produce new utterances and see whether they work. But one can also compare one's own utterances with those of other people speaking the language, or imagine what other people would say in a particular situation and then see whether they actually say it.

Scholars who hold the INNATIST HYPOTHESIS have claimed, in effect, that the number of hypotheses about a new language that need to be tested is not infinite. Some hypotheses are simply never formed, because of knowledge of LANGUAGE UNIVERSALS present in every normal human being at birth.

see also HYPOTHESIS FORMATION, DEDUCTIVE LEARNING

[*Further reading*: Elliot 1981]

I

ideal speaker/hearer /aɪˈdɪəl ˌspiːkər ˈhɪərər/ n
see under COMPETENCE

ideational function /aɪdiˈeɪʃənəl ˌfʌŋkʃən/ n
see under FUNCTIONS OF LANGUAGE[2]

ideogram /ˈɪdɪəɡræm/ n
see under IDEOGRAPHIC WRITING

ideographic writing /ɪdɪəˈɡræfɪk ˈraɪtɪŋ/ n
a WRITING SYSTEM using symbols (**ideograms**) to represent whole words
or concepts ("ideas"). The Chinese writing system is often
considered to be ideographic.
For example, in Chinese the ideogram 水 represents "water".

Chinese can create new LEXEMES by combining existing ideograms to
form COMPOUND WORDS. It can also combine existing ideograms into a
sequence whose pronunciation is like that of a foreign word the
Chinese wish to borrow, thus "transliterating" the foreign word into
Chinese characters.

idiolect/ˈɪdɪəˌlekt/ n **idiolectal** /ˌɪdɪəˈlektl/ adj
the language system of an individual as expressed by the way he or
she speaks or writes within the overall system of a particular
language.
In its widest sense, someone's idiolect includes their way of
communicating; for example, their choice of utterances and the
way they interpret the utterances made by others. In a narrower
sense, an idiolect may include those features, either in speech or
writing, which distinguish one individual from others, such as VOICE
QUALITY, PITCH, and SPEECH RHYTHM.
see also DIALECT, SOCIOLECT
[*Further reading*: Abercrombie 1969]

idiom /ˈɪdɪəm/ n **idiomatic** /ˌɪdɪəˈmætɪk/ adj
an expression which functions as a single unit and whose meaning
cannot be worked out from its separate parts.
For example:
He washed his hands of the matter.
means
"He refused to have anything more to do with the matter".

illiteracy /ɪˈlɪtərəsi/ n
see under LITERACY

illocutionary act /ɪləˈkjuːʃənəri ˈækt/ n

see under LOCUTIONARY ACT

illocutionary force /ɪləˈkjuːʃənəri ˈfɔːs ‖ -ɔr-/ n

see under SPEECH ACT, LOCUTIONARY ACT, PERFORMATIVE

imagery /ˈimədʒəri/ n

mental pictures or impressions ("images") created by, or accompanying, words or sentences.

Words or sentences that produce strong picture-like images may be easier to remember than those without visual imagery. For example, in the following pair of sentences, (a) may be easier to remember than (b) because it creates a stronger mental image.

(a) *The gloves were made by a tailor.*

(b) *The gloves were made by a machine.*

see also AUDIO-VISUAL METHOD

[*Further reading*: Glucksberg & Danks 1975]

imaginative function /ɪˈmædʒənətɪv ˌfʌŋkʃən/ n

see under DEVELOPMENTAL FUNCTIONS OF LANGUAGE

imitation /ˌiməˈteɪʃən/ n

(in language learning) the copying of the speech of another. The function of imitation has been studied to find out how important it is in language development (eg a child imitating its mother or a pupil repeating a SENTENCE PATTERN).

see also MIM-MEM METHOD, MODELLING, ELICITED IMITATION

[*Further reading*: Dale 1975]

immersion programme /ɪˈmɜːʃən ˌprəʊgræm, -ʒən ‖ -ɜr-/ n

a form of BILINGUAL EDUCATION in which children who speak only one language enter a school where a second language is the MEDIUM OF INSTRUCTION for all pupils.

For example, there are schools in Canada for English-speaking children, where French is the language of instruction.

If these children are taught in French for the whole day it is called a **total immersion programme**, but if they are taught in French for only part of the day it is called a **partial immersion programme**.

see also SUBMERSION PROGRAMME

[*Further reading*: Swain 1978]

imperative /ɪmˈperətɪv/ n

see under MOOD

imperative sentence /ɪmˈperətɪv ˈsentəns/ n

a sentence which is in the form of a command. For example:

Pick up the book!

Imperative sentences do not, however, always have the function of an order. For example:

Look what you've done now!

often functions as an expression of annoyance.

see also DECLARATIVE SENTENCE, INTERROGATIVE SENTENCE

[*Further reading*: Lyons 1977]

impersonal construction /ɪmˈpɜːsənəl kənˈstrʌkʃən ‖ -ɜr-/ *n*
a type of sentence in which there is no mention of who or what
does or experiences something. Examples include English *It's cold,
It's raining*, and French *Ici on parle anglais* (literally, "Here one
speaks English") "English is spoken here".

implication /ˌɪmpləˈkeɪʃən/ *n* **implicational** /ˌɪmpləˈkeɪʃənəl/ *adj*
imply /ɪmˈplaɪ/ *v*
(in semantics) a relationship between two or more statements. If we
know whether one is true or false we know whether the others are
true or false.
For example, if the statement *Tom is a widower* is true it implies
that the statement *Tom's wife has died* is true and that the
statement *Tom has never been married* is false. Similarly, if *Mary
likes onions* is false then *Mary likes all vegetables* is also false.
[*Further reading*: Lyons 1968]

implicational scaling /ˌɪmpləˈkeɪʃənəl ˌskeɪlɪŋ/ *n*
a method of showing relationships by means of an implicational
table or **scalogram**. For example, a group of students learning
English may acquire the rule for using the DEFINITE ARTICLE before
the rule for the INDEFINITE ARTICLE and they may acquire those two
rules before the rule for marking the PLURAL of nouns. This can be
shown by investigating their spoken or written language and
presenting the results in a table. The symbol + means 100% correct
use of the rule and the symbol × means that the rule is applied
sometimes but not at other times (variable use).

student	noun plural	indefinite article	definite article
C	×	×	×
A	×	×	+
D	×	×	+
B	×	+	+
F	×	+	+
E	+	+	+

The symbol + in any row in the table implies a + symbol in any
column to the right of it in the same row or in any row below it. In
this way the students are ranked from Student C through to Student
E, who is the best student, because he or she has 100% correct use
of all the rules.
Implicational scaling has been used to show the order of acquisition
of rules by FOREIGN-LANGUAGE and SECOND-LANGUAGE learners, and by
people who are moving from a CREOLE towards a STANDARD VARIETY.
see also VARIABLE[1]
[*Further reading*: Bickerton 1975; Hyltenstam 1977]

implicational universal /ˌɪmpləˈkeɪʃənəl ˌjuːnəˈvɜːsəl ‖ -ɜr-/ *n*
see under LANGUAGE UNIVERSAL

implicature /ˈɪmpləkəˌtʃʊəʳ ‖ -tʃər/ *n*
see under CONVERSATIONAL MAXIM

implicit performative /ɪmˈplɪsɪt pəˈfɔːmətɪv ‖ pərˈfɔr-/ *n*
see under PERFORMATIVE

inalienable possession /ɪnˈeɪlɪənəbəl pəˈzeʃən/ *n*
In many languages, there is a distinction between those objects which can change ownership, such as houses, or animals, and those which typically cannot, such as body parts, one's shadow, and one's footprints.
The first type of possession is called **alienable possession** and the latter type is called inalienable.
For example, in English, the verb *own* is typically not used with inalienable possessions: *George owns a car* but not **George owns a big nose* (if it is his own nose). On the other hand the verb *have* can be used with both types of possession: *George has a car* and *George has a big nose*.

inanimate noun /ɪnˈænəmət ˈnaʊn/ *n*
see under ANIMATE NOUN

inchoative verb /ɪnˈkəʊətɪv ˈvɜːb ‖ ˈvɜrb/ *n*
a verb which expresses a change of state. For example:
   yellowed in *The leaves yellowed.*
and
   matured in *The cheese matured.*
as the leaves "became yellow" and the cheese "became mature".
see also CAUSATIVE VERB

inclusive (first person) pronoun /ɪŋˈkluːsɪv ˈprəʊnaʊn/ *n*
see under EXCLUSIVE (FIRST PERSON) PRONOUN

indefinite article /ɪnˈdefənət ˈɑːtɪkəl ‖ ˈɑr-/ *n*
see under ARTICLE

indefinite pronoun /ɪnˈdefənət ˈprəʊnaʊn/ *n*
a pronoun that refers to something which is not thought of as definite or particular, such as *somebody, something, anybody, anyone, one, anything, everybody, everything.*

independent clause /ˌɪndəˈpendənt ˈklɔːz/ *n*
see under DEPENDENT CLAUSE

independent variable /ˌɪndəˈpendənt ˈveərɪəbəl/ *n*
see under DEPENDENT VARIABLE

indexical information /ɪnˈdeksɪkəl ˌɪnfəˈmeɪʃən ‖ -ər-/ *n*
(in communication) information which is communicated, usually indirectly, about the speaker or writer's social class, age, sex,

nationality, ethnic group, etc, or his or her emotional state (eg whether excited, angry, surprised, bored, etc).
[*Further reading*: Lyons 1977]

indicative /ɪnˈdɪkətɪv/ *n*
see under MOOD

indigenization /ɪnˌdɪdʒənaɪˈzeɪʃən/ *n*
another term for NATIVIZATION

indirect object /ˈɪndərekt ˈɒbdʒəkt, ˈɪndaɪ- ‖ ˈɑb-/ *n*
see under OBJECT[1]

indirect question /ˈɪndərekt ˈkwestʃən, ˈɪndaɪ-/ *n*
see under DIRECT SPEECH

indirect speech /ˈɪndərekt ˈspiːtʃ, ˈɪndaɪ-/ *n*
see under DIRECT SPEECH

indirect speech act /ˈɪndərekt ˈspiːtʃ ˈækt, ˈɪndaɪ-/ *n*
see under SPEECH ACT

individualized instruction /ˌɪndəˈvɪdʒuəlaɪzd ɪnˈstrʌkʃən/ *n*
also **individualized learning** /ˌɪndəˈvɪdʒuəlaɪzd ˈlɜːnɪŋ ‖ ˈlɜr-/
an approach to teaching in which:

(a) OBJECTIVEs are based on the needs of individual learners
(b) allowances are made in the design of a CURRICULUM for individual differences in what students wish to learn, how they learn, and the rate at which they learn.

Individualized instruction attempts to give learners more control over what they learn and how they learn it.
[*Further reading*: Disick 1975]

Indo-European languages /ˈɪndəʊ ˌjuərəˈpiːən ˈlæŋgwɪdʒəz/ *n*
languages which are related and which are supposed to have had a common ancestor language, called "Proto Indo-European".
Languages in this group include most European languages, eg English, French, German, and the Celtic and Slavonic languages. They also include the ancient Indian languages Sanskrit and Pali and such languages as Hindi, Urdu, Bengali, Sinhala, and Farsi.

induced error /ɪnˈdjuːst ˈerər ‖ -ˈduːst/ *n*
also **transfer of training**
(in language learning) an ERROR which has been caused by the way in which a language item has been presented or practised.
For example, in teaching *at* the teacher may hold up a box and say *I'm looking at the box*. However, the learner may infer that *at* means *under*. If later the learner uses *at* for *under* (thus producing **The cat is at the table* instead of *The cat is under the table*) this would be an induced error.
see also ERROR ANALYSIS, INFERENCING, INTERLANGUAGE
[*Further reading*: Stenson 1974]

inductive learning /ɪn'dʌktɪv 'lɜːnɪŋ ‖ 'lɜr-/ *n*
also **learning by induction**
see under DEDUCTIVE LEARNING

inferencing /'ɪnfərənsɪŋ/ *n*
(in learning) the process of arriving at a hypothesis, idea, or
judgment on the basis of other knowledge, ideas, or judgments (that
is, making inferences or inferring). In language learning, inferencing
has been discussed as a LEARNING STRATEGY used by learners to work
out grammatical and other kinds of rules.
[*Further reading*: Carton 1971]

inferential comprehension /,ɪnfə'renʃəl ,kɒmprə'henʃən ‖ ,kɑm-/ *n*
see under READING

infinitive /ɪn'fɪnətɪv/ *n*
the BASE FORM of a verb (eg *go, come*).
In English the infinitive usually occurs with the infinitive marker *to*
(eg *I want to go*) but can occur without *to* as with AUXILIARY VERBS
(eg *Do come! You may go*). The infinitive without *to* is known as the
bare infinitive or **simple form**. The infinitive with *to* is sometimes
called the "*to*-infinitive".
The infinitive is a non-finite form of the verb (see FINITE VERB).

infix /'ɪnfɪks/ *n*
a letter or sound or group of letters or sounds which are added
within a word, and which change the meaning or function of the
word.
see also under AFFIX

inflecting language /ɪn'flektɪŋ 'læŋgwɪdʒ/ *n*
also **fusional language** *n*
a language in which the form of a word changes to show a change
in meaning or grammatical function. Often there is no clear
distinction between the basic part of the word and the part which
shows a grammatical function such as number or tense.
For example:
  mice (= *mouse* + plural)
  came (= *come* + past tense)
Greek and Latin are inflecting languages, although there is no
clear-cut distinction between inflecting languages, AGGLUTINATING
LANGUAGES, and ISOLATING LANGUAGES.
Sometimes inflecting languages and agglutinating languages are called
synthetic languages.
see also INFLECTION
[*Further reading*: Fromkin & Rodman 1983]

inflection/inflexion /ɪn'flekʃən/ *n* **inflect** /ɪn'flekt/ *v*
(in MORPHOLOGY) the process of adding an AFFIX to a word or
changing it in some other way according to the rules of the grammar
of a language.

For example, in English, verbs are inflected for 3rd-person singular: *I work*, *he works* and for past tense: *I worked*. Most nouns may be inflected for plural: *horse – horses*, *flower – flowers*, *man – men*.
see also DERIVATION, CONJUGATION[2]

informal speech /ɪnˌfɔːməl 'spiːtʃ ‖ -ɔr-/ *n*
another term for COLLOQUIAL SPEECH

informant /ɪn'fɔːmənt ‖ -ɔr-/ *n*
(in research) a person who provides the researcher with data for analysis. The data may be obtained, for instance, by recording the person's speech or by asking him or her questions about language use.
see also FIELD WORK

information content /ˌɪnfə'meɪʃən 'kɒntent ‖ ˌɪnfər- 'kɑn-/ *n*
see under INFORMATION THEORY

information gap /ˌɪnfə'meɪʃən 'gæp ‖ ˌɪnfər-/ *n*
(in communication between two or more people) a situation where information is known by only some of those present.
In "communicative language teaching" (see COMMUNICATIVE APPROACH) it is said that in order to promote real communication between students, there must be an information gap between them, or between them and their teacher. Without such a gap the classroom activities and exercises will be mechanical and artificial.
[*Further reading*: Johnson 1982; Widdowson 1978]

information processing /ˌɪnfə'meɪʃən 'prəʊsesɪŋ ‖ ˌɪnfər- 'prɑ-/ *n*
(in psychology and PSYCHOLINGUISTICS) a general term for the processes by which meanings are identified and understood in communication, the processes by which information and meaning are stored, organized, and retrieved from MEMORY, and the different kinds of DECODING which take place during reading or listening.
The study of information processing includes the study of memory, decoding, and HYPOTHESIS TESTING, and the study of the processes and strategies (see STRATEGY) which learners use in working out meanings in the TARGET LANGUAGE[1].
see also HEURISTIC, HYPOTHESIS TESTING, INFORMATION THEORY, INPUT
[*Further reading*: McDonough 1981]

information structure /ˌɪnfə'meɪʃən 'strʌktʃər ‖ ˌɪnfər-/ *n*
the use of WORD ORDER, INTONATION, STRESS and other devices to indicate how the message expressed by a sentence is to be understood.
Information structure is communicated by devices which indicate such things as:
(a) which parts of the message the speaker assumes the hearer already knows and which parts of the message are new information (see FUNCTIONAL SENTENCE PERSPECTIVE)
(b) contrasts, which may be indicated by stressing one word and not

another (eg *I broke <u>MY</u> pen*; *I broke my <u>PEN</u>*; *I <u>BROKE</u> my pen*).

see also GROUNDING

[*Further reading*: Lyons 1977]

information theory /ˌɪnfəˈmeɪʃən ˈθɪəri ‖ ˌɪnfər-/ *n*
also **communication theory**

a theory which explains how communication systems carry information and which measures the amount of information according to how much choice is involved when we send information.

The **information content** of a unit (eg of a word or a sentence) is measured according to how likely it is to occur in a particular communication. The more predictable a unit is, the less information it is said to carry. The unit of information used in information theory is the "binary digit", or BIT. The related concept of REDUNDANCY refers to the degree to which a message contains more information than is needed for it to be understood.

A well-known model for describing the sending of information in human or man-made communication systems, proposed by Shannon and Weaver, is known as the Mathematical Model of Communication. It describes communication as a process consisting of the following elements. The information **source** (eg a speaker) selects a desired message out of a possible set of messages. The "transmitter" changes the messages into a **signal** which is sent over the communication CHANNEL (eg a telephone wire) where it is received by the RECEIVER (eg a telephone or earphones) and changed back into a MESSAGE which is sent to the "destination" (eg a listener). In the process of transmission certain unwanted additions to the signal may occur which are not part of the message (eg interference from a poor telephone line) and these are referred to as NOISE[2]. The different elements in the system may be shown as:

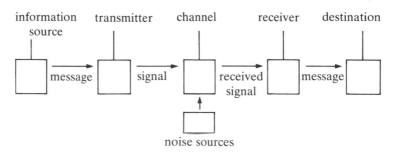

Communication system

In face-to-face communication, the speaker can be both information source and transmitter, while the listener can be both receiver and destination.

[*Further reading*: Sager, Dungworth, & McDonald 1980; DeVito 1970]

informative function /ɪnˈfɔːmətɪv ˌfʌŋkʃən ‖ -ɔr-/ *n*
see under DEVELOPMENTAL FUNCTIONS OF LANGUAGE

inhibition /ˌɪnhəˈbɪʃən/ *n*
see PROACTIVE INHIBITION

initial /ɪˈnɪʃəl/ *adj*
occurring at the beginning of a linguistic unit, eg as word-initial, clause-initial.
For example, a group of consonants at the beginning of a word, such as /spr/ in the English word *spray*, is an initial CONSONANT CLUSTER
see also MEDIAL, FINAL

Initial Teaching Alphabet /ɪˈnɪʃəl ˈtiːtʃɪŋ ˈælfəbet/ *n*
also **ITA**
a system which is used to teach beginners to read English. ITA uses 43 alphabetic characters and tries to make reading easier by reducing the amount of irregularity in the English spelling system. It is designed as an introduction to the normal alphabet and is not a replacement for it.

> Sœ when it's tiem for fœd, ov cors,
> heε ʃhouts, "hœrra,
> ie cœd eεt a hors!"
> but ſhis iʂ whot heε haʂ insted:
> milk, ʧheεʂ and frœt,
> and gœd broun bred.

[*Further reading*: Downing 1967]

innateness position /ɪˈneɪtnəs ˌpəˈzɪʃən/ *n*
another term for INNATIST HYPOTHESIS

innatist hypothesis /ɪˈneɪtəst haɪˈpɒθəsəs ‖ -ˈpɑ-/ *n*
also **innatist position** /ɪˈneɪtəst ˌpəˈzɪʃən/, **nativist position, innateness position, rationalist position**
a theory held by some philosophers and linguists which says that human knowledge develops from structures, processes, and "ideas" which are in the mind at birth (ie are innate), rather than from the environment, and that these are responsible for the basic structure of language and how it is learned. This hypothesis has been used to explain how children are able to learn language (see LANGUAGE ACQUISITION DEVICE). The innatist hypothesis contrasts with the belief that all human knowledge comes from experience (see EMPIRICISM).
see also MENTALISM
[*Further reading*: Chomsky 1968]

inner speech /ˌɪnəʳ ˈspiːtʃ/ *n*
a type of "speech" discussed by the Russian psychologist Vygotsky,

who distinguished between **external speech** and inner speech. External speech is spoken or written speech, and is expressed in words and sentences. Inner speech is speech for oneself. It takes place inside one's own mind and often takes place in "pure word meanings" rather than in words or sentences, according to Vygotsky.

[*Further reading*: Vygotsky 1962]

input /'ɪnpʊt/ *n*

(1) (in language learning) language which a learner hears or receives and from which he or she can learn. The language a learner produces is by analogy sometimes called **output**.

(2) In second or foreign language learning, a distinction is sometimes made between input (above) and **intake**. Intake is input which is actually helpful for the learner. Some of the language (ie the input) which a learner hears may be too rapid or difficult for the learner to understand, and therefore cannot be used in learning (ie cannot serve as intake).

see also INFORMATION PROCESSING

[*Further reading*: Davies, Criper, & Howatt 1984; Dulay, Burt, & Krashen 1982]

input hypothesis /'ɪnpʊt haɪ'pɒθəsəs ‖ -'pɑ-/ *n*

a hypothesis proposed by Krashen, which states that in second or foreign language learning, for language ACQUISITION to occur, it is necessary for the learner to understand INPUT language which contains linguistic items that are slightly beyond the learner's present linguistic COMPETENCE. Learners understand such language using cues in the situation. Eventually the ability to produce language is said to emerge naturally, and need not be taught directly.

see also MONITOR HYPOTHESIS

[*Further reading*: Krashen 1981, 1985]

instructional objective /ɪn'strʌkʃənəl əb'dʒektɪv/ *n*

another term for BEHAVIOURAL OBJECTIVE

instrumental case /ˌɪnstrə'mentl ˌkeɪs/ *n*

In CASE GRAMMAR, the noun or noun phrase that refers to the means by which the action of the verb is performed is in the instrumental case.

For example, in the sentences:

He dug the hole with a spade.
The hammer hit the nail.

a spade and *the hammer* are in the instrumental case.

[*Further reading*: Fillmore 1968]

instrumental function /ˌɪnstrə'mentl ˌfʌŋkʃən/ *n*

see under DEVELOPMENTAL FUNCTIONS OF LANGUAGE

instrumental motivation /ˌɪnstrə'mentl ˌməʊtɪ'veɪʃən/ *n*

see under MOTIVATION

intake /'ınteɪk/ n
see under INPUT

integrated approach /'ıntəgreɪtə́d ə'prəʊtʃ/ n
(in language teaching) the teaching of the language skills of reading,
writing, listening, and speaking, in conjunction with each other, as
when a lesson involves activities that relate listening and speaking to
reading and writing.
see also LANGUAGE ARTS

integrative motivation /'ıntəgreɪtɪv ˌməʊtɪ'veɪʃən/ n
see under MOTIVATION

integrative test /'ıntəgreɪtɪv 'test/ n
see under DISCRETE-POINT TEST

intelligibility /ınˌtelədʒə'bɪlə́ti/ n
the degree to which a message can be understood. Studies of speech
PERCEPTION have found that the intelligibility of speech is due to
various factors including ACCENT³ and INTONATION, the listener's ability
to predict parts of the message, the location of PAUSES in the
utterance, the grammatical complexity of sentences, and the speed
with which utterances are produced.
[*Further reading*: Foss & Hakes 1978]

intensifier /ın'tensə́faɪə r/ n
a class of words, generally adverbs, which are used to modify
gradable adjectives, adverbs, verbs, or -ed-PARTICIPLES, as in:
    It is <u>very</u> good.
    It was <u>completely</u> destroyed.
    I <u>absolutely</u> detest it.
see also GRADABLE
[*Further reading*: Close 1975]

intensive reading /ın'tensɪv 'riːdɪŋ/ n
see under EXTENSIVE READING

interactional function /ıntə'rækʃənəl 'fʌŋkʃən/ n
see under DEVELOPMENTAL FUNCTIONS OF LANGUAGE

interaction analysis /ıntə'rækʃən ə'næləsə́s/ n
also **interaction process analysis** /ıntə'rækʃən 'prəʊses
ə'næləsə́s ‖ 'prɑ-/
any of several procedures for measuring and describing the
behaviour of students and teachers in classrooms, (a) in order to
describe what happens during a lesson (b) to evaluate teaching (c)
to study the relationship between teaching and learning (d) to help
teacher-trainees learn about the process of teaching. In interaction
analysis, classroom behaviour is observed and the different types of
student and teacher activity are classified, using a classification
scheme. Several such schemes have been proposed.
[*Further reading*: Flanders 1970]

interactive /ˌɪntəˈræktɪv/ *adj*
(in COMPUTER ASSISTED INSTRUCTION) describes the ability of a user to "communicate" (or "interact") with a computer. Lessons in CAI materials may involve a question on the computer, a response from the student, and feedback from the computer telling the student if the answer is correct. In CAI such activities are said to be "interactive".

interdental /ˌɪntəˈdentl ‖ -tər-/ *adj*
describes a speech sound (a CONSONANT) produced with the tip of the tongue between the upper and lower teeth, eg /θ/ and /ð/ in the English words /θɪk/ *thick* and /ðɪs/ *this*.
see also MANNER OF ARTICULATION, PLACE OF ARTICULATION

interference /ˌɪntəˈfɪərəns ‖ -tər-/ *n*
see under LANGUAGE TRANSFER

intergroup communication /ɪntəˈgruːp kəˌmjuːnəˈkeɪʃən ‖ -tər-/ *n*
communication between different groups, especially those which are socially, ethnically, or linguistically different. Intergroup communication is often by means of a LINGUA FRANCA, a language known by speakers of both groups.
For example, in Indonesia, where many different languages are spoken, Bahasa Indonesia, the national language, is the language most frequently used for intergroup communication.
see also INTRAGROUP COMMUNICATION

interim grammar /ˈɪntərɪm ˈgræməʳ/ *n*
a temporary grammatical system used by children learning their first language at a particular stage in their language development. Children's grammatical systems change as they develop new grammatical rules; hence they may be said to pass through a series of interim grammars.
see also INTERLANGUAGE

interjection /ˌɪntəˈdʒekʃən ‖ -tər-/ *n*
a word such as *ugh!*, *gosh!*, *wow!*, which indicates an emotional state or attitude such as delight, surprise, shock, and disgust, but which has no referential meaning (see REFERENCE).
Interjections are often regarded as one of the PARTS OF SPEECH.
see also EXCLAMATION[1]

interlanguage /ˌɪntəˈlæŋgwɪdʒ ‖ -tər-/ *n*
the type of language produced by second- and foreign-language learners who are in the process of learning a language.
In language learning, learners' errors are caused by several different processes. These include:
(a) borrowing patterns from the mother tongue (see LANGUAGE TRANSFER)
(b) extending patterns from the target language, eg by analogy (see OVERGENERALIZATION)

(c) expressing meanings using the words and grammar which are already known (see COMMUNICATION STRATEGY)

Since the language which the learner produces using these processes differs from both the mother tongue and the TARGET LANGUAGE[1], it is sometimes called an interlanguage, or is said to result from the learner's interlanguage system or **approximative system**.

see also INTERIM GRAMMAR

[*Further reading*: Davies, Criper, & Howatt 1984; Selinker 1972]

interlingual error /ˌɪntə'lɪŋgwəl 'erəʳ ‖ -tər-/ n

(in ERROR ANALYSIS) an error which results from LANGUAGE TRANSFER, that is, which is caused by the learner's native language. For example, the incorrect French sentence *Elle regarde les* ("She sees them"), produced according to the word order of English, instead of the correct French sentence *Elle les regarde* (literally, "She them sees").

An **intralingual error** is one which results from faulty or partial learning of the TARGET LANGUAGE[1], rather than from language transfer. Intralingual errors may be caused by the influence of one target-language item upon another. For example a learner may produce *He is comes*, based on a blend of the English structures *He is coming*, *He comes*.

[*Further reading*: Richards 1974]

interlocutors /ˌɪntə'lɒkjʊtəz ‖ ˌɪntər'lɑkjətərz/ n

people who are actively engaged in conversation. Normally, the exchange is in the form of a dialogue or a number of dialogues. Apart from the interlocutors there may be other people present who are just silent participants, such as an audience.

The form and style of the conversation may be affected by the presence of these "silent participants".

internal consistency reliability /ɪn'tɜːnl kən'sɪstənsi rɪˌlaɪə'bɪləti ‖ -'tɜr-/ n

(in testing) a measure of the degree to which the items or parts of a test are homogeneous or consistent with each other.

Internal consistency reliability is often estimated by comparing the two halves of a test (SPLIT-HALF RELIABILITY) or by a KUDER-RICHARDSON RELIABILITY COEFFICIENT.

international language /ˌɪntə'næʃənəl 'læŋgwɪdʒ ‖ -tər-/ n

a language in widespread use as a FOREIGN LANGUAGE or SECOND LANGUAGE, ie as a language of international communication. English is the most widely used international language.

International Phonetic Alphabet /ˌɪntə'næʃənəl fə'netɪk 'ælfəbet ‖ -tər-/ n

also **IPA**

a system of symbols for representing the pronunciation of words in any language according to the principles of the International

Phonetic Association. The symbols consist of letters and DIACRITICS. Some letters are taken from the Roman alphabet (see ALPHABETIC WRITING), eg /p/, /e/, and /n/ as in the English word /pen/ *pen*. Others are special symbols, eg /ʃ/, /ə/, and /ʊ/ as in the English word /ʃəʊ/ *show*.

interpersonal function /ˌɪntəˈpɜːsənəl ˈfʌŋkʃən ‖ ˌɪntərˈpɜr-/ *n*
see under FUNCTIONS OF LANGUAGE[2]

interpretation /ɪnˌtɜːprəˈteɪʃən ‖ -ˌtɜr-/ *n*
the translation by an "interpreter" of what someone is saying into another language, to permit a speaker to communicate with people who do not understand the speaker's language.
If the interpretation takes place as the speaker is talking, providing a continuous translation which parallels the speaker's speech, it is called **simultaneous interpretation**.
If the speaker pauses during speaking to give the interpreter time to provide a translation of everything said up to that point, the result is called **consecutive interpretation**.

interpretive error /ɪnˈtɜːprətɪv ˈerər ‖ -ˈtɜr-/ *n*
see under ERROR

interpretive semantics /ɪnˈtɜːprətɪv sɪˈmæntɪks ‖ -ˈtɜr-/ *n*
a theory about the place of meaning in a model of GENERATIVE TRANSFORMATIONAL GRAMMAR. It considers a meaning component, called the **semantic component**, as part of the grammar. This component contains rules which interpret the meaning of sentences.
This theory differs from GENERATIVE SEMANTICS, which insists that the semantic component is the most basic part of a grammar from which all sentences of a language can be "generated" (see GENERATIVE GRAMMAR, RULE[2]).
In generative semantics, syntactic rules operate on the meaning of a sentence to produce its form. In interpretive semantics, semantic rules operate on the words and syntactic structure of a sentence to reveal its meaning.
[*Further reading*: Aitchison 1978; Katz & Fodor 1963]

inter-rater reliability /ˈɪntəˈreɪtər rɪˌlaɪəˈbɪləti/ *n*
(in testing) the degree to which different examiners or judges making different subjective ratings of ability (eg of language proficiency) agree in their evaluations of that ability. If different judges rank students in approximately the same order, using a RATING SCALE which measures different aspects of proficiency, the rating scale is said to have high inter-rater reliability.
Intra-rater reliability is the degree to which a teacher or examiner making subjective ratings of ability gives the same evaluation of that ability when he or she makes an evaluation on two or more different occasions.

interrogative pronoun /ˌɪntəˈrɒgətɪv ˈprəʊnaʊn ‖ -ˈrɑ-/ *n*

Wh-pronouns (*who, which, what, whose, who(m)* etc), which are used to form questions, eg:

Which is your book?

What is your name?

see also WH-QUESTION

[*Further reading*: Quirk et al 1985]

interrogative sentence /ˌɪntəˈrɒgətɪv ˈsentəns ‖ -ˈrɑ-/ *n*

A sentence which is in the form of a question. For example:

Did you open the window?

Interrogative sentences do not, however, always have the function of a question. For example:

Could you shut the window?

may be a request for someone to shut the window and not a question about whether or not the person is able to do so.

see also DECLARATIVE SENTENCE, IMPERATIVE SENTENCE

[*Further reading*: Lyons 1981]

interval scale /ˈɪntəvəl ˈskeɪl ‖ -tər-/ *n*

see under SCALE

intervocalic /ˌɪntəvəˈkælɪk, -vəʊ- ‖ -tər-/ *adj*

(of CONSONANTS) occurring between two vowels.

For example, English /d/ in /ˈleɪdi/ *lady* is an intervocalic CONSONANT.

intonation /ˌɪntəˈneɪʃən/ *n*

When speaking, people generally raise and lower the PITCH of their voice, forming pitch patterns. They also give some syllables in their utterances a greater degree of loudness and change their SPEECH RHYTHM. These phenomena are called intonation. Intonation does not happen at random but has definite patterns (see INTONATION PATTERNS) which can be analysed according to their structure and functions. Intonation is used to carry information over and above that which is expressed by the words in the sentence.

see also KEY², PITCH LEVEL, TONE UNIT

intonation contour /ˌɪntəˈneɪʃən ˈkɒntʊər ‖ ˈkɑn-/ *n*

see under TONE UNIT

intonation patterns /ˌɪntəˈneɪʃən ˈpætənz/ *n*

patterns in the spoken form of a language which are usually expressed by variations in pitch (see TONE UNIT), loudness, syllable length, and sometimes SPEECH RHYTHM.

Intonation patterns may, for instance:

(a) have grammatical functions, eg they may show that an utterance is a question and not a statement:

Ready?

(b) give additional information to that given by the words of an utterance:

I GOT the job. (it was doubtful whether I would)

(c) indicate the speaker's attitude to the matter discussed or to the listener:

But I TOLD you.

Intonation patterns often differ between languages or even between varieties of the same language, eg between Australian English and American English. In some communities, there is a difference in the intonation patterns of different age groups or speakers of different sex.

see also INTONATION

[*Further reading*: Brazil, Coulthard, & Johns 1980; Halliday 1970]

intragroup communication /ˌɪntrəˈgruːp kəˌmjuːnɪˈkeɪʃən/ *n*
communication among members of a group.
In some multi-ethnic countries or communities, a language may be used for communication within a particular ethnic group although it is not known or used by the majority of the population; for example, Spanish in parts of the USA among some Mexican-Americans.

see also COMMUNITY LANGUAGE, INTERGROUP COMMUNICATION

intralingual error /ˌɪntrəˈlɪŋgwəl ˈerəʳ/ *n*
see under INTERLINGUAL ERROR

intransitive verb /ɪnˈtrænsətɪv ˈvɜːb, -sə- ‖ ˈvɜrb/ *n*
see under TRANSITIVE VERB

intra-rater reliability /ˌɪntrəˈreɪtəʳ rɪˌlaɪəˈbɪləti/ *n*
see under INTER-RATER RELIABILITY

intrusion /ɪnˈtruːʒən/ *n* **intrusive** /ɪnˈtruːsɪv/ *adj*
When an extra consonant is added at the end of a word to link it to a following word starting with a vowel, this is known as intrusion.
In English, an intrusive /r/ is often added, especially before *and*.
For example:
  China and Japan /ˈtʃaɪnər ən dʒəˈpæn/
  Lena and Sue /ˈliːnər ən suː/
[*Further reading*: Gimson 1980]

IPA /ˌaɪ piː ˈeɪ/ *n*
an abbreviation for
(1) *I*nternational *P*honetic *A*ssociation
(2) INTERNATIONAL PHONETIC ALPHABET

irregular verb /ɪˈregjʊləʳ ˈvɜːb ‖ -gjə- ˈvɜrb/ *n*
see under REGULAR VERB

isolating language /ˈaɪsəleɪtɪŋ ˈlæŋgwɪdʒ/ *n*
also **analytic language**
a language in which word forms do not change, and in which grammatical functions are shown by WORD ORDER and the use of FUNCTION WORDS.

For example, in Mandarin Chinese:

júzi   wǒ chī le
orange I   eat (function word
                showing completion)
"I ate the orange"

wǒ chī le   júzi   le
I   eat (function orange (function
         word)   word)
"I ate an orange"

Languages which are highly isolating include Chinese and Vietnamese, although there is no clear-cut distinction between isolating languages, INFLECTING LANGUAGES, and AGGLUTINATING LANGUAGES. English is more isolating than many other European languages, such as French, German, and Russian, but is also an inflecting language.

[*Further reading*: Lyons 1968]

ITA /ˌaɪ tiː ˈeɪ/ n
an abbreviation for INITIAL TEACHING ALPHABET

item analysis /ˈaɪtəm əˈnæləsəs/ n
(in testing) the analysis of the responses to the items in a test, in order to find out how effective the test items are and to find out if they indicate differences between good and weak students.
see also ITEM FACILITY, ITEM DISCRIMINATION

item difficulty /ˈaɪtəm ˈdɪfɪkəlti/ n
another term for ITEM FACILITY

item discrimination /ˈaɪtəm dɪˌskrɪməˈneɪʃən/ n
(in testing) a measure of the extent to which a test item is sensitive to differences in ability among those who take the test. If a particular item in a test was answered in the same way by both the students who did well on the test as a whole and by those who did poorly, the item would be said to have poor discrimination: it could not discriminate between good students and bad students.

item facility /ˈaɪtəm fəˈsɪləti/ n
also **facility value, item difficulty**
(in testing) a measure of the ease of a test item. It is the proportion of the students who answered the item correctly, and may be determined by the formula:

Item Facility(IF) $= \dfrac{R}{N}$

where R = number of correct answers, N = number of students taking the test.
The higher the ratio of R to N, the easier the item.

J

jargon /ˈdʒɑːgən ‖ -ɑr-/ *n*

usually speech or writing containing specialized words or
constructions: *the jargon of law*; *medical jargon*.
The term "jargon" is typically used by those unfamiliar with that
particular type of language, and/or by those who dislike it.
see also LANGUAGES FOR SPECIAL PURPOSES, REGISTER, TERMINOLOGY

juncture /ˈdʒʌŋktʃər/ *n*

a type of BOUNDARY between two PHONEME*s*. Often, juncture helps
the listener to distinguish between pairs such as *see Mill* and *seem ill*
in *Did he see Mill?* and *Did he seem ill?*
[*Further reading*: Robins 1980]

key[1] /kiː/*n*

the tone, manner, or spirit in which a SPEECH ACT is carried out, for example whether mockingly or seriously. The key chosen would depend on the situation and the relationship of the speakers to each other. For example, the statement *If you do that I'll never speak to you again* may be either a real threat or a mock threat. The signalling of key may be verbal (eg by INTONATION) or non-verbal (eg by a wink, a gesture, or a certain posture).

[*Further reading*: Coulthard 1985; Hymes 1974]

key[2] *n*

(in INTONATION) a level of PITCH chosen by the speaker together with an intonation contour (see TONE UNIT) in order to convey a particular kind of meaning to the listener.

In English, a difference can be made between high key, mid key, and low key.

For example, the choice of a high key often signals a contrast as in:

But she's Peter's WIFE (where *wife* also has a fall in pitch)

This could be a reply to someone who had just stated that the person concerned was Peter's sister.

see also PITCH LEVEL

[*Further reading*: Brazil, Coulthard, & Johns 1980]

kinesics /kɪˈniːsɪks/ *n* **kinesic** *adj*

see under PARALINGUISTICS

KR21 /ˌkeɪ aːʳ ˌtwenti ˈwʌn/ *n*

another term for KUDER-RICHARDSON RELIABILITY COEFFICIENT

Kuder-Richardson Reliability Coefficient /ˈkuːdəʳ ˈrɪtʃədsən ‖ -ər-/ *n* also **KR 21**

a statistical formula used as one estimate of the RELIABLITY of a test. It is based on the number of items in the test, the MEAN score, and its STANDARD DEVIATION.

A similar reliability formula, based on information about the difficulty of the individual items, the test mean, and the standard deviation, is known as KR 20.

L

L1 /'el 'wʌn/ n

see under FIRST LANGUAGE

L2 /'el 'tuː/ n

another term for a TARGET LANGUAGE[1] or a SECOND LANGUAGE.

labial /'leɪbɪəl/ adj

(in PHONETICS) describes a pronunciation in which either one or both lips are used. The term comes from Latin *labia* "lip".

see also BILABIAL, LABIO-DENTAL

labialization /ˌleɪbɪəlaɪˈzeɪʃən/ n **labialize** /'leɪbɪəlaɪz/ v

rounding of the lips in the pronunciation of a speech sound. For example, in English, this may happen in the pronunciation of /r/ so that words like *very* and *red* are pronounced /vewi/ and /wed/. This type of pronunciation is heard mainly from children before they are able to produce an *r* sound but it may remain as a feature of adult speech.

[*Further reading*: Gimson 1980]

labio-dental /ˌleɪbɪəʊˈdentl/ adj

describes a speech sound (a CONSONANT) which is produced by the lower lip touching or nearly touching the upper teeth.

For example, in English the /f/ in /fæt/ *fat*, and the /v/ in /væt/ *vat* are labio-dental FRICATIVEs.

see also PLACE OF ARTICULATION, MANNER OF ARTICULATION

[*Further reading*: Gimson 1980]

LAD /ˌel eɪ 'diː/ n

an abbreviation for LANGUAGE ACQUISITION DEVICE

laminal /'læmənl/ adj

describes a speech sound (a CONSONANT) which is produced by the front upper surface of the tongue (the blade or **lamina**) touching the upper teeth or the gum ridge behind the upper teeth (the **alveolar ridge**).

In English, the /ʃ/ in /ʃuː/ *shoe* is a laminal FRICATIVE.

see also PLACE OF ARTICULATION, MANNER OF ARTICULATION

[*Further reading*: Gimson 1980]

language[1] /'læŋgwɪdʒ/ n

the system of human communication by means of a structured arrangement of sounds (or their written representation) to form larger units, eg MORPHEMES, WORDS, SENTENCEs.

In common usage it can also refer to non-human systems of communication such as the "language" of bees, the "language" of dolphins.

language² *n*

any particular system of human communication (see LANGUAGE¹), for example, the French language, the Hindi language. Sometimes a language is spoken by most people in a particular country, for example, Japanese in Japan, but sometimes a language is spoken by only part of the population of a country, for example Tamil in India, French in Canada.

Languages are usually not spoken in exactly the same way from one part of a country to the other. Differences in the way a language is spoken by different people are described in terms of regional and social variation (see DIALECT, SOCIOLECT). In some cases, there is a continuum from one language to another. Dialect A of Language X on one side of the border may be very similar to Dialect B of Language Y on the other side of the border if language X and language Y are related. This is the case between Sweden and Norway and between Germany and the Netherlands.
see also REGISTER

language achievement /ˈlæŋgwɪdʒ əˈtʃiːvmənt/ *n*

a learner's proficiency in a SECOND LANGUAGE or FOREIGN LANGUAGE as the result of what has been taught or learned after a period of instruction. Language achievement may be contrasted with LANGUAGE APTITUDE, which is measured before a course of instruction begins.
[*Further reading*: Carroll 1981]

language acquisition /ˈlæŋgwɪdʒ ækwəˈzɪʃən/ *n*

see ACQUISITION

language acquisition device /ˈlæŋgwɪdʒ ækwəˈzɪʃən dɪˈvaɪs/ *n*
also **LAD**

the capacity to acquire one's FIRST LANGUAGE, when this capacity is pictured as a sort of mechanism or apparatus.

In the 1960s and 1970s Chomsky and others claimed that every normal human being was born with an LAD (see INNATIST HYPOTHESIS). The LAD included basic knowledge about the nature and structure of human language.

The LAD was offered as an explanation of why children develop COMPETENCE in their first language in a relatively short time, merely by being exposed to it.
see also ACQUISITION
[*Further reading*: McNeill 1966]

language aptitude /ˈlæŋgwɪdʒ ˈæptətjuːd ‖ -tuːd/ *n*

the natural ability to learn a language, not including intelligence, MOTIVATION, interest, etc.

Language aptitude is thought to be a combination of various abilities, such as the ability to identify sound patterns in a new language, the ability to recognize the different grammatical functions of words in sentences, ROTE-LEARNING ability, and the ability to infer language rules (see INFERENCING, INDUCTIVE LEARNING). A person with

high language aptitude can learn more quickly and easily than a person with low language aptitude, all other factors being equal.
see also LANGUAGE APTITUDE TEST.
[*Further reading*: Carroll 1981]

language aptitude test /'læŋgwɪdʒ 'æptətjuːd 'test/ *n*
a test which measures a person's aptitude for SECOND-LANGUAGE or FOREIGN-LANGUAGE learning and which can be used to identify those learners who are most likely to succeed (see LANGUAGE APTITUDE). Language aptitude tests usually consist of several different tests which measure such abilities as:
(a) sound coding ability – the ability to identify and remember new sounds in a foreign or second language
(b) grammatical coding ability – the ability to identify the grammatical functions of different parts of sentences
(c) inductive learning ability – the ability to work out meanings without explanation in a new language (see INDUCTIVE LEARNING)
(d) memorization – the ability to remember words, rules, etc in a new language.
Two well-known language aptitude tests are *The Modern Language Aptitude Test* (Carroll and Sapon 1958) and the *Pimsleur Language Aptitude Battery* (Pimsleur 1966).
[*Further reading*: Carroll 1981]

language arts /'læŋgwɪdʒ 'ɑːts ‖ 'ɑrts/ *n*
those parts of an educational CURRICULUM which involve the development of skills related to the use of language, such as reading, writing, spelling, listening, and speaking. The term is used principally to describe approaches used in FIRST-LANGUAGE teaching which try to develop LANGUAGE SKILLS together rather than separately.

language attitudes /'læŋgwɪdʒ 'ætətjuːdz ‖ -tuːdz/ *n*
the attitudes which speakers of different languages or language varieties have towards each other's languages or to their own language. Expressions of positive or negative feelings towards a language may reflect impressions of linguistic difficulty or simplicity, ease or difficulty of learning, degree of importance, elegance, social STATUS, etc. Attitudes towards a language may also show what people feel about the speakers of that language.
Language attitudes may have an effect on SECOND-LANGUAGE or FOREIGN-LANGUAGE learning. The measurement of language attitudes provides information which is useful in language teaching and LANGUAGE PLANNING.
see also LANGUAGE EGO, MATCHED GUISE TECHNIQUE, MOTIVATION, SEMANTIC DIFFERENTIAL
[*Further reading*: Shuy & Fasold 1973]

language attrition /'læŋgwɪdʒ ə'trɪʃən/ *n*
LANGUAGE LOSS that is gradual rather than sudden.

language change /'læŋgwɪdʒ 'tʃeɪndʒ/ *n*

change in a language which takes place over time. All living languages have changed and continue to change.

For example, in English, changes which have recently been occurring include the following:

(a) the distinction in pronunciation between words such as *what* and *Watt* is disappearing

(b) *hopefully* may be used instead of *I hope, we hope, it is to be hoped*

(c) new words and expressions are constantly entering the language, eg *drop-out, alternative society, culture shock.*

Language change should not be confused with LANGUAGE SHIFT.

see also COMPARATIVE HISTORICAL LINGUISTICS, DIACHRONIC LINGUISTICS, NEOLOGISM

language contact /'læŋgwɪdʒ 'kɒntækt ‖ 'kɑn-/ *n*

contact between different languages, especially when at least one of the languages is influenced by the contact. This influence takes place typically when the languages are spoken in the same or adjoining regions and when there is a high degree of communication between the people speaking them. The influence may affect PHONETICS, SYNTAX, SEMANTICS, or communicative strategies such as ADDRESS FORMS and greetings.

Language contact occurs or has occurred in areas of considerable immigration such as the USA, Latin America, Australia and parts of Africa, as well as in language border areas such as parts of India.

see also **contact language** under PIDGIN

[*Further reading*: Fishman 1971]

language dominance /'læŋgwɪdʒ 'dɒmənəns ‖ 'dɑ-/ *n*

greater ability in, or greater importance of, one language than another.

(1) For an individual, this means that a person who speaks more than one language or dialect considers that he or she knows one of the languages better than the other(s) and/or uses it more frequently and with greater ease. The **dominant language** may be his or her NATIVE LANGUAGE or may have been acquired later in life at school or a place of employment.

(2) For a country or region where more than one language or dialect is used, this means that one of them is more important than the other(s). A language may become the dominant language because it has more prestige (higher STATUS) in the country, is favoured by the government, and/or has the largest number of speakers.

language ego /'læŋgwɪdʒ 'iːgəʊ, 'egəʊ/ *n*

(in SECOND-LANGUAGE or FOREIGN-LANGUAGE learning) the relation between people's feelings of personal identity, individual uniqueness, and value (ie their ego) and aspects of their FIRST LANGUAGE.

Guiora and others have suggested that a person's self-identity develops as he or she is learning the first language, that some aspects of language, especially pronunciation, may be closely linked to one's ego, and that this may hinder some aspects of second or foreign language learning.

[*Further reading*: Guiora et al 1972]

language enrichment /'læŋgwɪdʒ ɪn'rɪtʃmənt/ *n*
a term sometimes used to describe language teaching as part of a programme of COMPENSATORY INSTRUCTION.

language experience approach /'læŋgwɪdʒ ɪk'spɪərɪəns ə'prəʊtʃ/ *n*
an approach to the teaching of reading a FIRST LANGUAGE, which emphasizes the use of the child's recent experience as a basis for learning and which makes use of reading materials based on the child's own language.

For example, children may be given the opportunity to talk about recent events or experiences (eg a trip to the zoo), words and sentences produced may be written on the blackboard, and these may become the basis of reading instruction using a SENTENCE METHOD or WHOLE-WORD METHOD.

[*Further reading*: Goodacre 1978]

language functions /'læŋgwɪdʒ 'fʌŋkʃənz/ *n*
another term for FUNCTIONS OF LANGUAGE[1,2]

language laboratory /'læŋgwɪdʒ lə'bɒrətri ‖ 'læbrətori/ *n*
also **language lab** /'læŋgwɪdʒ ,læb/
a room that contains desks or individual booths with tape or cassette recorders and a control booth for teacher or observer and which is used for language teaching. The recorders usually have recording, listening, and playback facilities; students can practise recorded exercises and follow language programmes either individually or in groups, and the teacher can listen to each student's performance through earphones. Language laboratories are associated particularly with the AUDIOLINGUAL METHOD.

[*Further reading*: Dakin 1973]

language learning /'læŋgwɪdʒ 'lɜːnɪŋ ‖ 'lɜr-/ *n*
see ACQUISITION

language loss /'læŋgwɪdʒ 'lɒs ‖ 'lɑs/ *n*
the gradual forgetting and decay of the ability to use a language, usually through lack of opportunity to use it. Immigrants who move to a country where they have no occasion to use their mother tongue may eventually lose their ability to use it, in whole or in part.

Language loss may also occur suddenly as the result of illness (see APHASIA).

language loyalty /'læŋgwɪdʒ 'lɔɪəlti/ *n*
retention of a language by its speakers, who are usually in a
minority in a country where another language is the dominant
language (see LANGUAGE DOMINANCE).
For example, some immigrant groups in the USA, such as
Estonians, have shown a high degree of language loyalty.

language maintenance /'læŋgwɪdʒ 'meɪntənəns / *n*
the degree to which an individual or group continues to use their
language, particularly in a BILINGUAL or MULTILINGUAL area or among
immigrant groups. Many factors affect language maintenance, for
example:
(a) whether or not the language is an OFFICIAL LANGUAGE
(b) whether or not it is used in the media, for religious purposes, in
    education
(c) how many speakers of the language live in the same area. In
    some places where the use of certain languages has greatly
    decreased there have been attempts at revival, eg of Welsh in
    Wales and Gaelic in parts of Scotland.
see also DIGLOSSIA, LANGUAGE SHIFT, LANGUAGE REVITALIZATION
PROGRAMME
[*Further reading*: Fishman 1972]

language minority group /'læŋgwɪdʒ maɪ'nɒrəti 'gruːp ‖ mə'nɔ-,
mə'nɑ-/ *n*
also **minority language group**
a group of people in a country or community who have a language
other than the major or dominant language of the country or
community.
see also COMMUNITY LANGUAGE, MAJORITY LANGUAGE

language pedagogy /'læŋgwɪdʒ 'pedəgɒdʒi ‖ -gəʊ-/ *n*
a general term sometimes used to describe the teaching of a
language as a FIRST LANGUAGE, a SECOND LANGUAGE, or a FOREIGN
LANGUAGE.

language planning /'læŋgwɪdʒ 'plænɪŋ/ *n*
planning, usually by a government or goverment agency, concerning
choice of national or official language(s), ways of spreading the use
of a language, spelling reforms, the addition of new words to the
language, and other language problems. Through language planning,
an official **language policy** is established and/or implemented.
For example, in Indonesia, Malay was chosen as the national
language and was given the name Bahasa Indonesia (Indonesian
language). It became the main language of education. There were
several spelling reforms and a national planning agency was
established to deal with problems such as the development of
scientific terms.
see also LANGUAGE TREATMENT, SOCIOLINGUISTICS, SOCIOLOGY OF LANGUAGE
[*Further reading*: Fishman 1974]

language policy /'læŋgwɪdʒ 'pɒləsi ‖ 'pɑ-/ *n*
see under LANGUAGE PLANNING

language proficiency /'læŋgwɪdʒ prə'fɪʃənsi/ *n*
a person's proficiency in using a language for a specific purpose.
Whereas LANGUAGE ACHIEVEMENT describes language ability as a result
of learning, proficiency refers to the degree of skill with which a
person can use a language, such as how well a person can read, write,
speak, or understand language. Proficiency may be measured through
the use of a PROFICIENCY TEST.

language programme design /'læŋgwɪdʒ 'prəʊgræm dɪ'zaɪn/ *n*
another term for COURSE DESIGN

language revitalization programme /'læŋgwɪdʒ riːvaɪtəl-aɪ'zeɪʃən
'prəʊgræm ‖ -tələ-/ *n*
a programme intended to help to revive or strengthen a language
which is in danger of dying out, such as programmes for the
teaching of Irish in Ireland or several American Indian languages.

languages for special purposes /'læŋgwɪdʒəz fər 'speʃəl
'pɜːpəsəz ‖ 'pɜr-/ *n*
also **languages for specific purposes** /'læŋgwɪdʒəz fər spə'sɪfɪk
'pɜːpəsəz ‖ 'pɜr-/, **LSP**
second or foreign languages used for particular and restricted types
of communication (eg for medical reports, scientific writing, air-
traffic control) and which contain lexical, grammatical, and other
linguistic features which are different from ordinary language (see
REGISTER). In language teaching, decisions must be made as to
whether a learner or group of learners requires a language for
general purposes or for special purposes.
see also ENGLISH FOR SPECIAL PURPOSES
[*Further reading*: Sager, Dungworth, & McDonald 1980]

language shift /'læŋgwɪdʒ 'ʃɪft/ *n*
a change ("shift") from the use of one language to the use of
another language. This often occurs when people migrate to another
country where the main language is different, as in the case of
immigrants to the USA and Australia from non-English-speaking
countries. Language shift may be actively encouraged by official
government policy, for example by restricting the number of
languages used as media of instruction. It may also occur because
another language, usually the main language of the region, is
needed for employment opportunities and wider communication.
Language shift should not be confused with LANGUAGE CHANGE.
see also LANGUAGE PLANNING, MEDIUM OF INSTRUCTION, HOME-SCHOOL
LANGUAGE SWITCH
[*Further reading*: Fishman 1972]

language skills

language skills /'læŋgwɪdʒ skɪlz/ *n*
also **skills**
(in language teaching) the mode or manner in which language is used.
Listening, speaking, reading, and writing are generally called the four
language skills. Sometimes speaking and writing are called the
active/**productive skills** and reading and listening, the passive/**receptive
skills**. Often the skills are divided into subskills, such as discriminating
sounds in connected speech, or understanding relations within a
sentence.
see also MICRO-SKILLS
[*Further reading*: Munby 1978]

language survey /'læŋgwɪdʒ 'sɜːveɪ ‖ 'sɜr-/ *n*
investigation of language use in a country or region. Such a survey
may be carried out to determine, for example:
(a) which languages are spoken in a particular region
(b) for what purposes these languages are used
(c) what proficiency people of different age-groups have in these
languages.
A language survey may also be conducted in order to find out about
the USAGE[1] of a language. For example, The Survey of English
Usage at University College London has been accumulating
evidence about the way Standard British English (see STANDARD
VARIETY) is used in many different situations.
see also LANGUAGE PLANNING

language transfer /'læŋgwɪdʒ 'trænsfɜːʳ/ *n*
the effect of one language on the learning of another.
Two types of language transfer may occur. **Negative transfer**, also
known as **interference**, is the use of a native-language pattern or
rule which leads to an ERROR or inappropriate form in the TARGET
LANGUAGE[1]. For example, a French learner of English may produce
the incorrect sentence *I am here since Monday* instead of *I have
been here since Monday*, because of the transfer of the French
pattern *Je suis ici depuis lundi* ("I am here since Monday"). **Positive
transfer** is transfer which makes learning easier, and may occur
when both the native language and the target language have the
same form. For example, both French and English have the word
table, which can have the same meaning in both languages.
see also COMMUNICATIVE INTERFERENCE, ERROR ANALYSIS, INTERLANGUAGE
[*Further reading*: James 1980; Brown 1980]

language treatment /'læŋgwɪdʒ 'triːtmənt/ *n*
any kind of action which people take about language problems. This
includes LANGUAGE PLANNING by governments and government-
appointed agencies, but also includes such things as: language
requirements for employment in a private company, company policy
on style in business letters, trade-name spelling, publishers' style
sheets, and the treatment of language in dictionaries and usage
guides (see USAGE[2]).

language typology /'læŋgwɪdʒ taɪ'pɒlədʒi ‖ -'pɑ-/ *n*
see TYPOLOGY

language universal /'læŋgwɪdʒ juːnə'vɜːsəl ‖ -ɜr-/ *n*
(in general linguistic use) a language pattern or phenomenon which
occurs in all known languages.
For example, it has been suggested that:
(a) if a language has **dual** number for referring to just two of
something, it also has PLURAL number (for referring to more
than two). This type of universal is sometimes called an
implicational universal.
(b) there is a high probability that the word referring to the female
parent will start with a NASAL consonant, eg /m/ in English
mother, in German *Mutter*, in Swahili *mama*, in Chinese
(Mandarin) *mŭqin*.
The American linguist Chomsky has given the term "language
universal" a special meaning. He distinguishes between **formal
universals**, the types of rule that the grammars of all languages must
have (see GENERATIVE TRANSFORMATIONAL GRAMMAR), and **substantive
universals**, which are actual elements and constructions. These do
not necessarily occur in all languages, but they are available to all
languages. For example, it has been claimed that there is a universal
set of sounds of which each language uses only a certain number.
see also TYPOLOGY
[*Further reading*: Greenberg 1966; Chomsky 1965; Comrie 1981]

language variation /'læŋgwɪdʒ ˌveərɪ'eɪʃən/ *n*
see VARIATION

langue /lɒŋg(*Fr* lāg) ‖ lɔŋg/ *n*
The French word for "language". The term was used by the linguist
Saussure to mean the system of a language, that is the arrangement
of sounds and words which speakers of a language have a shared
knowledge of or, as Saussure said, "agree to use". Langue is the
"ideal" form of a language. Saussure called the actual use of
language by people in speech or writing "parole".
Saussure's distinction between "langue" and "parole" is similar to
Chomsky's distinction between COMPETENCE and PERFORMANCE. But
whereas for Saussure the repository of "langue" is the SPEECH
COMMUNITY, for Chomsky the repository of "competence" is the
"ideal speaker/hearer". So Saussure's distinction is basically
sociolinguistic (see SOCIOLINGUISTICS) whereas Chomsky's is basically
psycholinguistic (see PSYCHOLINGUISTICS).
see also USAGE[1]
[*Further reading*: Saussure 1966]

larynx /'lærɪŋks/ *n* **laryngeal** /ˌlærən'dʒɪəl, lə'rɪndʒəl/ *adj*
a casing of cartilage and muscles in the upper part of the windpipe
(in the throat) which contains the VOCAL CORDS.
see also PLACE OF ARTICULATION
[*Further reading*: Gimson 1980]

lateral /ˈlætərəl/ n

a speech sound (a CONSONANT) which is produced by partially blocking the airstream from the lungs, usually by the tongue, but letting it escape at one or both sides of the blockage.

For example, in English the /l/ in /laɪt/ *light* is a lateral.

see also MANNER OF ARTICULATION, PLACE OF ARTICULATION

[*Further reading*: Gimson 1980]

lateralization /ˌlætərəlaɪˈzeɪʃən/ n

see under BRAIN

Latin alphabet /ˈlætɪn ˈælfəbet/ n

another term for ROMAN ALPHABET

lax /læks/ adj

describes a speech sound (especially a VOWEL) which is produced with comparatively little movement of any part or parts of the VOCAL TRACT, for example the tongue. The vowels /ɪ/ in English *hit* and /ʊ/ in English *put* are lax vowels, as there is comparatively little movement of the tongue when these two vowels are articulated.

In GENERATIVE PHONOLOGY, lax sounds are sometimes marked [-tense] to distinguish them from TENSE[2] sounds.

[*Further reading*: Hyman 1975]

learning /ˈlɜːnɪŋ ‖ ˈlɜr-/ n

see ACQUISITION

learning by deduction /ˌlɜːnɪŋ baɪ dɪˈdʌkʃən ‖ ˌlɜr-/ n

another term for DEDUCTIVE LEARNING

learning by induction /ˌlɜːnɪŋ baɪ ɪnˈdʌkʃən ‖ ˌlɜr-/ n

another term for **inductive learning**

see under DEDUCTIVE LEARNING

learning strategy /ˈlɜːnɪŋ ˈstrætədʒi ‖ ˈlɜr-/ n

(in language learning) a way in which a learner attempts to work out the meanings and uses of words, grammatical rules, and other aspects of a language, for example by the use of GENERALIZATION and INFERENCING.

In FIRST-LANGUAGE learning, a child may not pay attention to grammatical words in a sentence, but in trying to understand a sentence may use the learning strategy that the first mentioned noun in a sentence refers to the person or thing performing an action. The child may then think that the sentence *The boy was chased by the dog* means the same thing as *The boy chased the dog*.

see also COMMUNICATION STRATEGY, COGNITIVE STYLE, HEURISTIC

[*Further reading*: Brown 1973]

learning style /ˈlɜːnɪŋ ˈstaɪl ‖ ˈlɜr-/ n

another term for COGNITIVE STYLE

left-ear advantage /ˈleft ɪəʳ ədˈvɑːntɪdʒ ‖ -ˈvæn-/ n

see under DICHOTIC LISTENING

left hemisphere /left ˈheməsfɪəʳ/ *n*
see under BRAIN

lenis /ˈliːnəs/ *adj*
see under FORTIS

LES /ˌel iː ˈes/ *n*
an abbreviation for LIMITED ENGLISH SPEAKER

lesson plan /ˈlesən ˌplæn/ *n*
a description or outline of (a) the OBJECTIVES a teacher has set for a lesson (b) the activities and procedures the teacher will use to achieve them and the order to be followed, and (c) the materials and resources which will be used.

level[1] /ˈlevəl/ *n*
a layer in a linguistic system, eg word level, phrase level. Often, these levels are considered to form a scale or hierarchy from lower levels containing the smaller linguistic units to higher levels containing larger linguistic units, eg MORPHEME level – WORD level – PHRASE level – CLAUSE level, etc.
It is also sometimes said that the items on each level consist of items on the next lower level: clauses consist of phrases, phrases of words, words of morphemes, etc.
see also RANK, STRATIFICATIONAL GRAMMAR, TAGMEMICS

level[2] *n*
see PITCH LEVEL

lexeme /ˈleksiːm/ *n*
also **lexical item**
the smallest unit in the meaning system of a language that can be distinguished from other similar units. A lexeme is an abstract unit. It can occur in many different forms in actual spoken or written sentences, and is regarded as the same lexeme even when inflected (see INFLECTION).
For example, in English, all inflected forms such as *give, gives, given, giving, gave* would belong to the one lexeme *give*.
Similarly, such expressions as *bury the hatchet*, *hammer and tongs*, *give up*, and *white paper* would each be considered a single lexeme. In a dictionary, each lexeme merits a separate entry or sub-entry.
[*Further reading*: Lyons 1981]

lexical ambiguity /ˈleksɪkəl ˌæmbɪˈgjuːəti/ *n*
see under AMBIGUOUS

lexical density /ˈleksɪkəl ˈdensəti/ *n*
also **Type-Token Ratio**
a measure of the ratio of different words to the total number of words in a text, sometimes used as a measure of the difficulty of a passage or text. Lexical density is normally expressed as a percentage and is calculated by the formula:

$$\text{Lexical density} = \frac{\text{number of separate words}}{\text{total number of words in the text}} \times 100$$

For example, the lexical density of this definition is:

$$\frac{29 \text{ separate words}}{57 \text{ total words}} \times 100 = 50.88$$

see also TYPE

[*Further reading*: Ure 1971]

lexical entry /'leksɪkəl 'entri/ *n*

a term widely used in GENERATIVE TRANSFORMATIONAL GRAMMAR for a word or phrase listed in the lexicon of the BASE COMPONENT and information about it. The information given in a lexical entry usually includes:

(a) its pronunciation (see DISTINCTIVE FEATURE, GENERATIVE PHONOLOGY)
(b) the other linguistic items it may co-occur with in a sentence, eg whether or not a verb can be followed by an OBJECT[1]
(c) its meaning, which is often given in a formalized way, eg <+human> <+male> (see SEMANTIC FEATURES).

[*Further reading*: Leech 1981; Chomsky 1971]

lexical field /'leksɪkəl 'fiːld/ *n*
also **semantic field**

the organization of related words and expressions (see LEXEME) into a system which shows their relationship to one another.

For example, kinship terms such as *father, mother, brother, sister, uncle, aunt* belong to a lexical field whose relevant features include generation, sex, membership of the father's or mother's side of the family, etc.

The absence of a word in a particular place in a lexical field of a language is called a **lexical gap**.

For example, in English there is no singular noun that covers both *cow* and *bull* as *horse* covers *stallion* and *mare*.

see also FIELD THEORY

[*Further reading*: Lyons 1977]

lexical gap /'leksɪkəl 'gæp/ *n*
see under LEXICAL FIELD

lexical item /'leksɪkəl 'aɪtəm/ *n*
another term for LEXEME

lexical meaning /'leksɪkəl 'miːnɪŋ/ *n*
see under CONTENT WORD

lexical verb /'leksɪkəl 'vɜːb ‖ 'vɜrb/ *n*
see under AUXILIARY VERB

lexical word /'leksɪkəl 'wɜːd ‖ 'wɜrd/ *n*
see under CONTENT WORD

lexicogrammar /ˌleksɪkəʊ'græmər/ *n*
see under SYSTEMIC LINGUISTICS

lexicography /ˌleksɪˈkɒgrəfi ‖ -ˈkɑ-/ *n* **lexicographic(al)**
/ˌleksɪkəˈgræfɪkəl/ *adj* **lexicographer** /ˌleksɪˈkɒgrəfəʳ ‖ -kɑ-/ *n*
the compiling of dictionaries.
see also LEXICOLOGY

lexicology /ˌleksɪˈkɒlədʒi ‖ -ˈkɑ-/ *n* **lexicological** /ˌleksɪkəˈlɒdʒɪkəl ‖
-ˈlɑ-/ *adj* **lexicologist** /ˌleksɪˈkɒlədʒəst ‖ -ˈkɑ-/ *n*
the study of the vocabulary items (LEXEMEs) of a language, including
their meanings and relations (see LEXICAL FIELD), and changes in their
form and meaning through time. The discoveries of lexicologists may
be of use to lexicographers.
see also ETYMOLOGY, LEXICOGRAPHY

lexicon[1] /ˈleksɪkən/ *n*
the set of all the words and idioms of any language (see LEXEME).
see also LEXICOGRAPHY, LEXICOLOGY

lexicon[2] *n*
a dictionary, usually of an ancient language such as Latin and
Greek.

lexicon[3] *n*
the words and phrases listed in the BASE COMPONENT of a GENERATIVE
TRANSFORMATIONAL GRAMMAR and information about them.
see also LEXICAL ENTRY

lexis /ˈleksəs/ *n* **lexical** /ˈleksɪkəl/ *adj*
the vocabulary of a language in contrast to its grammar (SYNTAX).
see also LEXEME

liaison /liˈeɪzən ‖ ˈliəzɑn, liˈeɪ-/ *n*
the linking of words in speech, in particular when the second word
begins with a vowel.
For example, in English, the phrase *an egg* is often pronounced
[əˈneg] with no noticeable break between the two words.

Likert Scale /ˈlaɪkət ˈskeɪl/ *n*
see under ATTITUDE SCALE

limited English proficiency /ˈlɪmətəd ˈɪŋglɪʃ prəˈfɪʃənsi/ *n*
see under LIMITED ENGLISH SPEAKER

limited English speaker /ˈlɪmətəd ˈɪŋglɪʃ ˈspiːkəʳ/ *n*
also **LES**
(in BILINGUAL EDUCATION or an ENGLISH AS A SECOND LANGUAGE
PROGRAMME) a person who has some proficiency in English but not
enough to enable him or her to take part fully and successfully in a
class where English is the only MEDIUM OF INSTRUCTION.
Such a person may be said to have **limited English proficiency**.

linear programme /ˈlɪnɪəʳ ˈprəʊgræm/ *n*
see under PROGRAMMED LEARNING

linear syllabus /ˈlɪnɪəʳ ˈsɪləbəs/ n

see under SPIRAL APPROACH

lingua franca /ˌlɪŋgwə ˈfræŋkə/ n

a language that is used for communication between different groups of people, each speaking a different language. The lingua franca could be an internationally used language of communication (eg English), it could be the NATIVE LANGUAGE of one of the groups, or it could be a language which is not spoken natively by any of the groups but has a simplified sentence structure and vocabulary and is often a mixture of two or more languages (see PIDGIN). The term *lingua franca* (Italian for "Frankish tongue") originated in the Mediterranean region in the Middle Ages among crusaders and traders of different language backgrounds.

The term **auxiliary language** is sometimes used as a synonym for lingua franca.

[*Further reading*: Todd 1984]

linguistically disadvantaged /lɪŋˈgwɪstɪkli ˌdɪsədˈvɑːntɪdʒd ‖ -ˈvæn-/ *adj*

a term sometimes used to refer to a person who has an insufficient command of the dominant language in a country. This term is not favoured by linguists since it suggests the person's home language is not useful or is unimportant.

see also DEFICIT HYPOTHESIS

linguistic analysis /lɪŋˈgwɪstɪk əˈnæləsəs/ n

investigation into the structure and functions of a particular language or language variety (see LANGUAGE²) or of language in general as a system of human communication (see LANGUAGE¹).

linguistic insecurity /lɪŋˈgwɪstɪk ɪnsəˈkjʊərəti/ n

a feeling of insecurity experienced by speakers or writers about some aspect of their language use or about the variety of language they speak. This may result, for instance, in MODIFIED SPEECH, when speakers attempt to alter their way of speaking in order to sound more like the speakers of a prestige variety.

see also SOCIOLECT

linguistic method /lɪŋˈgwɪstɪk ˈmeθəd/ n

a term used to refer to several methods of teaching first-language reading which claim to be based on principles of linguistics, and in particular to methods which reflect the views of two American linguists, Leonard Bloomfield and Charles Fries.

They argued that since the written language is based on the spoken language, the relationship between speech and written language should be emphasized in the teaching of reading. This led to reading materials which made use of words which had a regular sound-spelling correspondence and in which there was a systematic introduction to regular and irregular spelling patterns. In recent

years linguists have not supported any particular method for the teaching of reading.
[*Further reading*: Wardhaugh 1969]

linguistic relativity /lɪŋ'gwɪstɪk ˌrelə'tɪvəti/ *n*
a belief which was held by some scholars that the way people view the world is determined wholly or partly by the structure of their NATIVE LANGUAGE. As this hypothesis was strongly put forward by the American anthropological linguists Sapir and Whorf, it has often been called the **Sapir-Whorf hypothesis** or **Whorfian hypothesis**.
see also ANTHROPOLOGICAL LINGUISTICS

linguistics /lɪŋ'gwɪstɪks/ *n* **linguist** /'lɪŋgwɪst/ *n* **linguistic** /lɪŋ'gwɪstɪk/ *adj*
the study of language as a system of human communication. Although studies of language phenomena have been carried out for centuries, it is only fairly recently that linguistics has been accepted as an independent discipline. Linguistics now covers a wide field with different approaches and different areas of investigation, for example sound systems (PHONETICS, PHONOLOGY), sentence structure (SYNTAX), and meaning systems (SEMANTICS, PRAGMATICS, FUNCTIONS OF LANGUAGE).
In recent years, new branches of linguistics have developed in combination with other disciplines, eg ANTHROPOLOGICAL LINGUISTICS, PSYCHOLINGUISTICS, SOCIOLINGUISTICS.
see also APPLIED LINGUISTICS, COMPARATIVE LINGUISTICS, COMPUTATIONAL LINGUISTICS, CONTRASTIVE ANALYSIS, DIACHRONIC LINGUISTICS, GENERATIVE TRANSFORMATIONAL GRAMMAR, STRUCTURAL LINGUISTICS, SYSTEMIC LINGUISTICS, TAGMEMICS, PRAGUE SCHOOL, STRATIFICATIONAL GRAMMAR, TEXT LINGUISTICS

linguistic units /lɪŋ'gwɪstɪk 'juːnəts/ *n*
parts of a language system. Linguistic units can be the distinctive sounds of a language (PHONEMES), words, phrases, or sentences, or they can be larger units such as the UTTERANCES in a conversation.
see also CHUNKING, DISCOURSE, DISCOURSE ANALYSIS

linking verb /'lɪŋkɪŋ 'vɜːb ‖ 'vɜrb/ *n*
another term for COPULA

lipreading /'lɪp,riːdɪŋ/ *n* **lipread** /'lɪp,riːd/ *v*
also **speech reading**
a method used by deaf people and others to identify what a speaker is saying by studying the movements of the lips and face muscles.

liquid /'lɪkwəd/ *n, adj*
(used particularly by American linguists) a speech sound (a CONSONANT) such as /l/ in /laɪt/ *light* and /r/ in /red/ *red*. Liquids are FRICTIONLESS CONTINUANTS but not NASALS.
see also LATERAL
[*Further reading*: Hyman 1975]

literacy /'lɪtərəsi/ *n* **literate** /'lɪtərət/ *adj*
the ability to read and write in a language. The inability to read or write is known as **illiteracy**.
Functional literacy refers to the ability to use reading and writing skills sufficiently well for the purposes and activities which normally require literacy in adult life or in a person's social position. An inability to do this is known as **functional illiteracy**. People who are functionally illiterate are illiterate for all practical purposes. They may be able to write their names and read simple signs, but they can do little else. A person who is able to read and write in two languages is sometimes called (a) **biliterate**.
[*Further reading*: Hillerich 1978]

literal comprehension /'lɪtərəl ˌkɒmprɪ'henʃən ‖ ˌkɑm-/ *n*
see under READING

literal translation /'lɪtərəl trænz'leɪʃən, træns-/ *n*
see under TRANSLATION

literary culture /'lɪtərəri 'kʌltʃəʳ ‖ 'lɪtəreri/ *n*
see under ORAL CULTURE

loan translation /'ləʊn trænz'leɪʃən, træns-/ *n*
another term for CALQUE

loan word /'ləʊn ˌwɜːd ‖ ˌwɜrd/ *n*
see under BORROWING

local error /'ləʊkəl 'erəʳ/ *n*
see under GLOBAL ERROR

locative case /'lɒkətɪv ˌkeɪs ‖ 'lɑ-/ *n*
In CASE GRAMMAR, the noun or noun phrase which refers to the location of the action of the verb is in the locative case.
For example, in the sentence:
    Irene put the magazines on the table.
the table is in the locative case.
[*Further reading*: Fillmore 1968]

locutionary act /ləʊ'kjuːʃənəri 'ækt ‖ -neri/ *n*
A distinction is made by Austin in the theory of SPEECH ACTs between three different types of act involved in or caused by the utterance of a sentence.
A locutionary act is the saying of something which is meaningful and can be understood.
For example, saying the sentence *Shoot the snake* is a locutionary act if hearers understand the words *shoot*, *the*, *snake* and can identify the particular snake referred to. An **illocutionary act** is using a sentence to perform a function. For example *Shoot the snake* may be intended as an order or a piece of advice.

A **perlocutionary act** is the results or effects that are produced by means of saying something. For example, shooting the snake would be a perlocutionary act.

Austin's three-part distinction is less frequently used than a two-part distinction between the propositional content of a sentence (the PROPOSITION(s) which a sentence expresses or implies) and the **illocutionary force** or intended effects of speech acts (their function as requests, commands, orders etc).

[*Further reading*: Austin 1962; Searle 1981]

locutionary meaning /ləʊˈkjuːʃənəri ˈmiːnɪŋ ‖ -neri/ *n*
see under SPEECH ACT

logical subject /ˈlɒdʒɪkəl ˈsʌbdʒɪkt ‖ ˈlɑ-/ *n*
a NOUN PHRASE[1] which describes, typically, the performer of the action. Some linguists make a distinction between the grammatical subject (see SUBJECT) and the logical subject.
For example, in the passive sentence:
   The cake was eaten by Vera.
the cake is the grammatical subject but *Vera* is the logical subject as she is the performer of the action. In:
   Vera ate the cake.
Vera would be both the grammatical and the logical subject.
see also VOICE[1]

longitudinal method /ˌlɒndʒəˈtjuːdənəl ˈmeθəd ‖ ˌlɑndʒəˈtuː-/ *n*
also **longitudinal study** /ˌlɒndʒəˈtjuːdənəl ˈstʌdi ‖ ˌlɑndʒəˈtuː-/
see under CROSS-SECTION(AL) METHOD

long term memory /ˈlɒŋtɜːm ˈmeməri ‖ ˈlɔŋtɜrm/ *n*
see under MEMORY

look-and-say method /ˌlʊk ən ˈseɪ ˈmeθəd/ *n*
a method for teaching children to read, especially in their FIRST LANGUAGE, which is similar to the WHOLE-WORD-METHOD except that words are always taught in association with a picture or object and the pronunciation of the word is always required.

Low variety /ˈləʊ vəˈraɪəti/ *n*
see under DIGLOSSIA

low vowel /ˈləʊ ˈvaʊəl/ *n*
another term for **open vowel**
see under VOWEL

Lozanov method /ˈləʊzənɒf ˈmeθəd ‖ -ɑf/ *n*
another term for SUGGESTOPAEDIA

LSP /ˌel es ˈpiː/ *n*
an abbreviation for LANGUAGES FOR SPECIAL PURPOSES

L-variety /ˈel vəˈraɪəti/ *n*
see under DIGLOSSIA

machine translation /məˈʃiːn trænzˈleɪʃən, træns-/ *n*
also **mechanical translation**
the use of machines (usually computers) to translate texts from one
language to another.
Linguists and specialists in COMPUTATIONAL LINGUISTICS have worked on
machine translation for 30 years with limited results, but many
advances have been made in the development of some areas
relevant to machine translation (eg analysis of texts for different
lexical, semantic, and grammatical characteristics).

macro-sociolinguistics /ˈmækrəʊ ˌsəʊʃiəʊlɪŋˈgwɪstɪks, ˌsəʊʃəʊ-/ *n*
see under SOCIOLINGUISTICS

macro-structure /ˈmækrəʊ ˌstrʌktʃəʳ/ *n*
another term for SCHEME

main clause /ˈmeɪn ˈklɔːz/ *n*
see under DEPENDENT CLAUSE

maintenance bilingual education /ˈmeɪntənəns baɪˈlɪŋwəl
ˌedjʊˈkeɪʃən ‖ ˌedʒə-/ *n*
see under BILINGUAL EDUCATION

majority language /məˈdʒɒrəti ˈlæŋgwɪdʒ ‖ məˈdʒɑ-/ *n*
the language spoken by the majority of the population in a country,
such as English in the USA. A language spoken by a group of
people who form a minority within a country is known as a **minority
language**, such as Italian and Spanish in the USA.
see also COMMUNITY LANGUAGE, NATIONAL LANGUAGE

manner of articulation /ˈmænəʳ əv ɑːtɪkjʊˈleɪʃən ‖ ɑrtɪkjə-/ *n*
the way in which a speech sound is produced by the speech organs.
There are different ways of producing a speech sound. With
CONSONANTS the airstream may be:
(a) stopped and released suddenly (a STOP), eg /t/
(b) allowed to escape with friction (a FRICATIVE), eg /f/
(c) stopped and then released slowly with friction (an AFFRICATE), eg
/dʒ/ as in /dʒem/ *gem*.
The vocal cords may be vibrating (a voiced speech sound) or not (a
voiceless speech sound) (see VOICE²).
With VOWELS, in addition to the position of the tongue in the mouth,
the lips may be:
(a) rounded, eg for /uː/ in /ʃuː/ *shoe*; or
(b) spread, eg for /iː/ in /miːn/ *mean*.
see also FRICTIONLESS CONTINUANT, LATERAL, NASAL, PLACE OF
ARTICULATION
[Further reading: Gimson 1980]

markedness /'mɑːkədnəs/ *n* **marked** /mɑːkt/ *adj*
the theory that in the languages of the world certain linguistic
elements are more basic, natural, and frequent (**unmarked**) than
others which are referred to as "marked". For example, in English,
sentences which have the order:
  Subject – Verb – Object: *I dislike such people.*
are considered to be unmarked, whereas sentences which have the
order:
  Object – Subject – Verb: *Such people I dislike.*
are considered to be marked.
The concept of markedness has been discussed particularly within
GENERATIVE PHONOLOGY. Chomsky and Halle suggest that /p, t, k, s,
n/ are the least marked consonants and that they occur in most
languages. Other consonants such as /v, z/ are considered as more
highly marked and less common.
see also NATURALNESS
[*Further reading*: Hyman 1975; Chomsky & Halle 1968]

mass noun /'mæs 'naʊn/ *n*
see under COUNTABLE NOUN

matched guise technique /ˌmætʃt 'gaɪz tek'niːk/ *n*
(in studies of LANGUAGE ATTITUDES) the use of recorded voices of
people speaking first in one dialect or language and then in another;
that is, in two "guises". For example, BILINGUAL French Canadians
may first speak in French and then in English. The recordings are
played to listeners who do not know that the two samples of speech
are from the same person and who judge the two guises of the same
speaker as though they were judging two separate speakers each
belonging to a different ethnic or national group. The reactions of
the listeners to the speakers in one guise are compared to reactions
to the other guise to reveal attitudes towards different language or
dialect groups, whose members may be considered more or less
intelligent, friendly, co-operative, reliable.
[*Further reading*: Giles & Powesland 1975; Lambert 1967]

mathematical linguistics /ˌmæθəˈmætɪkəl lɪŋˈgwɪstɪks/ *n*
a branch of linguistics which makes use of statistical and
mathematical methods to study the linguistic structure of written or
spoken texts. This includes the study of the frequency of occurrence
of linguistic items (see FREQUENCY COUNT) and the study of literary style.
see also COMPUTATIONAL LINGUISTICS
[*Further reading*: Herdan 1964]

matrix /'meɪtrɪks/ *n*
a table consisting of rows and columns which is used in linguistics to
display data or results of an analysis.
For an example, see the matrix used in this dictionary under the
entry for IMPLICATIONAL SCALING.
The plural of *matrix* is *matrices* /'meɪtrəsiːz/.

mean /miːn/ *n*
also **meanscore, X̄**
the arithmetic average of a set of scores. The mean is the sum of all
the scores divided by the total number of items. The mean is the
most commonly used and most widely applicable measure of the
CENTRAL TENDENCY of a distribution.
If the scores on a test of four items are as follows:
2, 5, 7, 10
the mean is
$$\frac{2 + 5 + 7 + 10}{4} = \frac{24}{4} = 6.$$
see also MEDIAN, MODE

meaning /ˈmiːnɪŋ/ *n*
(in linguistics) what a language expresses about the world we live in
or any possible or imaginary world.
The study of meaning is called SEMANTICS. Semantics is usually
concerned with the analysis of the meaning of words, phrases, or
sentences (see CONNOTATION, DENOTATION, LEXICAL FIELD, SEMANTIC
FEATURES) and sometimes with the meaning of utterances in
discourse (see DISCOURSE ANALYSIS) or the meaning of a whole text.
see also FUNCTIONS OF LANGUAGE[1, 2], PRAGMATICS

meaningful drill /ˈmiːnɪŋfəlˈdrɪl/ *n*
In language teaching, a distinction between different types of DRILLS
is made according to the degree of control the drill makes over the
response produced by the student.
A **mechanical drill** is one where there is complete control over the
student's response, and where comprehension is not required in
order to produce a correct response. For example:

Teacher	Student
book	*Give me the book.*
ladle	*Give me the ladle.*

A meaningful drill is one in which there is still control over the
response, but understanding is required in order for the student to
produce a correct response. For example:

Teacher reads a sentence	Student chooses a response
I'm hot.	*I'll get you something to eat.*
I'm cold.	*I'll turn on the air conditioning.*
I'm thirsty.	*I'll get you something to drink.*
I'm hungry.	*I'll turn on the heater.*

A **communicative drill** is one in which the type of response is
controlled but the student provides his or her own content or
information. For example in practising the past tense, the teacher
may ask a series of questions:

Teacher	Student completes cues
What time did you get up on Sunday?	*I got up _____*

What did you have for breakfast?	*I had _____*
What did you do after breakfast?	*I _____*

[*Further reading*: Paulston 1980]

meaningful learning /'miːnɪŋfəl 'lɜːnɪŋ ‖ 'lɜr-/ *n*

(in COGNITIVE PSYCHOLOGY) learning in which learned items become part of a person's mental system of concepts and thought processes. The psychologist Ausubel contrasted meaningful learning with ROTE LEARNING and other types of learning in which learned items are not integrated into existing mental structures. Meaningful learning is said to be important in classroom language learning.

[*Further reading*: Ausubel 1968; Brown 1980]

meaning potential /'miːnɪŋ pə,tenʃəl/ *n*

a term used by Halliday to refer to the semantic system in language. The "semantic system" means the range of meaning alternatives which are open to a speaker when he or she wishes to communicate with others. Grammar and vocabulary (the "lexicogrammatical" system) express this meaning in words and these are then turned into sounds or writing through the phonological system or the orthographical system.

see also DEVELOPMENTAL FUNCTIONS OF LANGUAGE, FUNCTIONS OF LANGUAGE[2], SYSTEMIC LINGUISTICS

[*Further reading*: Halliday 1978]

mean length of utterance /'miːn 'leŋθ əv 'ʌtərəns/ *n*
also **MLU, mean utterance length**

(in language ACQUISITION research) a measure of the linguistic complexity of children's utterances, especially during the early stages of FIRST-LANGUAGE learning. It is measured by counting the average length of the utterances a child produces, using the MORPHEME rather than the word as the unit of measurement. As a simple countable measure of grammatical development the MLU has been found to be a more reliable basis for comparing children's language development than the age of the children.

[*Further reading*: Brown 1973]

meanscore /'miːnskɔːr/ *n*
another term for MEAN

mean utterance length /'miːn 'ʌtərəns 'leŋθ/ *n*
another term for MEAN LENGTH OF UTTERANCE

mechanical drill /mɪ'kænɪkəl 'drɪl/ *n*
see under MEANINGFUL DRILL

mechanical translation /mɪ'kænɪkəl trænz'leɪʃən, træns-/ *n*
another term for MACHINE TRANSLATION

medial /'miːdɪəl/ *adj*
occurring in the middle of a linguistic unit.
For example, in English the /ɪ/ in /pɪt/ *pit* is in a medial position in the word.
see also INITIAL, FINAL

median /'miːdɪən/ *n*
the value of the middle item or score when the scores in a SAMPLE are arranged in order from lowest to highest. The median is therefore the score which divides the sample into two equal parts. It is the most appropriate measure of CENTRAL TENDENCY for data arranged in an "ordinal scale" or a "rank scale" (see SCALE).
For example the median of the following set of scores is 5:
    2 4 5 7 10
see also MEAN, MODE

mediation theory /ˌmiːdɪˈeɪʃən ˈθɪəri/ *n*
(in psychology) a theory which explains certain types of learning in terms of links which are formed between a "stimulus" and a "response" (see STIMULUS-RESPONSE THEORY). A simple model of mediation learning is shown below, where Stimulus A becomes linked to Response C, through the mediation of B.

	Stimulus	Response
Learn	A	B
Then learn	B	C
Test whether	A	C

Mediation theories exist in many complex forms and have been used to explain different aspects of VERBAL LEARNING, thought, and language learning. Such theories are particularly associated with BEHAVIOURISM.
[*Further reading*: Osgood 1957; Mowrer 1960]

medium /'miːdɪəm/ *n*
the means by which a message is conveyed from one person to another.
For example, an invitation to a party can be made in writing or in speech.
The plural of *medium* is *media* /'miːdɪə/ or *mediums*.
see also MESSAGE, DECODING, ENCODING

medium of instruction /'miːdɪəm əv ɪnˈstrʌkʃən/ *n*
the language used in education. In many countries, the medium of instruction is the STANDARD VARIETY of the main or NATIONAL LANGUAGE of the country, eg French in France. In some countries, the medium of instruction may be different in various parts of the country, as in Belgium where both French and Dutch are used. In MULTILINGUAL countries or regions there may be a choice, or there may be schools in which some subjects are taught in one language and other subjects in another, as in Singapore and Hong Kong.

The plural of *medium of instruction* is *media of instruction* or *mediums of instruction*.

see also BILINGUAL EDUCATION

membershipping /ˈmembəʃɪpɪŋ ‖ -ər-/ *n* **membership** /ˈmembəʃɪp ‖ -ər-/ *v*

classifying a person as a member of a group or category, eg shop assistant, student, or resident of a particular town. Once a category has been assigned to a person, conversation with that person may be affected.

For example, a visitor to a town may ask a passer-by whom he or she, correctly or incorrectly, memberships as a local resident: *Could you please tell me how to get to the station?* Wrong membershipping may result in misunderstanding or may cause annoyance, eg if a customer in a department store is wrongly membershipped as a shop assistant.

[*Further reading*: Coulthard 1985; Schegloff 1972]

memorizing /ˈmeməraɪzɪŋ/ *n* **memorize** *v* **memorization** /ˌmeməraɪˈzeɪʃən/ *n*

the process of establishing information etc in memory. The term "memorizing" usually refers to conscious processes. Memorizing may involve ROTE LEARNING, practice, ASSOCIATIVE LEARNING, etc.

memory /ˈmeməri/ *n*

the mental capacity to store information, either for short or long periods. Two different types of memory are often distinguished:

(a) **Short-term memory** refers to that part of the memory where information which is received is stored for short periods of time while it is being analysed and interpreted. Once the message or information in an utterance is understood the data may become part of permanent memory (or **long term memory**). The utterance itself is now no longer needed and may fade from short-term memory.

(b) **Long-term memory** is that part of the memory system where information is stored more permanently. Information in long-term memory may not be stored in the same form in which it is received. For example, a listener may hear sentence A below, and be able to repeat it accurately immediately after hearing it. The listener uses short-term memory to do this. On trying to remember the sentence a few days later the listener may produce sentence B, using information in long-term memory which is in a different form from the original message.

A *The car the doctor parked by the side of the road was struck by a passing bus.*

B *The doctor's car was hit by a bus.*

see also EPISODIC MEMORY

[*Further reading*: Clark & Clark 1977]

mentalism /ˈmentəlɪzəm/ *n* **mentalist** /ˈmentələst/ *n*, *adj*
the theory that a human being possesses a mind which has
consciousness, ideas, etc, and that the mind can influence the
behaviour of the body.
see also INNATIST HYPOTHESIS

mesolect /ˈmesəʊlekt/ *n*
see under POST-CREOLE CONTINUUM

message /ˈmesɪdʒ/ *n*
what is conveyed in speech or writing from one person to one or
more other people. The message may not always be stated in verbal
form but can be conveyed by other means, eg a wink, gestures.
A distinction can be made between message form and message
content. In a spoken request, for example, the message form is how
the request is made (eg type of sentence structure, use or non-use of
courtesy words, type of intonation) and the message content is what
is actually requested (eg the loan of some money).
see also DECODING, ENCODING, KEY[1]
[*Further reading*: Hymes 1974]

meta-language /ˈmetəˌlæŋgwɪdʒ/ *n*
the language used to analyse or describe a language. For example,
the sentence: *In English, the phoneme /b/ is a voiced bilabial stop* is
in meta-language. It explains that the *b*-sound in English is made
with vibration of the vocal cords and with the two lips stopping the
airstream from the lungs.

metaphor /ˈmetəfəʳ, -fɔːʳ ǁ -fɔr/ *n*
see under FIGURE OF SPEECH

metathesis /məˈtæθəsəs/ *n* **metathesize** /məˈtæθəsaɪz/ *v*
change in the order of two sounds in a word, eg /flɪm/ for /fɪlm/
film. Metathesis sometimes occurs in the speech of language learners
but it may also occur with native speakers. When a metathesized
form becomes commonly and regularly used by most native speakers
of a language, it may lead to a change in the word. For example,
Modern English *bird* developed by metathesis from Old English *brid*
"young bird".

method /ˈmeθəd/ *n*
(in language teaching) a way of teaching a language which is based
on systematic principles and procedures, ie, which is an application
of views on how a language is best taught and learned.
Different methods of language teaching such as the DIRECT METHOD,
the AUDIOLINGUAL METHOD, the AUDIO-VISUAL METHOD, the GRAMMAR
TRANSLATION METHOD, the SILENT WAY and COMMUNICATIVE APPROACH
result from different views of:
(a) the nature of language
(b) the nature of language learning
(c) goals and OBJECTIVES in teaching

(d) the type of SYLLABUS to use

(e) the role of teachers, learners, and instructional materials

(f) the techniques and procedures to use.

see also APPROACH

[*Further reading*: Richards & Rodgers 1982]

methodology /ˌmeθəˈdɒlədʒi ‖ -ˈdɑ-/ *n*

(1) (in language teaching) the study of the practices and procedures used in teaching, and the principles and beliefs that underlie them. Methodology includes:

(a) study of the nature of LANGUAGE SKILLS (eg reading, writing, speaking, listening) and procedures for teaching them

(b) study of the preparation of LESSON PLANS, materials, and textbooks for teaching language skills

(c) the evaluation and comparison of language teaching METHODS (eg the AUDIOLINGUAL METHOD)

(2) such practices, procedures, principles, and beliefs themselves. One can for example criticize or praise the methodology of a particular language course.

see also CURRICULUM, SYLLABUS

[*Further reading*: Rivers 1981]

micro-skills /ˈmaɪkrəʊ ˌskɪlz/ *n*
also enabling skills, part skills

(in language teaching) a term sometimes used to refer to the individual processes and abilities which are used in carrying out a complex activity.

For example, among the micro-skills used in listening to a lecture are: identifying the purpose and scope of the lecture; identifying the role of conjunctions, etc, in signalling relationships between different parts of the lecture; recognizing the functions of PITCH and INTONATION. For the purposes of SYLLABUS DESIGN, reading, writing, speaking, and listening may be further analysed into different micro-skills.

see also LANGUAGE SKILLS

[*Further reading*: Munby 1978]

micro-sociolinguistics /ˈmaɪkrəʊ ˌsəʊʃiəʊlɪŋˈgwɪstɪks, ˌsəʊʃəʊ-/ *n*
see under SOCIOLINGUISTICS

microteaching /ˈmaɪkrəʊˌtiːtʃɪŋ/ *n*

a technique used in the training of teachers, in which different teaching skills are practised under carefully controlled conditions. It is based on the idea that teaching is a complex set of activities which can be broken down into different skills. These skills can be practised individually, and later combined with others. Usually in microteaching, one trainee teacher teaches a part of a lesson to a small group of his or her classmates. The lesson may be recorded on tape or videotape and later discussed in individual or group tutorials. Each session generally focusses on a specific teaching task.

Microteaching thus involves a scaling-down of teaching because class size, lesson length, and teaching complexity are all reduced.

mid vowel /'mɪd 'vaʊəl/ *n*
see under VOWEL

mim-mem method /ˌmɪm 'mem 'meθəd/ *n*
a term for the AUDIOLINGUAL METHOD, because the method uses exercises such as pattern practice (see DRILL) and dialogues which make use of the *mim*icry (imitation) and *mem*orization of material presented as a model.

minimal-distance principle /'mɪnəməl 'dɪstəns 'prɪnsəpəl/ *n*
the principle that in English, a COMPLEMENT or a NON-FINITE VERB refers to the NOUN PHRASE[1] which is closest to it (ie which is minimally distant from it). For example in the following sentences:
   John wants Mary to study.
   Penny made the children happy.
the non-finite verb *to study* refers to *Mary* (not *John*) and the complement *happy* refers to *the children* (not *Penny*).
Some sentences do not follow the principle, however. For example, in:
   John promised Mary to wash the clothes.
the non-finite verb phrase *to wash the clothes* refers to *John* (not *Mary*). Such sentences are believed to cause comprehension problems for children learning English.
[*Further reading*: Chomsky 1969]

minimal pair /'mɪnəməl 'peər/ *n*
two words in a language which differ from each other by only one distinctive sound (one PHONEME) and which also differ in meaning. For example, the English words *bear* and *pear* are a minimal pair as they differ in meaning and in their initial phonemes /b/ and /p/. The term "minimal pair" is also sometimes used of any two pieces of language that are identical except for a specific feature or group of related features.
For example, the sentences:
   The boy is here.
   The boys are here.
may be called a minimal pair because they are the same except for the contrast between singular and plural expressed in both noun and verb.

minimal pair drill /ˌmɪnəməl 'peər 'drɪl/ *n*
a DRILL in which MINIMAL PAIRS are practised together, especially in order to help students to learn to distinguish a sound contrast. For example if a teacher wanted to practise the contrast between /b/ and /p/, the teacher could (a) explain how the sounds differ; (b) present pairs of words containing the contrast, for listening practice; eg *bore – pour, big – pig, buy – pie*; (c) get the students to show that they

know which member of the pair they have heard; (d) get them to pronounce such pairs themselves.

Minimal Terminable Unit /'mɪnəməl 'tɜːmɪnəbəl 'juːnət ‖ -ɜr-/ *n*
another term for T-UNIT

minority language /maɪ'nɒrəti 'læŋgwɪdʒ ‖ mə'nɔ-, mə'nɑ-/ *n*
see under MAJORITY LANGUAGE

minority language group /maɪ'nɒrəti 'læŋgwɪdʒ 'gruːp ‖ mə'nɔ-, mə'nɑ-/ *n*
another term for LANGUAGE MINORITY GROUP

miscue /mɪs'kjuː/ *n*
see under MISCUE ANALYSIS

miscue analysis /mɪs'kjuː ə'næləsəs/ *n*
the analysis of errors or unexpected responses which readers make in reading, as part of the study of the nature of the reading process in children learning to read their mother tongue.
Among the different types of **miscue** which occur are:
(a) insertion miscue: the adding of a word which is not present in the text (eg the child may read *Mr Barnaby was a busy old man* instead of *Mr Barnaby was a busy man*).
(b) reversal miscue: the reader reverses the order of words (eg the child reads *Mrs Barnaby was a rich kind old lady* instead of *Mrs Barnaby was a kind rich old lady*).
[*Further reading*: Goodman & Goodman 1977]

mistake /mɪ'steɪk/ *n*
see under ERROR

MLAT /ˌem el eɪ 'tiː/ *n*
an abbreviation for the *M*odern *L*anguage *A*ptitude *T*est, a test of LANGUAGE APTITUDE

MLU[1] /ˌem el 'juː/ *n*
an abbreviation for MEAN LENGTH OF UTTERANCE

MLU[2]
an abbreviation for *M*ulti-*W*ord *L*exical *U*nit, a LEXEME consisting of more than one word. For example, COMPOUND NOUNS and PHRASAL VERBS are MLUs.

modal /'məʊdl/ *n*
also **modal verb** /ˌməʊdl 'vɜːb ‖ 'vɜrb/, **modal auxiliary** /ˌməʊdl ɔːg'zɪljəri, ɔːk- ‖ ɔg'zɪljəri, -'zɪləri/
any of the AUXILIARY VERBS which indicate attitudes of the speaker/writer towards the state or event expressed by another verb, ie which indicate different types of **modality**. The following are modal verbs in English:
may, might, can, could, must, have (got) to, will, would, shall, should

Modal meanings are shown in the following examples; all are in contrast to simple assertion:

I may be wrong. (*may* = possibility)
That will be Tom at the door. (*will*=prediction)
You can smoke here. (*can*=permission)
I can play the piano. (*can*=ability)

Modality can be expressed in other ways, too:

I may be wrong. = *Perhaps I'm wrong.*

modality /məʊˈdæləti/ *n*
see under MODAL

mode /məʊd/ *n*
the most frequently occurring score or scores in a SAMPLE. It is a measure of the CENTRAL TENDENCY of a DISTRIBUTION. For example, in the following test scores, the mode is equal to 20.

score	number of students with the score
10	2
20	10
30	3
40	4
50	3

A frequency distribution with two modes is known as a **bimodal distribution**, as when the two most frequently occurring scores are 60 and 40. The mode(s) of a distribution can be pictured graphically as the "peaks" in the distribution. A NORMAL DISTRIBUTION has only one peak. The following shows a bimodal distribution:

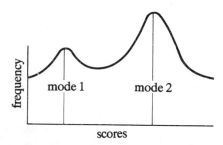

model[1] /ˈmɒdl ‖ ˈmɑdl/ *n*
(in linguistics) a systematic way of setting out some aspects or features of language in order to show their structure or function. For example, the whole sound system of a language may be represented by a model using contrastive features (DISTINCTIVE FEATURES), such as [+consonantal] and [−consonantal], [+nasal] and [−nasal].

In its wider sense, the term may mean the representation of a theory, eg the "Communication Model" (see INFORMATION THEORY), the "Aspects Model" (see GENERATIVE TRANSFORMATIONAL GRAMMAR).

model[2] *n*

(in language teaching) someone or something which is used as a standard or goal for the learner, eg the pronunciation of an educated native speaker.

see also MODELLING

modelling /'mɒdəlɪŋ ‖ 'mɑ-/ *n*

providing a model (eg a sentence, a question) as an example for someone learning a language.

In SECOND-LANGUAGE and FOREIGN-LANGUAGE learning, some teaching methods emphasize the need for teachers to provide accurate models for learners to imitate, for example the AUDIO-LINGUAL METHOD.

In FIRST-LANGUAGE learning, parents sometimes provide correct sentences for children to repeat, and this may be referred to as modelling. The effect of modelling on children's language development has been compared with that of **expansion** and **prompting**.

In expansion the parent repeats part of what the child has said, but expands it. The expansion usually contains grammatical words which the child did not use. This is thought to be one of the ways children develop their knowledge of the rules of a language. For example:

Child: *Doggy sleeping.*
Parent: *Yes, the doggy is sleeping.*

Prompting refers to stating a sentence in a different way. For example:

Parent: *What do you want?*
Child: (no answer)
Parent: *You want what?*

By presenting the question in two different forms the parent may assist the child in understanding the structure of questions and other language items.

[*Further reading*: Dale 1975]

mode of discourse /ˌməʊd əv 'dɪskɔːs ‖ -ɔr-/ *n*

see under SOCIAL CONTEXT

modified speech /'mɒdɪfaɪd 'spiːtʃ ‖ 'mɑ-/ *n*

a term used by linguists to describe speech which is deliberately changed in an attempt to make it sound more educated or refined. The change is usually temporary and the speaker lapses back to his or her normal speech pattern.

modifier /'mɒdɪfaɪəʳ ‖ 'mɑ-/ *n* **modification** /ˌmɒdɪfɪ'keɪʃən ‖ ˌmɑ-/ *n* **modify** /'mɒdɪfaɪ ‖ 'mɑ-/ *v*

a word or group of words which gives further information about ("modifies") another word or group of words (the HEAD).

Modification may occur in a NOUN PHRASE[1], a VERB PHRASE, an ADJECTIVAL PHRASE, etc.

(a) Modifiers before the head are called **premodifiers**, for example *expensive* in *this expensive camera*.

(b) Modifiers after the head are called **postmodifiers**, for example
with a stumpy tail in *The cat with a stumpy tail*.
Halliday restricts the term "modifier" to premodifiers and calls
postmodifiers QUALIFIERS.
In earlier grammars, the term "modifier" referred only to words,
phrases, or clauses which modified verbs, adjectives, or other
adverbials, but not to those which modified nouns.
[*Further reading*: Quirk et al 1985; Halliday 1982]

monitor hypothesis /ˈmɒnətəʳ haɪˈpɒθəsəs ‖ ˈmɑ- -ˈpɑ-/ *n*
also **monitor model of second language development** /ˈmɒnətəʳ
ˈmɒdl əv ˈsekənd ˈlæŋgwɪdʒ dɪˈveləpmənt ‖ ˈmɑ- ˈmɑdl/
a theory proposed by Krashen which distinguishes two distinct
processes in second and foreign language development and use. One,
called "acquisition", is said to be a subconscious process which
leads to the development of "competence" and is not dependent
on the teaching of grammatical rules. The second process,
called "learning", refers to the conscious study and knowledge
of grammatical rules. In producing utterances, learners initially use
their acquired system of rules. Learning and learned rules have only
one function: to serve as a monitor or editor of utterances initiated
by the acquired system, and learning cannot lead to acquisition.
see also INPUT HYPOTHESIS
[*Further reading*: Krashen 1978]

monitoring /ˈmɒnətərɪŋ ‖ ˈmɑ-/ *n* **monitor** *v*
listening to one's own UTTERANCES to compare what was said with
what was intended, and to make corrections if necessary.
People generally try to speak fluently (see FLUENCY) and
appropriately (see APPROPRIATENESS), and try to make themselves
understood. The interjections and self-corrections that speakers
make while talking show that monitoring is taking place, and are
usually for the purposes of making meaning clearer. For example:
He is, well, rather difficult.
Can I have, say, a glass of beer.
They own, I mean rent, a lovely house.
see also AUDITORY FEEDBACK, PAUSING
[*Further reading*: Clark & Clark 1977]

monolingual /ˌmɒnəˈlɪŋgwəl ‖ ˌmɑ-/ *n, adj* **monolingualism** *n*
(1) a person who knows and uses only one language.
(2) a person who has an active knowledge of only one language,
though perhaps a passive knowledge of others.
see also ACTIVE/PASSIVE LANGUAGE KNOWLEDGE, BILINGUAL, MULTILINGUAL

monophthong /ˈmɒnəfθɒŋ ‖ ˈmɑnəfθɔːŋ/ *n* **monophthongal**
/ˌmɒnəfˈθɒŋgəl ‖ ˌmɑnəfˈθɔːŋgəl/ *adj*
also **pure vowel**
a vowel which is produced without any noticeable change in vowel

quality. For example, in English:
/ʌ/ as in /hʌt/ *hut*
is a monophthong.
see also DIPHTHONG
[*Further reading*: Gimson 1980]

monosyllabic /ˌmɒnəsə̍'læbɪk ‖ ˌmɑ-/ *adj* **monosyllable**
/'mɒnəˌsɪləbəl/ *n*
consisting of one SYLLABLE, eg the English word *cow*.
see also DISYLLABIC

mood /muːd/ *n*
a set of contrasts which are often shown by the form of the verb
and which express the speaker's or writer's attitude to what is said
or written.
Three moods have often been distinguished:

(1) **indicative** mood: the form of the verb used in DECLARATIVE
SENTENCE*s* or QUESTION*s*. For example:
She sat down.
Are you coming?

(2) **imperative** mood: the form of the verb used in IMPERATIVE
SENTENCE*s*. For example:
Be quiet!
Put it on the table!
In English, imperatives do not have tense or perfect aspect (see
ASPECT) but they may be used in the progressive aspect. For
example:
Be waiting for me at five.

(3) **subjunctive** mood: the form of the verb often used to express
uncertainty, wishes, desires, etc. In contrast to the indicative mood,
the subjunctive usually refers to non-factual or hypothetical situations.
In English, little use of the subjunctive forms remains. The only
remaining forms are:
(a) *be* (present subjunctive), *were* (past subjunctive) of *be*
(b) the stem form, eg *have, come, sing* of other verbs (present
   subjunctive only).
The use of the subjunctive forms is still sometimes found in:
(a) *that* clauses after certain verbs. For example:
   It is required that he be present.
   I demand that he come at once.
(b) past subjunctive of *be* in *if* clauses. For example:
   If I were you, I'd go there.
(c) in some fixed expressions. For example:
   So be it.
[*Further reading*: Quirk et al 1985]

morpheme /'mɔːfiːm ‖ 'mɔr-/ *n* **morphemic** /mɔː'fiːmɪk ‖ mɔr-/ *adj*
the smallest meaningful unit in a language. A morpheme cannot be

morpheme boundary

divided without altering or destroying its meaning. For example, the English word *kind* is a morpheme. If the *d* is removed, it changes to *kin*, which has a different meaning. Some words consist of one morpheme, eg *kind*, others of more than one. For example, the English word *unkindness* consists of three morphemes: the STEM[1] *kind*, the negative prefix *un-*, and the noun-forming suffix *-ness*. Morphemes can have grammatical functions. For example, in English the *-s* in *she talks* is a **grammatical morpheme** which shows that the verb is the third-person singular present-tense form.

see also AFFIX, ALLOMORPH, BOUND FORM, COMBINING FORM

[*Further reading*: Aitchison 1978; Bloomfield 1933]

morpheme boundary /ˈmɔːfiːm ˈbaʊndəri ‖ -ər-/ *n*

the boundary between two MORPHEMES.

For example, in *kindness* there is a clear morpheme boundary between the STEM[1] *kind* and the suffix *-ness*. On the other hand, in the adverb *doubly* (from *double* + *-ly*) it is hard to establish the boundary. Does the *l* go with *double*, with *-ly*, or with both?

see also AFFIX, COMBINING FORM

morphology /mɔːˈfɒlədʒi ‖ mɔrˈfɑ-/ *n* **morphological** /ˌmɔːfəˈlɒdʒɪkəl ‖ ˌmɔrfəˈlɑ-/ *adj*

(1) the study of MORPHEMES and their different forms (ALLOMORPHs), and the way they combine in WORD FORMATION. For example, the English word *unfriendly* is formed from *friend*, the adjective-forming suffix *-ly* and the negative prefix *un-*.

(2) a morphemic system: in this sense, one can speak of "comparing the morphology of English with the morphology of German".

see also AFFIX, COMBINING FORM

[*Further reading*: Aitchison 1978; Bloomfield 1933]

morphophonemics /ˌmɔːfəʊfəˈniːmɪks ‖ ˌmɔr-/ *n* **morphophonemic** *adj*

variation in the form of MORPHEMES because of PHONETIC factors, or the study of this variation.

For example, in English, the regular past tense is formed by adding /d/, /t/ or /əd/ to the stem of the verb according to the final sound in the stem: *begged* /begd/, *tripped* /trɪpt/, *needed* /niːdəd/

see also MORPHOLOGY

motherese /ˌmʌðəˈriːz/ *n*

another term for CARETAKER SPEECH

mother talk /ˈmʌðəʳ ˌtɔːk/ *n*

another term for CARETAKER SPEECH

mother tongue /ˈmʌðəʳ ˌtʌŋ/ *n*

(usually) a FIRST LANGUAGE which is acquired at home.

motivation /məʊtə'veɪʃən/ *n*

the factors that determine a person's desire to do something. In SECOND-LANGUAGE and FOREIGN-LANGUAGE learning, learning may be affected differently by different types of motivation. Two types of motivation are sometimes distinguished:

(a) **instrumental motivation**: wanting to learn a language because it will be useful for certain "instrumental" goals, such as getting a job, reading a foreign newspaper, passing an examination.

(b) **integrative motivation**: wanting to learn a language in order to communicate with people of another culture who speak it.

[*Further reading*: Gardner & Lambert 1972]

move /muːv/ *n*

(in DISCOURSE ANALYSIS) a unit of DISCOURSE which may be smaller than an UTTERANCE.

For example, a teacher's utterance: *That's right, Jessica, and can you give me another example*? would consist of two moves:

(a) *That's right, Jessica*, which gives the teacher's reaction to a correct answer by the student

(b) *can you give me another example*? which attempts to elicit another response from the student.

see also SPEECH ACT

[*Further reading*: Coulthard 1985]

multicultural education /ˌmʌlti'kʌltʃərəl ˌedjʊ'keɪʃn ‖ ˌedʒə-/ *n*

see under CULTURAL PLURALISM

multilingual /ˌmʌlti'lɪŋgwəl/ *n, adj*

a person who knows and uses three or more languages. Usually, a multilingual does not know all the languages equally well. For example, he/she may:

(a) speak and understand one language best

(b) be able to write in only one

(c) use each language in different types of situation (DOMAINS), eg one language at home, one at work, and one for shopping

(d) use each language for different communicative purposes, eg one language for talking about science, one for religious purposes, and one for talking about personal feelings.

see also BILINGUAL, MULTILINGUALISM

multilingualism /ˌmʌlti'lɪŋgwəlɪzəm/ *n*

the use of three or more languages by an individual (see MULTILINGUAL) or by a group of speakers such as the inhabitants of a particular region or a nation. Multilingualism is common in, for example, some countries of West Africa (eg Nigeria, Ghana), Malaysia, Singapore, and Israel.

see BILINGUALISM, NATIONAL LANGUAGE

multiple-choice item /'mʌltəpəl 'tʃɔɪs 'aɪtəm/ *n*

a TEST ITEM in which the examinee is presented with a question along with four or five possible answers from which one must be selected. Usually the first part of a multiple choice item will be a question or incomplete statement. This is known as the **stem**. The different possible answers are known as **alternatives**. The alternatives contain (usually) one correct answer and several wrong answers or **distractors**. For example:

> Yesterday I _____ several interesting magazines. (a) have bought (b) buying (c) was bought (d) bought

[*Further reading*: Heaton 1975]

multiple correlation /'mʌltəpəl kɒrə'leɪʃən ‖ ˌkɔ- ˌkɑ-/ n
a coefficient of CORRELATION among three or more VARIABLES[2]. For example, if we wish to study the correlation between a DEPENDENT VARIABLE (eg the level of students' language proficiency) and several other variables (the INDEPENDENT VARIABLES, eg the amount of homework the students do each week, their knowledge of grammar, and their motivation) the multiple correlation is the correlation between the dependent variable and all the predictors (the independent variables).

multiple regression /ˌmʌltəpəl rɪ'greʃən/ n
see under REGRESSION ANALYSIS

multivariate analysis /ˌmʌltə'veərɪ-ət ə'næləsəs/ n
a general term for various statistical techniques which are used to analyse MULTIVARIATE DATA, such as FACTOR ANALYSIS and REGRESSION ANALYSIS.

multivariate data /ˌmʌltə'veərɪ-ət 'deɪtə, 'dɑːtə/ n
(in statistics) data which contain measurements based on more than one VARIABLE[2]. For example, if we were measuring a student's language proficiency and tests were given for reading, writing, and grammar, the resulting information would be multivariate data because it is based on three separate scores (three variables).

mutation /mjuː'teɪʃən/ n
a change in a sound, as in the formation of some irregular noun plurals in English by a change in an internal vowel, eg *foot – feet*, *man – men*, *mouse – mice*.
The term "mutation" is used when the sound change is due to the PHONETIC environment of the sound that changes. In the examples mutation was due to other vowels that were present in earlier forms of the words but have since disappeared.

N /en/ *n*
(in testing and statistics) a symbol for the *n*umber of students, subjects, scores, or observations involved in a study (as in, eg, N = 15).

narrow notation /ˈnærəʊ nəʊˈteɪʃən/ *n*
also **narrow transcription** /ˈnærəʊ trænˈskrɪpʃən/
see under NOTATION

nasal /ˈneɪzəl/ *adj*
describes a speech sound (consonant or vowel) which is produced by stopping the airstream from the lungs at some place in the mouth (for example by closing the lips) and letting the air escape through the nose.
The English nasal consonants are /m/, /n/, and /ŋ/.
see also MANNER OF ARTICULATION, ORAL², PLACE OF ARTICULATION, NASALIZATION
[*Further reading*: Gimson 1980; Hyman 1975]

nasal cavity /ˈneɪzəl ˈkævəti/ *n*
see under VOCAL TRACT, PLACE OF ARTICULATION

nasalization /ˌneɪzəlaɪˈzeɪʃən ‖ -zələ-/ *n* **nasalize** /ˈneɪzəlaɪz/ *v*
(in the production of speech sounds) letting the air from the lungs escape through the nose and the mouth. This can be done by lowering the soft palate (the **velum**) at the back of the mouth. In a number of languages, some of the VOWELs are nasalized, as in French *un bon vin blanc* /œ̃ bɔ̃ vɛ̃ blɑ̃/ "a good white wine".
see also MANNER OF ARTICULATION, PLACE OF ARTICULATION

national language /ˈnæʃənəl ˈlæŋgwɪdʒ/ *n*
a language which is usually considered to be the main language of a nation.
For example, German is the national language of Germany.
A government may declare a particular language or dialect to be the national language of a nation, eg Bahasa Malaysia (standard Malay) in Malaysia and Pilipino in the Philippines.
Usually, the national language is also the **official language**; that is, the language used in government and courts of law, and for official business. However, in multilingual nations, there may be more than one official language, and in such cases the term "official language" is often used rather than "national language". For example, the Republic of Singapore has four official languages: English, Chinese (Mandarin), Malay, and Tamil.
see also STANDARD VARIETY

native language /'neɪtɪv 'læŋgwɪdʒ/ *n*
(usually) the language which a person acquires in early childhood
because it is spoken in the family and/or it is the language of the
country where he or she is living. The native language is often the
first language a child acquires but there are exceptions. Children
may, for instance, first acquire some knowledge of another language
from a nurse or an older relative and only later on acquire a second
one which they consider their native language. Sometimes, this term
is used synonymously with FIRST LANGUAGE.

native speaker (of a language) /'neɪtɪv 'spiːkəʳ/ *n* **natively** /'neɪtɪvli/
adv
a person considered as a speaker of his or her NATIVE LANGUAGE.
In GENERATIVE TRANSFORMATIONAL GRAMMAR, the intuition of a
native speaker about the structure of his or her language is one
basis for establishing or confirming the rules of the grammar.
A native speaker is said to speak his or her native language
"natively".

nativist position /'neɪtəvəst pə'zɪʃən/ *n*
another term for INNATIST HYPOTHESIS

nativization /ˌneɪtəvaɪ'zeɪʃən/ *n* **nativize** /'neɪtəvaɪz/ *v*
also **indigenization**
the adaptation a language may undergo when it is used in a
different cultural and social situation. English in India, for example,
is said to have undergone nativization because changes have
occurred in aspects of its phonology, vocabulary, grammar, etc so
that it is now recognized as a distinct variety of English – Indian
English.
[*Further reading*: Kachru 1981]

natural approach /'nætʃərəl ə'prəʊtʃ/ *n*
also **natural method**
(1) a term for a number of language-teaching METHODs which were
developed in the 19th century as a reaction to the GRAMMAR
TRANSLATION METHOD. These methods emphasized:
(a) the use of the spoken language
(b) the use of objects and actions in teaching the meanings of words
and structures
(c) the need to make language teaching follow the natural principles
of first language learning.
These methods lead to the DIRECT METHOD.
(2) a term for an APPROACH proposed by Terrell, to develop teaching
principles which:
(a) emphasize natural communication rather than formal grammar
study
(b) are tolerant of learners' errors
(c) emphasize the informal ACQUISITION of language rules.
[*Further reading*: Rivers 1981; Richards & Rogers 1986; Terrell 1977]

natural language /'nætʃərəl 'læŋgwɪdʒ/ *n*
a language which has NATIVE SPEAKERS, in contrast with an ARTIFICIAL
LANGUAGE.

natural method /'nætʃərəl 'meθəd/ *n*
another term for NATURAL APPROACH

naturalness /'nætʃərəlnə̀s/ *n* **natural** /'nætʃərəl/ *adj*
(in GENERATIVE PHONOLOGY), the probability that particular sounds,
classes of sounds, or phonological rules occur in any language. For
example, the VOWELS /i/ and /u/ are considered to be more frequent
and therefore more "natural" than the vowels /y/ (an /i/ pronounced
with rounded lips) and /ɯ/ (a /u/ pronounced with spread lips). In
general, a language will have a /y/, as in German /ryːmən/ *rühmen* "to
praise", only if it has an /i/, as in German /riːmən/ *Riemen* "strap".
[*Further reading*: Hyman 1975]

natural order hypothesis /'nætʃərəl 'ɔːdə haɪ'pɒθəsəs ‖ 'ɔrdər
haɪ'pɑ-/ *n*
the hypothesis that children acquiring their first language acquire
linguistic forms, rules, and items in a similar order. For example, in
English children acquire progressive *-ing*, plural *-s*, and active
sentences before they acquire third person *-s* on verbs, or passive
sentences. This is said to show a natural order of development. In
SECOND-LANGUAGE and FOREIGN-LANGUAGE learning grammatical forms
may also appear in a natural order, though this is not identical with the
ORDER OF ACQUISITION in FIRST-LANGUAGE learning.
[*Further reading*: Brown 1973; Dulay & Burt 1974]

needs analysis /'niːdz ə'næləsə̀s/ *n*
also **needs assessment** /'niːdz ə'sesmənt/
(in language teaching) the process of determining the needs for
which a learner or group of learners requires a language and
arranging the needs according to priorities. Needs assessment makes
use of both subjective and objective information (eg data from
questionnaires, tests, interviews, observation) and seeks to obtain
information on:
(a) the situations in which a language will be used (including *who* it
    will be used *with*)
(b) the OBJECTIVES and purposes for which the language is needed
(c) the types of communication that will be used (eg written,
    spoken, formal, informal)
(d) the level of proficiency that will be required.
Needs assessment is a part of CURRICULUM DEVELOPMENT and
is normally required before a SYLLABUS can be developed for language
teaching.
[*Further reading*: Munby 1978]

negative politeness strategies /'negətɪv pə'laɪtnə̀s 'strætə̀dʒɪz/ *n*
see under POLITENESS

negative pronoun /'nəgətɪv 'prəʊnaʊn/ *n*

a PRONOUN which stands for a negative NOUN PHRASE[1]. The following words in English are negative pronouns:

nobody, no one, none, neither, nothing

For example:

<u>*Nobody*</u> *has passed the test.*

That's <u>*none*</u> *of your business.*

Negative pronouns can function as NEGATOR*s*.

negative question /'negətɪv 'kwestʃən/ *n*

a question which includes a negative word or PARTICLE. For example,

Can'<u>t</u> you drive?

Isn'<u>t</u> it awful?

In English, negative questions are answered in the same way as positive questions:

	If you can drive	If you can't drive
Can you drive?		
Can't you drive?	*Yes, I can.*	*No, I can't.*

negative reinforcement /'negətɪv ˌriːɪn'fɔːsmənt ‖ -ɔr-/ *n*

see under OPERANT CONDITIONING, STIMULUS-RESPONSE THEORY

negative transfer /'negətɪv 'trænsfɜːʳ/ *n*

see under LANGUAGE TRANSFER

negator /nɪ'geɪtəʳ/ *n*

a word which makes a sentence a negative sentence. For example, English negators include *not, hardly ever, never, seldom, neither, nothing*.

see also NEGATIVE PRONOUN

negotiation /nɪˌgəʊʃi'eɪʃən/ *n*

(in conversation) what speakers do in order to achieve successful communication. For conversation to progress naturally and for speakers to be able to understand each other it may be necessary for them to:

(a) indicate that they understand or do not understand, or that they want the conversation to continue (see FEEDBACK)

(b) help each other to express ideas (see FOREIGNER TALK)

(c) make corrections when necessary to what is said or how it is said (see REPAIR).

These aspects of the work which speakers do in order to make successful conversation is known as negotiation, in CONVERSATIONAL ANALYSIS.

see also ACCOMMODATION, CONVERSATIONAL MAXIMS, ETHNOMETHODOLOGY

[*Further reading*: Garfinkel 1967]

neologism /niː'ɒlədʒɪzəm ‖ -'ɑlə-/ *n*

a new word or expression which is introduced into a language. For example, *non-restrictive* came into English in 1916, *non-standard* in 1923, and *null hypothesis* in 1935.

network /'netwɜːk ‖ -ɜr-/ *n*

a group of people within a larger community who are in a relatively fixed relationship to one another and who communicate among themselves in certain more or less predictable ways, eg a family group, a tutorial group at a university, the staff in an office. Recognition of networks and their structures is of importance for studies of language variation, language use, and language learning. There are two differences between a network and a PEER GROUP:

(a) in a peer group all members have equal STATUS, but in a network members may be of unequal status (eg parents and children in a family).

(b) in a network all members know one another, but in a peer group this need not be so. For example, a lexicographer may consider all lexicographers to be his or her peer group without knowing them all personally.

Nevertheless, most peer groups are networks and many networks are peer groups.

[*Further reading*: Milroy 1980]

neurolinguistics /ˌnjʊərəʊlɪŋ'gwɪstɪks ‖ ˌnʊərə-/ *n* **neurolinguistic** *adj*

the study of the function the BRAIN performs in language learning and language use. Neurolinguistics includes research into how the structure of the brain influences language learning, how and in which parts of the brain language is stored (see MEMORY), and how damage to the brain affects the ability to use language (see APHASIA).

[*Further reading*: Lamendella 1979]

neutralization /ˌnjuːtrəlaɪ'zeɪʃən ‖ ˌnuːtrələ-/ *n* **neutralize** /'njuːtrəlaɪz ‖ 'nuː-/ *v*

the process which takes place when two distinctive sounds (PHONEMEs) in a language are no longer distinctive (ie in contrast). This usually occurs in particular positions in a word. For example, in German /t/ and /d/ are neutralized at the end of a word. *Rad* "wheel" and *Rat* "advice" are both pronounced /raːt/.

node /nəʊd/ *n*

(in GENERATIVE TRANSFORMATIONAL GRAMMAR) each position in a **tree diagram** where lines ("branches") meet. At each node is a symbol for a GRAMMATICAL CATEGORY[2].

For example, in the tree diagram for a noun phrase, *the child*:

the category symbols NP (NOUN PHRASE[1]), Det (DETERMINER), N (NOUN) are all at nodes in the diagram.

noise[1]

The NP node is said to **dominate** the Det node and the N node.
see also BASE COMPONENT

noise[1] /nɔɪz/ *n*

When speech sounds are produced, the moving particles of air from the lungs may form regular patterns (see SOUND WAVE) or irregular patterns. These irregular patterns are called noise and occur in the production of certain consonants such as /s/.
[*Further reading*: Gimson 1980]

noise[2] *n*

(in INFORMATION THEORY) any disturbance or defect which interferes with the transmission of the message from one person to another. In speech, this interference could be caused by other sounds, eg a pneumatic drill, a voice on the radio. Because of the presence of noise, a certain degree of REDUNDANCY is necessary in any communication.
[*Further reading*: Cherry 1957]

nominal /ˈnɒmənəl ‖ ˈnɑ-/ *n*

(1) a term used instead of NOUN
(2) a term for a linguistic unit which has some but not all characteristics of a noun, eg *wounded* in *The wounded were taken by helicopter to the hospital*.
Although *wounded* is the HEAD of the noun phrase *the wounded* and is preceded by an article, it would not be modified by an adjective but by an adverb, eg *the seriously wounded*.

nominal clause /ˈnɒmənəl ˈklɔːz ‖ ˈnɑ-/ *n*
also **noun clause**

a clause which functions like a noun or noun phrase; that is, which may occur as subject, object COMPLEMENT, in APPOSITION, or as prepositional COMPLEMENT. For example:
nominal clause as subject: *What he said is awful*.
nominal clause as object: *I don't know what he said*.

nominalization /ˌnɒmənəlaɪˈzeɪʃən ‖ ˌnɑ-/ *n* **nominalize**
/ˈnɒmənəlaɪz ‖ ˈnɑ-/ *v*

the grammatical process of forming nouns from other parts of speech, usually verbs or adjectives. For example, in English:
nominalized forms from the verb *to write*: *writing*, *writer*
as in: *His writing is illegible. Her mother is a writer*.

nominal scale /ˈnɒmənəl ˌskeɪl ‖ ˈnɑ-/ *n*
see under SCALE

nominative case /ˈnɒmənətɪv ˌkeɪs, ˈnɒmnə- ‖ ˈnɑ-/ *n*
the form of a noun or NOUN PHRASE[1] which usually shows that the noun or noun phrase can function as the subject of a sentence.

In TRADITIONAL GRAMMAR, the pronoun *I* could be described as in the nominative case, in contrast to the pronoun *me*.
see also CASE[1]
[*Further reading*: Lyons 1968]

non-defining relative clause /ˌnɒndɪˈfaɪnɪŋ ˈrelətɪv ˈklɔːz ‖ ˌnɑn-/ *n*
also **non-restrictive relative clause**
see under DEFINING RELATIVE CLAUSE

non-finite verb /ˌnɒnˈfaɪnaɪt ˈvɜːb ‖ ˌnɑn- ˈvɜrb/ *n*
see under FINITE VERB

non-native varieties of English /ˌnɒn ˈneɪtɪv vəˈraɪətiz əv ˈɪŋglɪʃ ‖ ˌnɑn-/ *n*
a term sometimes used for varieties of English used in countries where English is a SECOND LANGUAGE, such as Singapore English, Nigerian English, Indian English.
see also NATIVIZATION
[*Further reading*: Kachru 1981; Platt & Weber 1980]

non-past /ˈnɒnˈpɑːst ‖ ˈnɑnˈpæst/ *n*, *adj*
a term sometimes used for the PRESENT TENSE form of a verb in languages such as English. It emphasizes that this verb form is generally used to describe time periods other than the past, but not necessarily the present. For example:
  I leave tomorrow. (future reference)
  The sun rises in the east. (general truth)

non-restrictive relative clause /ˌnɒn rɪˈstrɪktɪv ˈrelətɪv ˈklɔːz ‖ ˌnɑn-/ *n*
another term for **non-defining relative clause**
see under DEFINING RELATIVE CLAUSE

nonstandard /nɒnˈstændəd ‖ nɑnˈstændərd/ *adj*
used of speech or writing which differs in pronunciation, GRAMMAR, or vocabulary from the STANDARD VARIETY of the language. Sometimes the expression SUBSTANDARD is used but linguists prefer the term nonstandard as it is a more neutral term.
see also NORM, STANDARD VARIETY

non-verbal communication /nɒnˈvɜːbəl kəˌmjuːnəˈkeɪʃən ‖ nɑnˈvɜr-/ *n*
communication without the use of words. This could be done, for instance, by gestures (see PARALINGUISTICS) or signs (see SIGN LANGUAGE).

norm[1] /nɔːm ‖ -ɔr-/ *n* **normative** /ˈnɔːmətɪv ‖ -ɔr-/ *adj*
that which is considered appropriate in speech or writing for a particular situation or purpose within a particular group or community. The norm for an informal situation may be very different from the norm for a formal one.
For example, in English, a first name (*Joe*) may be the norm for

addressing people in an informal situation but title and surname (*Mr Smith*) for a formal one.

see also STANDARD VARIETY, STYLE

[*Further reading*: Richards 1982]

norm[2] *n*

(in testing and statistics) the scores or typical performance of a particular group (the "norm group") as measured in some way. Norms may be used to compare the performance of an individual or group with the norm group. Norms may be expressed by reference to such factors as age, length of previous instruction, or PERCENTILE rank on a test.

normal distribution /'nɔːməl ˌdɪstrə'bjuːʃən ‖ 'nɔr-/ *n*

(in statistics) a commonly occurring DISTRIBUTION of scores in a SAMPLE, in which scores rise and fall gradually from a single peak. It forms a symmetrical bell-shaped curve. In a normal distribution the MEAN, MEDIAN, and MODE all coincide, and the information necessary for describing the distribution is given in the mean and the STANDARD DEVIATION (SD).

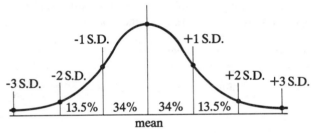

The normal curve

normalized standard score /'nɔːməlaɪzd 'stændəd skɔːʳ ‖ 'nɔr- -dərd skɔr/ *n*

(in statistics) a STANDARD SCORE which has been converted to a NORMAL DISTRIBUTION through a statistical procedure. For example a PERCENTILE ranking is a normalized standard score.

normative grammar /'nɔːmətɪv 'græməʳ ‖ 'nɔr-/ *n*

a grammar which contains rules for what is considered to be correct or appropriate usage. The rules may be based on classical literary works or the speech of those people who are considered as models for others to copy. In a nation in which many different DIALECTS are spoken, a NATIONAL LANGUAGE may be developed and a normative grammar and dictionary produced.

see also PRESCRIPTIVE GRAMMAR, STANDARD VARIETY

norm referenced test /'nɔːm 'refərənst 'test ‖ -ɔr-/ *n*

see under CRITERION REFERENCED TEST

notation /nəʊ'teɪʃən/ *n* **notate** /nəʊ'teɪt/ *v*
also **transcription**

the use of symbols (see PHONETIC SYMBOLS) to show sounds or sound
sequences in written form. There are different systems of phonetic
symbols. One of the most commonly used is that of the
International Phonetic Association.

A distinction is made between two types of notation:

(1) **Phonemic notation** uses only the distinctive sounds of a language
(PHONEMES). It does not show the finer points of pronunciation.
Phonemic notation is written within slanting brackets.

For example, the English word *foot* may appear in phonemic
notation as /fʊt/. /f/, /ʊ/, and /t/ are phonemes of English. Phonemic
notation may be used, for example:

(a) for languages which have no writing system of their own

(b) for teaching purposes, to show differences in pronunciation, eg
/hed/ *head* and /hæt/ *hat*.

(2) **Phonetic notation** (also **phonetic script**) uses phonetic symbols
for various sounds, including symbols to show in detail how a
particular sound is pronounced. It is used to show finer points of
pronunciation. Phonetic notation is written in square brackets.

For example, the English word *pin* may appear in phonetic notation
as [pʰɪn] with the raised *h* showing the ASPIRATION of the [p].
In phonemic notation, *pin* would be rendered as /pɪn/.

Phonetic notation may be used, for example:

(a) to show the different pronunciation of closely related dialects

(b) to show the pronunciation of individual speakers or groups of
speakers. For example, students learning English may use a
DENTAL t-sound, shown by [t̪], instead of the ALVEOLAR [t]
commonly used in English.

Phonemic notation is sometimes referred to as **broad notation** and
phonetic notation as **narrow notation**.

see also INTERNATIONAL PHONETIC ALPHABET
[*Further reading*: Gimson 1980]

notion /'nəʊʃən/ *n*

see under NOTIONAL SYLLABUS

notional-functional syllabus /'nəʊʃənəl 'fʌŋkʃənəl 'sɪləbəs/ *n*

another term for NOTIONAL SYLLABUS

notional grammar[1] /'nəʊʃənəl 'græməʳ/ *n*

a grammar which is based on the belief that there are categories
such as TENSE, MOOD, GENDER, NUMBER, and CASE which are available
to all languages although not all languages make full use of them.
For example, a case system (see CASE[1]) is found in German, Latin,
and Russian, but not in modern English.

TRADITIONAL GRAMMAR was often notional in its approach but
sometimes attempted to apply some categories to a language without

notional grammar²

first investigating whether they were useful and appropriate for describing that language.

[*Further reading*: Lyons 1968]

notional grammar² *n*

a grammar based on the meanings or concepts that people need to express through language (eg time, quantity, duration, location) and the linguistic items and structures needed to express them.

[*Further reading*: Leech & Svartvik 1975]

notional syllabus /ˈnəʊʃənəl ˈsɪləbəs/ *n*
also **notional-functional syllabus**

(in language teaching) a SYLLABUS in which the language content is arranged according to the meanings a learner needs to express through language and the functions the learner will use the language for.

The term NOTIONAL is taken from NOTIONAL GRAMMAR². A notional syllabus is contrasted with a grammatical syllabus or STRUCTURAL SYLLABUS (one which consists of a sequence of graded language items) or a situational syllabus (one which consists of situations and the relevant language items (see SITUATIONAL METHOD)).

A notional syllabus contains:

(a) the meanings and concepts the learner needs in order to communicate (eg time, quantity, duration, location) and the language needed to express them. These concepts and meanings are called **notions**.

(b) the language needed to express different functions or SPEECH ACTS (eg requesting, suggesting, promising, describing).

These notions and functions are then used to develop learning/teaching units in a language course.

see also COMMUNICATIVE APPROACH

[*Further reading*: Wilkins 1976]

noun /naʊn/ *n*

a word which (a) can occur as the subject or object of a verb or the object (COMPLEMENT) of a preposition (b) can be modified by an adjective (c) can be used with DETERMINERS.

Nouns typically refer to people, animals, places, things, or abstractions.

see also ADJECTIVAL NOUN, ANIMATE NOUN, COLLECTIVE NOUN, COMPOUND NOUN, CONCRETE NOUN, COUNTABLE NOUN, UNCOUNTABLE NOUN, PROPER NOUN, PARTS OF SPEECH

noun clause /ˈnaʊn ˌklɔːz/ *n*

another term for NOMINAL CLAUSE

noun phrase¹ /ˈnaʊn ˌfreɪz/ *n*
also **NP**

(in STRUCTURALIST LINGUISTICS, GENERATIVE TRANSFORMATIONAL GRAMMAR and related grammatical theories) a group of words with a noun or pronoun as the main part (the HEAD).

The noun phrase may consist of only one word (for example *George* in *George arrived yesterday*) or it may be long and complex (for example, all the words before *must* in: *The students who enrolled late and who have not yet filled in their cards must do so by Friday*).

noun phrase[2] *n*

(in some TRADITIONAL GRAMMARS) a participial (see PARTICIPLES) or INFINITIVE phrase which could be replaced by a noun or pronoun. For example, the participial phrase *mowing the lawn* in:

George just hates mowing the lawn.

could be replaced by *it*:

George just hates it.

NP /ˌen ˈpiː/ *n*

an abbreviation for NOUN PHRASE[1]

nucleus /ˈnjuːklɪəs ‖ ˈnuː-/ *n*

see under SYLLABLE

null hypothesis /ˈnʌl haɪˈpɒθəsəs ‖ -ˈpɑ-/ *n*

see under HYPOTHESIS

number[1] /ˈnʌmbər/ *n*

a grammatical distinction which determines whether nouns, verbs, adjectives, etc in a language are singular or plural. In English this is seen particularly in NOUNS and DEMONSTRATIVES.

For example:

	singular	plural
count noun	*book*	*books*
demonstrative	*this*	*these*

number[2] *n*

numbers are used either as **cardinal numbers** (or **cardinals**) or **ordinal numbers** (or **ordinals**).

Cardinal numbers are used when counting; eg *6 boys, 200 dollars, a million years*, and they may be used as nouns (eg *count up to ten*) Ordinal numbers are used when we put things in a numerical order; eg *first, second, third, fourth, fifth*, etc.

Both cardinal numbers and ordinal numbers can be written with figures (eg *6, 6th*) or with words (*six, sixth*).

number concord /ˈnʌmbər ˈkɒŋkɔːd ‖ ˈkɑŋkɔrd/ *n*

see under CONCORD

numeral /ˈnjuːmərəl ‖ ˈnuː-/ *n*

a word or phrase which is used to name a number.

In English, numerals may be **cardinal numbers** – *one, two, three*, etc – or **ordinal numbers** – *first, second, third*, etc.

see also DETERMINER, QUANTIFIER, NUMBER[2]

[*Further reading*: Quirk et al 1985]

object¹ /ˈɒbdʒɪkt ‖ ˈɑb-/ *n*

the noun, noun phrase or clause, or pronoun in sentences with
TRANSITIVE VERBS, which is traditionally described as being affected by
the action of the verb. The object of a verb can be affected by the
verb either directly or indirectly.

If it is affected directly, it may be called the **direct object.** In
English, the direct object of a verb may be:

(a) created by the action of the verb, as in:
   Terry baked <u>a cake</u>.

(b) changed in some way by the action of the verb as in:
   Terry baked <u>a potato</u>.

(c) perceived by the SUBJECT of the verb, as in:
   Terry saw <u>the cake</u>.

(d) evaluated by the subject of the verb, as in:
   Terry liked <u>the cake</u>.

(e) obtained or possessed by the subject of the verb, as in:
   Terry bought <u>the cake</u>.

If the object of a verb is affected by the verb indirectly, it is usually
called the **indirect object.** In English, the indirect object may be:

(a) the receiver of the direct object, as in:
   Terry gave <u>me</u> the cake. (= "Terry gave the cake *to* me")

(b) the beneficiary of the action of the verb, as in:
   Terry baked <u>me</u> the cake. (= "Terry baked the cake *for* me")

In English, direct objects and many indirect objects can become
subjects when sentences in the active voice are changed to the
passive voice (see VOICE¹):
   <u>The cake</u> was given (to) me.
   <u>I</u> was given the cake.

see also GOAL¹, OBJECT OF RESULT

object² **(of a preposition)** *n*

another term for **prepositional complement**
see under COMPLEMENT

object case /ˈɒbdʒɪkt ˈkeɪs ‖ ˈɑb-/ *n*

another term for OBJECTIVE CASE

object complement /ˈɒbdʒɪkt ˈkɒmpləmənt ‖ ˈɑb- ˈkɑm-/ *n*

see under COMPLEMENT

objective /əbˈdʒektɪv/ *n*

a goal of a course of instruction. Two different types of objectives
may be distinguished.

General objectives, or **aims,** are the underlying reasons for or
purposes of a course of instruction. For example, the aims of the
teaching of a foreign language in a particular country might be: to

teach students to read and write a foreign language, to improve students' knowledge of a foreign culture, to teach conversation in a foreign language, etc. Aims are long-term goals, described in very general terms.

Specific objectives (or simply objectives), are descriptions of what is to be achieved in a course. They are more detailed descriptions of exactly what a learner is expected to be able to do at the end of a period of instruction. This might be a single lesson, a chapter of a book, a term's work, etc. For instance, specific objectives of a classroom lesson might be: Use of the linking words *and, but, however, although*. These specific objectives contribute to the general objective of paragraph writing. A description of specific objectives in terms which can be observed and measured is known as a BEHAVIOURAL OBJECTIVE.

[*Further reading*: Pratt 1980]

objective case /ɒb'dʒektɪv 'keɪs ‖ ɑb-/ *n*
also **object case**

In CASE GRAMMAR, the noun or NOUN PHRASE[1] that refers to whoever or whatever has the most neutral relationship to the action of the verb is in the objective case.

The noun or noun phrase in the objective case neither performs the action, nor is the instrument of the action.

For example, in the sentences:

They sliced *the sausage* with a knife.
The sausage sliced easily.
The sausage was thick.

the sausage is neither agent (like *they*) nor instrument (like *a knife*). It is in the objective case.

The notion of the objective case is related to the traditional notion of OBJECT[1]. But not everything in the objective case would be an object, and not all objects would be considered to be in the objective case.

see also CASE GRAMMAR

[*Further reading*: Fillmore 1968]

objective test /əb'dʒektɪv 'test/ *n*
see under SUBJECTIVE TEST

objective test item /əb'dʒektɪv 'test 'aɪtəm/ *n*
a TEST ITEM which requires the choice of a single correct answer, such as a MULTIPLE-CHOICE ITEM or a TRUE-FALSE ITEM.
see also SUBJECTIVE TEST

object of result /'ɒbdʒɪkt əv rɪ'zʌlt ‖ 'ɑb-/ *n*
also **effected object**

an object of a verb which refers to something that is produced through the action indicated by the verb, eg *a cake* in:

Terry baked a cake.

as the cake is the result of the baking.

obstruent

However, in:
Terry baked a potato.
a potato is not an object of result as it is not produced by baking. It is, however, affected by baking, and so may be called an **affected object**.

see also FACTITIVE CASE
[*Further reading*: Quirk et al 1985]

obstruent /ˈɒbstruːənt ‖ ˈɑb-/ *n, adj*
a speech sound (a CONSONANT) where the passage of the air from the lungs is obstructed in some way or other (eg the /p/ in *pin*, the /s/ in *sing*). Sounds such as /n/ and /m/ are not usually considered obstruents because although the air is stopped in the mouth, it is allowed free passage through the nose.
In GENERATIVE PHONOLOGY, obstruents are often marked [-sonorant] to distinguish them from sounds such as VOWELS, NASALS, etc, which are marked [+sonorant].

see also DISTINCTIVE FEATURE
[*Further reading*: Hyman 1975]

official language /əˈfɪʃəl ˈlæŋgwɪdʒ/ *n*
see under NATIONAL LANGUAGE

onomatopoeia /ˌɒnəmætəˈpiːə ‖ ˌɑ-/ *n* **onomatopoeic** /ˌɒnəmætəˈpiːɪk/ *adj*
imitation of natural sounds by means of words or groups of words, as in English *moo*, *baa*, *cuckoo*. There are other words which are examples of "semi-onomatopoeia", such as the English words *swish*, *growl*, *splash*.
Languages differ in their choice of onomatopoeic words. An English cock goes *cock-a-doodle-do*; a Japanese one goes *kokekokko*.

onset /ˈɒnset ‖ ˈɑn-/ *n*
see under SYLLABLE, TONE UNIT

ontogeny /ɒnˈtɒdʒəni ‖ ɑnˈtɑ-/ *n* **ontogenetic** /ˌɒntədʒəˈnetɪk ‖ ˌɑn-/ *adj*
also **ontogenesis** /ˌɒntəˈdʒenəsəs ‖ ˌɑn-/
In studies of child language ACQUISITION, the development of language in an individual is sometimes referred to as ontogeny, and the historical development of language in a speech community as **phylogeny**. Linguists are interested in whether the ontogeny of language in the child shows similar stages to those which a language has gone through in its historical development. In other words, they are interested in the famous question whether ontogeny recapitulates phylogeny.

open class /ˈəʊpən ˈklɑːs ‖ ˈklæs/ *n*
also **open set**
a group of words (a WORD CLASS), which contains an unlimited number of items.

Nouns, verbs, adjectives, and adverbs are open-class words. New words can be added to these classes, eg *laser*, *Chomskyan*.

The word classes conjunctions, prepositions, and pronouns consist of relatively few words, and new words are not usually added to them. These are called **closed classes**, or **closed sets**.

[*Further reading*: Quirk et al 1985]

open-ended question /ˈəʊpən endəd ˈkwestʃən/ *n*
a TEST ITEM which allows the person taking the test to answer in his or her own way, in contrast to questions with limited multiple-choice possibilities.

open-ended response /ˈəʊpən endəd rɪˈspɒns ‖ -ˈspɑns/ *n*
see under TEST ITEM

open set /ˈəʊpən ˈset/ *n*
another term for OPEN CLASS

open syllable /ˈ əʊpən ˈsɪləbəl/ *n*
see under SYLLABLE

open vowel /ˈəʊpən ˈvaʊəl/ *n*
also **low vowel**
see under VOWEL

operant /ˈɒpərənt ‖ ˈɑ-/ *n*
see under OPERANT CONDITIONING

operant conditioning /ˈɒpərənt kənˈdɪʃənɪŋ ‖ ˈɑ-/ *n*
a learning theory proposed by the American psychologist Skinner, and an important aspect of behaviourist psychology (see BEHAVIOURISM). It is a type of conditioning (see CONDITIONED RESPONSE) in which an organism (eg a child learning its first language) produces an action (eg an UTTERANCE) which achieves an outcome or purpose for the child (eg to get food). This action is called the **operant**. If the outcome is favourable the operant is likely to occur again, and is said to be reinforced. It is positively reinforced (**positive reinforcement**) if the operant is followed by something pleasant, and negatively reinforced (**negative reinforcement**) if it is followed by the removal of something unpleasant. If there is no outcome (ie no reinforcement), or if the outcome is unpleasant, the operant is less likely to occur again. Skinner believed that children learn language according to the principle of operant conditioning.
[*Further reading*: Skinner 1957; Elliot 1981]

operating principle /ˈɒpəreɪtɪŋ ˈprɪnsəpəl ‖ ˈɑpə-/ *n*
see under HEURISTIC

operator /ˈɒpəreɪtəʳ ‖ ˈɑ-/ *n*
(in English) the first AUXILIARY VERB to occur in a verb phrase, so called because it is the verb which "operates" as the question-

forming word, by moving to the initial position in the sentence in questions. For example:

(a) *He will   be   coming*
      aux 1   aux 2
      (operator)

(b) *She couldn't   have been   there.*
      aux 1   aux 2 aux 3
      (operator)

(a) becomes *Will he be coming?*

(b) becomes *Couldn't she have been there?*

[*Further reading*: Quirk et al 1985]

opposition /ɒpəˈzɪʃən ‖ ˈɑpə-/ *n*

the relationship between pairs of elements in a language, such as the distinctive sounds (PHONEME*s*).

For example, the opposition between /k/ and /g/ in English distinguishes between the MINIMAL PAIR *cut* /kʌt/ and *gut* /gʌt/. In general, the term "opposition" is used when two elements differ in only one feature. So English /k/ and /g/ are said to be in opposition because they differ only in that /g/ is **voiced** and /k/ is **voiceless** (see VOICE[2]). One is less likely to speak of the opposition between /k/ and /b/ (as in *cut* /kʌt/ and *but* /bʌt/), because they differ in several ways involving both PLACE OF ARTICULATION and MANNER OF ARTICULATION.

see also MARKEDNESS

optimum age hypothesis /ˈɒptəməm ˈeɪdʒ haɪˌpɒθəsəs ‖ ˌɑp-haɪˌpɑ-/ *n*

the hypothesis that there is an ideal or optimal age (below puberty) during which languages can be learned relatively easily, and after which language learning is more difficult. This hypothesis has not been supported by direct evidence but is based on the observation that children often learn a second or foreign language more easily than older learners.

see also BRAIN

[*Further reading*: Penfield & Lamar Roberts 1959]

oral[1] /ˈɔːrəl ‖ ˈo-/ *adj*

a term used to stress that a spoken form of language is used as opposed to a written form, as in *an oral test, an oral examination*.

oral[2] *adj, n*

(of) a speech sound which is produced while the soft palate (the **velum**) at the back of the mouth is raised so that the airstream from the lungs cannot escape through the nose.

In English, all vowels, and all consonants except /m/, /n/, and /ŋ/ as in /sɪŋ/ *sing*, are oral.

In GENERATIVE PHONOLOGY, oral sounds are marked [-nasal] to distinguish them from NASAL sounds.

see also MANNER OF ARTICULATION, PLACE OF ARTICULATION

[*Further reading*: Hyman 1975]

oral approach /ˈɔːrəl əˈprəʊtʃ ‖ ˈo-/ n
another term for SITUATIONAL LANGUAGE TEACHING

oral cavity /ˈɔːrəl ˈkævəti ‖ ˈo-/ n
see under VOCAL TRACT, PLACE OF ARTICULATION

oral culture /ˈɔːrəl ˌkʌltʃəʳ ‖ ˈo-/ n
the culture of a society in which culture and cultural values are communicated through spoken language rather than through writing. A society in which written language plays an important part in culture and cultural values is said to have a **literary culture**.

oral reading /ˈɔːrəl ˈriːdɪŋ ‖ ˈo-/ n
see under READING

order of acquisition /ˈɔːdər əv ˌækwəˈzɪʃən ‖ ˌɔr-/ n
also **acquisition order**
the order in which linguistic forms, rules, and items are acquired in first- or second-language learning.
see also ACQUISITION, NATURAL ORDER HYPOTHESIS
[*Further reading*: Brown 1973]

ordinal number /ˈɔːdənəl ˈnʌmbəʳ ‖ ˈɔr-/ n
also **ordinal**
see under NUMBER[2]

ordinal scale /ˈɔːdənəl ˈskeɪl ‖ ˈɔr-/ n
see under SCALE

orthography /ɔːˈθɒɡrəfi ‖ ɔrˈθɑ-/ n **orthographic** /ˌɔːθəˈɡræfɪk ‖ ˌɔr-/ adj
The term "orthography" is used:
(1) for spelling in general.
(2) for correct or standard spelling.
For some languages, the orthography is based on generally accepted usage and is not prescribed by an official body. For other languages, eg Swedish, it is laid down by official or semi-official organizations. Like the term "spelling" itself, the term "orthography" is more likely to be used of alphabetic writing than of syllabic writing, and is unlikely to be used of ideographic writing (see WRITING SYSTEMS).

other repair /ˈʌðəʳ rɪˈpeəʳ/ n
see under REPAIR

output /ˈaʊtpʊt/ n
see under INPUT

over-extension /ˈəʊvər ɪkˈstenʃən/ n
another term for OVERGENERALIZATION

overgeneralization /ˈəʊvəʳˌdʒenərəlaɪˈzeɪʃən/ n **overgeneralize** /ˌəʊvəʳˈdʒenərəlaɪz/ v
also **over-extension, over-regularization, analogy**
a process common in both first- and second-language learning, in

which a learner extends the use of a grammatical rule or linguistic item beyond its accepted uses, generally by making words or structures follow a more regular pattern. For example, a child may use *ball* to refer to all round objects, or use *mans* instead of *men* for the plural of *man*.

see also LANGUAGE TRANSFER, ERROR ANALYSIS, INTERLANGUAGE

[*Further reading*: Dulay, Burt, & Krashen 1982]

over-regularization /ˈəʊvəʳ regjʊləraɪˈzeɪʃən ‖ -gjə̣-/ *n*
another term for OVERGENERALIZATION

paired-associate learning /ˌpeəd əˈsəʊʃi-ət ˈlɜːnɪŋ, -ʃət ‖ ˌpeərd lɜr-/ n

a type of learning task used in studies of VERBAL LEARNING. Pairs of words or other learning items are presented and the learner is required to make associations between them. For example:

  horse – brown
  bird – blue
  table – white

The learner is tested with the first member of the pair to see if the second item can be remembered.

see also ASSOCIATIVE LEARNING

[*Further reading*: Gagné 1970]

pair work /ˈpeər ˌwɜːk ‖ ˌwɜrk/ n
also **pair practice**

(in language teaching) a learning activity which involves learners working together in pairs.

see also GROUP WORK

palatal /ˈpælətl/ adj

describes a speech sound (typically a CONSONANT) which is produced by the front upper surface of the tongue touching or nearly touching the hard palate at the top of the mouth.

For example, in German the /ç/ in /ɪç/ *ich* "I", and in /nɪçt/ *nicht* "not" is a palatal FRICATIVE. And in English, the /j/ in /jes/ "yes" may be called an unrounded palatal SEMI-VOWEL.

see also PLACE OF ARTICULATION, MANNER OF ARTICULATION

[*Further reading*: Gimson 1980]

palatalization /ˌpælətəlaɪˈzeɪʃən/ n **palatalize** /ˈpælətəlaɪz/ v

the raising of the front upper surface of the tongue towards the hard palate at the top of the mouth. Palatalization of speech sounds may occur when the sound is followed by a close front vowel such as /i/ (see VOWEL).

For example, in the Paris dialect of French, the /k/ is palatalized in /ki/ *qui* "who".

see also PLACE OF ARTICULATION, MANNER OF ARTICULATION

[*Further reading*: Gimson 1980]

palate /ˈpælət/ n

see under PLACE OF ARTICULATION

paradigm /ˈpærədaɪm/ n **paradigmatic** /ˌpærədɪgˈmætɪk/ adj

a list or pattern showing the forms which a word can have in a grammatical system. For example, in English:

singular	plural
boy	*boys*
boy's	*boys'*
(of the boy)	(of the boys)

Paradigms may be used to show the different forms of a verb. For example, in French:

singular	plural
je parle "I speak"	*nous parlons* "we speak"
tu parles "you speak"	*vous parlez* "you speak"
il parle "he speaks"	*ils parlent* "they speak"
elle parle "she speaks"	*elles parlent* "they speak"

Paradigms typically show a word's INFLECTIONS rather than its derivatives (see DERIVATION).

[*Further reading*: Palmer 1971]

paradigmatic relations /ˌpærədɪgˈmætɪk rɪˈleɪʃənz/ *n*
also **paradigmatic relationships**

see under SYNTAGMATIC RELATIONS

paragraph /ˈpærəgrɑːf ‖ -græf/ *n*

a unit of organization of written language, which serves to indicate how the main ideas in a written text are grouped. In TEXT LINGUISTICS, paragraphs are treated as indicators of the macro-structure of a text (see SCHEME). They group sentences which belong together, generally, those which deal with the same topic. A new paragraph thus indicates a change in topic or sub-topic. In English a paragraph begins on a new line and the opening sentence of a new paragraph is usually set in from the margin (ie is indented).

see also DISCOURSE ANALYSIS

[*Further reading*: Van Dijk 1977]

paralinguistic features /ˌpærəlɪŋˈgwɪstɪk ˈfiːtʃəz ‖ -ərz/ *n*

see under PARALINGUISTICS

paralinguistics /ˌpærəlɪŋˈgwɪstɪks/ *n* **paralinguistic** *adj*

the study or use of non-vocal phenomena such as facial expressions, head or eye movements, and gestures, which may add support, emphasis, or particular shades of meaning to what people are saying. These phenomena are known as **paralinguistic features**.

For example, in many English-speaking countries, nodding the head could be used instead of various spoken ways of showing agreement, such as *yes*, *that's right*, or *agreed*. Sometimes head-nodding accompanies and emphasizes verbal agreement.

The use of paralinguistic features in this sense is also called **kinesics**. For some linguists, paralinguistic features would also include those vocal characteristics such as TONE OF VOICE which may express the speaker's attitude to what he or she is saying.

see also PROXEMICS

parallel form reliability /ˈpærəlel fɔːm rɪˌlaɪəˈbɪləti ‖ -ɔr-/ *n*
another term for ALTERNATE FORM RELIABILITY

parallel forms /ˈpærəlel ˈfɔːmz ‖ -ɔr-/ *n*
also **equivalent forms, alternate forms**
different forms of a test which try to measure exactly the same skills
or abilities, which use the same methods of testing, and which are of
equal length and difficulty.
In general, if people get similar scores on parallel forms of a test,
this suggests that the test is reliable (see RELIABILITY).

parameter /pəˈræmətər/ *n*
(in statistics) any measurable characteristic of a POPULATION which is
believed to affect that population.
For example, a group of children of the same age may be classified
by the parameters of height and weight, or a group of language-
learners by the parameters of their skill at reading, writing,
speaking, and understanding.

paraphrase /ˈpærəfreɪz/ *n, v*
an expression of the meaning of a word or phrase using other words
or phrases, often in an attempt to make the meaning easier to
understand.
For example, *to make (someone or something) appear or feel
younger* is a paraphrase of the English verb *rejuvenate*.
Dictionary definitions often take the form of paraphrases of the
words they are trying to define.

parsing /ˈpɑːzɪŋ ‖ ˈpɑrsɪŋ/ *n* **parse** *v*
the identification of parts of a sentence as SUBJECT, VERB, OBJECT[1],
etc) and of words in a sentence as noun (plural), verb (past tense),
etc.
For example, in English:

subject			verb	object
The	*noisy*	*frogs*	*disturbed*	*us*
definite	adjective	noun	verb (past	pronoun
article		(plural)	tense)	(1st-person
				plural)

Parsing is a well-established technique of TRADITIONAL GRAMMAR.
Attempts are now being made to carry out parsing with the help of
a computer.

participant /pɑːˈtɪsəpənt ‖ pɑr-/ *n*
a person who is present in a SPEECH EVENT and whose presence may
have an influence on what is said and how it is said. He or she may
actually take part in the exchange of speech or be merely a silent
participant; for example, as part of an audience to whom a political
speech is made.
see also INTERLOCUTORS
[*Further reading*: Hymes 1974]

participant observation /pɑːˈtɪsəpənt ˌɒbzəˈveɪʃən ‖ pɑr- ˌɑbzər-/ *n*
  participant observer /pɑːˈtɪsəpənt əbˈzɜːvəʳ ‖ pɑr- -ɜr-/ *n*
  a research procedure used in different types of research, including
  language research, in which the researcher or observer takes part in
  the situation he or she is studying as a way of collecting data for
  further study.
  It is claimed that an observer who is also a participant can
  understand a situation more fully than an observer who is merely
  looking on from the outside.

participle /ˈpɑːtəsɪpəl ‖ ˈpɑr-/ *n* **participial** /ˌpɑːtəˈsɪpɪəl ‖ ˌpɑr-/ *adj*
  a non-finite verb form (see FINITE VERB) which functions as an
  adjective, and is used in passive sentences (see VOICE¹) and to form
  PERFECT and PROGRESSIVE ASPECT. There are two participles in English,
  the **present participle** and the **past participle**.
  The present participle is formed by adding *-ing* to a verb base. It
  functions as an adjective (eg *a smiling girl, a self-winding watch*); it
  is used with *BE* to form the PROGRESSIVE (eg *It is raining*); it occurs
  in constructions such as *Let's go shopping*.
  The past participle is usually formed by adding *-ed* to a verb base;
  exceptions are the *-en*-suffix (*break – broken; fall – fallen*) and some
  irregular verbs (eg *build – built*). It is used as an adjective (eg *a
  broken window*); it is used with *BE* to form the passive (eg *I was
  amused by her*); it is used to form the PERFECT ASPECT (eg *She has
  finished*).

particle /ˈpɑːtɪkəl ‖ ˈpɑr-/ *n*
  a term sometimes used for a word which cannot readily be identified
  with any of the main PARTS OF SPEECH (ie as a noun, verb, adverb
  etc). The word *not* and the *to* used with INFINITIVES are sometimes
  called particles for this reason, as well as *up, down* and similar
  adverbs when they function as ADVERB PARTICLES.

partitive /ˈpɑːtətɪv ‖ ˈpɑr-/ *n*
also **partitive construction** /ˌpɑːtətɪv kənˈstrʌkʃən ‖ ˈpɑr-/
  a phrase used to express quantity and used with an UNCOUNTABLE
  NOUN. There are three types of partitive in English:
  (a) measure partitives, eg *a yard of cloth, an acre of land, two pints
      of milk*
  (b) typical partitives (ie where a particular partitive collocates with a
      particular noun), eg *a slice of cake, a stick of chalk, a lump of
      coal*
  (c) general partitives (ie those which are not restricted to specific
      nouns), eg *a piece of paper/cake, a bit of cheese/cloth*.
  see also COLLOCATION
  [*Further reading*: Quirk et al 1985]

part learning /ˈpɑːt ˈlɜːnɪŋ ‖ ˈpɑrt ˈlɜr-/ *n*
  see under GLOBAL LEARNING

part skills /'pɑːt skɪlz ‖ -ɑr-/ *n*
another term for MICRO-SKILLS

parts of speech /ˌpɑːts əv 'spiːtʃ ‖ -ɑr-/ *n*
a traditional term to describe the different types of word which are
used to form sentences, such as noun, pronoun, verb, adjective,
adverb, preposition, conjunction, interjection. From time to time
other parts of speech have been proposed, such as DETERMINER.
Parts of speech may be identified by:
(a) their meaning (eg a verb is the name of a state or event: *go*)
(b) their form (eg a verb has an *-ing*-form, a past tense, and a past
 participle: *going, went, gone*)
(c) their function (eg a verb may form or be part of the PREDICATE
 of a sentence: *They went away*).
These criteria will identify the most typical representatives of each
part of speech. However, many problems still remain. For example,
in the sentence:
 Their going away surprised me.
is *going* a verb or a noun?
see also GERUND, PARTICIPLE, PARTICLE

passive language knowledge /'pæsɪv 'læŋgwɪdʒ 'nɒlɪdʒ ‖ 'nɑ-/ *n*
see ACTIVE/PASSIVE LANGUAGE KNOWLEDGE

passive vocabulary /'pæsɪv və'kæbjʊləri, vəʊ- ‖ -bjəleri/ *n*
see under ACTIVE/PASSIVE LANGUAGE KNOWLEDGE

passive voice /'pæsɪv 'vɔɪs/ *n*
see under VOICE[1]

past continuous /'pɑːst kən'tɪnjʊəs/ *n*
see under PROGRESSIVE

past participle /'pɑːst 'pɑːtəsɪpəl ‖ 'pæst 'pɑr-/ *n*
see under PARTICIPLE

past perfect /'pɑːst 'pɜːfɪkt ‖ 'pæst 'pɜr-/ *n*
see under PERFECT

past tense /'pɑːst 'tens ‖ 'pæst/ *n*
the form of a verb which is usually used to show that the act or
state described by the verb occurred at a time before the present.
For example, in English:

present tense	past tense
is	*was*
walk	*walked*
try	*tried*

The form of the past which is used without an AUXILIARY VERB (eg I
left, he *wept*) is sometimes known as the **simple past** or **preterite**.

pattern practice /'pætn 'præktəs ‖ -ərn/ *n*
see under DRILL

pausing /ˈpɔːzɪŋ/ *n*
also **hesitation phenomena**
    a commonly occurring feature of natural speech in which gaps or
    hesitations appear during the production of utterances. The
    commonest types of pauses are:
    (a) **silent pauses**: silent breaks between words
    (b) **filled pauses**: gaps which are filled by such expressions as *um,*
        er, mm.
    People who speak slowly often use more pauses than people who
    speak quickly. When people speak, up to 50% of their speaking
    time may be made up of pauses.
    see also FLUENCY
    [*Further reading*: Clark & Clark 1977]

peak (of a syllable) /piːk/ *n*
    see under SYLLABLE

pedagogic grammar /ˌpedəˈgɒdʒək ˈgræməʳ ‖ -ˈgɑ-, -ˈgəʊ-/ *n*
also **pedagogical grammar**
    a grammatical description of a language which is intended for
    pedagogical purposes, such as language teaching, syllabus design, or
    the preparation of teaching materials. A pedagogic grammar may be
    based on:
    (a) grammatical analysis and description of a language
    (b) a particular grammatical theory, such as GENERATIVE
        TRANSFORMATIONAL GRAMMAR
    (c) the study of the grammatical problems of learners (see ERROR
        ANALYSIS)
    or on a combination of approaches. An example of a pedagogic
    grammar of English is Close's *A reference grammar for students of*
    English (Close 1975).

peer group /ˈpɪəʳ ˌgruːp/ *n*
    a group of people with whom a person associates or identifies, eg
    neighbourhood children of the same age, or members of the same
    class at school or of the same sports team.
    see also NETWORK

peer teaching /ˈpɪəʳ ˌtiːtʃɪŋ/ *n*
also **peer mediated instruction** /ˈpɪəʳ ˈmiːdieɪtəd ɪnˈstrʌkʃən/
    classroom teaching in which one student teaches another,
    particularly within an individualized approach to teaching (see
    INDIVIDUALIZED INSTRUCTION). For example, when students have learnt
    something, they may teach it to other students, or test other
    students on it.

percentile /pəˈsentaɪl ‖ pər-/ *n*
    (in statistics) a term indicating the position of a given score or test-
    taker in a distribution divided into 100 ranks. For example, a score

at the 9th percentile will be among the top 10% of all the scores. The higher one's percentile score, the better, on most tests.
see also DISTRIBUTION[1]

perception /pə'sepʃən ‖ pər-/ *n*
the recognition and understanding of events, objects, and stimuli through the use of senses (sight, hearing, touch, etc). Several different types of perception are distinguished:
(a) **Visual perception**: the perception of visual information and stimuli
(b) **Auditory perception**: the perception of information and stimuli received through the ears. Auditory perception requires a listener to detect different kinds of acoustic signals, and to judge differences between them according to differences in such acoustic characteristics as their frequency, amplitude, duration, order of occurrence, and rate of presentation.
(c) **Speech perception**: the understanding or comprehension of speech (see CHUNKING, HEURISTIC (2)).

perceptual salience /pə'septʃuəl 'seɪlɪəns ‖ pər'septʃəl/ *n*
another term for SALIENCE

perfect /'pɜːfɪkt ‖ 'pɜr-/ *n*
(in grammar) an ASPECT which shows a relationship between one state or event and a later state, event, or time. In English the perfect is formed from the AUXILIARY VERB *have* and the past PARTICIPLE. For example:
I have finished.   She has always loved animals.
If the auxiliary is in the present tense, the verb group is described as the **present perfect** (eg *They have eaten*) and if the auxiliary is in the past tense, the verb group is described as the **past perfect** (eg *They had finished*).
English also has a fairly rare **future perfect** (*They will have finished before noon tomorrow*).
In English the perfect generally refers
(a) to a state or event that extends up to a point in time (eg *I have lived here for six years* – up to now)
(b) to an event that occurred within a time period (eg *Have you ever been to Paris* – in your life up to now)
(c) to an event that has results which continue up to a point in time (eg *I have broken my watch* – and it's still broken now).
[*Further reading*: Leech 1971]

performance /pə'fɔːməns ‖ pər'fɔr-/ *n*
(in GENERATIVE TRANSFORMATIONAL GRAMMAR) a person's actual use of language. A difference is made between a person's knowledge of the language (COMPETENCE) and how a person uses this knowledge in producing and understanding sentences (performance). The difference between linguistic competence and linguistic performance can be seen, for example, in the production of long and complex

sentences (see RECURSIVE RULES). People may have the competence to produce an infinitely long sentence but when they actually attempt to use this knowledge (to "perform") there are many reasons why they restrict the number of adjectives, adverbs, and clauses in any one sentence. They may run out of breath, or their listeners may get bored or forget what has been said if the sentence is too long. Psycholinguists attempt to describe how competence is used in the actual production and understanding of sentences (performance). In second and foreign language learning, a learner's performance in a language may indicate his or her competence (see PERFORMANCE ANALYSIS).

There is also a somewhat different way of using the term "performance". In using language, people make errors (see SPEECH ERRORS) or false starts. These may be due to **performance factors** such as fatigue, lack of attention, excitement, nervousness. Their actual use of language on a particular occasion may not reflect their competence. The errors they make are described as examples of performance.

see also USAGE[1]

[*Further reading*: Fromkin & Rodman 1983; Chomsky 1965]

performance analysis /pə'fɔːməns ə'næləsəs ‖ pər'fɔr-/ *n*
(in SECOND LANGUAGE ACQUISITION research) an approach to the study of a learner's COMPETENCE in a language, based on the study of a learner's total linguistic performance (ie what the learner is able to say and do in the language) and not just the learner's errors (see ERROR ANALYSIS).

[*Further reading*: Svartvik 1973]

performance factors /pə'fɔːməns 'fæktəz ‖ pər'fɔr- -tərz/ *n*
see under PERFORMANCE

performance grammar /pə'fɔːməns 'græməʳ ‖ pər'fɔr-/ *n*
a description of the rules or strategies which people use when they produce and understand sentences. A performance grammar may be contrasted with a competence grammar (see COMPETENCE), which is a description of the linguistic knowledge of speakers and hearers, but not an explanation of how they use that knowledge in speaking and listening.

[*Further reading*: Carroll 1973]

performance objective /pə'fɔːməns əb'dʒektɪv/ *n*
another term for BEHAVIOURAL OBJECTIVE

performative /pə'fɔːmətɪv ‖ pər'fɔr-/ *n*
(in SPEECH ACT theory) an utterance which performs an act, such as *Watch out* (= a warning), *I promise not to be late* (= a promise). The philosopher Austin distinguished between performatives and **constatives**. A constative is an utterance which asserts something that is either true or false; for example, *Chicago is in the United*

States. Austin further distinguished between **explicit performatives**
(those containing a "performative verb", such as *promise, warn,
deny*, which names the speech act or **illocutionary force** of the
sentence) and **implicit performatives**, which do not contain a
performative verb, eg *There is a vicious dog behind you* (= an
implied warning).

It has even been suggested that there is no real difference between
constatives and implicit performatives, because the sentence *Chicago
is in the United States* can be understood to mean (*I state that*)
Chicago is in the United States, with the implicit performative verb
state.

[*Further reading*: Austin 1962; Searle 1981]

perlocutionary act /ˌpɜːləʊˈkjuːʃənəri ˈækt ‖ ˌpɜrləʊˈkjuːʃəneri/ *n*
see under LOCUTIONARY ACT

perseveration error /pəˌsevəˈreɪʃən ˈerər ‖ pər-/ *n*
see under SPEECH ERRORS

person /ˈpɜːsən ‖ ˈpɜr-/ *n*
a grammatical category which determines the choice of pronouns in
a sentence according to such principles as:
(a) whether the pronoun represents or includes the person or
persons actually speaking or writing ("first person", eg *I, we*)
(b) whether the pronoun represents the person or persons being
addressed ("second person", eg *you*)
(c) whether the pronoun represents someone or something other
than the speaker/writer or the listener/reader ("third person",
eg *he, she, it, they*).

personal function /ˈpɜːsənəl ˈfʌŋkʃən ‖ ˈpɜr-/ *n*
see under DEVELOPMENTAL FUNCTIONS OF LANGUAGE

personal pronouns /ˈpɜːsənəl ˈprəʊnaʊnz ‖ ˈpər-/ *n*
the set of pronouns which represent the grammatical category of
PERSON, and which in English is made up of *I, you, he, she, it, we,
they*, and their derived forms (eg *me, mine, yours, him, his, hers*,
etc).

pharyngeal /ˌfəˈrɪndʒɪəl, ˌfærənˈdʒɪəl/ *n, adj*
a speech sound (a CONSONANT) which is produced by pushing the very
back of the tongue (the **root**) towards the back of the throat (the
PHARYNX). The airstream from the lungs can be either completely
blocked and then released, or allowed to escape with friction (a
pharyngeal FRICATIVE).
Pharyngeal sounds are used, for example, in some dialects of
Arabic.
see also PLACE OF ARTICULATION, MANNER OF ARTICULATION
[*Further reading*: Gimson 1980]

pharynx /ˈfærɪŋks/ *n*
that part of the throat which extends from above the VOCAL CORDS up
to the soft palate (**velum**) at the back of the mouth. The pharynx is
like a large chamber and in the production of speech sounds its
shape and volume can be changed in various ways:
(a) by tightening the muscles which enclose it
(b) by movement of the back of the tongue
(c) by either raising or lowering the soft palate.
Changes in the shape of the pharynx affect the quality of the sounds
produced.
see also PLACE OF ARTICULATION

phatic communion /ˈfætɪk kəˈmjuːnɪən/ *n*
a term used by the British-Polish anthropologist Malinowski to refer
to communication between people which is not intended to seek or
convey information but has the social function of establishing or
maintaining social contact. Examples of phatic communion in
English include such expressions as *How are you?* and *Nice day,
isn't it?*

philology /fɪˈlɒlədʒi ‖ -ˈlɑ-/ *n* **philological** /ˌfɪləˈlɒdʒɪkəl ‖ -ˈlɑ-/ *adj*
another term for COMPARATIVE HISTORICAL LINGUISTICS

phone /fəʊn/ *n* **phonic** /ˈfɒnɪk ‖ ˈfɑ-/ *adj*
individual sounds as they occur in speech. Phones are grouped by
PHONEMIC ANALYSIS into the distinctive sound units (PHONEMES) of a
language.
For example, in English, the different ways of pronouncing the
vowel in the word *can*, eg long [æː], shorter [æ], with nasalization
[æ̃], are all phones of the phoneme /æ/.
see also ALLOPHONE, PHONEMICS, PHONOLOGY

phoneme /ˈfəʊniːm/ *n* **phonemic** /fəˈniːmɪk/ *adj*
the smallest unit of sound in a language which can distinguish two
words. For example:
(a) in English, the words *pan* and *ban* differ only in their initial
    sound: *pan* begins with /p/ and *ban* with /b/
(b) *ban* and *bin* differ only in their vowels: /æ/ and /ɪ/.
Therefore, /p/, /b/, /æ/, and /ɪ/ are phonemes of English. The
number of phonemes varies from one language to another. English
is often considered to have 44 phonemes: 24 CONSONANTS and 20
VOWELS.
see also ALLOPHONE, GRAPHEME, MINIMAL PAIR, PHONEMICS, PHONOLOGY
[*Further reading*: Gimson 1980; Bloomfield 1933]

phonemic analysis /fəˈniːmɪk əˈnæləsəs/ *n*
the grouping of words and sounds (PHONES) in a particular language
in order to decide which are the distinctive sound units (PHONEMES)
of that language and which are only variants of these.
For example, the two English words *nip* and *nib* differ only because

nip ends with /p/ and *nib* ends with /b/. So /p/ and /b/ are two separate English phonemes.
On the other hand, pronouncing *nip* with an aspirated /p/, [pʰ], does not make it into another word. So [pʰ] is a variant (an ALLOPHONE) of /p/ and not a separate phoneme.
There are different approaches to phonemic analysis (see DISTINCTIVE FEATURES, MINIMAL PAIRS.
See also ALLOPHONE, ASPIRATION, PHONEMICS, PHONOLOGY

phonemic notation /fəˈniːmɪk nəʊˈteɪʃən/ *n*
see under NOTATION

phonemics /fəˈniːmɪks/ *n* **phonemic** *adj*
(1) the study or description of the distinctive sound units (PHONEME*s*) of a language and their relationship to one another.
(2) procedures for finding the phonemes of a language (see PHONEMIC ANALYSIS).
The term "phonemics" has been used by American linguists, particularly in STRUCTURAL LINGUISTICS. Lately, the term PHONOLOGY has been preferred.
(3) the phonemic system of a language, as in a phrase like "the phonemics of English".
see also MORPHOPHONEMICS

phonetic method /fəˈnetɪk ˈmeθəd/ *n*
another term for PHONICS

phonetic notation /fəˈnetɪk nəʊˈteɪʃən/ *n*
also **phonetic script**
see under NOTATION, PHONETIC SYMBOLS

phonetics /fəˈnetɪks/ *n* **phonetic** *adj*
the study of speech sounds. There are three main areas of phonetics:
(1) **Articulatory phonetics** deals with the way in which speech sounds are produced. Sounds are usually classified according to the position of the lips and the tongue, how far open the mouth is, whether or not the VOCAL CORDS are vibrating, etc.
(2) **Acoustic phonetics** deals with the transmission of speech sounds through the air. When a speech sound is produced it causes minor air disturbances (SOUND WAVE*s*). Various instruments are used to measure the characteristics of these sound waves.
(3) **Auditory phonetics** deals with how speech sounds are perceived by the listener.
For example, a listener may perceive:
(a) differences in ASPIRATION eg between the aspirated /p/ of [pʰɪt] *pit* and the unaspirated /p/ of [tɪp] *tip*.
(b) other differences in sound quality, eg between the "clear" /l/ of [laɪt] *light* and the "dark" /l/ of [hɪɫ] *hill*.
see also PHONEMICS, PHONOLOGY
[*Further reading*: Gimson 1980; Denes & Pinson 1963]

phonetic script /fə'netɪk 'skrɪpt/ *n*
another term for **phonetic notation**
see under NOTATION, PHONETIC SYMBOLS

phonetic symbols /fə'netɪk 'sɪmbəlz/ *n*
special symbols which express the sounds of an actual spoken
utterance in writing. A transcription of such an utterance in
phonetic symbols is said to be in **phonetic notation** or **script**.
For example, the sound which is written *sh* in English, *sch* in
German and *ch* in French can be expressed by the symbols [ʃ] or
[š], eg English [ʃɪp] *ship*, German [ʃɪf] *Schiff* "ship". French [ʃik]
chic "smart, stylish".
see also INTERNATIONAL PHONETIC ALPHABET, NOTATION, PHONETICS

phonics /'fɒnɪks ‖ 'fɑ-/ *n*
also **phonetic method**
a method of teaching children to read. It is commonly used in
teaching reading in the mother tongue.
Children are taught to recognize the relationship between letters and
sounds. They are taught the sounds which the letters of the alphabet
represent, and then try to build up the sound of a new or unfamiliar
word by saying it one sound at a time.
see also ALPHABETIC METHOD
[*Further reading*: Smith 1971]

phonological component /ˌfɒnə'lɒdʒɪkəl kəm'pəʊnənt ‖ ˌfɑnə'lɑ-/ *n*
see under GENERATIVE TRANSFORMATIONAL GRAMMAR

phonological rule /ˌfɒnə'lɒdʒɪkəl 'ruːl ‖ ˌfɑnə'lɑ-/ *n*
see under GENERATIVE PHONOLOGY

phonology /fə'nɒlədʒi ‖ -'nɑ-/ *n* **phonological**
/ˌfɒnə'lɒdʒɪkəl ‖ ˌfɑnə'lɑ-/ *adj*
(1) another term for PHONEMICS.
(2) (for some linguists) a cover term for both PHONETICS and
PHONEMICS.
(3) the establishment and description of the distinctive sound units
of a language (PHONEMES) by means of DISTINCTIVE FEATURES.
Each phoneme is considered as consisting of a group of these
features and differing in at least one feature from the other
phonemes, eg:

/iː/	/uː/
+ high	+ high
− low	− low
− back	+ back
− round	+ round

where the features + or − *high*, + or − *low*, + or − *back* refer to
the position of the tongue in the mouth and + or − *round* to
whether the lips are rounded or not.

Phonology is also concerned with:

(a) the study of word-to-word relations in sentences; that is, how sound patterns are affected by the combination of words. For example, /gɪv/ *give* and /hɪm/ *him* may combine to /gɪvɪm/ *give him*.

(b) the investigation of INTONATION PATTERNS.

see also BOUNDARIES, GENERATIVE PHONOLOGY, SUPRASEGMENTALS

phonotactics /ˌfəʊnə'tæktɪks/ *n* **phonotactic** *adj*
(in PHONOLOGY) the arrangements of the distinctive sound units (PHONEMES) in a language.
For example, in English, the consonant groups (CONSONANT CLUSTERS) /spr/ and /str/ can occur at the beginning of a word, as in *sprout*, *strain*, but they cannot occur at the end of a word. A description of the phonotactics of English consonant clusters would include this information.

phrasal-prepositional verb /'freɪzəl ˌprepə'zɪʃənəl 'vɜːb ‖ 'vɜrb/ *n*
see under PHRASAL VERB

phrasal verb /'freɪzəl 'vɜːb ‖ 'vɜrb/ *n*
a verbal construction consisting of a verb plus an ADVERB PARTICLE. A distinction may be made between phrasal verbs, **prepositional verbs**, and **phrasal-prepositional verbs**, according to the different grammatical patterns in which they occur. For example:

	phrasal verb		prepositional verb
Particle may be stressed	*Turn OFF the light.*	Verb may be stressed	*I'll APPLY for the job.*
Particle can occur after the object	*Turn the light off.*	Particle cannot occur after the object	(*I'll apply the job for*)
Short pronouns occur between the verb and the particle	*Turn it off.* (*Turn off it*)	Pronouns occur after the verb + particle	*I'll apply for it.* (*I'll apply it for*)

A phrasal-prepositional verb consists of a verb, an adverb particle, and a PREPOSITION:

We must cut down on expenses.
They put their failure down to bad advice.

The meaning of some of these verbal constructions can be guessed from the meanings of their parts (eg *cut down on*). But the meaning of others is idiomatic (eg *put down to*).

phrase

Nowadays the term "phrasal verb" is often used to include phrasal verbs, prepositional verbs, and phrasal-prepositional verbs.

see also IDIOM

[*Further reading*: Quirk et al 1985]

phrase /freɪz/ *n*

see under CLAUSE

phrase marker /'freɪz ˌmɑːkəʳ ‖ ˌmɑrkər/ *n*
also **P-marker**

(in GENERATIVE TRANSFORMATIONAL GRAMMAR) the representation of the structure of a sentence. This could be its basic syntactic structure (DEEP STRUCTURE) or the structure after the application of transformational rules.

see also BASE COMPONENT, TRANSFORMATIONAL COMPONENT

[*Further reading*: Chomsky 1965]

phrase-structure component /'freɪz 'strʌktʃəʳ kəm'pəʊnənt/ *n*

another term for BASE COMPONENT

phrase-structure grammar /'freɪz 'strʌktʃəʳ 'græməʳ/ *n*

a grammar which analyses the structure of different sentence types in a language. It consists of phrase-structure rules (see BASE COMPONENT) which show how a sentence can be broken up into its various parts (CONSTITUENTs) and how each part can be expanded. The structure of a sentence can be illustrated by a diagram called a **tree diagram**. For example, the structure of the English sentence:

The parrot shrieked noisily.

can be shown by the simplified diagram:

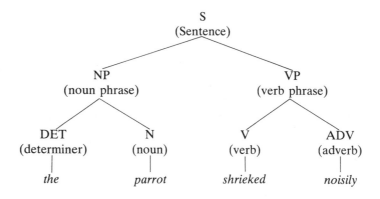

A phrase-structure grammar is a major part of the BASE COMPONENT of a GENERATIVE TRANSFORMATIONAL GRAMMAR.

see also GENERATIVE TRANSFORMATIONAL GRAMMAR

[*Further reading*: Aitchison 1978; Chomsky 1957]

phrase-structure rule /'freɪz 'strʌktʃər 'ruːl/ *n*
see under BASE COMPONENT

phylogeny /fɪ'lɒdʒəni ‖ -'lɑ-/ *n*
also **phylogenesis** /ˌfaɪləʊ'dʒenəsəs/
see under ONTOGENY

pidgin /'pɪdʒən/ *n* **pidginized** /'pɪdʒənaɪzd/ *adj*
a language which develops as a **contact language** when groups of
people who speak different languages come into contact and
communicate with one another, as when foreign traders
communicate with the local population or workers on plantations or
in factories communicate with one another or with their bosses. A
pidgin usually has a limited vocabulary and a very reduced
grammatical structure which may expand when a pidgin is used over
a long period of time or for many purposes. For example, Tok Pisin
(New Guinea Pidgin):
    yu   ken kisim   long olgeta bik pela   stua.
    You   can get (it) at   all   big (noun marker) stores.
see also CREOLE, PIDGINIZATION[1], PIDGINIZED FORM
[*Further reading*: Todd 1984]

pidginization[1] /ˌpɪdʒənaɪ'zeɪʃən/ *n*
the process by which a PIDGIN develops.

pidginization[2] *n*
(in second and foreign language learning) the development of a
grammatically reduced form of a TARGET LANGUAGE[1]. This is usually a
temporary stage in language learning. The learner's INTERLANGUAGE
may have a limited system of auxiliary verbs, simplified question and
negative forms, and reduced rules for TENSE[1], NUMBER[1], and other
grammatical categories.
If learners do not advance beyond this stage, the result may be a
PIDGINIZED FORM of the target language.
see also PIDGINIZATION HYPOTHESIS

pidginization hypothesis /ˌpɪdʒənaɪ'zeɪʃən haɪ'pɒθəsəs ‖ -'pɑ-/ *n*
(in SECOND LANGUAGE ACQUISITION theory) the hypothesis that a
PIDGINIZED FORM of a language may develop (a) when learners regard
themselves as socially separate from speakers of the TARGET
LANGUAGE[1] (b) when a language is used for a very limited range of
functions.
see also PIDGINIZATION[2]
[*Further reading*: Schumann 1978]

pidginized form (of a language) /'pɪdʒənaɪzd ˌfɔːm ‖ -ɔr-/ *n*
a variety of a language in which the sentence structure and the
vocabulary of the original language have been greatly reduced.

Generally, elements from another language have been absorbed, either in the form of vocabulary items or in the way sentences are structured (see PIDGIN).

An example is Bahasa Pasar (Bazaar Malay), a pidginized form of Malay, which was spoken extensively by Chinese and other non-Malays in Malaysia and Singapore.

pitch /pɪtʃ/ n

When we listen to people speaking, we can hear some sounds or groups of sounds in their speech to be relatively higher or lower than others. This relative height of speech sounds as perceived by a listener is called "pitch".

For example, in the English question *Ready?* meaning "Are you ready?" the second syllable *-dy* will be heard as having a higher pitch than the first syllable, though pitch movement upwards will begin on the first syllable *rea-* (see TONE[2]). What we can hear as pitch is produced by the VOCAL CORDS vibrating. The faster the vocal cords vibrate, the higher the pitch.

see also SOUND WAVES

pitch level /'pɪtʃ ˌlevəl/ n

the relative height of the PITCH of a speaker's voice, as this is perceived by the listener.

For English, three pitch levels have often been recognized: normal pitch level, higher than normal level, lower than normal level. These three levels cannot be identified in absolute terms. One person's high pitch will not be the same as another person's high pitch. Differences in pitch level are therefore relative (see KEY[2])

see also TONE UNIT

[*Further reading*: Brazil, Coulthard, & Johns 1980; Crystal 1969]

pitch movement /'pɪtʃ ˌmuːvmənt/ n

another term for TONE[2]

pitch range[1] /'pɪtʃ ˌreɪndʒ/ n

variations in PITCH height that an individual speaker is able to produce.

Differences in the pitch of individual speakers are related to differences in the size of their VOCAL CORDS and the structure of their VOCAL TRACT. Usually, women can speak with a higher pitch than men, but there are exceptions.

pitch range[2] n

variations in height which are used by a speaker or group of speakers in communication. Whether the pitch range used by individuals in a speech community is wide or narrow often depends on social or cultural conventions and may be a convention of a whole speech community.

For example, the pitch range of the average Australian when speaking English is narrower than that of many British English speakers.

When speakers are in certain emotional states, they may either extend their normal pitch range, eg to express anger or excitement, or narrow it, eg to express boredom or misery.

[*Further reading*: Brazil, Coulthard, & Johns 1980]

pivot grammar /ˈpɪvət ˌgræməʳ/ n
a term for a now-discarded theory of grammatical development in first-language learning. Children were said to develop two major grammatical classes of words: a pivot class (a small group of words which were attached to other words, eg *on, allgone, more*) and an "open class" (eg *shoe, milk*) to which pivot words were attached. The child's early grammar was thought to be a set of rules which determined how the two classes of words could be combined to produce utterances such as *allgone milk, shoe on*.

[*Further reading*: McNeill 1970]

PLAB /ˌpiː el eɪ ˈbiː/ n
an abbreviation for the *P*imsleur *L*anguage *A*ptitude *B*attery, a test of LANGUAGE APTITUDE.

placement test /ˈpleɪsmənt ˌtest/ n
a test which is designed to place students at an appropriate level in a programme or course. The term "placement test" does not refer to what a test contains or how it is constructed, but to the purpose for which it is used. Various types of test or testing procedure (eg dictation, an interview, a grammar test) can be used for placement purposes.

[*Further reading*: Valette 1977]

place of articulation /ˈpleɪs əv ɑːtɪkjʊˈleɪʃən ‖ ɑrtɪkjə-/ n
there are many parts of the mouth and throat (the **oral cavity**) that are used in the production of speech sounds. The main ones for the articulation of English CONSONANTs are:
(a) the two lips (BILABIAL), eg /p/
(b) the lower lip touching the upper teeth (LABIODENTAL), eg /f/
(c) the tongue touching the upper teeth (INTERDENTAL), eg /θ/ *th* in *thick*
(d) the tongue touching the alveolar ridge (**alveolum**) (ALVEOLAR), eg /t/
(e) the back of the tongue touching the soft palate (**velum**) (VELAR), eg /k/

The production of VOWELs is conditioned by the position of the tongue in the mouth, eg FRONT VOWELs, BACK VOWELs, HIGH VOWELs, LOW VOWELs.

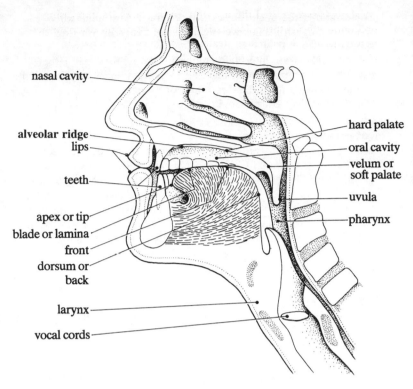

- nasal cavity
- alveolar ridge
- lips
- teeth
- apex or tip
- blade or lamina
- front
- dorsum or back
- larynx
- vocal cords
- hard palate
- oral cavity
- velum or soft palate
- uvula
- pharynx

see also CARDINAL VOWELS, MANNER OF ARTICULATION
[*Further reading*: Gimson 1980]

plosive /ˈpləʊsɪv/ *n*
another term for STOP

plural /ˈplʊərəl/ *n*
(with English COUNTABLE NOUNS, and PRONOUNS,) the form referring to more than one. For example, *books, geese, they* are the plurals of *book, goose*, and *he/she/it*.

P-marker /ˈpiː ˌmɑːkəʳ ‖ -ɑr-/ *n*
an abbreviation for PHRASE MARKER

politeness /pəˈlaɪtnəs/ *n*
(in language study) (a) how languages express the SOCIAL DISTANCE between speakers and their different ROLE RELATIONSHIPS; (b) how face-work (see FACE); that is, the attempt to establish, maintain, and save face during conversation, is carried out in a speech community. Languages differ in how they express politeness. In English, phrases like *I wonder if I could* . . . can be used to make a request more polite. In other languages the same effect can be expressed by a word or PARTICLE.
Politeness markers include differences between FORMAL SPEECH and

COLLOQUIAL SPEECH, and the use of ADDRESS FORMS. In expressing politeness, the anthropologists Brown and Levinson distinguished between **positive politeness strategies** (those which show the closeness, intimacy, and rapport between speaker and hearer) and **negative politeness strategies** (those which indicate the social distance between speaker and hearer).
[*Further reading*: Brown & Levinson 1978]

politeness formula /pə'laɪtnəs 'fɔːmjʊlər ‖ 'fɔrmjə-/ *n*
see under ROUTINE

polysemous /pə'lɪsəməs/ *adj* **polysemy** /pə'lɪsémi/ *n*
(of a word) having two or more meanings, eg *foot* in:
   He hurt his <u>foot</u>.
   She stood at the <u>foot</u> of the stairs.
A well-known problem in SEMANTICS is how to decide whether we are dealing with a single polysemous word (like *foot* above) or with two or more HOMONYMS[3].
see also HOMOGRAPHS, HOMOPHONES
[*Further reading*: Palmer 1981]

polysyllabic /,pɒlɪsə'læbɪk ‖ ,pɑ-/ *adj*
(of a word) consisting of more than one SYLLABLE.
For example, in English:
   baby: *ba-by*
   telephone: *tel-e-phone*
are polysyllabic words.

population /,pɒpjʊ'leɪʃən ‖ ,pɑpjə-/ *n*
(in statistics) any set of items, individuals, etc which share some common and observable characteristics and from which a SAMPLE can be taken. Thus, one can speak of comparing test scores across a sample of a population of students.

positive politeness strategies /'pɒzətɪv pə'laɪtnəs 'strætədʒɪz ‖ 'pɑ-/ *n*
see under POLITENESS

positive reinforcement /,pɒzətɪv ,riːɪn'fɔːsmənt ‖ ,pɑ- -'fɔrs-/ *n*
see under OPERANT CONDITIONING, STIMULUS-RESPONSE THEORY

positive transfer /'pɒzətɪv 'trænsfɜːr ‖ 'pɑ-/ *n*
see under LANGUAGE TRANSFER

possessive /pə'zesɪv/ *n*
a word or part of a word which is used to show ownership or possession. In English, there are many kinds of possessives, for example:
(a) possessive pronouns, such as *my, her, your, mine, hers, yours,* etc
(b) *'s*, as in *Helen's shoes*, and *s'*, as in *the three boys' books*
(c) the *of* construction, as in *the home of the doctor*

The possessive pronouns that are used before a noun (eg *my, her, your*) are often called "possessive adjectives" to distinguish them from those that are used after a verb (eg *mine, hers, yours*). The distinction can be seen in a pair of sentences like:

My book is here. This book is mine.

see also DETERMINER

[*Further reading*: Quirk et al 1985]

post-creole continuum /ˈpəʊst ˈkriːəʊl kənˈtɪnjʊəm/ *n*

When people in a CREOLE-speaking community are taught in the standard language to which the creole is related, they form a post-creole continuum.

For example, in Jamaica and Guyana, an English-based creole is spoken and Standard English is taught in schools. Those with higher levels of education speak something close to Standard English, the **acrolect**. Those with little or no education speak the creole or something close to it, the **basilect**, and the rest speak a range of varieties in between, the **mesolects**.

speech varieties	speakers
acrolect	higher education and social status
mesolects	
basilect	little or no education, low social status

The use of the terms "acrolect", "mesolects", "basilect" has recently been extended. They are now sometimes used in describing any range of speech varieties from the most prestigious (acrolect) to the least prestigious (basilect).

see also DECREOLIZATION, SPEECH CONTINUUM

[*Further reading*: Bickerton 1975]

postmodifier /ˌpəʊstˈmɒdəfaɪəʳ ‖ -ˈmɑ-/ *n*

see under MODIFIER

postponed subject /pəsˈpəʊnd ˈsʌbdʒɪkt/ *n*

see under EXTRAPOSITION

postposition /ˌpəʊstpəˈzɪʃən/ *n*

a word or MORPHEME which follows a noun or NOUN PHRASE[1] and indicates location, direction, possession, etc.

For example, in Japanese:

Tokyo – kara

"Tokyo" "from"

"from Tokyo"

English prefers PREPOSITIONs to postpositions, but a word like *notwithstanding* can be used in either way:

The plan went ahead, notwithstanding my protests. (prepositional use)

The plan went ahead, my protests notwithstanding. (postpositional use)

post-test /'pəʊst ˌtest/ *n*
a test given after learning has occurred or is supposed to have occurred. A test given before learning has occurred is a pre-test. In teaching, the comparison of pre-test and post-test results measures the amount of progress a learner has made.

practice effect /'præktəs ɪˌfekt/ *n*
the effect of previous practice on later performance. For example, in testing how much grammar improvement had occurred in students after a grammar course, if the same items appeared on a pre-test and a post-test (see POST-TEST), students might perform better on the post-test simply because they had already had practice on the items during the pre-test, rather than because of what they had learned from the course.

practice stage /'præktəs ˌsteɪdʒ/ *n*
also **repetition stage**
see under STAGE

pragmatic error /præg'mætɪk 'erəʳ/ *n*
see under ERROR

pragmatics /præg'mætɪks/ *n* **pragmatic** *adj*
the study of the use of language in communication, particularly the relationships between sentences and the contexts and situations in which they are used. Pragmatics includes the study of:
(a) how the interpretation and use of UTTERANCES depends on knowledge of the real world
(b) how speakers use and understand SPEECH ACTS
(c) how the structure of sentences is influenced by the relationship between the speaker and the hearer.
Pragmatics is sometimes contrasted with SEMANTICS, which deals with meaning without reference to the users and communicative functions of sentences.
see also USAGE[2]
[*Further reading*: Leech 1983; Levinson 1983; Palmer 1981]

Prague School /'prɑːg ˌskuːl/ *n*
a linguistic tradition which began with the founding of the "Prague Linguistic Circle" in 1926. Many ideas which have influenced modern linguistic thought were developed by the linguists belonging to the Prague School.
Among the things of interest to these linguists were:
(a) research into the DISTINCTIVE FEATURES of sounds
(b) the relationship between the grammatical forms and the sounds of a language (see MORPHOPHONEMICS)
(c) stylistic variation in a language
(d) the inclusion of extralinguistic factors, such as the social environment, in linguistic investigations (see COMMUNICATIVE COMPETENCE, DISCOURSE ANALYSIS).

Some well-known linguists connected with the Prague School include Jakobson, Trubetzkoy, Isačenko, Vachek, Daneš and Firbas.
see also FUNCTIONAL SENTENCE PERSPECTIVE
[*Further reading*: Ivic 1963]

predeterminer /ˌpriːdɪˈtɜːmənər ‖ -ɜr-/ *n*
a word which occurs before DETERMINERs in a NOUN PHRASE[1]. For example, in English the QUANTIFIERs *all, both, half, double, twice,* etc can be predeterminers.

all the bread
| determiner
predeterminer

[*Further reading*: Quirk et al 1985]

predicate /ˈpredɪkət/ *n* **predicate** /ˈpredɪkeɪt/ *v*
that part of a sentence which states or asserts something about the SUBJECT and usually consists of a verb either with or without an OBJECT[1], COMPLEMENT, or ADVERB. For example:

John is tired.
The children saw the play.
The sun rose.

Adjectives, nouns, etc which occur in the predicate are said to be used "predicatively". For example:

Her behaviour was friendly. (PREDICATIVE ADJECTIVE)
These books are dictionaries. (predicative noun)

see also ATTRIBUTIVE ADJECTIVE

predication /ˌpredɪˈkeɪʃən/ *n*
see under PROPOSITION

predicative adjective /preˈdɪkətɪv ˈædʒəktɪv/ *n*
an adjective that is used after a verb
see also under ATTRIBUTIVE ADJECTIVE

predictive validity /prɪˈdɪktɪv vəˈlɪdəti/ *n*
a type of VALIDITY based on the degree to which a test accurately predicts future performance. A LANGUAGE APTITUDE test, for example, should have predictive validity, because the results of the test should predict the ability to learn a second or foreign language.

prefabricated language /priːˈfæbrɪkeɪtəd ˈlæŋgwɪdʒ/ *n*
also **prefabricated speech** /priːˈfæbrɪkeɪtəd ˈspiːtʃ/
another term for ROUTINE

prefix /ˈpriːfɪks/ *n*
a letter or sound or group of letters or sounds which are added to the beginning of a word, and which change the meaning or function of the word.
Some COMBINING FORMs can be used like prefixes. For example, the word *pro-French* uses the prefix *pro-* "in favour of", and the word *Anglo-French* uses the combining form *Anglo-* "English".
see also under AFFIX

premodifier /priː'mɒdᵻfaɪəʳ ‖ -'mɑ-/ *n*
see under MODIFIER

pre-operational stage /ˌpriːɒpə'reɪʃənəl 'steɪdʒ ‖ -əpə-/ *n*
see under GENETIC EPISTEMOLOGY

preposition /ˌprepə'zɪʃən/ *n*
a word used with NOUNs, PRONOUNs and GERUNDs, to link them
grammatically to other words. The phrase so formed, consisting of a
preposition and its COMPLEMENT, is a **prepositional phrase**. In English,
a prepositional phrase may be "discontinuous", as in:
   Who(m) did you speak to?
Prepositions may express such meanings as possession (eg *the leg of
the table*), direction (eg *to the bank*), place (eg *at the corner*), time
(eg *before now*). They can also mark the cases discussed in CASE
GRAMMAR. For example, in the sentence:
   Smith killed the policeman with a revolver.
the preposition *with* shows that a revolver is in the INSTRUMENTAL
CASE.
In English, too, there are groups of words (eg *in front of, owing to*)
that can function like single-word prepositions.
see also POSTPOSITION
[*Further reading*: Quirk et al 1985]

prepositional adverb /ˌprepə'zɪʃənəl 'ædvɜːb ‖ -ɜr-/ *n*
another term for ADVERB PARTICLE

prepositional complement /ˌprepə'zɪʃənəl 'kɒmpləmənt ‖ 'kʌm-/ *n*
also **prepositional object** /ˌprepə'zɪʃənəl 'ɒbdʒɪkt ‖ 'ab-/, **object (of a
preposition)**
see under COMPLEMENT

prepositional phrase /ˌprepə'zɪʃənəl 'freɪz/ *n*
see under PREPOSITION

prepositional verb /ˌprepə'zɪʃənəl 'vɜːb ‖ 'vɜrb/ *n*
see under PHRASAL VERB

prescriptive grammar /prɪ'skrɪptɪv ˌgræməʳ/ *n*
a grammar which states rules for what is considered the best or most
correct usage. Prescriptive grammars are often based not on
descriptions of actual usage but rather on the grammarian's views of
what is best. Many TRADITIONAL GRAMMARs are of this kind.
see also DESCRIPTIVE GRAMMAR, NORMATIVE GRAMMAR

presentation stage /ˌprezən'teɪʃən ˌsteɪdʒ/ *n*
see under STAGE

present continuous /'prezənt kən'tɪnjʊəs/ *n*
see under PROGRESSIVE

present participle /'prezənt 'pɑːtᵻsɪpəl ‖ 'pɑr-/ *n*
see under PARTICIPLE

present perfect /'prezənt 'pɜːfɪkt ‖ 'pɜr-/ *n*
see under PERFECT

present perfect continuous /'prezənt 'pɜːfɪkt kən'tɪnjuəs ‖ 'pɜr-/ *n*
see under PROGRESSIVE

present tense /'prezənt 'tens/ *n*
a tense which typically relates the time of an action or state to the present moment in time. In English the present tense can also be used to refer to future time (eg *We leave tomorrow*) or to timeless expressions (eg *Cats have tails*), and for this reason it is sometimes called the NON-PAST tense.
see also ASPECT

presupposition /ˌpriːsʌpə'zɪʃən/ *n* **presuppose** /ˌpriːsə'pəʊz/ *v*
what a speaker or writer assumes that the receiver of the message already knows.
For example:
> speaker A: *What about inviting Simon tonight?*
> speaker B: *What a good idea; then he can give Monica a lift.*
Here, the presuppositions are, amongst others, that speakers A and B know who Simon and Monica are, that Simon has a vehicle, most probably a car, and that Monica has no vehicle at the moment. Children often presuppose too much. They may say:
> . . .*and he said "let's go" and we went there.*
even if their hearers do not know who *he* is and where *there* is.
see also COHERENCE, COHESION

pre-teaching /'priː 'tiːtʃɪŋ/ *n*
selecting new or difficult items that students will meet in a future classroom activity, and teaching such items before the activity.
For example, difficult words in a listening-comprehension exercise may be taught before students do the exercise.

preterite /'pretərət/ *n*
see under PAST TENSE

pre-test /'priːˌtest/ *n* **pre-test** /ˌpriː'test/ *v*
the try-out phase of a newly written but not yet fully developed test. Tests under development may be revised on the basis of the ITEM ANALYSIS obtained from the results of pre-testing.
see also under POST-TEST

pretonic /priː'tɒnɪk ‖ -'tɑ-/ *n, adj*
see under TONE UNIT

primary cardinal vowel /'praɪməri 'kɑːdənəl 'vauəl ‖ -meri 'kɑr-/ *n*
see under CARDINAL VOWEL

primary language /'praɪməri ˌlæŋgwɪdʒ ‖ -meri/ *n*
the language which a person uses most frequently in his or her daily life, although it may not be the person's MOTHER TONGUE.

principal clause /'prɪnsə̇pəl 'klɔːz/ *n*
see under DEPENDENT CLAUSE

proactive inhibition /prəʊ'æktɪv ˌɪnhə̇'bɪʃən/ *n*
also **proactive interference** /prəʊ'æktɪv ɪntə'fɪərəns ‖ -tər-/
the interfering effect of earlier learning on later learning.
For example, if a learner first learns how to produce questions
which require AUXILIARY VERB inversion (eg *I can go → Can I go?*)
this may interfere with the learning of patterns where auxiliary
inversion is not required. The learner may write **I don't know
where can I find it* instead of *I don't know where I can find it*.
By contrast, **retroactive inhibition/interference** is the effect of later
learning on earlier learning. For example, children learning English
may learn irregular past-tense forms such as *went, saw*. Later, when
they begin to learn the regular-*ed* past-tense inflection, they may
stop using *went* and *saw* and produce **goed* and **seed*.

problem solving /'prɒbləm 'sɒlvɪŋ ‖ 'prɑ- 'sɑl-/ *n*
a learning STRATEGY which involves selecting from several
alternatives in order to reach a desired goal. In second and foreign
language learning, problem-solving strategies are often used, for
example, in choosing whether to use *a* or *the* before a noun.

procedural syllabus /prə'siːdʒərəl 'sɪləbəs/ *n*
another term for TASK SYLLABUS

proclaiming tone /prə'kleɪmɪŋ 'təʊn/ *n*
see under REFERRING TONE

production stage /prə'dʌkʃən ˌsteɪdʒ/ *n*
also **transfer stage, free practice**
see under STAGE

productive/receptive language knowledge /prə'dʌktɪv rɪ'septɪv
'læŋgwɪdʒ ˌnɒlɪdʒ ‖ -ˌnɑ-/ *n*
another term for ACTIVE/PASSIVE LANGUAGE KNOWLEDGE

productive skills /prə'dʌktɪv 'skɪlz/ *n*
see under LANGUAGE SKILLS

product-process distinction /'prɒdʌkt 'prəʊses dɪ'stɪŋkʃən ‖ 'prɑdʌkt
'prɑ-/ *n*
(in language teaching and SECOND LANGUAGE ACQUISITION research) a
distinction sometimes made between completed acts of
communication or language output (products) and the underlying
abilities and skills used in producing them (processes).
For example: in writing, letters, compositions, and long essays are
examples of the products of writing. But in order to write a long
essay, a number of processes are involved, such as collecting
information, note-taking, outlining, drafting, and revising. These are
among the processes of writing the essay (the product). Language

teaching and the study of language learning are concerned both with products, and with underlying processes.

[*Further reading*: Murray 1980]

proficiency /prə'fɪʃənsi/ *n*
see LANGUAGE PROFICIENCY

proficiency test /prə'fɪʃənsi ˌtest/ *n*
a test which measures how much of a language someone has learned. The difference between a proficiency test and an ACHIEVEMENT TEST is that the latter is usually designed to measure how much a student has learned from a particular course or SYLLABUS. A proficiency test is not linked to a particular course of instruction, but measures the learner's general level of language mastery. Although this may be a result of previous instruction and learning the latter are not the focus of attention. Some proficiency tests have been standardized for worldwide use, such as the American TOEFL TEST which is used to measure the English language proficiency of foreign students who wish to study in the USA. A proficiency test measures what the student has learned relative to a specific purpose, eg does he or she know enough English to follow a lecture in English.
see also ACHIEVEMENT TEST

[*Further reading*: Vallette 1977]

profile /'prəʊfaɪl/ *n*
(in testing, statistics, etc) a graphic representation of scores or VARIABLES[2] of an individual or group on a number of tests or measures for the purposes of comparison. For example, the profile below is based on PERCENTILE scores of a student in English, French, and Mathematics.

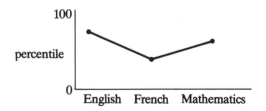

pro-forms /'prəʊˌfɔːmz ‖ -ɔr-/ *n*
forms which can serve as replacements for different elements in a sentence. For example:
(a) A: *I hope you can come.*
    B: *I hope so.* (*so* replaces *that I can come*)
(b) A: *Mary is in London.*
    B: *John is there too.* (*there* replaces *in London*)
(c) *We invited Mary and John to eat with us because we liked them.*
    (*them* replaces *Mary and John*)

(d) A: *I like coffee.*
   B: *We do too.* (*do* replaces *like coffee*)
see also PRONOUN, PRO-VERB
[*Further reading*: Quirk et al 1985]

programme design /ˈprəʊɡræm dɪˌzaɪn/ *n*
another term for COURSE DESIGN

programmed learning /ˌprəʊɡræmd ˈlɜːnɪŋ ‖ ˈlɜr-/ *n*
also **programmed instruction** /ˌprəʊɡræmd ɪnˈstrʌkʃən/
an APPROACH to the design of teaching/learning in which the subject
matter to be learned is presented as an ordered sequence of items,
each of which requires a response from the learner. The student
then compares his or her response with the correct response which
is provided.
In a **linear programme** students work through learning material
which is presented in graded units, at their own pace.
In a **branching programme** a student who has difficulty with a
particular item is directed to supplementary or revision material in a
separate part (a "branch") of the programme. Then the student is
returned to the main programme.
Linear programmes and branching programmes may be combined.
[*Further reading*: Lane 1964; Lumsdaine & Glaser 1960]

progressive /prəˈɡresɪv/ *n, adj*
also **continuous**
a grammatical ASPECT which indicates that an action is incomplete, in
progress, or developing. The progressive in English is formed with
the AUXILIARY VERB BE and the *-ing* form of the verb (eg *She is
wearing contact lenses. They were crossing the road when the
accident occurred*). The progressive aspect may be used (a) with the
present tense (*Today I am wearing glasses*: present tense;
progressive aspect) This is called the **present continuous**. (b) with
the past tense (*Yesterday I was wearing glasses*: past tense;
progressive aspect) This is called the **past continuous**. (c) with
PERFECT aspect: (*I have been wearing glasses for six years*: present
tense; perfect and progressive aspects). This is called the **present
perfect continuous**. Verbs which describe states in English (eg *know,
believe*) are not usually used in the progressive.
see also STATIVE VERB
[*Further reading*: Comrie 1976]

progressive assimilation /prəˈɡresɪv əˌsɪməˈleɪʃən/ *n*
see under ASSIMILATION[1]

progress test /ˈprəʊɡres ˌtest ‖ ˈprɑ-/ *n*
an ACHIEVEMENT TEST linked to a particular set of teaching materials
or a particular course of instruction. Tests prepared by a teacher
and given at the end of a chapter, course, or term are progress

tests. Progress tests may be regarded as similar to achievement tests but narrower and much more specific in scope.
They help the teacher to judge the degree of success of his or her teaching and to identify the weakness of the learners.
[*Further reading*: Heaton 1975]

prominence /ˈprɒmə̇nəns ‖ ˈprɑ-/ *n* **prominent** *adj*
(in DISCOURSE), greater STRESS on the words or syllables which the speaker wishes to emphasize. Prominence may be given to different words according to what has been said before by another speaker, eg:

> *He may come to*MORow.
> (as a reply to *"When is Mr Jones coming?"*)
> *He* MAY *come tomorrow.*
> (as a reply to *"Is Mr Jones likely to come tomorrow?"*)

Prominence may be accompanied by pitch movement (see TONE²) on the **prominent syllable**.
[*Further reading*: Brazil, Coulthard, & Johns 1980]

prominent syllable /ˌprɒmə̇nənt ˈsɪləbəl ‖ ˌprɑ-/ *n*
see under PROMINENCE

prompting /ˈprɒmptɪŋ ‖ ˈprɑmptɪŋ/ *n*
see under MODELLING

pronoun /ˈprəʊnaʊn/ *n*
a word which may replace a noun or noun phrase (eg English *it, them, she*).
see also PERSONAL PRONOUNS, POSSESSIVE, DEMONSTRATIVE, INTERROGATIVE PRONOUN, REFLEXIVE PRONOUN, INDEFINITE PRONOUN, RELATIVE CLAUSE

pronunciation /prəˌnʌnsiˈeɪʃən/ *n* **pronounce** /prəˈnaʊns/ *v*
the way a certain sound or sounds are produced. Unlike ARTICULATION, which refers to the actual production of speech sounds in the mouth, pronunciation stresses more the way sounds are perceived by the hearer, eg:

> *You haven't* pronounced *this word correctly.*

and often relates the spoken word to its written form, eg:

> *In the word* knife, *the* k *is not pronounced.*

proper noun /ˈprɒpəʳ ˈnaʊn ‖ ˈprɑ-/ *n*
a noun which is the name of a particular person, place, or thing, Proper nouns are spelt with a capital letter. For example: *London, Richard*.
A noun which is not the name of a particular person, place or thing is called a **common noun**. For example, *book, woman, sugar*. In English, common nouns are spelt with a lower-case (small) letter.
see also NOUN, ABSTRACT NOUN, ADJECTIVAL NOUN, ANIMATE NOUN, COLLECTIVE NOUN, COMPOUND NOUN, CONCRETE NOUN, COUNTABLE NOUN, UNCOUNTABLE NOUN

proposition /ˌprɒpə'zɪʃən ‖ ˌprɑ-/ *n* **propositional** *adj*
(in philosophy, LINGUISTICS and SEMANTICS) the basic meaning which a
sentence expresses. Propositions consist of (a) something which is
named or talked about (known as the **argument**, or entity) (b) an
assertion or **predication** which is made about the argument.
A sentence may express or imply (see PRESUPPOSITION) more than one
proposition. For example:

sentence	underlying propositions
John's friend, Tony, who is a	John has a friend.
dentist, likes apples.	The friend's name is Tony.
	Tony is a dentist.
	Tony likes apples.

In SPEECH ACT theory a distinction is made between the propositional
meaning of a sentence, and its **illocutionary force** (ie the use made
of the sentence in communication, eg as a request, a warning, a
promise).
[*Further reading*: Austin 1962; Lyons 1977]

proprioceptive feedback /prəʊpriəʊ'septɪv 'fiːdbæk, -priə-/ *n*
FEEDBACK involving muscular movements which are used in the
production of speech and which can be used in MONITORING speech.
Deaf people make use of this form of feedback rather than AUDITORY
FEEDBACK.
[*Further reading*: Dalton & Hardcastle 1977]

prosodic features /prəˌsɒdɪk 'fiːtʃəz ‖ -ˌsɑ- -ərz/ *n*
sound characteristics which affect whole sequences of syllables. They
may involve, for instance, the relative loudness or duration of
syllables, changes in the pitch of a speaker's voice (see TONE^2) and
the choice of pitch level (see KEY^2).
see also INTONATION PATTERNS, PROMINENCE, SUPRASEGMENTALS

prosody /'prɒsədi ‖ 'prɑ-/ *n* **prosodic** /prə'sɒdɪk ‖ -'sɒ-/ *adj*
(in PHONETICS) a collective term for variations in loudness, PITCH and
SPEECH RHYTHM.

protocol /'prəʊtəkɒl ‖ -kɑl/ *n*
a sample containing observation(s) of a phenomenon which is being
described, observed, or measured. For example, if a researcher were
studying the use of a grammatical feature, and recorded a person's
speech for purposes of analysis, a transcription of the recording
could be called a protocol. A completed test script and responses of
subjects to an experiment are also sometimes called protocols.
Nowadays the term "protocol" is often used for a person's own
account of his or her thoughts and ideas while doing a task. Such a
protocol can give information of value in the study of
PSYCHOLINGUISTICS and COGNITIVE PROCESSes.

pro-verb /'prəʊ ˌvɜːb ‖ -ɜr-/ n
a verb form that may be used instead of a full verb phrase. For example, in English, various forms of *do* can be pro-verbs, as in:
A: *I like coffee*   A: *She broke the window.*
B: *I do too.*   B: *So she did.*
   So do I.
   Alan does too.
see also PRO-FORMS

proxemics /prɒk'siːmɪks ‖ prɑk-/ n **proxemic** adj
the study of the physical distance between people when they are talking to each other, as well as their postures and whether or not there is physical contact during their conversation. These factors can be looked at in relation to the sex, age, and social and cultural background of the people involved, and also their attitudes to each other and their state of mind.
see also PARALINGUISTICS, SOCIAL DISTANCE

pseudo-cleft sentence /'sjuːdəʊ 'kleft 'sentəns ‖ 'suː-/ n
see under CLEFT SENTENCE

psycholinguistics /ˌsaɪkəʊlɪŋ'gwɪstɪks/ n **psycholinguistic** adj
the study of (a) the mental processes that a person uses in producing and understanding language, and (b) how humans learn language. Psycholinguistics includes the study of SPEECH PERCEPTION, the role of MEMORY, CONCEPTs and other processes in language use, and how social and psychological factors affect the use of language.
[*Further reading*: Clark & Clark 1977; Foss & Hakes 1978]

pure vowel /'pjʊəʳ 'vaʊəl/ n
another term for MONOPHTHONG

qualifier[1] /ˈkwɒlə̇faɪəʳ ‖ ˈkwɑ-/ *n* **qualify** /ˈkwɒlə̇faɪ ‖ ˈkwɑ-/ *v*
(in TRADITIONAL GRAMMAR) any linguistic unit (eg an adjective, a
phrase, or a clause) that is part of a NOUN PHRASE[1] and gives added
information about the noun.
For example, *her, expensive,* and *from Paris* are qualifiers in the
noun phrase:
    her expensive blouse from Paris
see also MODIFIER[1]

qualifier[2] *n* **qualify** *v*
(in Halliday's SYSTEMIC GRAMMAR) any linguistic unit that is part of a
group, gives added information about the HEAD of the group, and
follows the head.
For example, *from Paris* is a qualifier in the noun group
    her expensive blouse from Paris
see also MODIFIER[2]
[*Further reading*: Berry 1975]

quantifier /ˈkwɒntə̇faɪəʳ ‖ ˈkwɑn-/ *n*
a word or phrase which is used with a noun, and which shows
quantity.
Some quantifiers in English are: *many, few, little, several, much, a
lot of, plenty of, a piece of, a loaf of, three kilograms of,* etc.
see also NUMERAL, DETERMINER
[*Further reading*: Quirk et al 1985]

question /ˈkwestʃən/ *n*
a sentence which is addressed to a listener/reader and asks for an
expression of fact, opinion, belief etc. In English, questions may be
formed:
(a) by the use of a **question word** such as *what, how, when, where,
    why*
(b) by the use of an OPERATOR in the first position in a sentence, as
    in *Can she come?*
(c) through the use of intonation, as in:
    She isn't married?
(d) by the use of a **question tag** such as *isn't it, is it, can he, won't
    she, do you* etc. For example:
    Patricia is a student isn't she?

question tag /ˈkwestʃən ˌtæg/ *n*
see under QUESTION

question word /ˈkwestʃən ˌwɜːd ‖ ˌwɜrd/ *n*
see under QUESTION

R

r²

an abbreviation for COEFFICIENT OF DETERMINATION

random sample /'rændəm 'sɑmpəl ‖ 'sæm-/ *n*
see under SAMPLE

range /reɪndʒ/ *n*
(1) In statistics, the DISPERSION of a DISTRIBUTION. The range of a sample is the distance between the smallest and the largest values in a set of measurements or observations. For example if the top score in a test is 80 and the bottom score is 32, the range is 48. Since the range does not take the distribution of scores into account it is usually supplemented in statistical reports by the STANDARD DEVIATION.
(2) In a FREQUENCY COUNT, a measure of the distribution of linguistic items throughout a sample, and generally expressed as a measure of the number of texts or samples in which a linguistic item occurs.

rank /ræŋk/ *n*
a term used in a type of linguistic analysis in which linguistic units (eg sentences, clauses, words) are arranged in a certain order (**rank scale**) to show that higher units include lower ones.
For example, on the rank scale below, each unit consists of one or more units of the next lower rank.

higher rank

clause
group (verbal, nominal, etc)
word (verb, noun, etc)
morpheme

lower rank

The term was first used by Halliday (see SYSTEMIC GRAMMAR, SYSTEMIC LINGUISTICS).
[*Further reading*: Kress 1976; Halliday 1978]

rank correlation /ˌrænk kɒrə'leɪʃən ‖ kɔ-, kɑ-/ *n*
a type of coefficient of CORRELATION in which the two VARIABLES[1] are measured in ranks, or on ordinal scales (see SCALE). For example, a rank correlation could be determined between the frequency of occurrence of words in two different texts based on their ranks in each text.

TEXT A		TEXT B	
rank frequency	word	rank frequency	word
1st	*a*	1st	*the*
2nd	*the*	2nd	*and*
3rd	*and*	3rd	*a*

236

In this data there is a negative correlation between the "rank order" of the words in Text A and Text B.

rank scale /'ræŋk ˌskeɪl/ *n*
see under RANK

rapid reading /'ræpəd 'riːdɪŋ/ *n*
another term for SPEED READING

rate of articulation /ˌreɪt əv ɑːtɪkjʊ'leɪʃən ‖ ɑrtɪkjə-/ *n*
see under RATE OF SPEECH

rate of reading /ˌreɪt əv 'riːdɪŋ/ *n*
another term for READING SPEED

rate of speech /ˌreɪt əv 'spiːtʃ/ *n*
also **rate of utterance, speech rate**
the speed at which a person speaks. This may depend on a number of factors, such as the speaker's personality, the type of topic, the number of people present, and the speaker's reactions to them. Another factor is the speaker's familiarity with the language or dialect he or she is using.
A distinction is often made between the rate of speech, measured by the number of syllables per minute, and the **rate of articulation**, measured by the number of syllables per minute minus the time taken up by PAUSING. Usually, the longer and more frequent the pauses, the slower the speech rate.
[*Further reading*: Goldman-Eisler 1968]

rate of utterance /ˌreɪt əv 'ʌtərəns/ *n*
another term for RATE OF SPEECH

rating scale /'reɪtɪŋ ˌskeɪl/ *n*
(in language testing) a technique for measuring language proficiency in which aspects of a person's language use are judged using scales that go from worst to best performance in a number of steps.
For example, the components of FLUENCY in a foreign language could be rated on the following scales:
naturalness of language   unnatural   1 2 3 4 5 natural
style of expression   foreign   1 2 3 4 5 native-speaker-like
clarity of expression   unclear   1 2 3 4 5 clear
For each component skill, the listener rates the speaker on a scale of 1 to 5. Overall fluency can then be measured by taking account of the three scores for each speaker.
see also SCALE
[*Further reading*: Cohen 1980]

rationalist position /'ræʃənələst pə'zɪʃən/ *n*
another term for INNATIST HYPOTHESIS

ratio-scale /'reɪʃiəʊ ˌskeɪl/ *n*
see under SCALE

raw score /ˌrɔː ˈskɔːʳ/ *n*

(in testing, statistics, etc) a score that is presented in terms of its original numerical value, not converted into some other value. For example, raw scores may be the number of correct answers in a test, or, in some cases, the number of errors. Usually it is necessary to convert such values into percentages, PERCENTILE*s*, ranks, or some other form (eg STANDARD SCORE*s*), in order to make the scores easier to interpret.

readability /ˌriːdəˈbɪlə̩ti/ *n*

how easily written materials can be read and understood. Readability depends on many factors, including (a) the average length of sentences in a passage (b) the number of new words a passage contains (c) the grammatical complexity of the language used. Procedures used for measuring readability are known as "readability formulae".

see also LEXICAL DENSITY

[*Further reading*: Klare 1978]

reading /ˈriːdɪŋ/ *n*

(1) perceiving a written text in order to understand its contents. This can be done silently (**silent reading**). The understanding that results is called reading comprehension.

(2) saying a written text aloud (**oral reading**). This can be done with or without an understanding of the contents.

Different types of reading comprehension are often distinguished, according to the reader's purposes in reading and the type of reading used. The following are commonly referred to:

(a) **literal comprehension**: reading in order to understand, remember, or recall the information explicitly contained in a passage

(b) **inferential comprehension**: reading in order to find information which is not explicitly stated in a passage, using the reader's experience and intuition, and by inferring (INFERENCING)

(c) **critical** or **evaluative comprehension**: reading in order to compare information in a passage with the reader's own knowledge and values

(d) **appreciative comprehension**: reading in order to gain an emotional or other kind of valued response from a passage.

see also SCANNING, READING SPEED, EXTENSIVE READING

[*Further reading*: Alderson & Urquhart 1983]

reading approach /ˈriːdɪŋ əˌprəʊtʃ/ *n*
also **reading method** /ˈriːdɪŋ ˌmeθəd/

in foreign language teaching, a programme or method in which reading comprehension is the main objective. In a reading approach (a) the foreign language is generally introduced through short passages written with simple vocabulary and structures (b) comprehension is taught through translation and grammatical

analysis (c) if the spoken language is taught, it is generally used to reinforce reading and limited to the oral reading of texts.
[*Further reading*: Mackey 1965]

reading speed /ˈriːdɪŋ ˌspiːd/ *n*
also **rate of reading**
The speed with which a person reads depends on (a) the type of reading material (eg fiction or non-fiction) (b) the reader's purpose (eg to gain information, to find the main ideas in a passage) (c) the level of comprehension required (eg to extract the main ideas or to gain complete understanding) (d) the reader's individual reading skills. The following are typical reading speeds:

speed	purpose	good reader
slow	study reading, used when material is difficult and/or high comprehension is required	200–300 words per minute (wpm) 80–90% comprehension
average	used for everyday reading of magazines, newspapers, etc	250–500 wpm 70% comprehension
fast	skimming, used when highest speed is required comprehension is intentionally lower	800+ wpm 50% comprehension

[*Further reading*: Fry 1965]

reading vocabulary /ˈriːdɪŋ vəˈkæbjʊləri, vəʊ- ‖ -bjəleri/ *n*
the number of words a person can understand in reading.
see also ACTIVE/PASSIVE LANGUAGE KNOWLEDGE

realia /riˈɑːlɪə ‖ -ˈæ-/ *n plural*
(in language teaching) actual objects and items which are brought into a classroom as examples or as aids to be talked or written about and used in teaching. Realia may include such things as photographs, articles of clothing, and kitchen objects.

reality principle /riˈæləti ˈprɪnsəpəl/ *n*
(in SPEECH ACT theory) the principle that in conversation, people are expected to talk about things that are real and possible if there is no evidence to the contrary.
For example, in the following exchange:
   A: *How are you going to New York?*
   B: *I'm flying.*
A understands B to mean that B is travelling by plane and not literally flying through the air.
see also CONVERSATIONAL MAXIM

realization /ˌrɪəlaɪˈzeɪʃən ‖ -lə-/ *n* **realize** /ˈrɪəlaɪz/ *v*
the actual occurrence in speech or writing of an abstract linguistic unit.

For example, the PHONEME /ɪ/ as in /bɪg/ *big* can be realized with more or less length, eg as [ɪ], [ɪː] or [ɪːː], where : means "with some length" and :: means "particularly long". The last example may be used when someone wants to put particular emphasis on the word *big*, or to suggest by the duration of the vowel the size of the "big" thing:

It's really bíg!

received pronunciation /rɪˌsiːvd prəˌnʌnsiˈeɪʃən/ *n*
also **RP**

the type of British STANDARD ENGLISH pronunciation which has been regarded as the prestige variety and which shows no REGIONAL VARIATION. It has often been popularly referred to as "BBC English" because it was until recently the standard pronunciation used by most British Broadcasting Corporation newsreaders.

RP differs from Standard American English pronunciation in various ways. For example, it uses the PHONEME /ɒ/ where most Americans would use another phoneme, as in *hot* /hɒt ‖ hɑt/. Speakers of RP do not have an *r* sound before a CONSONANT, though most Americans do, as in *farm* /fɑːm ‖ fɑrm/.

receiver /rɪˈsiːvəʳ/ *n*

see under COMMUNICATION

receptive language knowledge /rɪˈsɛptɪv ˈlæŋgwɪdʒ ˌnɒlɪdʒ ‖ ˌnɑ-/ *n*

see ACTIVE/PASSIVE LANGUAGE KNOWLEDGE

receptive skills /rɪˈsɛptɪv ˈskɪlz/ *n*

see under LANGUAGE SKILLS

reciprocal pronoun /rɪˈsɪprəkəl ˈprəʊnaʊn/ *n*

a PRONOUN which refers to an exchange or mutual interaction between people or groups.

English uses the phrases *each other* and *one another* like reciprocal pronouns. For example, the sentence *X and Y smiled at each other* implies that X smiled at Y and that Y smiled at X.

reciprocal verb /rɪˌsɪprəkəl ˈvɜːb ‖ ˈvɜrb/ *n*

A verb is called reciprocal when it suggests that the people or things represented by the SUBJECT of the sentence are doing something to one another.

For example, the sentence *Jeremy and Basil were fighting* may imply that Jeremy and Basil were fighting each other. In that case, the sentence uses *fight* as a reciprocal verb.

recursive rule /rɪˈkɜːsɪv ˌruːl ‖ -ˈkɜr-/ *n*

(in GENERATIVE TRANSFORMATIONAL GRAMMAR), a rule which can be applied repeatedly without any definite limit. For example, a recursive rule for the addition of relative clauses could produce:

The man saw the dog which bit the girl who was stroking the cat which had caught the mouse which had eaten the cheese which . . .

reduction /rɪ'dʌkʃən/ *n* **reduce** /rɪ'djuːs ‖ -'duːs/ *v*

(in PHONETICS and PHONOLOGY), change in a vowel to a centralized vowel when it is in an unstressed position.

For example, *could* /kʊd/ is often reduced to /kəd/ in a sentence like:
We could go to the park this afternoon.

see also ELISION

redundancy /rɪ'dʌndənsi/ *n* **redundant** /rɪ'dʌndənt/ *adj*

the degree to which a message contains more information than is needed for it to be understood. Languages have built-in redundancy, which means that utterances contain more information than is necessary for comprehension.

For example, in English, PLURAL may be shown on the demonstrative, the noun, and the verb, as in:
These books are expensive.

However, if the *s* on *books* is omitted, the message would still be understood. Therefore, the *s* is redundant in this context. 50% of normal language is said to be redundant.

reduplication /rɪ,djuːplɪ̣'keɪʃən ‖ rɪ,duː-/ *n*

repetition of a syllable, a MORPHEME, or a word. For example:
(a) in Tagalog (a Philippine language) *tatlo* "three", *tatatlo* "only three"
(b) in Malay *anak* "child", *anak anak* "children".

reference /'refərəns/ *n* **referent** /'refərənt/ *n* **refer** /rɪ'fɜːʳ/ *v*
referential /ˌrefə'renʃəl/ *adj*

(in SEMANTICS) the relationship between words and the things, actions, events, and qualities they stand for.

An example in English is the relationship between the word *tree* and the object "tree" (referent) in the real world.

Reference in its wider sense would be identical with DENOTATION. In its narrower sense it is used only for the relationship between linguistic expressions and specific phenomena, such as the phrase *Peter's horse* and "Peter's horse", and not classes and types, such as the word *horse* and "horse" meaning the type of animal.

see also SENSE

[*Further reading*: Lyons 1981]

referring tone /rɪ'fɜːrɪŋ ˌtəʊn/ *n*

an intonation pattern which indicates that something that is said is part of the knowledge shared between the speaker and the listener. In Standard British English, the referring tone (r) is often a fall and then a rise in PITCH ⌄ or a rise in pitch ⁄ whereas the **proclaiming tone** (p), often shown by a fall in pitch ⟍ , suggests that the speaker is introducing information which is new to the listener:

(a) (r) He'll be twenty (p) in August.
(b) (p) He'll be twenty (r) in August.

In example (a) the new information is *August*. In example (b) the new information is the age of the person discussed.

see also KEY[2], TONE[2], TONE UNIT

[*Further reading*: Brazil, Coulthard, & Johns 1980]

reflexive pronoun /rɪ'fleksɪv 'prəʊnaʊn/ *n*

a form of a PRONOUN which is used when the direct or indirect OBJECT in a sentence refers to the same person or thing as the subject of the sentence. In English these are formed in the same way as EMPHATIC PRONOUNS, ie by adding -*self*, -*selves* to the pronoun, as in:
I hurt myself.

reflexive verb /rɪ'fleksɪv 'vɜːb ‖ -ɜr-/ *n*

a verb used so as to imply that the subject is doing something to himself or herself.

In English, this is typically expressed by means of a REFLEXIVE PRONOUN added to the verb, eg *They hurt themselves*. But the same meaning may be expressed by the verb on its own, as in *I was shaving.*

regional dialect /'riːdʒənəl 'daɪəlekt/ *n*

see under DIALECT

regional variation /ˌriːdʒənəl veəri'eɪʃən/ *n*

variation in speech according to the particular area where a speaker comes from (see DIALECT). Variation may occur with respect to pronunciation, vocabulary, or syntax.

For example, in the southwest of England and in the American Midwest, many speakers use an /r/ sound in words such as *her, four, part*, whereas speakers from some other places, such as the London region and New England, do not.

register /'redʒəstər/ *n*

(1) see STYLE

(2) a SPEECH VARIETY used by a particular group of people, usually sharing the same occupation (eg doctors, lawyers) or the same interests (eg stamp collectors, baseball fans).

A particular register often distinguishes itself from other registers by having a number of distinctive words, by using words or phrases in a particular way (eg in tennis: *deuce, love, tramlines, van*), and sometimes by special grammatical constructions (eg legal language).

regression /rɪ'greʃən/ *n*

a backward movement of the eye along a line of print when reading. Poor readers tend to make more regressions than good readers. In reading aloud, a regression is the repetition of a syllable, word, or phrase that has already been read.

regression analysis /rɪ'greʃən əˌnæləsəs/ *n*

a statistical technique for estimating or predicting a value for a DEPENDENT VARIABLE from a set of INDEPENDENT VARIABLES. For example, if a student scored 60% on a test of reading comprehension and 70% on a grammar test (the independent variables) regression analysis could be used to predict his or her likely score on a test of language proficiency (the dependent variable). When two or more independent variables are present, as in this example, the statistical technique is called **multiple regression**.

regressive assimilation /rɪ'gresɪv ə,sɪmə'leɪʃən/ *n*
see under ASSIMILATION[1]

regular verb /'regjʊlər 'vɜːb ‖ -gjə- -ɜr-/ *n*
a verb which has the most typical forms in its language for grammatical categories such as TENSE or PERSON. In written English regular verbs form the past tense (a) by adding *-ed* to the verb base; *walk → walked*; (b) by adding *-d* to the base; *smile → smiled*; (c) by changing *-y → -ied*; *cry → cried*. A verb which does not have regular forms for tense, person, etc is known as an **irregular verb**. Irregular verbs in English may form the past tense (a) by using the same form as the present tense; *upset → upset*; *put → put* (b) by having an irregular past tense form which is also used as past participle; *keep → kept*; *catch → caught* (c) by having an irregular past tense form which is different from the past participle; *drive → drove → driven*.

regulatory function /'regjʊlətəri 'fʌŋkʃən ‖ -gjələteri/ *n*
see under DEVELOPMENTAL FUNCTIONS OF LANGUAGE

reinforcement /,riːən'fɔːsmənt ‖ -ər-/ *n*
see under STIMULUS-RESPONSE THEORY

relative clause /'relətɪv 'klɔːz/ *n*
a CLAUSE which modifies a noun or noun phrase. For example in English:
People who smoke annoy me.
The book which I am reading is interesting.
The pronoun which introduces a relative clause is known as a **relative pronoun**, eg *who, which, that*.
see also DEFINING RELATIVE CLAUSE

relative pronoun /'relətɪv 'prəʊnaʊn/ *n*
see under RELATIVE CLAUSE

relativity /,relə'tɪvəti/ *n*
see LINGUISTIC RELATIVITY

reliability /rɪ,laɪə'bɪləti/ *n* **reliable** /rɪ'laɪəbəl/ *adj*
(in testing) a measure of the degree to which a test gives consistent results. A test is said to be reliable if it gives the same results when it is given on different occasions or when it is used by different people.
see also PARALLEL FORMS, ALTERNATE FORM RELIABILITY, SPLIT-HALF RELIABILITY, INTERNAL CONSISTENCY RELIABILITY, SPEARMAN-BROWN FORMULA

remedial grammar /rɪˈmiːdɪəl ˈɡræməʳ/ n

(in language teaching) a term sometimes used to describe grammatical explanation, teaching, etc which is intended to remedy, correct, or compensate for the learner's inadequate understanding or use of any aspect of the grammar of a language.

repair /rɪˈpeəʳ/ n, v

(in CONVERSATIONAL ANALYSIS) a term for ways in which errors, unintended forms, or misunderstandings are corrected by speakers or others during conversation. A repair which is made by the speaker (ie which is self-initiated) is known as a **self repair**. For example:

I bought a, uhm . . . what do you call it . . . a floor polisher.

A repair made by another person (ie which is other-initiated) is known as **other repair**. For example:

A: *How long you spend?*
B: *Hmm?*
A: *How long did you spend there?*

B's response serves to indicate that a repair is needed to A's original utterance.

[*Further reading*: Schegloff, Jefferson, & Sacks 1977]

repetition drill /ˌrepəˈtɪʃən ˌdrɪl/ n
see under DRILL

repetition stage /ˌrepəˈtɪʃən ˌsteɪdʒ/ n
another term for **practice stage**
see under STAGE

reported speech /rɪˈpɔːtəd ˈspiːtʃ ‖ -ɔr-/ n
see under DIRECT SPEECH

representative /ˌreprɪˈzentətɪv/ n
see under SPEECH ACT CLASSIFICATION

representative sample /ˌreprɪˌzentətɪv ˈsɑːmpəl ‖ ˈsæm-/ n
see under SAMPLE

response /rɪˈspɒns ‖ -ˈspɑns/ n
(1) see under STIMULUS-RESPONSE THEORY, BEHAVIOURISM
(2) see under CUE

restricted code /rɪˈstrɪktəd ˈkəʊd/ n
see under CODE²

restrictive relative clause /rɪˈstrɪktɪv ˈrelətɪv ˈklɔːz/ n
another term for DEFINING RELATIVE CLAUSE

result(ative) case /rɪˈzʌltətɪv ˌkeɪs/ n
see under FACTITIVE CASE

retention /rɪˈtenʃən/ n
the ability to recall or remember things after an interval of time. In

language teaching, retention of what has been taught (eg grammar rules, vocabulary) may depend on the quality of teaching, the interest of the learners, or the meaningfulness of the materials.

retroactive inhibition/interference /ˌretrəʊˈæktɪv ɪnhəˈbɪʃən/ *n*
see under PROACTIVE INHIBITION

retroflex /ˈretrəfleks/ *adj*
describes a speech sound (a CONSONANT) which is produced with the tip of the tongue curled back to touch or nearly touch the hard palate at the top of the mouth.
Many Indian languages use retroflex /t/ and /d/, – [t] and [d] – and many native speakers of these languages continue to use these sounds when they speak English.
The /r/ used by some speakers in the south-west of England, and in many varieties of American English, is a retroflex sound.
see also PLACE OF ARTICULATION, MANNER OF ARTICULATION
[*Further reading*: Gimson 1980]

retrospective syllabus /ˌretrəˈspektɪv ˈsɪləbəs/ *n*
see under A PRIORI SYLLABUS

reversal error /rɪˈvɜːsəl ˈerəʳ ‖ -ɜr-/ *n*
see under SPEECH ERRORS

rewrite rule /ˈriːraɪt ˈruːl/ *n*
see under BASE COMPONENT

rheme /riːm/ *n*
see under FUNCTIONAL SENTENCE PERSPECTIVE

rhetoric /ˈretərɪk/ *n*
the study of how effective writing achieves its goals. The term "rhetoric" in this sense is common in North American college and university courses in rhetoric or "rhetorical communication", which typically focus on how to express oneself correctly and effectively in relation to the topic of writing or speech, the audience, and the purpose of communication.
In traditional grammar, rhetoric was the study of style through grammatical and logical analysis. Cicero, the ancient Roman orator and writer, described rhetoric as "the art or talent by which discourse is adapted to its end".

rhetorical question /rɪˈtɒrɪkəl ˈkwestʃən ‖ -ˈtɔ-, -ˈtɑ-/ *n*
a forceful statement which has the form of a question but which does not expect an answer. For example, "*What difference does it make?*", which may function like the statement, "*It makes no difference*".

rhetorical structure /rɪˈtɒrɪkəl ˌstrʌktʃər ‖ -ˈtɔ-, -ˈtɑ-/ *n*
another term for SCHEME

rhythm /'rɪðəm/ *n*
see SPEECH RHYTHM

right-ear advantage /'raɪt 'ɪəʳ əd'vɑːntɪdʒ ‖ -'væn-/ *n*
see under DICHOTIC LISTENING

right hemisphere /'raɪt 'heməsfɪəʳ/ *n*
see under BRAIN

ritual /'rɪtʃʊəl/ *n*
a SPEECH EVENT which follows a more or less strictly defined pattern, eg part of a religious service, an initiation ceremony. Often UTTERANCES must follow each other in a particular sequence and may have to be of a particular kind.
For example, the **ritual insults** in the BLACK ENGLISH VERNACULAR of some American cities are a verbal exchange between two speakers, each attempting to out-do the other. Each successive insult has to be more ingenious and obscene than the preceding one.

ritual insults /'rɪtʃʊəl 'ɪnsʌlts/ *n*
see under RITUAL

role /rəʊl/ *n*
(1) the part taken by a participant in any act of communication. Some roles are more or less permanent, eg that of teacher or student, while other roles are very temporary, eg the role of someone giving advice. The same person could have a number of different roles in his or her daily activities. For example, a man may be father, brother, son, husband in his family life but colleague, teacher, employee, treasurer, counsellor in his working life. Roles affect the way people communicate with each other (see ROLE RELATIONSHIPS).
(2) people also sometimes talk of the "roles" of *speaker* or *listener* in a SPEECH EVENT.
[*Further reading*: Hymes 1974]

role-play /'rəʊl,pleɪ/ *n, v*
also **role playing** *n*
drama-like classroom activities in which students take the ROLES of different participants in a situation and act out what might typically happen in that situation. For example, to practise how to express complaints and apologies in a foreign language, students might have to role-play a situation in which a customer in a shop returns a faulty article to a salesperson.
see also SIMULATION

role relationship /'rəʊl rɪ'leɪʃənʃɪp/ *n*
the relationship which people have to each other in an act of communication and which influences the way they speak to each other. One of the speakers may have a ROLE which has a higher STATUS than that of the other speaker(s), eg school principal ⟶

teacher, teacher↔student(s), lieutenant↔sergeant. Sometimes people temporarily take on superior roles, either because of the situation, eg bank manager↔loan seeker, or because one of them has a stronger personality, eg student A↔student B.

roll /rəʊl/ *n*
also **trill**
a speech sound (a CONSONANT) which is produced by a series of rapid closures or taps by a flexible speech organ, eg the tip of the tongue, against a firm surface, eg the gum ridge behind the upper teeth (the **alveolar ridge**).
For example, in some varieties of Scottish English the /r/ in /əˈɡriːd/ *agreed* is a roll.
see also MANNER OF ARTICULATION, PLACE OF ARTICULATION, FLAP
[*Further reading*: Gimson 1980]

Roman alphabet /ˈrəʊmən ˈælfəbet/ *n*
also **Latin alphabet**
an alphabetic writing system used for many languages, including English. It consists of letters which may represent different sounds or sound combinations in different languages. For example, the letter *w* represents /w/ in English as /ˈwɔːtər/ *water* but /v/ in German /vasər/ *Wasser* "water".
see also ALPHABET

root /ruːt/ *n*
also **base form**
a MORPHEME which is the basic part of a word and which may, in many languages, occur on its own (eg English *man, hold, cold, rhythm*). Roots may be joined to other roots (eg English *house + hold → household*) and/or take AFFIXes (eg *manly, coldness*) or COMBINING FORMs (eg *biorhythm*).
see also STEM[1]

rote learning /ˈrəʊt ˌlɜːnɪŋ ‖ ˌlɜr-/ *n*
the learning of material by repeating it over and over again until it is memorized, without paying attention to its meaning.

rounded vowel /ˈraʊndəd ˈvaʊəl/ *n*
see under VOWEL

routine /ruːˈtiːn/ *n*
also **formula, formulaic speech/expressions/language, conventionalized speech, prefabricated language/speech**
(generally) a segment of language made up of several morphemes or words which are learned together and used as if they were a single item. For example *How are you? with best wishes, To Whom it May Concern, You must be kidding*. Researchers use different names for these routines. A routine or formula which is used in conversation is sometimes called a **conversational routine**, (eg *that's all for now, How awful!, you don't say, the thing is . . . Would you believe it!*)

and one used to show politeness, a **politeness formula** (eg *Thank you very much*).

see also GAMBIT, IDIOM, UTTERANCE

[*Further reading*: Coulmas 1981]

RP /ˌɑːˈ ˈpiː/ n

an abbreviation for RECEIVED PRONUNCIATION

rule[1] /ruːl/ n

(in TRADITIONAL GRAMMAR) a statement

(1) about the formation of a linguistic unit, eg how to form the PAST TENSE of VERBS, or

(2) about the CORRECT usage of a linguistic unit or units, eg that verbs are modified by adverbs (*Come here quickly*) and not by adjectives (**Come here quick*).

rule[2] n

(in GENERATIVE TRANSFORMATIONAL GRAMMAR) a statement about the formation of a linguistic unit or about the relationship between linguistic units. Rules describe and analyse (**generate**) structures in a language and change the structures into sentences.

see also BASE COMPONENT, GENERATIVE GRAMMAR, TRANSFORMATIONAL COMPONENT

rule-governed behaviour /ˈruːlˌgʌvənd bɪˈheɪvɪəʳ/ ‖ -vərnd/ n

A person's knowledge of a language (COMPETENCE) can be described as a system made up of rules for linguistic units such as MORPHEMES, words, clauses, and sentences. Although speakers of a language may not be able to explain why they construct sentences in a particular way in their language, they generally use their language in a way which is governed by the rules of this linguistic system. Language is thus described as "rule-governed behaviour".

rules of speaking /ˌruːlz əv ˈspiːkɪŋ/ n

rules shared by a group of people which govern their spoken behaviour. Rules of speaking may, for instance, regulate when to speak in a conversation, what to say, and how to start and end a conversation. These rules may vary not only between different countries but also between different regions of a country or different social groups.

see also CONVERSATIONAL ANALYSIS, SPEECH EVENT

[*Further reading*: Hymes 1972]

salience /'seɪlɪəns/ *n* **salient** /'seɪlɪənt/ *adj*
also **perceptual salience**
    (in language learning, speech PERCEPTION, and INFORMATION
    PROCESSING) the ease with which a linguistic item is perceived. In
    language learning, the salience of linguistic items has been studied
    to see if it affects the order in which the items are learned. For
    example, the salience of a spoken word may depend on:
    (a) the position of a phoneme in the word
    (b) the emphasis given to the word in speech, ie whether it is
        STRESS*ed* or unstressed
    (c) the position of the word in a sentence.
    see also NATURAL ORDER HYPOTHESIS
    [*Further reading*: Dulay, Burt, & Krashen 1982]

sample /'sɑːmpəl ‖ 'sæm-/ *n*
    (in statistics and testing) any group of individuals which is selected
    to represent a POPULATION.
    A sample in which every member of the population has an equal
    and independent chance of being selected is known as a **random
    sample**.
    A sample in which the population is grouped into several strata (eg
    of high, medium, and low scores), and a selection drawn from each
    level, is known as a **stratified sample**.
    A sample which contains a good representation of the population
    from which it is selected is known as a **representative sample**.

sampling /'sɑːmplɪŋ ‖ 'sæm-/ *n*
    the procedure of selecting a SAMPLE. This selection can be done in
    various ways, eg by selecting a random sample or a stratified
    sample.

Sapir-Whorf hypothesis /ˌsæpɪəʳ 'wɔːf haɪ'pɒθəsəs ‖ -ɔr- -'pɑ-/ *n*
    see under LINGUISTIC RELATIVITY

scale /skeɪl/ *n*
    (in statistics and testing) the level or type of quantification produced
    by a measurement. Four different scales are often used:
    (a) a **nominal scale** is used to assign values to items or individuals
        which belong to different groups or categories. For example, we
        may assign the number 1 to all students in one class, 2 to those
        in another, 3 to students in another class, and so on.
    (b) An **ordinal scale** makes use of ORDINAL NUMBER*s* (eg first, second,
        third). It ranks things in order (eg because the examiner judges
        that there is a greater amount of skill required by one task than
        another, without knowing precisely how much). The difference
        between the values on the scale are not necessarily the same (eg

the difference in points between being first or second on a test may not be the same as the difference between being 21st or 22nd).

(c) An **interval scale** is similar to an ordinal scale except that it has the additional quality that the intervals between the points on the scale are equal (as on the centigrade scale). The difference between 6 and 8 on the centigrade scale is the same as the difference between 26 and 28.

(d) A **ratio-scale** is similar to an interval scale except that it has an absolute zero, enabling actual scores to be compared rather than the intervals between scores. A scale for measuring distance or time would be a "ratio-scale".

scalogram /ˈskeɪləgræm/ n
see under IMPLICATIONAL SCALING

scanning /ˈskænɪŋ/ n
(in READING) a type of SPEED-READING technique which is used when the reader wants to locate a particular piece of information without necessarily understanding the rest of a text or passage. For example, the reader may read through a chapter of a book as rapidly as possible in order to find out information about a particular date, such as when someone was born.
Scanning may be contrasted with **skimming** or **skim-reading**, which is a type of rapid reading which is used when the reader wants to get the main idea or ideas from a passage. For example a reader may skim-read a chapter to find out if the writer approves or disapproves of something.
see also READING SPEED

scatter diagram /ˈskætər ˌdaɪəgræm/ n
also **scattergram** /ˈskætəˌgræm ‖ -tər-/, **scatterplot** /ˈskætəˌplɒt ‖ -tərˌplɑt/
a representation on a graph of two separate variables, in such a way as to display their relationship as shown below:

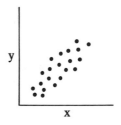

Y axis: scores on test Y
X axis: scores on test X
see also CORRELATION

scheme /'skiːm/ *n*

also **schema** /'skiːmə/, **macro-structure, genre-scheme, discourse structure, rhetorical structure**

(in TEXT LINGUISTICS and DISCOURSE ANALYSIS) the underlying structure which accounts for the organization of a TEXT or DISCOURSE. Different kinds of texts and discourse (eg stories, descriptions, letters, reports, poems) are distinguished by the ways in which the TOPIC, PROPOSITION*s*, and other information are linked together to form a unit. This underlying structure is known as the "scheme" or "macro-structure". For example the scheme underlying many stories is:

Story = Setting(= state + state + . . .) + Episodes(= Event(s) + Reaction)

ie stories consist of a setting in which the time, place, and characters are identified, followed by episodes leading towards a reaction.

A text or discourse in which a suitable underlying scheme or macro-structure is used is said to be "coherent" (see COHERENCE).

Note that the plural of *scheme* is *schemes*, but the plural of *schema* is either *schemes* or *schemata*.

see also SCRIPT

[*Further reading*: van Dijk 1977]

schwa /ʃwɑː/ *n*

also **shwa**

a short vowel usually produced with the tongue in a central position in the mouth and lips unrounded. The phonetic symbol for a schwa is [ə].

In English, it occurs very frequently in unaccented syllables, eg *-mous* in /'feɪməs/ *famous*, *-ment* in /'muːvmənt/ *movement* and in unstressed words in rapid speech, eg *to* in /tə 'teɪk/ *to take*.

see also MANNER OF ARTICULATION, PLACE OF ARTICULATION

[*Further reading*: Gimson 1980]

scoring /'skɔːrɪŋ/ *n*

procedures for giving numerical values or scores to the responses in a test.

script /skrɪpt/ *n*

also **frame**

(in COGNITIVE PSYCHOLOGY) units of meaning consisting of sequences of events and actions that are related to particular situations. For example a "restaurant script" is our knowledge that a restaurant is a place where waitresses, waiters, and cooks work, where food is served to customers, and where customers sit at tables, order food, eat, pay the bill, and depart. A person's knowledge of this "script" helps in understanding the following paragraph:

Tom was hungry. He went into a restaurant. At 8 pm he paid the bill and left.

Although Tom was most probably shown to a table, sat down, ordered a meal, and ate it, these facts are not mentioned in the paragraph. The reader's knowledge of a restaurant script, ie the usual sequence of events for this situation, provides this information. Script theory has been used in studies of problem solving, reading, memory, and comprehension.

see also SCHEME

[*Further reading*: Schank & Abelson 1977]

SD¹ /ˌes 'diː/ *n*
an abbreviation for STANDARD DEVIATION

SD² *n*
an abbreviation for STRUCTURAL DESCRIPTION

SE /ˌes 'iː/ *n*
an abbreviation for STANDARD ERROR

secondary cardinal vowel /'sekəndəri 'kɑːdə̇nəl 'vauəl ‖ -deri 'kɑr-/ *n*
see under CARDINAL VOWEL

second language /'sekənd 'læŋgwidʒ/ *n*
see under FOREIGN LANGUAGE

second language acquisition /'sekənd 'læŋgwidʒ ˌækwə̇'ziʃən/ *n*
(in APPLIED LINGUISTICS) the processes by which people develop proficiency in a second or foreign language. These processes are often investigated with the expectation that information about them may be useful in language teaching. The term "second language acquisition" has been used particularly in the USA by researchers interested in:
(a) longitudinal studies and case studies of the development of syntax and phonology in second and foreign language learners (see CROSS-SECTIONAL METHOD, CASE STUDY)
(b) analysis of the spoken and written discourse of second and foreign language learners (see DISCOURSE ANALYSIS)
(c) the study of other aspects of language development.
[*Further reading*: Hatch 1978]

segment /'segmənt/ *n* **segment** /seg'ment/ *v*
any linguistic unit in a sequence which may be isolated from the rest of the sequence, eg a sound in an UTTERANCE or a letter in a written text.

segmental phonemes /seg,mentl 'fəuniːmz/ *n*
Sometimes a distinction is made between the vowels and consonants of a particular language, which are referred to as segmental phonemes, and such sound phenomena as accent (see ACCENT¹) and INTONATION, which stretch over more than one segment (SUPRASEGMENTALS).
see also PHONEME

selection /səˈlekʃən/ *n*
(in language teaching) the choice of linguistic content (vocabulary, grammar, etc) for a language course, textbook, etc. Procedures for selecting language items to include in a language course include the use of FREQUENCY COUNTS, NEEDS ANALYSIS, and PEDAGOGIC GRAMMARS.
see also SYLLABUS
[*Further reading*: Mackey 1965]

self concept /ˈself ˌkɒnsept ‖ ˌkɑn-/ *n*
the image a person has of himself or herself. A measure of a person's self concept is sometimes included in the study of affective variables (see COGNITIVE VARIABLE) in language learning.

self-rating /ˈself ˈreɪtɪŋ/ *n*
also **self report**
(in language testing) an individual's own evaluation of their language ability, generally according to how good they are at particular language skills (eg reading, speaking), how well they are able to use the language in different DOMAINS or situations (eg at the office, at school) or how well they can use different styles of the language (eg a formal style or an informal style). Self-ratings are a way of obtaining indirect information about a person's proficiency in a language.

self repair /ˌself rɪˈpeəʳ/ *n*
see under REPAIR

self report /ˈself ˈrɪˈpɔːt ‖ -ort/ *n*
another term for SELF-RATING

semantic component /sɪˈmæntɪk kəmˈpəʊnənt/ *n*
see under GENERATIVE TRANSFORMATIONAL GRAMMAR, INTERPRETIVE SEMANTICS

semantic components /sɪˈmæntɪk kəmˈpəʊnənts/ *n*
another term for SEMANTIC FEATURES

semantic differential /sɪˈmæntɪk ˌdɪfəˈrenʃəl/ *n*
a technique for measuring people's attitudes or feelings about words. The semantic differential makes use of a RATING SCALE which contains pairs of adjectives with opposite meanings (**bi-polar adjectives**) which are used to rate different impressions of meaning. The following scale, for example, could be used to measure the subjective meanings of words:

WORD (eg *democracy*)

good	—	—	—	— *bad*
weak	—	—	—	— *strong*
rough	—	—	—	— *smooth*
active	—	—	—	— *passive*

Subjects rate the word on each dimension. The ratings of different words can be compared. The semantic differential has been used in SEMANTICS, PSYCHOLINGUISTICS, and in the study of LANGUAGE ATTITUDES.
[*Further reading*: Osgood 1964]

semantic features /sɪˈmæntɪk ˈfiːtʃəz ‖ -ərz/ *n*
also **semantic components**
The smallest units of meaning in a word. The meaning of words may be described as a combination of semantic features.
For example, the feature <+ male> is part of the meaning of *father*, and so is the feature <+ adult> but other features are needed to make up the whole CONCEPT or SENSE of *father*.
Often, semantic features are established by contrast and can be stated in terms of <+> and <−>, eg:

child	<+ animate>	<− adult>	
man	<+ animate>	<+ adult>	<+ male>
woman	<+ animate>	<+ adult>	<− male>

see also BINARY FEATURE, COMPONENTIAL ANALYSIS
[*Further reading*: Aitchison 1978]

semantic field /sɪˈmæntɪk ˈfiːld/ *n*
another term for LEXICAL FIELD

semantic memory /sɪˈmæntɪk ˈmeməri/ *n*
see under EPISODIC MEMORY

semantics /sɪˈmæntɪks/ *n* **semantic** *adj*
the study of MEANING. There are many different approaches to the way in which meaning in language is studied. Philosophers, for instance, have investigated the relation between linguistic expressions, such as the words of a language, and persons, things, and events in the world to which these words refer (see REFERENCE, SIGNS). Linguists have investigated, for example, the way in which meaning in a language is structured (see COMPONENTIAL ANALYSIS, LEXICAL FIELD, SEMANTIC FEATURES) and have distinguished between different types of meanings (see CONNOTATION, DENOTATION). There have also been studies of the semantic structure of sentences (see PROPOSITIONS).
In recent years, linguists have generally agreed that meaning plays an important part in grammatical analysis but there has been disagreement on how it should be incorporated in a grammar (see BASE COMPONENT, GENERATIVE SEMANTICS, INTERPRETIVE SEMANTICS).
see also PRAGMATICS
[*Further reading*: Aitchison 1978; Leech 1981; Lyons 1977; Palmer 1981]

semi-consonant /ˈsemi ˌkɒnsənənt ‖ ˌkɑn-/ *n*
see under CONSONANT

semilingual /ˌsemɪˈlɪŋgwəl/ *adj* **semilingualism** /ˌsemɪˈlɪŋgwəlɪzəm/ *n*
sometimes used for people who have acquired several languages at

different periods of their lives, but who have not developed a native-speaker level of proficiency in any of them. This issue is regarded as controversial by many linguists.

[*Further reading*: Skutnabb-Kangas & Toukomaa 1976]

semiotics /ˌsemiˈɒtɪks ‖ -ˈɑtɪks/ *n* **semiotic** *adj*
(1) the theory of SIGNS.
(2) the analysis of systems using signs or signals for the purpose of communication (**semiotic systems**). The most important semiotic system is human language, but there are other systems, eg Morse code, SIGN LANGUAGE, traffic signals.

semiotic systems /ˌsemiˈɒtɪk ˈsɪstəmz ‖ -ˈɑtɪk/ *n*
see under SEMIOTICS

semi-vowel /ˈsemi ˌvaʊəl/ *n*
a speech sound (a CONSONANT) which is produced by allowing the airstream from the lungs to move through the mouth and/or nose with only very slight friction.
For example, in English the /j/ in /jes/ *yes* is a semi-vowel.
In terms of their articulation, semi-vowels are very like vowels, but they function as consonants.
see also under CONSONANT
[*Further reading*: Gimson 1980]

sender /ˈsendəʳ/ *n*
see under COMMUNICATION

sense /sens/ *n*
the place which a word or phrase (a LEXEME) holds in the system of relationships with other words in the vocabulary of a language.
For example, the English words *bachelor* and *married* have the sense relationship of *bachelor = never married*.
A distinction is often made between sense and REFERENCE. see also CONNOTATION, DENOTATION
[*Further reading*: Lyons 1981]

sensorimotor stage /ˌsensəriˈməʊtəʳ ˌsteɪdʒ/ *n*
see under GENETIC EPISTEMOLOGY

sentence /ˈsentəns/ *n*
(in GRAMMAR[1, 2]) the largest unit of grammatical organization within which parts of speech (eg nouns, verbs, adverbs) and grammatical classes (eg word, phrase, clause) are said to function. In English a sentence normally contains one INDEPENDENT CLAUSE with a FINITE VERB. Units which are larger than the sentence (eg a paragraph) are regarded as examples of DISCOURSE.

sentence combining /ˈsentəns kəmˈbaɪnɪŋ/ *n*
a technique used in the teaching of grammar and writing, in which the student combines basic sentences to produce longer and more complex sentences and paragraphs. For example:

The teacher has doubts.
The doubts are grave.
The doubts are about Jackie.
↓
The teacher has grave doubts about Jackie.

sentence method /'sentəns ˌmeθəd/ *n*
a method used to teach reading in the mother tongue, which uses
sentences as the basic units of teaching, rather than words or sounds
(see PHONICS, WHOLE-WORD METHOD). The reading material uses whole
sentences from the beginning, and less importance is given to letter
names or sounds.
[*Further reading*: Goodacre 1978]

sentence pattern /'sentəns ˌpætn ‖ -tərn/ *n*
(in language teaching) a structure which is considered a basic
grammatical pattern for sentences in the language being taught, and
which can be used as a model for producing other sentences in the
language. For example:

<u>sentence pattern</u>

Determiner +	Noun +	Verb +	Article +	Adjective +	Noun
Our	*house*	*has*	*a*	*large*	*garden.*
My	*dog*	*has*	*a*	*big*	*tail.*

sentential adverb /sen'tenʃəl 'ædvɜːb ‖ -ɜr-/ *n*
another term for **disjunct**
see under ADJUNCT

sequencing[1] /'siːkwənsɪŋ/ *n*
(in CONVERSATIONAL ANALYSIS) the relationship between UTTERANCES,
that is, which type of utterance may follow another one. Sequencing
is governed by rules known as **sequencing rules**, which may be
different for different languages or different varieties of the same
language. In some cases, the sequence of utterances is quite strictly
regulated, as in greetings and leave-takings (see ADJACENCY PAIRS) but
often there is a range of possibilities depending on the situation, the
topic, the speakers, and their intentions at the moment.
For example, a question is usually followed by an answer but can, in
certain circumstances, be followed by another question:
　A: *What are you doing tonight?*
　B: *Why do you want to know?*
see also TURN-TAKING
[*Further reading*: Coulthard 1985; Schegloff 1972]

sequencing[2]
another term for GRADATION

sequencing rules /'siːkwənsɪŋ ˌruːlz/ *n*
see under SEQUENCING[1]

serial learning /ˈsɪərɪəl ˌlɜːnɪŋ ‖ ˌlɜr-/ *n*
also **serial-order learning** /ˌsɪərɪəl ˈɔːdəʳ ˌlɜːnɪŋ ‖ ˈɔr- ˌlɜr-/
the learning of items in a sequence or order, as when a list of words is memorized. In PSYCHOLINGUISTICS, serial-order learning theories (also known as "linear" or "left-to-right" theories) have been compared with **top-to-bottom** or hierarchical theories of how people produce sentences. For example in producing the sentence *The dog chased the cat*, in a serial-order model each word the speaker produces determines the word which comes after it:
  The + dog + chased + the + cat.
In a top-to-bottom model, items which build the PROPOSITION are produced before other items. For example:
(a) *dog, cat, chase* (unordered)
(b) *dog + chase + cat* (ordered)
(c) *the + dog + chased + the + cat* (modified)
[*Further reading*: Foss & Hakes 1978]

setting /ˈsetɪŋ/ *n*
the time and place of a SPEECH EVENT.
For example, a conversation can take place in a classroom, a garden, a church, and it can take place at any hour of the day. The setting of a speech event may have an effect on what is being said and how it is said.
see also COMMUNICATIVE COMPETENCE
[*Further reading*: Hymes 1974]

short-term memory /ˈʃɔːt ˌtɜːm ˈmeməri ‖ -ɔr- -ɜr-/ *n*
see under MEMORY

shwa /ʃwɑː/ *n*
another spelling of SCHWA

sibilant /ˈsibɘlənt/ *n*
a speech sound (a CONSONANT) which is produced with friction and which has an *s*-like quality.
For example, in English the /s/ in /siː/ *sea* and the /z/ in /heɪz/ *haze* are sibilants.
A sibilant is a type of FRICATIVE.
[*Further reading*: Gimson 1980]

sight method /ˈsaɪt ˌmeθəd/ *n*
another term for WHOLE-WORD METHOD

sight vocabulary /ˈsaɪt və,kæbjʊləri, vəʊ- ‖ -bjəleri/ *n*
(in teaching reading in the mother tongue) those words which a child can recognize at sight in a reading passage or text and which he or she does not need to decode using phonic or other reading skills (see PHONICS).

signal /ˈsɪgnəl/ *n*
see under INFORMATION THEORY

signification /ˌsɪgnɪfəˈkeɪʃən/ *n*
see under SIGNS, USAGE[2]

signify /ˈsɪgnəfaɪ/ *v*
see under SIGNS

sign language /ˈsaɪn ˌlæŋgwɪdʒ/ *n* **sign** *v*
a language used by many deaf people and by some who
communicate with deaf people, which makes use of movements of
the hands, arms, body, head, face, eyes, and mouth to communicate
meanings. Different sign languages have developed in different parts
of the world, for example American Sign Language or **Ameslan**,
British Sign Language, Danish Sign Language, French Sign
Language. These are true languages with their own grammars and
are not simply attempts to "spell out" the language spoken in the
country where they are used. The visual-gestural units of
communication used in sign languages are known as "signs".
[*Further reading*: Baker & Cokely 1980; Deuchar 1984]

signs /saɪnz/ *n*
in linguistics, the words and other expressions of a language which
signify, that is, "stand for", other things. In English, the word *table*,
for instance, stands for a particular piece of furniture in the real
world. Some linguists and philosophers include a third item in the
process of **signification**, that is, an abstract CONCEPT of the thing for
which the sign stands, eg:

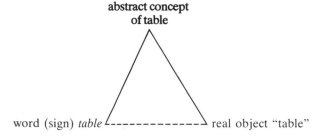

[*Further reading*: Lyons 1977; Ogden & Richards 1923]

silent pause /ˈsaɪlənt ˈpɔːz/ *n*
see under PAUSING

silent reading /ˈsaɪlənt ˈriːdɪŋ/ *n*
see under READING

silent way /ˈsaɪlənt ˌweɪ/ *n*
a METHOD of foreign-language teaching developed by Gattegno which
makes use of gesture, mime, visual aids, wall charts, and in
particular Cuisinière rods (wooden sticks of different lengths and
colours) that the teacher uses to help the students to talk. The

method takes its name from the relative silence of the teacher using these techniques.

[*Further reading*: Gattegno 1976; Richards & Rogers 1986]

simile /'sıməli/ *n*
see under FIGURE OF SPEECH

simple form /'sımpəl ,fɔ:m ‖ -ɔr-/ *n*
see under INFINITIVE

simple past /'sımpəl 'pɑ:st ‖ 'pæst/ *n*
see under PAST TENSE

simple sentence /'sımpəl 'sentəns/ *n*
see under COMPLEX SENTENCE

simplification[1] /,sımpləfə'keıʃən/ *n*
(in the study of SECOND LANGUAGE ACQUISITION and ERROR ANALYSIS) a term sometimes used to describe what happens when learners make use of rules which are grammatically (or morphologically/ phonologically, etc) less complex than TARGET-LANGUAGE[1] rules, often as a result of an OVERGENERALIZATION. For example, a learner may have a single rule for forming the past tense (by adding *-ed* to the verb base) ignoring exceptions and producing incorrect forms such as *breaked*, *standed*. In studies of the INTERLANGUAGE of second- and foreign-language learners, simplifications may be contrasted with errors which result from other processes, such as LANGUAGE TRANSFER.

simplification[2] *n*
(in language teaching) the rewriting or adaptation of original texts or materials, generally using a WORD LIST and sometimes also a structure list or grammatical SYLLABUS, to produce simplified reading or other materials suitable for second- or foreign-language learners.
see also GRADED READER

simplified reader /'sımpləfaıd 'ri:dər/ *n*
another term for GRADED READER

simulation /,sımjʊ'leıʃən ‖ -mjə-/ *n*
classroom activities which reproduce or simulate real situations and which often involve dramatization and group discussion (see ROLE-PLAY, which does not include group discussion). In simulation activities, learners are given roles in a situation, TASKS, or a problem to be solved, and are given instructions to follow (for example, an employer-employee discussion over wage increases in a factory). The participants then make decisions and proposals. Consequences are "simulated" on the basis of decisions the participants take. They later discuss their actions, feelings, and what happened.

simultaneous interpretation /sıməl,teınıəs ın,tɜ:prə'teıʃən ‖ saı- -tɜr-/ *n*
see under INTERPRETATION

singular /ˈsɪŋgjʊləʳ ‖ -gjə-/ *n, adj*
the form of nouns, verbs, pronouns, etc used to refer to only one in number.
For example:

singular	plural
machine	*machines*
it	*they/them*

Situational Language Teaching /ˌsɪtʃʊˈeɪʃənəl ˈlæŋgwɪdʒ ˈtiːtʃɪŋ/ *n*
also **oral approach**
a language teaching METHOD developed by British language teaching specialists between 1940 and 1960. Situational Language Teaching is a grammar-based method in which principles of grammatical and lexical GRADATION are used and new teaching points presented and practised through situations. Although no longer in fashion, techniques derived from Situational Language Teaching are found in many widely used language teaching textbooks.
[*Further reading*: Richards & Rodgers 1986]

situational method /ˌsɪtʃʊˈeɪʃənəl ˌmeθəd/ *n*
(in language teaching) a term sometimes used to refer to a programme or method in which the selection, organization, and presentation of language items is based on situations (eg *at the bank, at the supermarket, at home*). A SYLLABUS for such a language course or textbook may be referred to as a **situational syllabus**. Many methods make use of simulated situations as a way of practising language items, but use other criteria for selecting and organizing the content of the course (see NOTIONAL SYLLABUS, FUNCTIONAL SYLLABUS, for example). Only if situations are used to select, organize, and practise language would the term "situational method" strictly apply.

situational syllabus /ˌsɪtʃʊˈeɪʃənəl ˈsɪləbəs/ *n*
see under SITUATIONAL METHOD

skills /skɪlz/ *n*
(in language teaching) another term for LANGUAGE SKILLS

skimming /ˈskɪmɪŋ/ *n*
also **skim-reading** /ˈskɪm ˈriːdɪŋ/
see under SCANNING

social context /ˈsəʊʃəl ˈkɒntekst ‖ ˈkɑn-/ *n*
the environment in which meanings are exchanged. (According to Halliday) the social context of language can be analysed in terms of three factors:
(a) The **field of discourse** refers to what is happening, including what is being talked about.
(b) The **tenor of discourse** refers to the participants who are taking part in this exchange of meaning, who they are and what kind of relationship they have to one another (see ROLE RELATIONSHIP).

(c) The **mode of discourse** refers to what part the language is playing in this particular situation, for example, in what way the language is organized to convey the meaning, and what CHANNEL is used – written or spoken or a combination of the two.

Example: A foreign language lesson in a secondary school.

field: language study, a defined area of information about the foreign language, eg the use of tenses. Teacher imparting, students acquiring knowledge about tenses and their use.

tenor: participants: teacher – students. Fixed role relationships defined by the educational institution. Teacher in higher role. Temporary role relationships between students, depending on personality.

mode: language used for instruction and discussion. Channel: spoken (eg questions eliciting information, answers supplying information, acted dialogues by students) and written (eg visual presentation on blackboard, textbooks, additional reading material).

see also FUNCTIONS OF LANGUAGE[2], SYSTEMIC LINGUISTICS

[*Further reading*: Halliday 1978]

social dialect /ˈsəʊʃəl ˈdaɪəlekt/ *n*
another term for SOCIOLECT

social dialectal variation /ˌsəʊʃəl daɪəˈlektl veəriˈeɪʃən/ *n*
another term for **sociolectal variation**
see under SOCIOLECT

social distance /ˈsəʊʃəl ˈdɪstəns/ *n*
the feeling a person has that his or her social position is relatively similar to or relatively different from the social position of someone else. The social distance between two different groups or communities influences communication between them, and may affect the way one group learns the language of another (for example, an immigrant group, learning the language of the dominant group in a country). Social distance may depend on such factors as differences in the size, ethnic origin, political STATUS, social status of two groups, and has been studied in SECOND LANGUAGE ACQUISITION research.

see also PIDGINIZATION HYPOTHESIS, ASSIMILATION[2], ACCULTURATION

[*Further reading*: Schumann 1978]

social function /ˈsəʊʃəl ˈfʌŋkʃən/ *n*
see under FUNCTIONS OF LANGUAGE[1]

socialized speech /ˈsəʊʃəlaɪzd ˈspiːtʃ/ *n*
see under EGOCENTRIC SPEECH

social psychology of language /ˌsəʊʃəl saɪˌkɒlədʒi əv ˈlæŋgwɪdʒ ‖ -ˌkɑ-/ *n*
the study of how society and its structures affect the individual's language behaviour. The term is used particularly in that branch of

sociolect

psychology known as social psychology. Investigations in this field deal, for instance, with attitudes to different languages or language varieties and to their speakers.

[*Further reading*: Giles & St Clair 1979]

sociolect /'səʊʃɪəlekt/ *n* **sociolectal** /ˌsəʊʃɪə'lektl/ *adj*
also **social dialect**
a variety of a language (a DIALECT) used by people belonging to a particular social class. The speakers of a sociolect usually share a similar socioeconomic and/or educational background. Sociolects may be classed as high (in STATUS) or low (in status).
For example:
He and I were going there. (higher sociolect)
'Im 'n me was goin' there. (lower sociolect)
The sociolect with the highest status in a country is often the STANDARD VARIETY.
The difference between one sociolect and another can be investigated by analysing the recorded speech of large samples of speakers from various social backgrounds. The differences are referred to as **sociolectal variation** or **social dialectal variation**.
see also DIALECT, ACCENT[3], SPEECH VARIETY

sociolectal variation /ˌsəʊʃɪə'lektl veəri'eɪʃən/ *n*
also **social dialectal variation**
see under SOCIOLECT

sociolinguistics /ˌsəʊʃiəʊlɪŋ'gwɪstɪks, ˌsəʊʃəʊ-/ *n* **sociolinguistic** *adj*
the study of language in relation to social factors, that is, social class, educational level and type of education, age, sex, ethnic origin, etc. Linguists differ as to what they include under sociolinguistics. Many would include the detailed study of interpersonal communication, sometimes called **micro-sociolinguistics**, eg SPEECH ACTS, SPEECH EVENTS, SEQUENCING[1] of UTTERANCES, and also those investigations which relate variation in the language used by a group of people to social factors (see SOCIOLECT). Such areas as the study of language choice in BILINGUAL or MULTILINGUAL communities, LANGUAGE PLANNING, LANGUAGE ATTITUDES, etc may be included under sociolinguistics and are sometimes referred to as **macro-sociolinguistics**, or they are considered as being part of the SOCIOLOGY OF LANGUAGE or the SOCIAL PSYCHOLOGY OF LANGUAGE.
see also ETHNOGRAPHY OF COMMUNICATION

[*Further reading*: Pride & Holmes 1972; Trudgill 1980]

sociology of language /səʊsiˌɒlədʒi əv 'læŋgwɪdʒ, ˌsəʊʃi- ‖ -'ɑlə-/ *n*
the study of language varieties and their users within a social framework, for example the study of language choice in BILINGUAL or MULTILINGUAL nations, LANGUAGE PLANNING, LANGUAGE MAINTENANCE and LANGUAGE SHIFT.

The sociology of language is considered either as including the branch of linguistics called SOCIOLINGUISTICS or as an extension of sociolinguistics.
[*Further reading*: Fishman 1971]

soft palate /'sɒft 'pælət ‖ 'sɑft/ *n*
another term for **velum**
see under PLACE OF ARTICULATION, VELAR

software /'sɒft,weəʳ ‖ 'sɑft-/ *n*
see under HARDWARE

sonorant /'sɒnərənt ‖ 'sɑ-/ *n*
a speech sound which is produced with a relatively free passage of air from the lungs, either through the mouth or through the nose. For example, /e/ in *bed*, /l/ in *lid* and /n/ in *nose* are sonorants. In GENERATIVE PHONOLOGY these sounds are marked [+sonorant] to distinguish them from OBSTRUENTs, which are marked [-sonorant].
see also DISTINCTIVE FEATURES
[*Further reading*: Hyman 1975]

sound change /'saʊnd ˌtʃeɪndʒ/ *n*
change in the pronunciation of words over a period of time. For example, there has been a sound change from Middle English /aː/ to Modern English /eɪ/:
　　Middle English /naːmə/　　Modern English /neɪm/ *name*.
Such sound changes are still continuing and often differences can be observed between the pronunciation of older and younger speakers in a community.
[*Further reading*: Aitchison 1981; Labov 1972a]

sound wave /'saʊnd ˌweɪv/ *n*
wave-like movements of air which transmit sounds. In speech, sound waves are caused by the vibration of the VOCAL CORDS.
The rate at which the air in a sound wave moves backwards and forwards in a given time is called **frequency**. The faster the movement, the higher the frequency. A speech sound is a combination of simple sound waves vibrating at different frequencies and forming a complex sound wave, eg:

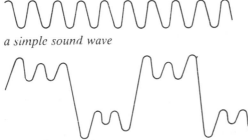

a simple sound wave

a complex sound wave

The lowest frequency in a complex sound wave is called the
fundamental frequency. It is the same frequency as that at which the
vocal cords are vibrating.
[*Further reading*: Denes & Pinson 1963]

source¹ /sɔːs ‖ -ɔr-/ *n*
see under INFORMATION THEORY

source² *n*
(in CASE GRAMMAR) the place from which someone or something
moves or is moved.
For example, *the station* in:
   He came from the station.
[*Further reading*: Fillmore 1971]

source language¹ /'sɔːs ˌlæŋgwɪdʒ ‖ -ɔr-/ *n*
(in language BORROWING) a language from which words have been
taken into another language. French was the source language for
many words which entered English after the Norman Conquest
(1066), eg *prince, just, saint, noble*, as well as for words which
entered English at a later stage, eg *garage, restaurant*.

source language² *n*
the language out of which a translation is made (eg in a bilingual
dictionary).
see also TARGET LANGUAGE²

SOV language /ˌes əʊ 'viː 'læŋgwɪdʒ/ *n*
see under TYPOLOGY

Spearman-Brown Formula /ˌspɪəmən 'braʊn ˌfɔːmjʊlə ‖ ˌspɪər-
ˌfɔrmjə-/ *n*
a formula for estimating the RELIABILITY of a test by calculating the
reliability of a shorter or longer version of the same test. This
formula is most frequently used in estimating the reliability of two
independent halves of a test (see SPLIT-HALF RELIABILITY).

special languages /'speʃəl 'læŋgwɪdʒəz/ *n*
a term used for the varieties of language used by specialists in
writing about their subject matter, such as the language used in
botany, law, nuclear physics or linguistics. The study of special
languages includes the study of TERMINOLOGY (the special LEXEMEs
used in particular disciplines) and REGISTER (2) the distinctive
linguistic features which occur in special languages).
see also ENGLISH FOR SPECIAL PURPOSES
[*Further reading*: Sager, Dungworth, & McDonald 1980]

specific question /spə'sɪfɪk 'kwestʃən/ *n*
see under GLOBAL QUESTION

speech act /'spiːtʃ ˌækt/ *n*

an UTTERANCE as a functional unit in communication. In speech act theory, utterances have two kinds of meaning:

(a) propositional meaning (also known as **locutionary meaning**). This is the basic literal meaning of the utterance which is conveyed by the particular words and structures which the utterance contains (see PROPOSITION, LOCUTIONARY ACT).

(b) illocutionary meaning (also known as **illocutionary force**). This is the effect the utterance or written text has on the reader or listener.

For example, in *I am thirsty* the propositional meaning is what the utterance says about the speaker's physical state. The illocutionary force is the effect the speaker wants the utterance to have on the listener. It may be intended as a request for something to drink.

A speech act is a sentence or utterance which has both propositional meaning and illocutionary force.

There are many different kinds of speech acts, such as requests, orders, commands, complaints, promises (see SPEECH ACT CLASSIFICATION).

A speech act which is performed indirectly is sometimes known as an **indirect speech act**, such as the speech act of requesting above. Indirect speech acts are often felt to be more polite ways of performing certain kinds of speech act, such as requests and refusals.

In language teaching, and SYLLABUS design, speech acts are often referred to as "functions" or "language functions" (see NOTIONAL SYLLABUS, FUNCTIONAL SYLLABUS).

see also PERFORMATIVE, PRAGMATICS, UPTAKE

[*Further reading*: Austin 1962; Searle 1981]

speech act classification /'spiːtʃ ˌækt ˌklæsəfəˈkeɪʃən/ *n*

The philosopher Searle established a five-part classification of SPEECH ACTS:

a) **commissive**: a speech act that commits the speaker to doing something in the future, such as a promise or a threat. For example:

If you don't stop fighting I'll call the police. (threat)
I'll take you to the movies tomorrow. (promise)

b) **declarative**: a speech act which changes the state of affairs in the world. For example, during the wedding ceremony the act of marriage is performed when the phrase *I now pronounce you man and wife* is uttered.

c) **directive**: a speech act that has the function of getting the listener to do something, such as a suggestion, a request, or a command. For example:

Please sit down.
Why don't you close the window.

d) **expressive**: a speech act in which the speaker expresses feelings and

attitudes about something, such as an apology, a complaint, to thank someone, to congratulate someone. For example:
The meal was delicious.

e) **representative**: a speech act which describes states or events in the world, such as an assertion, a claim, a report. For example, the assertion:
This is a German car.

[*Further reading*: Searle 1965]

speech community /'spiːtʃ kə'mjuːnɪ̀ti/ *n*

a group of people who form a community, eg a village, a region, a nation, and who have *at least* one SPEECH VARIETY in common.

In BILINGUAL and MULTILINGUAL communities, people would usually have more than one speech variety in common (see SPEECH REPERTOIRE).

[*Further reading*: Hymes 1974]

speech continuum /'spiːtʃ kən,tɪnjʊəm/ *n*

a range of speech varieties (see SPEECH VARIETY). Although it is common to think of a language as being divided into separate regional DIALECTs or social dialects (SOCIOLECTs), there is often no clear division between them but rather a **continuum** from one to another.

speech defect /'spiːtʃ ˌdiːfekt/ *n*

also **speech disorder** /'spiːtʃ dɪsˌɔːdəʳ ‖ -ɔr-/

any abnormality in the production of speech which interferes with communication, such as APHASIA, or stuttering.

speech errors /'spiːtʃ ˌerəz ‖ -ərz/ *n*

faults made by speakers during the production of sounds, words, and sentences.

Both NATIVE SPEAKERs and non-native speakers of a language make unintended mistakes when speaking. Some of the commonest speech errors include:

(a) **anticipation error**: when a sound or word is brought forward in a sentence and used before it is needed. For example:
I'll put your cat in the cupboard instead of *I'll put your hat in the cupboard.*

(b) **perseveration error**: when a sound or word which has already been uttered reappears. For example:
the president of Prance instead of *the president of France.*

(c) **reversal error**, also **spoonerism**: when the position of sounds, syllables, or words is reversed. For example:
let's have chish and fips instead of *let's have fish and chips*

Speech errors have been studied by psycholinguists in order to find out how people store language items in long term memory and how they select items from memory when speaking.

see also MEMORY

[*Further reading*: Clark & Clark 1977]

speech event /'spiːtʃ ɪˌvent/ *n*
a particular instance when people exchange speech, eg an exchange of greetings, an enquiry, a conversation. For example:

Child: *Mum, where's my red jumper?*
Mother: *Bottom drawer in your bedroom.*
Child: *Right, I'll have a look.*

Speech events are governed by rules and norms for the use of speech, which may be different in different communities. The structure of speech events varies considerably according to the GENRE they belong to.

The components of a speech event are its SETTING, the PARTICIPANTS and their ROLE RELATIONSHIPS, the MESSAGE, the key (see KEY[1]) and the CHANNEL.

The term **speech situation** is sometimes used instead of speech event, but usually it refers to any situation which is associated with speech, eg a classroom lesson, a party.

A speech situation may consist of just one speech event, eg two people meeting in the street and having a brief conversation, or it may contain a number of speech events, some going on at the same time, eg a large dinner party.

[*Further reading*: Coulthard 1985; Hymes 1974]

speech pathology /'spiːtʃ pə'θɒlədʒi ‖ -'θɑ-/ *n*
the study of speech abnormalities and disorders, such as APHASIA and stuttering.

Speech therapists (see SPEECH THERAPY) are sometimes called "speech pathologists" or "speech-language pathologists", especially in the USA.

speech perception /ˌspiːtʃ pə'sepʃən ‖ pər-/ *n*
see under PERCEPTION

speech rate /'spiːtʃ ˌreɪt/ *n*
another term for RATE OF SPEECH

speech reading /'spiːtʃ ˌriːdɪŋ/ *n*
another term for LIPREADING

speech repertoire /'spiːtʃ ˌrepətwɑːr ‖ -ər-/ *n*
the languages or language varieties that a person knows and uses within his or her SPEECH COMMUNITY in everyday communication. A particular group of speakers may use not just one language or language variety to communicate with one another but several, each appropriate for certain areas of everyday activity (see DOMAIN). The speech repertoire of a French Canadian in Montreal could include Standard Canadian French, Colloquial Canadian French and English (perhaps in more than one variety).
see also DIGLOSSIA, VERBAL REPERTOIRE

speech rhythm /'spiːtʃ ˌrɪðəm/ *n*
rhythm in speech is created by the contracting and relaxing of chest

muscles (pulses). This causes changes in air pressure. There are two different patterns of pulses:

(a) a more regular type of contraction with regular rises in air pressure (chest pulses)

(b) less frequent but stronger contractions with more sudden rises in air pressure (stress pulses).

The way these two systems operate together in any one language is said to cause different types of speech rhythm.

see also STRESS-TIMED RHYTHM, SYLLABLE-TIMED RHYTHM

[*Further reading*: Abercrombie 1965]

speech situation /'spiːtʃ sɪtʃʊ'eɪʃən/ *n*
see under SPEECH EVENT

speech styles /'spiːtʃ ˌstaɪlz/ *n*
alternative ways of speaking within a community, often ranging from more colloquial to more formal. Usually, the range of styles available to a person varies according to his or her own background and the type of SPEECH COMMUNITY. The choice of a particular style has social implications. For example, choosing a formal style in a casual context may sound funny and using a very colloquial style in a formal context, such as in a sermon at a funeral service, may offend. Generally, a native speaker knows when a certain speech style is or is not appropriate (see APPROPRIATENESS).

Two types of rules which are connected with speech styles are **co-occurrence rules** and **alternation rules**. Co-occurrence rules determine which linguistic unit may follow or precede, that is, "co-occur with", another unit or units. For example:

formal style: *I should most certainly like to attend your ball, Sir Reginald.*

colloquial style: *I'd love to come to your do, Reg.*

Alternation rules determine the possible choice of "alternatives" from a number of speech styles or stylistic features which are at the speaker's disposal, eg:

formal style: *Good morning, Mrs Smith . . .*

semi-formal style: *Hullo . . .*

colloquial style: *Hi, Penny . . .*

[*Further reading*: Coulthard 1985; Ervin-Tripp 1972]

speech synthesis /'spiːtʃ 'sɪnθəsəs/ *n*
see under COMPUTATIONAL LINGUISTICS

speech therapy /'spiːtʃ 'θerəpi/ *n*
activities and exercises which are designed to help to alleviate or cure a language or speech defect (eg stuttering) or to help someone to regain their use of speech after having suffered speech loss (eg after a stroke).

see also SPEECH PATHOLOGY

speech variety /ˈspiːtʃ vəˈraɪəti/ *n*

a term sometimes used instead of LANGUAGE², DIALECT, SOCIOLECT, PIDGIN, CREOLE, etc because it is considered more neutral than such terms. It may also be used for different varieties of one language, eg American English, Australian English, Indian English.

speed reading /ˈspiːd ˌriːdɪŋ/ *n*
also **rapid reading**

techniques used to teach people to read more quickly and to achieve a greater degree of understanding of what they read. Readers are usually trained to use more effective eye movements when reading (see REGRESSIONS), and to use better ways of understanding words and meanings in written texts.

see also READING, TACHISTOSCOPE

spelling pronunciation /ˈspelɪŋ prəˌnʌnsiˈeɪʃən/ *n*

a way of pronouncing a word which is based on its spelling and which may differ from the way the word is generally pronounced. For example, a non-native speaker of English might pronounce *yacht* as /jɒkt/ instead of /jɒt/. Native speakers also sometimes use spelling pronunciations, and some have become acceptable ways of pronouncing words, such as /ˈɒftən/ for *often* rather than /ˈɒfən/.

spiral approach /ˈspaɪərəl əˈprəʊtʃ/ *n*
also **cyclical approach**

a SYLLABUS in which items recur throughout the syllabus but are treated in greater depth or in more detail when they recur. This may be contrasted with a **linear syllabus**, in which syllabus items are dealt with once only.

[*Further reading*: Howatt 1974]

spirant /ˈspaɪərənt/ *n*

a term used by some American linguists for a FRICATIVE

split-half reliability /ˈsplɪt ˌhɑːf rɪˌlaɪəˈbɪləti ‖ ˌhæf/ *n*

(in TESTING and statistics) an estimate of RELIABILITY based on the coefficient of CORRELATION between two halves of a test (eg between the odd and even scores or between the first and second half of the items of the test). Usually the SPEARMAN-BROWN FORMULA is applied to the results in order to estimate the reliability of the full test rather than its separate halves.

spoonerism /ˈspuːnərɪzəm/ *n*

see under SPEECH ERROR

S-R theory /ˌes ˈɑːʳ ˈθɪəri/ *n*

an abbreviation for STIMULUS-RESPONSE THEORY

stage /steɪdʒ/ *n*

In language teaching, a lesson is sometimes divided into three stages:

(a) **presentation stage**: the introduction of new items, when their meanings are explained, demonstrated, etc, and other necessary information is given

(b) **practice stage** (also, **repetition stage**): New items are practised, either individually or in groups. Practice activities usually move from controlled to less controlled practice.

(c) **production stage** (also, **transfer stage**, **free practice**): Students use the new items more freely, with less or little control by the teacher.

standard /'stændəd ‖ -dərd/ n **standard** adj
another term for STANDARD VARIETY

Standard American English /'stændəd ə'merɪkən 'ɪŋglɪʃ ‖ -dərd/ n
see under STANDARD VARIETY

Standard British English /'stændəd 'brɪtɪʃ 'ɪŋglɪʃ ‖ -dərd/ n
see under STANDARD VARIETY

standard deviation /'stændəd ˌdiːvi'eɪʃən ‖ -dərd/ n
also **SD**

(in statistics) the commonest measure of the DISPERSION of a DISTRIBUTION[2], that is, of the degree to which scores vary from the MEAN. It is defined as the square root of the VARIANCE.

$$SD = \sqrt{\frac{\Sigma x^2}{N}}$$

x = a score minus the mean
N = the number of items
Σ = the sum of

standard dialect /'stændəd 'daɪəlekt ‖ -dərd/ n
another term for STANDARD VARIETY

Standard English /'stændəd 'ɪŋglɪʃ ‖ -dərd/ n
see under STANDARD VARIETY

standard error /'stændəd 'erər ‖ -dərd/ n
also **SE**

(in TESTING and statistics) a statistic used for determining the degree to which the estimate of a POPULATION PARAMETER is likely to differ from the computed sample statistic. The standard error of a statistic provides an indication of how accurate an estimate it is of the population parameter. One commonly used standard error is the standard error of the MEAN, which indicates how close the mean of the observed sample is to the mean of the entire population.

standardization /ˌstændədaɪ'zeɪʃən ‖ -dər-/ n **standardize**
/'stændədaɪz ‖ -dər-/ v

the process of making some aspect of language USAGE[1] conform to a STANDARD VARIETY. This may take place in connection with the WRITING SYSTEM or the spelling system of a particular language and is usually implemented by a government authority. For example, a standardized system has been introduced in Malaysia and Indonesia, which provides a common standard for the spelling of Malay and Indonesian.

	Indonesian	Malay	
old spelling	*tjantik*	*chantek*	"pretty, good-
new spelling	*cantik*	*cantik*	looking"
old spelling	*burung*	*burong*	"bird"
new spelling	*burung*	*burung*	

standardized test /'stændədaɪzd 'test ‖ -dər-/ *n*
a test (a) which has been developed from tryouts and experimentation to ensure that it is reliable and valid (see RELIABILITY, VALIDITY)
(b) for which NORMS[2] have been established
(c) which provides uniform procedures for administering (time limits, response format, number of questions) and for scoring the test.

standard language /'stændəd 'læŋgwɪdʒ ‖ -dərd/ *n*
another term for STANDARD VARIETY

standard nine /ˌstændəd 'naɪn ‖ -dərd/ *n*
another term for STANINE

standard score /'stændəd 'skɔːʳ ‖ -dərd 'skɔr/ *n*
(in TESTING and statistics) a type of DERIVED SCORE by which scores or values from different measures can be reported or compared using a common scale. For example, in order to compare a student's scores on two tests of different lengths, a standard score might be used. A standard score expresses a RAW SCORE as a function of its relative position in a DISTRIBUTION[1] of scores, and is thus usually easier to interpret than the raw score. Commonly used standard scores are the Z-SCORE and the T-SCORE.

Standard Theory /'stændəd 'θɪəri ‖ -dərd/ *n*
see under GENERATIVE TRANSFORMATIONAL GRAMMAR

standard variety /'stændəd və'raɪəti ‖ -dərd/ *n*
also **standard dialect, standard language, standard**
the variety of a language which has the highest STATUS in a community or nation and which is usually based on the speech and writing of educated native speakers of the language.
A standard variety is generally:
(a) used in the news media and in literature
(b) described in dictionaries and grammars (see NORMATIVE GRAMMAR)
(c) taught in schools and taught to non-native speakers when they learn the language as a foreign language.
Sometimes it is the educated variety spoken in the political or cultural centre of a country, eg the standard variety of French is based on educated Parisian French.
The standard variety of American English is known as **Standard American English** and the standard variety of British English is **Standard British English**.

A standard variety may show some variation in pronunciation according to the part of the country where it is spoken, eg Standard British English in Scotland, Wales, Southern England. **Standard English** is sometimes used as a cover term for all the national standard varieties of English. These national standard varieties have differences in spelling, vocabulary, grammar, and particularly pronunciation, but there is a common core of the language. This makes it possible for educated native speakers of the various national standard varieties of English to communicate with one another.

see also RECEIVED PRONUNCIATION, NATIONAL LANGUAGE

[*Further reading*: Trudgill 1975]

stanine /'steɪnaɪn/ *n*
also **standard nine**

a NORMALIZED STANDARD SCORE sometimes used in testing, in which standardized scores are arranged on a nine-step scale. A stanine equals one ninth of the range of the standard scores of a DISTRIBUTION[1].

statement /'steɪtmənt/ *n*

an utterance which describes a state of affairs, action, feeling or belief, eg *It's very cold here in winter; I don't think she looks very well.*

A statement occurs in the form of a DECLARATIVE SENTENCE but not all declarative sentences make statements. For example:

I suppose you'll be there.

could be said to be more a question than a statement.

statistical hypothesis /stə,tɪstɪkəl haɪ'pɒθəsəs ‖ -'pɑ-/ *n*

see under HYPOTHESIS

statistical significance /stə,tɪstɪkəl sɪg'nɪfɪkəns/ *n*

a term used when testing a statistical hypothesis (see HYPOTHESIS), which refers to the likelihood that an obtained sample MEAN can be expected to represent the mean of the population. The level of significance, symbolized as p (for probability) is expressed as a proportion of 1. The most common levels of significance are $p < .05$ and $p < .01$ (where the symbol $<$ means "less than"). If the difference between two means, for instance, is given as significant at the $p < .05$ or at the 0.05 level, this indicates that such a difference could be expected to occur by chance in only 5 out of 100 samplings. A level of significance of 0.01 means that the difference can be expected to occur by chance only one time in 100 samplings. Thus, the *lower* the probability of chance occurrence (p), the *higher* the level of significance, and the *greater* the probability that the observed difference is a true one and not due to chance.

stative verb /'steɪtɪv 'vɜːb ‖ -ɜr-/ *n*

a verb which usually refers to a state (ie an unchanging condition), for example *believe, have, belong, contain, cost, differ, own*, as in:

This <u>contains</u> calcium.

She <u>believes</u> in God.

Stative verbs are not usually used in the PROGRESSIVE ASPECT.

A verb which can be used in the progressive aspect is known as a **dynamic verb**, for example *read, wear*.

I <u>am reading</u> a good book.

She <u>is wearing</u> dark glasses.

[*Further reading*: Quirk et al 1985]

status /'steɪtəs ‖ 'steɪtəs, 'stæ-/ *n*

higher, lower, or equal position, particularly in regard to prestige, power, and social class.

Speech varieties (see SPEECH VARIETY) may have different statuses in a SPEECH COMMUNITY. For example, a variety which is limited to use in markets and for very informal situations would have a low status whereas another variety which is used in government, education, administration, etc, would have a high status (see DIGLOSSIA).

The status of people, when they are communicating in speech or writing, is also important, as it may affect the SPEECH STYLE they use to each other, eg ADDRESS FORMS, courtesy formulae.

see also ROLE RELATIONSHIPS

stem[1] /stem/ *n*

also **base form**

that part of a word to which an inflectional AFFIX is or can be added. For example, in English the inflectional affix *-s* can be added to the stem *work* to form the plural *works* in *the <u>works</u> of Shakespeare*.

The stem of a word may be:

(a) a simple stem consisting of only one morpheme (ROOT), eg *work*

(b) a root plus a derivational affix, eg *work+-er = worker*

(c) two or more roots, eg *work+shop = workshop*.

Thus we can have *work+-s = works, (work + -er) + -s = workers*, or *(work+shop)+-s = workshops*.

see also DERIVATION, INFLECTION,

stem[2] *n*

see under MULTIPLE CHOICE ITEM

stimulus /'stɪmjʊləs ‖ -mjə-/ *n*

see under STIMULUS-RESPONSE THEORY, BEHAVIOURISM

stimulus-response theory /'stɪmjʊləs rɪ'spɒns 'θɪəri ‖ -mjə- -'spɑns/ *n*

also **S-R theory**

a learning theory associated particularly with the American psychologist B.F. Skinner (1904—) (see BEHAVIOURISM), which describes learning as the formation of associations between responses. A **stimulus** is that which produces a change or reaction in an individual or organism. A **response** is the behaviour which is produced as a reaction to a stimulus. **Reinforcement** is a stimulus which follows the occurrence of a response and affects the probability of that response occurring or not occurring again. Reinforcement which increases the likelihood of a response is known as **positive reinforcement**. Reinforcement which decreases the likelihood of a response is known as **negative reinforcement**. If no reinforcement is associated with a response the response may eventually disappear. This is known as **extinction**. If a response is produced to similar stimuli with which it was not originally associated this is known as "stimulus generalization". Learning to distinguish between different kinds of stimuli is known as **discrimination**.

There are several S-R theories which contain these general principles or variations of them, and they have been used in studies of VERBAL LEARNING and language learning.

see also OPERANT CONDITIONING

[*Further reading*: Gagné 1970]

stop /stɒp ‖ stɑp/ *n*
also **plosive**

a speech sound (a CONSONANT) which is produced by stopping the airstream from the lungs and then suddenly releasing it.

For example, /p/ is a BILABIAL stop, formed by stopping the air with the lips and then releasing it.

see also CONSONANT, MANNER OF ARTICULATION, PLACE OF ARTICULATION

[*Further reading*: Gimson 1980]

strategy /ˈstrætədʒi/ *n*

procedures used in learning, thinking, etc, which serve as a way of reaching a goal. In language learning, learning strategies (see LEARNING STRATEGY) and communication strategies (see COMMUNICATION STRATEGY) are those conscious or unconscious processes which language learners make use of in learning and using a language.

see also HEURISTIC, HYPOTHESIS TESTING, OVERGENERALIZATION, SIMPLIFICATION[1]

stratificational grammar /ˌstrætəfəˈkeɪʃənəl ˈɡræməʳ/ *n*

a theory of language developed by the American linguist Lamb. According to this theory there are a number of "strata" (levels) within a language: a "PHONEMIC stratum" (level) which relates to the sound system of a language, a "sememic stratum" which is connected with SEMANTIC concepts, and several strata between these two. For each stratum there is a system, which includes patterns such as the "tactic patterns" of arrangement. For example at the phonemic stratum, the PHONOTACTIC patterns would specify what arrangements of sound units are possible in a language. For English, the combination /tr/ is possible, as in *trip*, but /tl/ as in **tlip* is not.

[*Further reading*: Lockwood 1972]

strong verb

stratified sample /ˈstrætəfaɪd ˈsɑːmpəl ‖ ˈsæm-/ *n*
see under SAMPLE

stress /stres/ *n, v*
the pronunciation (see ARTICULATION) of a word or syllable with more
force than the surrounding words or syllables, ie, when it is
produced by using more air from the lungs.
Syllables may be stressed or unstressed. A listener hears a stressed
syllable or word as being louder and/or of longer duration and/or
produced with a higher PITCH than the surrounding words or
syllables.
A syllable may be stressed because:
(a) the ACCENT[1] is on that syllable, eg *dismay*, *ever*, *confusion*
(b) the speaker wishes to emphasize (give PROMINENCE to) the
syllable, eg:
    I said INduce, not DEduce.
[*Further reading*: Brazil, Coulthard, & Johns 1980; Halliday 1970]

stress-timed rhythm /ˈstres ˌtaɪmd ˈrɪðəm/ *n*
A SPEECH RHYTHM in which the stressed syllables are said to recur at
equal intervals of time. English has often been called stress-timed.
For example, in:
Álison didn't / fínish her / éssay
      1   2   3
each of the three segments (marked 1, 2, 3) would take the same
time to utter, although each segment has a different number of
syllables. The effect is that the stressed syllables (marked ´) occur at
equal intervals.
However, recorded speech of British English shows that, although
English has a tendency to stress-timed rhythm, it is not strictly
stress-timed.
see also SYLLABLE-TIMED RHYTHM
[*Further reading*: Abercrombie 1965; Brazil, Coulthard, & Johns
1980]

strong form /ˈstrɒŋ ˌfɔːm ‖ ˈstrɔŋ ˌfɔrm/ *n*
one of the possible forms in which a word appears in speech. If a
word is said in isolation or if it is stressed (eg *he cán pay us*), the
strong form is used (eg /kæn/ *can*). If a word is unstressed, it often
appears in its **weak form**. For example, the vowel sound in *can* does
not have the same quality in the weak form and is reduced in length
(eg /kən/).

strong verb /ˈstrɒŋ ˈvɜːb ‖ ˈstrɔŋ ˈvɜrb/ *n*
(in grammar) a term sometimes used to refer to a verb which forms
the past tense and the past participle by a change in a vowel (eg
begin-began-begun, sing-sang-sung). A regular verb which forms the
past tense and participle by adding *-ed* is known as a **weak verb** (eg
open-opened).

structural description /'strʌktʃərəl dɪ'skrɪpʃən/ *n*
also **SD**
> (in GENERATIVE TRANSFORMATIONAL GRAMMAR) a complete grammatical
> analysis of a sentence typically in the form of tree-like structures
> (**tree diagram**) or strings of labelled constituents. The structural
> description shows the most abstract syntactic form of the sentence
> (DEEP STRUCTURE) and the changes made to it by various rules
> ("transformational rules").
> see also BASE COMPONENT, TRANSFORMATIONAL COMPONENT

structural global method /ˌstrʌktʃərəl 'gləʊbəl 'meθəd/ *n*
> another term for AUDIO-VISUAL METHOD

structural(ist) linguistics /'strʌktʃərəlɪst lɪŋ'gwɪstɪks/ *n*
> an approach to linguistics which stresses the importance of language
> as a system and which investigates the place that linguistic units such
> as sounds, words, sentences have within this system.
> Structural linguists, for example, studied the distribution of sounds
> within the words of a language; that is, whether certain sounds
> appear only at the beginning of words or also in the middle or at
> the end. They defined some sounds in a language as distinctive and
> used in the identification of words (see PHONEME), and some as
> variants (see ALLOPHONE). Similar studies of distribution and
> classification were carried out in MORPHOLOGY and SYNTAX.
> In its widest sense, the term has been used for various groups of
> linguists, including those of the PRAGUE SCHOOL, but most often it is
> used to refer to a group of American linguists such as Bloomfield
> and Fries, who published mainly in the 1930s to 1950s. The work of
> these linguists was based on the theory of BEHAVIOURISM and had a
> considerable influence on some language teaching methods (see
> AUDIOLINGUAL METHOD).
> [*Further reading*: Bolinger 1975]

structural syllabus /'strʌktʃərəl 'sɪləbəs/ *n*
> a SYLLABUS for the teaching of a language which is based on a
> selection of the grammatical items and structures (eg tenses,
> grammatical rules, sentence patterns) which occur in a language and
> the arrangement of them into an order suitable for teaching. The
> order of introducing grammatical items and structures in a structural
> syllabus may be based on such factors as frequency, difficulty,
> usefulness, or a combination of these.
> see also NOTIONAL SYLLABUS, SITUATIONAL METHOD
> [*Further reading*: Alexander et al 1975]

structural word /'strʌktʃərəl ˌwɜːd ‖ -ɜr-/ *n*
> see under CONTENT WORD

structure /'strʌktʃərʳ/ *n*
> (in linguistics) the term often refers to a sequence of linguistic units
> that are in a certain relationship to one another.

For example, one of the structures of a NOUN PHRASE[1] may be "article + adjective + noun" as in *the friendly ape*. One of the possible SYLLABLE structures in English is CVC (consonant + vowel + consonant) as in *con* in *concert*.

see also SYNTAGMATIC RELATIONS

structured response item /ˌstrʌktʃəd rɪˈspɒns ˈaɪtəm ‖ -tʃərd -ˈspɑns/ *n*
see under TEST ITEM

structure word /ˈstrʌktʃəʳ ˌwɜːd ‖ -ɜr-/ *n*
see under CONTENT WORD

student-centred learning /ˈstjuːdənt ˈsentəd ˈlɜːnɪŋ ‖ ˈstuː- -tərd ˈlɜr-/ *n*
(in education) learning situations in which:
(a) students take part in setting goals and OBJECTIVES
(b) there is a concern for the student's feelings and values (see HUMANISTIC APPROACH)
(c) there is a different role of the teacher; the teacher is seen as a helper, adviser, or counsellor.
Language-teaching methods such as COMMUNITY LANGUAGE LEARNING and SILENT WAY give the students an active role in learning and are hence said to be less teacher-centred and more student-centred than many traditional methods.

study skills /ˈstʌdi ˌskɪlz/ *n*
abilities, techniques, and strategies (see MICRO-SKILLS) which are used when reading, writing, or listening for study purposes. For example, study skills needed by university students studying from English-language textbooks include: adjusting reading speeds according to the type of material being read (see READING SPEED), using the dictionary, guessing word meanings from context, interpreting graphs, diagrams, and symbols, note-taking and summarizing.

style /staɪl/ *n* **stylistic** /staɪˈlɪstɪk/ *adj*
(1) variation in a person's speech or writing. Style usually varies from casual to formal according to the type of situation, the person or persons addressed, the location, the topic discussed, etc.
A particular style, eg a formal style or a colloquial style, is sometimes referred to as a **stylistic variety**.
Some linguists use the term "register" for a stylistic variety whilst others differentiate between the two (see REGISTER).
(2) style can also refer to a particular person's use of speech or writing at all times or to a way of speaking or writing at a particular period of time, eg Dickens' style, the style of Shakespeare, an 18th-century style of writing.
see also STYLISTIC VARIATION

style shift /ˈstaɪl ˌʃɪft/ *n*
a change in STYLE during a verbal or written communication.
Usually, a style shift takes place if the writer reassesses or redefines a particular situation. For example, a writer may add an informal

note at the end of a formal invitation because he or she is on familiar terms with the person the invitation is addressed to. In a job interview, an applicant may change his or her formal style to a less formal style if the interviewer adopts a very informal manner.

see also STYLISTIC VARIATION

stylistics /staɪˈlɪstɪks/ n

the study of that variation in language (STYLE) which is dependent on the situation in which the language is used and also on the effect the writer or speaker wishes to create on the reader or hearer. Although stylistics sometimes includes investigations of spoken language, it usually refers to the study of written language, including literary texts. Stylistics is concerned with the choices that are available to a writer and the reasons why particular forms and expressions are used rather than others.

see also DISCOURSE ANALYSIS

[*Further reading*: Bolinger 1975]

stylistic variation /staɪˌlɪstɪk veəriˈeɪʃən/ n

differences in the speech or writing of a person or group of people according to the situation, the topic, the addressee(s) and the location. Stylistic variation can be observed in the use of different speech sounds, different words or expressions, or different sentence structures.

For example, in English:

(a) Pronunciation: People are more likely to say /sɪtn̩/ *sitt'n* /wɜːkn̩/ *work'n* instead of /sɪtɪŋ/ *sitting* /wɜːkɪŋ/ *working* if the style is more informal.

(b) Words and sentence structures:

more formal: *We were somewhat dismayed by his lack of response to our invitation.*

less formal: *We were rather fed up that he didn't answer when we invited him.*

The stylistic variation of an individual or group can be measured by analysing recorded speech and making comparisons.

see also STYLE

stylistic variety /staɪˌlɪstɪk vəˈraɪəti/ n

see under STYLE

subject /ˈsʌbdʒɪkt/ n

(in English grammar) generally the noun, pronoun or NOUN PHRASE[1] which:

(a) typically precedes the main verb in a sentence and is most closely related to it

(b) determines CONCORD

(c) refers to something about which a statement or assertion is made in the rest of the sentence.

That part of the sentence containing the verb, or VERB GROUP (and which may include OBJECTs, COMPLEMENTs, or ADVERBIALs) is known as the PREDICATE. The predicate is that part of the sentence which predicates something of the subject. For example:

subject	predicate
The woman	*smiled.*
Fish	*is good for you.*

see also OBJECT[1]

subject complement /ˌsʌbdʒɪkt 'kɒmpləmənt ‖ 'kɑm-/ *n*
see under COMPLEMENT

subjective test /səb'dʒektɪv 'test/ *n*
a test which is scored according to the personal judgment of the marker, such as an essay examination. A subjective test may be contrasted with an **objective test** which is a test that can be marked without the use of the examiner's personal judgment. TRUE-FALSE and MULTIPLE-CHOICE tests are examples of objective tests.

Subject-Prominent language /'sʌbdʒɪkt 'prɒmənənt 'læŋgwɪdʒ ‖ 'prɑ-/ *n*
a language in which the grammatical units of SUBJECT and PREDICATE are basic to the structure of sentences and in which sentences usually have subject-predicate structure. English is a Subject-Prominent language, since sentences such as the following are a usual sentence type:

I	*have already seen Peter.*
(Subject)	(Predicate)

A language in which the grammatical units of topic and comment (see TOPIC[2]) are basic to the structure of sentences is known as a **Topic-Prominent language**. Chinese is a Topic-Prominent language, since sentences with Topic-Comment structure are a usual sentence type in Chinese. For example:

Zhāngsān	wǒ	yǐjīng	jiàn	guo	le
Zhangsan	I	already	see	aspect marker	particle

ie *Zhangsan, I have already seen (him).*

(Topic)	(Comment)

[*Further reading*: Li & Thompson 1981]

subjunctive /səb'dʒʌŋktɪv/ *n*
see under MOOD

submersion programme /səb'mɜːʃən 'prəʊgræm ‖ -ɜr-/ *n*
a form of BILINGUAL EDUCATION in which the language of instruction is not the FIRST LANGUAGE of some of the children, but *is* the first language of others. This happens in many countries where immigrant children enter school and are taught in the language of the host country.
see also IMMERSION PROGRAMME
[*Further reading*: Swain 1978]

subordinate clause /sə'bɔːdənət 'klɔːz ‖ -ɔr-/ *n*
another term for DEPENDENT CLAUSE

subordinating conjunction /sə,bɔːdəneɪtɪŋ kən'dʒʌŋkʃən ‖ -ɔr-/ *n*
see under CONJUNCTION

subordination /sə,bɔːdə́'neɪʃən ‖ -ɔr-/ *n*
see under CONJUNCTION

subordinator /sə'bɔːdə́neɪtəʳ ‖ -ɔr-/ *n*
see under CONJUNCTION

substandard /ˌsʌb'stændəd ‖ -dərd/ *adj*
a term which expresses a negative value judgment on any part of
the speech or writing of a person or group that does not conform to
the STANDARD VARIETY of a language and is therefore thought to be
undesirable.
For example, the double negative used in some dialects of English:
   I don't know nothing.
would be considered by some people as substandard. A more
neutral term used by linguists for forms which do not belong to the
standard variety of a language is NONSTANDARD.

substantive /səb'stæntɪv ‖ 'sʌbstəntɪv/ *n*
a term sometimes used for a NOUN or any word which can function
as a noun, such as a pronoun, an adjective (eg in *the old*), *a*
GERUND, etc.

substantive universal /'sʌbstəntɪv juːnə́'vɜːsəl ‖ -ɜr-/ *n*
see under LANGUAGE UNIVERSAL

substitution drill /ˌsʌbstə́'tjuːʃən ˌdrɪl ‖ -'tuː-/ *n*
see under DRILL

substitution table /ˌsʌbsté'tjuːʃən 'teɪbəl ‖ -'tuː-/ *n*
(in language teaching) a table which shows the items that may be
substituted at different positions in a sentence. A substitution table
can be used to produce many different sentences by making
different combinations of items. For example:

The post office	is	behind	the park.
The bank		near	the hotel.
The supermarket		across from	the station.

subtest /'sʌbˌtest/ *n*
a test which is given as a part of a longer test. For example, a
language-proficiency test may contain subtests of grammar, writing,
and speaking.

subtractive bilingual education /səb,træktɪv baɪ,lɪŋgwəl
edjʊ'keɪʃən ‖ edʒə-/ *n*
also **subtractive bilingualism** /səb,træktɪv baɪ'lɪŋgwəlɪzəm/
see under ADDITIVE BILINGUAL EDUCATION

subvocal reading /ˌsʌbˈvəʊkəl ˈriːdɪŋ/ *n*

a type of reading said to be characteristic of all readers (by some researchers) and of poor readers (by other researchers), in which the reader pronounces words silently while reading, sometimes also making slight movements of the tongue, lips, and vocal cords.

suffix /ˈsʌfɪks/ *n*

a letter or sound or group of letters or sounds which are added to the end of a word, and which change the meaning or function of the word.

see also under AFFIX

suggestopaedia /səˌdʒestəʊˈpiːdɪə, -stə-/ *n*
also **suggestopedia, suggestopedy** /səˌdʒeˈstɒpədi ‖ -ˈstɑ-/, **Lozanov method**

a METHOD of foreign-language teaching developed by the Bulgarian Lozanov. It makes use of dialogues, situations, and translation to present and practise language, and in particular, makes use of music, visual images, and relaxation exercises to make learning more comfortable and effective. Suggestopaedia is said to be a pedagogical application of "Suggestology", the influence of suggestion on human behaviour.

[*Further reading*: Lozanov 1979; Richards & Rogers 1986]

summative evaluation /ˌsʌmətɪv ɪˌvæljʊˈeɪʃən/ *n*
see under FORMATIVE EVALUATION

summative test /ˌsʌmətɪv ˈtest/ *n*
see under FORMATIVE TEST

superlative /suːˈpɜːlətɪv, sjuː- ‖ sʊˈpɜr-/ *n, adj*
also **superlative degree** /suːˈpɜːlətɪv dɪˈɡriː, sjuː- ‖ sʊˈpɜr-/
see under COMPARATIVE

superordinate /ˌsuːpərˈɔːdənət, sjuː- ‖ -ɔr-/ *n, adj*
see under HYPONYMY

suppletion /səˈpliːʃən/ *n*

(in MORPHOLOGY) a type of irregularity in which there is a complete change in the shape of a word in its various inflected forms (see INFLECTION).

For example, English *good – better – best* does not follow the normal pattern as in *tall – taller – tallest* but uses different forms for the comparative and the superlative (see COMPARATIVE) of the adjective *good*.

suprasegmentals /ˌsuːprəseɡˈmentəlz/ *n*

(in PHONETICS and PHONOLOGY) units which extend over more than one sound in an utterance, eg STRESS and tone (see TONE[1], TONE[2]). The term suprasegmentals is used particularly by American linguists.

see also INTONATION, PROMINENCE, SEGMENTAL PHONEMES

[*Further reading*: Hyman 1975]

surface structure

surface structure /ˈsɜːfəs ˌstrʌktʃər ‖ ˈsɜr-/ n
see under DEEP STRUCTURE, BASE COMPONENT, GENERATIVE
TRANSFORMATIONAL GRAMMAR

surrender value /səˈrendər ˌvæljuː/ n
(in language teaching) a term borrowed from life insurance and
sometimes used to refer to the functional skills which a learner has
acquired at any given point in a language course, and which the
learner would be able to use even if he or she did not continue
learning beyond that point.

SVO language /ˌes viː ˈəʊ ˈlæŋgwɪdʒ/ n
see under TYPOLOGY

syllabic writing /səˈlæbɪk ˈraɪtɪŋ/ n
a WRITING SYSTEM in which each symbol represents a SYLLABLE, eg the
Japanese syllabic systems Katakana and Hiragana:
Examples from Katakana:

イ ギ リ ス

Igirisu (Great Britain)

ト ラ ン プ

toranpu (playing cards)

see also ALPHABETIC WRITING, IDEOGRAPHIC WRITING

syllabification /səˌlæbəfəˈkeɪʃən/ n **syllabify** /səˈlæbəfaɪ/ v
dividing a word up into SYLLABLES.
For example, *locomotive* can be divided up into four syllables:
lo-co-mo-tive.
The syllabification of the spelling of a word can differ from the
syllabification of its pronunciation. For example, in
    styl-is-tics /staɪˈlɪstɪks/
the first syllable of the spelling is *styl*, but the first syllable of the
pronunciation is /staɪ-/.

syllable /ˈsɪləbəl/ n **syllabic** /səˈlæbɪk/ adj
a unit in speech which is often longer than one sound and smaller than
a whole word. For example, the word *terminology* consists of five
syllables: *ter-mi-no-lo-gy*.
In PHONETICS, the syllable is often related to chest pulses. These are the
contractions of certain chest muscles. Each chest pulse is accompanied
by increased air pressure. This air pressure is most noticeable in the
"central" part, the **peak** of a syllable. The hearer may distinguish the
central part of a syllable because it has more sound quality than the
surrounding sounds, but people often have difficulty in hearing when

one syllable ends and another one begins. For example, the word
bitter may be heard as *bi-tter, bit-ter* or *bitt-er*.
In PHONOLOGY, the syllable is defined by the way in which VOWELS and
CONSONANTS combine to form various sequences. Vowels can form a
syllable on their own or they can be the "centre" of a syllable, eg /e/ in
/bed/ *bed*. Consonants are at the beginning or the end of syllables and,
with a few exceptions, do not usually form syllables on their own.
Syllables may be classified according to whether they end in a vowel
(**open syllables**) or in a consonant (**closed syllables**). For example, in
English, *to, try, show* are open syllables and *bet, ask* and *snap* are
closed syllables.
A syllable can be divided into three parts:
(a) the beginning, called the **onset**
(b) the central part, called the **nucleus** or **peak**
(c) the end, called the **coda**.
In the English word *bed*, /bed/, /b/ would be the onset, /e/ the
nucleus and /d/ the coda.
Speech sounds which can be in the nucleus of a syllable are
sometimes called **syllabic** or [+syllabic]. Speech sounds which cannot
be in the nucleus are called **asyllabic** or [-syllabic].
[*Further reading*: Gimson 1980; Hyman 1975]

syllable-timed rhythm /ˈsɪləbəl ˌtaɪmd ˈrɪðəm/ *n*
a SPEECH RHYTHM in which all syllables are said to recur at equal
intervals. French is usually referred to as syllable-timed. For example,
in:
Il / est / ar/ri/vé / à / six / heures
1　2　3 4 5 6 7　8
"he arrived (is arrived) at six o'clock"
the segments marked 1, 2, 3, etc would each take the same time to
utter, and each segment consists of a single syllable.
However, recorded speech of French speakers shows that although
French has a tendency towards syllable-timed rhythm, it is usually
not strictly syllable-timed.
see also STRESS-TIMED RHYTHM
[*Further reading*: Abercrombie 1965; Brazil, Coulthard, & Johns 1980]

syllabus /ˈsɪləbəs/ *n*
also **curriculum**
a description of the contents of a course of instruction and the order
in which they are to be taught. Language-teaching syllabuses may be
based on (a) grammatical items and vocabulary (see STRUCTURAL
SYLLABUS) (b) the language needed for different types of situations
(see SITUATIONAL METHOD) (c) the meanings and communicative
functions which the learner needs to express in the TARGET
LANGUAGE[1] (see NOTIONAL SYLLABUS).
see also CURRICULUM[2], GRADATION, LANGUAGES FOR SPECIAL PURPOSES,
SPIRAL APPROACH, SYNTHETIC APPROACH
[*Further reading*: Wilkins 1976]

syllabus design /ˈsɪləbəs dɪˈzaɪn/ n
see under COURSE DESIGN, CURRICULUM DEVELOPMENT

synchronic /sɪŋˈkrɒnɪk ‖ -ˈkrɑ-/ adj
see under DIACHRONIC LINGUISTICS

synchronic linguistics /sɪŋˌkrɒnɪk lɪŋˈgwɪstɪks ‖ -ˌkrɑ-/ n
see under DIACHRONIC LINGUISTICS

synonym /ˈsɪnənɪm/ n **synonymous** /səˈnɒnəməs ‖ -ˈnɑ-/ n
synonymy /səˈnɒnəmi ‖ -ˈnɑ-/ n
a word which has the same, or nearly the same, meaning as another
word.
For example, in English *hide* and *conceal* in:
   He hide the money under the bed.
   He concealed the money under the bed.
Often one word may be more appropriate than another in a
particular situation, eg *conceal* is more formal than *hide*.
Sometimes two words may be synonymous in certain sentences
only.
For example, in the sentences:
   I must buy some more stamps at the post office.
   I must get some more stamps at the post office.
buy and *get* are synonyms, as it would usually be thought that *get* in
the second sentence means *buy* and not *steal*.
see also ANTONYM, HYPONYMY
[*Further reading*: Palmer 1981]

syntactic /sɪnˈtæktɪk/ adj
see SYNTAX

syntactic structure /sɪnˈtæktɪk ˈstrʌktʃər/ n
the arrangement of words and MORPHEMES into larger units (PHRASES,
CLAUSES and SENTENCES). Languages may be compared for differences
in syntactic structure.
For example, in English, the word order in a NOUN PHRASE[1] is
usually:
   demonstrative + adjective + noun
   this   *big*   *house*
whereas in Malay the order is:
   noun + adjective + demonstrative
   rumah *besar*   *ini*
   house   big   this

syntagm /ˈsɪntægəm/ n **syntagmatic** /ˌsɪntægˈmætɪk/ adj
also **syntagma** /sɪnˈtægmə/
a structurally significant combination of two or more units in a
language. For example, a syntagm may consist of:
(a) two or more morphemes forming a word, eg:
   re- + write = rewrite
or

(b) combinations of words forming PHRASES, CLAUSES, and SENTENCES, eg:
   the + train + is + leaving + now
see also SYNTAGMATIC RELATIONS, SYNTAX

syntagmatic relations /ˌsɪntæɡˈmætɪk rɪˈleɪʃənz/ *n*
the relationship that linguistic units (eg words, clauses) have with other units because they may occur together in a sequence. For example, a word may be said to have syntagmatic relations with the other words which occur in the sentence in which it appears, but **paradigmatic relations** with words that could be substituted for it in the sentence.
For example:

I ↔ gave ↔ Tracy ↔ the ↔ book

    passed

    handed   ↔ = syntagmatic relations

             ↕ = paradigmatic relations

    threw

see also STRUCTURE

syntax /ˈsɪntæks/ *n* **syntactic** /sɪnˈtæktɪk/ *adj*
the study of how words combine to form sentences and the rules which govern the formation of sentences.
In GENERATIVE TRANSFORMATIONAL GRAMMAR, the syntactic component is one of the three main parts of the grammar. This component contains the rules for forming syntactic structures (see BASE COMPONENT) and rules for changing these structures (see TRANSFORMATIONAL COMPONENT).
see also MORPHOLOGY, PHONOLOGY, SYNTACTIC STRUCTURE

synthetic approach /sɪnˈθetɪk əˈprəʊtʃ/ *n*
(in language teaching) a term sometimes used to refer to procedures for developing a SYLLABUS or a language course, in which the language to be taught is first analysed into its basic parts (eg the grammar is analysed into parts of speech and grammatical constructions) and these are taught separately. The learner's task is to put the individual parts together again (ie to synthesize them). A syllabus which consisted of a list of grammatical items arranged in order of difficulty would be part of a synthetic approach to language teaching. In this sense, many traditional syllabuses would be called "synthetic".
This may be contrasted with an **analytic approach** in which units of language behaviour are the starting point in syllabus and course design (eg descriptions, requests, apologies, enquiries, and other SPEECH ACTS). At a later stage, if necessary, the vocabulary and grammar used for different functions can be analysed. In this sense, a NOTIONAL SYLLABUS would be called "analytic".
[*Further reading*: Wilkins 1976]

synthetic language /sɪn'θetɪk 'læŋgwɪdʒ/ *n*
a cover term for AGGLUTINATING LANGUAGE or INFLECTING LANGUAGE

systematic phonemics /ˌsɪstə'mætɪk fə'niːmɪks/ *n*
a theory that a native speaker's knowledge of a language includes
knowledge of the phonological relationships between different forms
of words. It is claimed that the forms of words as they occur in
actual speech (eg the English words *serene* and *serenity*) are
produced from an underlying abstract level called the "systematic
phonemic level". The abstract form, called the **underlying form**, for
both *serene* and *serenity* is said to be //serēn//, with //ē//
representing a long //e// SEGMENT. This form does not exist in actual
speech.
see also GENERATIVE PHONOLOGY
[*Further reading*: Hyman 1975; Chomsky & Halle 1968]

systemic grammar /sɪ'stiːmɪk 'græmər, -'stemɪk/ *n*
an approach to grammatical analysis which is based on a series of
systems. Each system is a set of options of which one must be
chosen at each relevant point in the production of an UTTERANCE.
For example, in English, the speaker or writer makes choices among
the systems of NUMBER[1]: singular or plural; TENSE[1]: past, present, or
future; MOOD: declarative, interrogative, or imperative, and many
others.
Choices made in the sentence:
She jumped.
include:
singular, third person, and feminine (for *she*)
past, active, and action process (for *jumped*)
see also SYSTEMIC LINGUISTICS, TRANSITIVITY[2]
[*Further reading*: Berry 1975; Fawcett & Halliday 1985]

systemic linguistics /sɪ'stiːmɪk lɪŋ'gwɪstɪks, -'stemɪk/ *n*
an approach to linguistics developed by Halliday which sees
language in a social context. The theory behind this approach is
functional rather than formal, that is, it considers language as a
resource used for communication and not as a set of rules. In this way,
the scope of systemic linguistics is wider than that of many other
linguistic theories (see GENERATIVE TRANSFORMATIONAL GRAMMAR).
PHONOLOGY and **lexicogrammar** (words and grammatical structures)
are closely related to meaning and cannot be analysed without
reference to it. An essential concept of the theory is that each time
language is used, no matter in what situation, the user is making
constant choices. These choices are essentially choices in meaning
but are expressed, for instance, by INTONATION, words, and
GRAMMATICAL structures.
see also SOCIAL CONTEXT, SYSTEMIC GRAMMAR, TRANSITIVITY[2]
[*Further reading*: de Joia & Stenton 1980; Fawcett & Halliday 1985]

systems approach /ˈsɪstəmz əˈprəʊtʃ/ *n*
(in education, language teaching, and COURSE DESIGN) an approach to
analysis, planning and development in which (a) all the different
elements involved are identified (eg society, parents, teachers,
learners, time, materials, etc) (b) their interactions are analysed and
studied (c) a plan or system is developed which enables OBJECTIVES
to be reached.

T

tachistoscope /'tækɪstəʊˌskəʊp, -stə-/ *n*

a mechanical apparatus which presents printed material (eg words, sentences) very briefly when a shutter or similar device is opened and closed rapidly, and which is used in research on PERCEPTION and READING, and sometimes in SPEED READING courses.

tag /tæg/ *n*

a word, phrase, or clause added to a sentence in order to give emphasis or to form a question.

For example:

They're lovely and juicy, these oranges.
Jill's coming tomorrow, isn't she?

The latter is called a **tag question**.

[*Further reading*: Quirk et al 1985]

tagmeme /'tægmiːm/ *n* **tagmemic** /tæg'miːmɪk/ *adj*

(in TAGMEMICS) the basic unit of grammatical analysis. A tagmeme is a unit in which there is a relationship between the GRAMMATICAL FUNCTION, for instance the function of SUBJECT, OBJECT[1] or PREDICATE, and a class of **fillers**.

For example, in the sentence:

The baby bit Anthea.

the subject tagmeme is filled by the NOUN PHRASE[1] *the baby*, the predicate tagmeme is filled by the TRANSITIVE VERB *bite* in its past tense form *bit*, and the object tagmeme is filled by the proper noun *Anthea*.

tagmemics /tæg'miːmɪks/ *n*

a theory of language originated by Pike. In tagmemic analysis there are three hierarchies or systems: grammatical, phonological, and lexical. In each of these systems there are a number of levels. For example, in the grammatical system there are: the morpheme level, the word level, the phrase level, the clause level, the sentence level, the paragraph level. On each level of the grammatical system there are TAGMEMES displaying relationships between grammatical functions and classes of linguistic items which can fill these functions (**fillers**).

[*Further reading*: Pike 1967]

tag question /'tæg ˌkwestʃən/ *n*

see under TAG

tap /tæp/ *n*

another term for FLAP

target language[1] /'tɑːɡət ˌlæŋgwɪdʒ ‖ 'tɑr-/ *n*

also **L2**

(in language teaching) the language which a person is learning, in contrast to a FIRST LANGUAGE or mother tongue.

target language[2] *n*

the language into which a translation is made (eg in a bilingual dictionary).

see also SOURCE LANGUAGE[2]

task /taːsk ‖ tæsk/ *n*

(in language teaching) an activity or action which is carried out as the result of processing or understanding language (ie as a response). For example, drawing a map while listening to a tape, listening to an instruction and performing a command, may be referred to as tasks. Tasks may or may not involve the production of language. A task usually requires the teacher to specify what will be regarded as successful completion of the task. The use of a variety of different kinds of tasks in language teaching is said to make language teaching more communicative (COMMUNICATIVE APPROACH), since it provides a purpose for a classroom activity which goes beyond the practice of language for its own sake.

see also TASK SYLLABUS

[*Further reading*: Johnson 1982]

task syllabus /'taːsk ˌsɪləbəs ‖ 'tæsk/ *n*

also **task-based syllabus** /'taːsk beɪst ˌsɪləbəs ‖ 'tæsk/, **procedural syllabus**

(in language teaching) a SYLLABUS which is organized around TASKS, rather than in terms of grammar or vocabulary. For example the syllabus may suggest a variety of different kinds of tasks which the learners are expected to carry out in the language, such as using the telephone to obtain information; drawing maps based on oral instructions; performing actions based on commands given in the target language; giving orders and instructions to others, etc. It has been argued that this is a more effective way of learning a language since it provides a purpose for the use and learning of a language other than simply learning language items for their own sake.

[*Further reading*: Prabhu 1983; Johnson 1982]

taxonomic /tæksə'nɒmik ‖ -'na-/ *adj* **taxonomy** /tæk'sɒnəmi ‖ -'sa-/ *n*

(in linguistics) classification of items into classes and sub-classes. Taxonomic approaches have been used in PHONOLOGY, SYNTAX and SEMANTICS.

For example, in taxonomic PHONEMICS, the distinctive speech sounds of a language are classified as VOWELS and CONSONANTS, the consonants are classified as STOPS, FRICATIVES, NASALS, etc, the stops are classified as voiced or voiceless (see VOICE[2]) and so on.

see also CLASS

teacher talk /'tiːtʃər ˌtɔːk/ *n*

that variety of language sometimes used by teachers when they are in the process of teaching. In trying to communicate with learners, teachers often simplify their speech, giving it many of the characteristics of FOREIGNER TALK and other simplified styles of speech addressed to language learners.

see also CARETAKER SPEECH

[*Further reading*: Sinclair & Brazil 1982]

technique /tek'niːk/ *n*

see under APPROACH

TEFL /'tefəl/ *n*

an acronymn for *T*eaching *E*nglish as a *F*oreign *L*anguage, used to describe the teaching of English in situations where it is a FOREIGN LANGUAGE.

telegraphic speech /ˌteləˈgræfɪk 'spiːtʃ/ *n*

a term sometimes used to describe the early speech of children learning their first language, so called because children's early speech lacks the same sorts of words which adults leave out of telegrams (eg prepositions, AUXILIARY VERBS, articles). For example:

Baby no eat apple.

tenor of discourse /ˌtenər əv 'dɪskɔːs ‖ -ors/ *n*

see under SOCIAL CONTEXT

tense[1] /tens/ *n*

the relationship between the form of the verb and the time of the action or state it describes.

In English, verbs may be in the PAST or PRESENT TENSE. However, the present tense form of the verb is also used in:

(a) timeless expressions: *The sun rises in the east.*

(b) for future events: *I leave/am leaving next Monday.*

(c) past events for dramatic effect: *Suddenly she collapses on the floor.*

The past tense form of the verb may also occur in conditional clauses (see CONDITIONAL): *If you worked harder, you would pass the exam.*

see also MOOD

[*Further reading*: Quirk et al 1985]

tense[2] *adj*

describes a speech sound which is produced with a comparatively greater degree of movement and muscular tension in the VOCAL TRACT. The vowel /iː/ as in English /siːp/ *seep* is a tense vowel as the lips are spread and the tongue moves towards the roof of the mouth.

[*Further reading*: Hyman 1975]

terminology /ˌtɜːməˈnɒlədʒi ‖ ˌtɜrməˈnɑ-/ *n*

(1) the special lexical items which occur in a particular discipline or subject matter. For example *clause*, *conjunction*, and *aspect* are part of the terminology of English grammar.

(2) the development or selection of lexical items for concepts in a

language. Terminology is often a part of LANGUAGE PLANNING, since when languages are being adapted or developed for different purposes (eg when a NATIONAL LANGUAGE is being developed) new terms are often needed for scientific or technical concepts.
see also SPECIAL LANGUAGES, STANDARDIZATION
[*Further reading*: Sager, Dungworth, & McDonald 1980]

TESL /'tesəl/ *n*
an acronymn for *T*eaching *E*nglish as a *S*econd *L*anguage, used either to describe the teaching of English in situations where it is a SECOND LANGUAGE or to refer to any situation where English is taught to speakers of other languages.

TESOL /'tesəl, 'tiːsɒl ‖ 'tiːsɑl/ *n*
an acronymn for *T*eaching *E*nglish to *S*peakers of *O*ther *L*anguages, used, particularly in the USA, to describe the teaching of English in situations where it is either a SECOND LANGUAGE or a FOREIGN LANGUAGE. In British usage this is usually referred to as ELT, ie *E*nglish *L*anguage *T*eaching.

test /test/ *n*
any procedure for measuring ability, knowledge, or performance.
see also ACHIEVEMENT TEST, CLOZE PROCEDURE, DISCRETE POINT TEST, LANGUAGE APTITUDE TEST, PLACEMENT TEST, PROFICIENCY TEST, PROGRESS TEST, STANDARDIZED TEST, TOEFL TEST

test battery /'test ˌbætəri/ *n*
another term for BATTERY OF TESTS

testing /'testɪŋ/ *n*
the use of TESTs, or the study of the theory and practice of their use, development, evaluation, etc.

test item /'test 'aɪtəm/ *n*
a question or element in a test which requires an answer or response. Several different types of test item are commonly used in language tests, including:
(a) **alternate response item**: one in which a correct response must be chosen from two alternatives, such as True/False, Yes/No, or A/B.
(b) **fixed response item**, also **closed-ended response**: one in which the correct answer must be chosen from among several alternatives. A MULTIPLE-CHOICE ITEM is an example of a fixed response item. For example:
Choose (a), (b), (c), or (d).
Yesterday we _____ a movie. (a) has seen (b) saw (c) have seen (d) seen.
(*b*) is the correct response, while (*a*), (*b*) and (*d*) are called **distractors**.
(c) **free response item**, also **open-ended response**: one in which the student is free to answer a question as he or she wishes without having to choose from among alternatives provided.

(d) **structured response item**: one in which some control or guidance is given for the answer, but the students must contribute something of their own. For example, after a reading passage, a comprehension question such as the following:
What is astrology?
Astrology is the ancient _____ of telling what will _____ in the future by studying the _____ of the stars and the planets.
[*Further reading*: Cohen 1980]

test-retest reliability /ˌtest ˈriːtest rɪˌlaɪəˈbɪləti/ *n*
an estimate of the RELIABILITY of a test determined by the extent to which a test gives the same results if it is administered at two different times. It is estimated from the coefficient of CORRELATION which is obtained from the two administrations of the test.

text /tekst/ *n* **textual** /ˈtekstʃuəl/ *adj*
a piece of spoken or written language. A text may be considered from the point of view of its structure and/or its functions, eg warning, instructing, carrying out a transaction.
A full understanding of a text is often impossible without reference to the context in which it occurs.
A text may consist of just one word, eg *DANGER* on a warning sign, or it may be of considerable length, eg a sermon, a novel, or a debate.
see also CONTEXT OF SITUATION, DISCOURSE, TEXT LINGUISTICS

text linguistics /ˈtekst lɪŋˌgwɪstɪks/ *n*
a branch of linguistics which studies spoken or written TEXT*s*, eg a descriptive passage, a scene in a play, a conversation. It is concerned, for instance, with the way the parts of a text are organized and related to one another in order to form a meaningful whole.
Some linguists prefer to include the study of all spoken texts, particularly if they are longer than one sentence, under DISCOURSE ANALYSIS.

textual function /ˈtekstʃuəl ˌfʌŋkʃən/ *n*
see under FUNCTIONS OF LANGUAGE[2]

TG grammar /ˌtiː ˈdʒiː ˈgræməʳ/ *n*
another term for GENERATIVE TRANSFORMATIONAL GRAMMAR

theme /θiːm/ *n*
see under FUNCTIONAL SENTENCE PERSPECTIVE

theory /ˈθɪəri/ *n*
(1) a statement of a general principle, based upon reasoned argument and supported by evidence, that is intended to explain a particular fact, event, or phenomenon. A theory is more strongly supported by evidence than a HYPOTHESIS.
(2) the part of a science or art that deals with general principles and

methods as opposed to practice: a set of rules or principles for the study of a subject.

theory of semantic fields /'θɪəri əv sɪ'mæntɪk 'fiːldz/ *n*
another term for FIELD THEORY

thesaurus /θɪ'sɔːrəs/ *n*
an arrangement of the words and phrases of a language not in alphabetical order but according to the ideas they express. A thesaurus is different from a dictionary. Whereas a dictionary aims at explaining the meaning of words and expressions, a thesaurus suggests a range of words and phrases associated with an idea. For example, an excerpt from *Roget's Thesaurus of English Words and Phrases* shows under "*Amusement*" expressions such as:
    fun, frolic, merriment, whoopee, jollity, joviality, laughter

threshold hypothesis /'θreʃhəʊld haɪ'pɒθəsəs, -ʃəʊld ‖ -'pɑ-/ *n*
a hypothesis first proposed by Cummins which states that in learning a second language, a certain minimum "threshold" level of proficiency must be reached in that language before the learner can benefit from the use of the language as a medium of instruction in school. This hypothesis is related by Cummins to the **developmental interdependence hypothesis** which says that the development of proficiency in a second language depends upon the level of proficiency the child learner has reached in the first language at the time when extensive exposure to the second language begins.
[*Further reading*: Cummins 1979]

threshold level /'θreʃhəʊld ˌlevəl, -ʃəʊld/ *n*
a term used by the European regional organization The Council of Europe, to refer to the minimal level of language proficiency which is needed to achieve functional ability in a foreign language. It serves as an OBJECTIVE for foreign language teaching. The threshold level is defined according to the situations in which the language will be used, the activities it will be used for, the topics to be referred to, the functions the language will be used for, and the language forms (eg vocabulary and grammar) which will be needed.
see also NOTIONAL SYLLABUS
[*Further reading*: Van Ek 1975]

timbre /'tæmbəʳ, 'tɪm-(*Fr* tɛ̃br)/ *n*
see under VOICE QUALITY

TOEFL test /'təʊfəl ˌtest/ *n*
a name containing an acronym for the *T*est *O*f *E*nglish as a *F*oreign *L*anguage, a STANDARDIZED TEST of English proficiency administered by the Educational Testing Service, and widely used to measure the English-language proficiency of foreign students wishing to enter American universities.

token /'təʊkən/ *n*
see under TYPE

tone[1] /təʊn/ *n*
Height of PITCH and change of pitch which is associated with the
pronunciation of syllables or words and which affects the meaning of
the word.

A **tone language** is a language in which the meaning of a word
depends on the tone used when pronouncing it.

For example, Mandarin Chinese, a tone language, makes a
distinction between four different tones:

mā (high level tone)	"mother"
má (high rising tone)	"hemp"
mǎ (fall-rise)	"horse"
mà (high falling tone)	"scold"

Other tone languages are spoken in Vietnam, Thailand, West
Africa, and Central America.

tone[2] *n*
also **pitch movement**
A change in PITCH which affects the meaning and function of
utterances in discourse.

In English, linguists have distinguished four or five different tones:
Tone 1 fall in pitch
Tone 2 rise in pitch
Tone 3 a slight rise in pitch
Tone 4 fall in pitch followed by a rise
Tone 5 rise in pitch followed by a fall

In a unit of intonation (see TONE UNIT) the syllable on which pitch
movement begins is often called the **tonic** or the **tonic syllable**. The
tonic syllable is often the last prominent syllable in the unit.
For example, in:
They flew to Frankfurt.
the pitch of the speaker's voice begins to fall on the syllable *Frank*.
see also KEY[2], REFERRING TONE
[*Further reading*: Brazil, Coulthard, & Johns 1980; Halliday 1970]

tone group /'təʊn ˌgruːp/ *n*
another term for TONE UNIT

tone language /'təʊn ˌlæŋgwɪdʒ/ *n*
see under TONE[1]

tone unit /'təʊn ˌjuːnət/ *n*
also **tone group**
the basic unit of INTONATION in a language. A tone unit is usually
divided into several parts. The most important part contains the
syllable on which a change of pitch begins: the **tonic syllable.** The
ways in which linguists have divided the tone unit into its different
parts and the terms they have used for these parts are not always

the same. The simplified diagram below shows the main parts of a tone unit together with different divisions and terms which have been used.

	unstressed syllables	*onset* first stressed syllable	*tonic syllable* where major pitch movement begins	continuation and completion of pitch movement
Crystal 1969	(prehead)	head	nucleus	(tail)
Halliday 1967, 1970	pretonic		tonic	
Brazil et al, 1980	(proclitic segment)		tonic segment	(enclitic segment)

eg   *That's a*   VERY TALL   STO   *ry*
where the first syllable of *very* is the **onset**, the first prominent syllable in the tone unit, and the first syllable of *story* is the tonic syllable, where the pitch of the speaker's voice begins to fall.
Some linguists refer to a tone unit as an **intonation contour**.
see also PROMINENCE, TONE[2]
[*Further reading*: Brazil, Coulthard, & Johns 1980; Crystal 1969, 1975; Halliday 1967, 1970]

tonic /ˈtɒnɪk ‖ ˈtɑ-/ *n, adj*
See under TONE[2]

tonicity /ˌtɒˈnɪsəti ‖ ˌtə-, ˌtəʊ-/ *n*
the choice of the places in an utterance or part of an utterance where a movement in pitch begins (see **tonic syllable** under TONE UNIT). The choice depends on what the speaker wishes to emphasize. For example, in *She came last SATurday* the change in pitch would often be placed on the *SAT* of *Saturday* but in a dialogue such as:
    A: *She never comes on Saturdays.*
    B: *But she came LAST Saturday.*
a change in pitch would start on *LAST*.
[*Further reading*: Halliday 1970]

tonic segment /ˌtɒnɪk ˈsegmənt ‖ ˌtɑ-/ *n*
see under TONE UNIT

tonic syllable /ˌtɒnɪk ˈsɪləbəl ‖ ˌtɑ-/ *n*
see under TONE[2], TONE UNIT

top-down process /ˌtɒp ˈdaʊn ˈprəʊses ‖ ˌtɑp/ *n*
in PSYCHOLINGUISTICS, COGNITIVE PSYCHOLOGY, and INFORMATION PROCESSING, a contrast is made between two different ways in which humans analyse and process language as part of the process of

comprehension and learning. One way, known as a top-down process or approach, makes use of previous knowledge ("higher-level knowledge") in analysing and processing information which is received (words, sentences, etc). The other way, a **bottom-up process**, makes use principally of information which is already present in the data (ie the words, sentences etc). As applied to reading comprehension for example, bottom-up processing would be understanding a text mainly by analysing the words and sentences in the text itself. Top-down processing on the other hand would make use of the reader's previous knowledge, his or her expectations, experience, SCRIPTs, and SCHEMEs, in reading the text.

The term "top-down process" should not be confused with the term "top-to-bottom" (see SERIAL LEARNING).

topic[1] /'tɒpɪk ‖ 'tɑ-/ *n*

what is talked about or written about. In different speech communities (see SPEECH COMMUNITY) there are different rules about what topics may or may not be discussed. For example, in some communities, illness, death, a person's income, and a person's age may be considered unsuitable topics for conversation.

[*Further reading*: Coulthard 1985]

topic[2] *n*

in describing the INFORMATION STRUCTURE of sentences, a term for that part of a sentence which names the person, thing, or idea about which something is said (the **comment**). The concept of Topic and Comment is not identical with SUBJECT and PREDICATE. Subject-Predicate refers to the grammatical structure of a sentence rather than to its information structure (see SUBJECT-PROMINENT LANGUAGE). The difference is illustrated in the following example:

As for your drycleaning, I will bring it tomorrow.

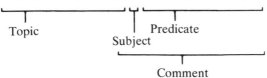

In some sentences in English, however, Topic-Comment and Subject-Predicate are identical. For example:

Hilary	*is a dancer.*
Subject	Predicate
Topic	Comment

Topic-Prominent language /'tɒpɪk 'prɒmɪnənt 'læŋgwɪdʒ ‖ 'tɑ-'prɑ-/ *n*

see under SUBJECT-PROMINENT LANGUAGE

topic sentence /'tɒpɪk 'sentəns ‖ 'tɑ-/ *n*

the sentence in a PARAGRAPH or passage which contains the main idea.

top-to-bottom /ˌtɒp tə ˈbɒtəm ‖ ˌtɑp tə ˈbɑtəm/ *adj*
see under SERIAL LEARNING
see also TOP-DOWN PROCESS

total physical response method /ˈtəʊtl ˈfɪzɪkəl rɪˈspɒns ˈmeθəd ‖
-ˈspɑns/ *n*
a language teaching METHOD developed by Asher in which items are
presented in the foreign language as orders, commands, and
instructions requiring a physical response from the learner (eg
opening a window or standing up). This is thought to lead to more
meaningful and effective learning.
[*Further reading*: Asher 1977; Richards & Rogers 1986]

traditional grammar /trəˈdɪʃənəl ˈgræmər/ *n*
a grammar which is usually based on earlier grammars of Latin or
Greek and applied to some other language, often inappropriately. For
example, some grammarians stated that English had six CASES[1]
because Latin had six cases. These grammars were often notional and
prescriptive in their approach (see NOTIONAL GRAMMAR, PRESCRIPTIVE
GRAMMAR). Although there has been a trend towards using grammars
which incorporate more modern approaches to language description
and language teaching, some schools still use traditional grammars.

transcription /trænˈskrɪpʃən/ *n*
another term for NOTATION

transfer /ˈtrænsfɜːr/ *n*
(in learning theory) the carrying over of learned behaviour from one
situation to another. **Positive transfer** is learning in one situation
which helps or facilitates learning in another later situation. **Negative
transfer** is learning in one situation which interferes with learning in
another later situation.
see also LANGUAGE TRANSFER, PROACTIVE INHIBITION
[*Further reading*: Brown 1980]

transfer of training /ˈtrænsfɜːr əv ˈtreɪnɪŋ/ *n*
see under INDUCED ERROR

transfer stage /ˈtrænsfɜːr ˌsteɪdʒ/ *n*
another term for **production stage**
see under STAGE

transformational component /ˌtrænsfəˈmeɪʃənəl kəmˈpəʊnənt ‖
-fər-/ *n*
the part of a GENERATIVE TRANSFORMATIONAL GRAMMAR which contains
the **transformational rules**. These are rules which change a basic
syntactic structure (see BASE COMPONENT) into a sentence-like structure.
Another part of the grammar (the "phonological component") is
needed to supply the rules for pronouncing a sentence (phonetic
interpretation).
[*Further reading*: Aitchison 1978; Chomsky 1965]

transformational grammar /ˌtrænsfə'meɪʃənəl 'græməʳ ‖ -fər-/ *n*
another term for GENERATIVE TRANSFORMATIONAL GRAMMAR

transformational rules /ˌtrænsfə'meɪʃənəl 'ruːlz ‖ -fər-/ *n*
see under TRANSFORMATIONAL COMPONENT

transformation drill /ˌtrænsfə'meɪʃən 'drɪl ‖ -fər-/ *n*
see under DRILL

transitional bilingual education /træn'zɪʃənəl baɪ'lɪŋgwəl
edjʊ'keɪʃən, træn'sɪ- ‖ edʒə-/ *n*
see under BILINGUAL EDUCATION

transitive verb /'trænsətɪv 'vɜːb, -zə- ‖ 'vɜrb/ *n*
a verb which takes an OBJECT[1]. For example:
They saw the accident.
A verb which takes an indirect and a direct object is known as a
ditransitive verb. For example:
I gave the money to my mother. = I gave my mother the money.
      DO   IO   IO   DO
A verb which takes a direct object and an object complement (see
COMPLEMENT) is known as a **complex transitive verb.** For example:
We elected Mary chairman.
            DO   object complement
A verb which does not take an object is an **intransitive verb**. For
example:
The children danced.
see also COMPLEMENT

transitivity[1] /ˌtrænsə'tɪvəti, -zə-/ *n*
the state of being a TRANSITIVE VERB. In this sense, one can speak of
the transitivity of the verb *saw* in the sentence:
They saw the accident.

transitivity[2] *n*
(in SYSTEMIC GRAMMAR) a choice between the three main processes
that can be represented in a sentence:
(a) a physical or "material" process as in *Fred cut the lawn.*
(b) a "mental" process as in *David saw Rosemary.*
(c) a "relational" process as in *This view is magnificent.*
Related to this choice of processes is:
(a) the choice of participants. A participant is someone or
    something involved in the process, eg, in the above examples,
    Fred and *the lawn*, *David* and *Rosemary* and
(b) the choice of circumstances, eg David saw Rosemary
    yesterday/in the garden/by accident.
Further choices associated with transitivity would be which roles the
participants had in a process and how processes, participants, and
circumstances are combined.
see also SYSTEMIC LINGUISTICS
[*Further reading*: Berry 1975; Halliday 1967; de Joia & Stenton 1980]

translation /trænz'leɪʃən, træns-/ *n*

the process of changing speech or writing from one language (the SOURCE LANGUAGE[2]) into another (the TARGET LANGUAGE[2]), or the target-language version that results from this process. A translation which reproduces the general meaning and intention of the original but which does not closely follow the grammar, style, or organization of it is known as a **free translation**. A translation which approximates to a word-for-word representation of the original is known as a **literal translation**.

see also SIMULTANEOUS INTERPRETATION

translation equivalence /trænz'leɪʃən ɪ'kwɪvələns, træns-/ *n*

the degree to which linguistic units (eg words, syntactic structures) can be translated into another language without loss of meaning. Two items with the same meaning in two languages are said to be **translation equivalents**.

tree diagram /'tri: 'daɪəgræm/ *n*

see under BASE COMPONENT, CONSTITUENT STRUCTURE, NODE, PHRASE-STRUCTURE GRAMMAR

trill /trɪl/ *n*

another term for ROLL

triphthong /'trɪfθɒŋ, 'trɪp- ‖ -θɔŋ/ *n*

(in PHONETICS) a term sometimes used for a combination of three vowels. For example, in English:

/aɪə/ as in /faɪəʳ/ *fire*

is a triphthong.

see also DIPHTHONG, MONOPHTHONG

true beginner /'tru: bɪ'gɪnəʳ/ *n*

see under FALSE BEGINNER

true-false item /ˌtru: 'fɔːls 'aɪtəm/ *n*

an item in a test which requires True or False as the answer or response.

T-score /'ti: ˌskɔːʳ ‖ ˌskɔr/ *n*

(in statistics) a STANDARD SCORE whose DISTRIBUTION has a MEAN of 50 and a STANDARD DEVIATION of 10.

T-test /'ti: 'test/ *n*

(in testing and statistics) a quantitative procedure for determining the STATISTICAL SIGNIFICANCE of the difference between the MEANS on two sets of scores.

see also CHI-SQUARE

T-unit /'ti: ˌjuːnət/ *n*

also **Minimal Terminable Unit**

a measure of the linguistic complexity of sentences, defined as the shortest unit (the Terminable Unit, Minimal Terminable Unit, or T-Unit) which a sentence can be reduced to, and consisting of one independent clause together with whatever DEPENDENT CLAUSES are attached to it. For example the sentence *After she had eaten, Kim went to bed* would be described as containing one T-Unit.

Compound sentences (see COMPLEX SENTENCE) contain two or more T-Units. The study of T-Units in written language has been used in the study of children's language development.

[*Further reading*: Hunt 1966]

turn /tɜːn ‖ tɜrn/ *n*
see under TURN-TAKING

turn-taking /'tɜːn ˌteɪkɪŋ ‖ 'tɜrn/ *n*
In conversation, the roles of speaker and listener change constantly. The person who speaks first becomes a listener as soon as the person addressed takes his or her **turn** in the conversation by beginning to speak.

The rules for turn-taking may differ from one community to another as they do from one type of SPEECH EVENT (eg a conversation) to another (eg an oral test). Turn-taking and rules for turn-taking are studied in CONVERSATIONAL ANALYSIS and DISCOURSE ANALYSIS.

see also SEQUENCING[1]

[*Further reading*: Coulthard 1985; Sacks et al 1974]

type /taɪp/ *n*
In linguistics, a distinction is sometimes made between classes of linguistic items (eg PHONEMES, WORDS, UTTERANCES) and actual occurrences in speech or writing of examples of such classes. The class of linguistic units is called a **type** and examples or individual members of the class are called **tokens**.

For example, *hello, hi, good morning* are three different tokens of the type "Greeting".

In MATHEMATICAL LINGUISTICS the total number of words in a text may be referred to as the number of text tokens, and the number of different words as the number of text types. The ratio of *different* words in a text to *total* words in the text is known as the LEXICAL DENSITY or **Type-Token Ratio** for that text.

see also LEXICAL DENSITY

[*Further reading*: Mackey 1965]

Type-Token Ratio /ˌtaɪp 'təʊkən 'reɪʃiəʊ ‖ 'reɪʃəʊ/ *n*
another term for LEXICAL DENSITY

typology /taɪ'pɒlədʒi ‖ -'pɑ-/ *n*
classification of languages into types.

For example, languages may be classified according to whether or not they are tone languages (see TONE[1]) or according to their most typical SYNTACTIC STRUCTURES, eg whether they are **SVO languages** (Subject – Verb – Object languages) like English or **SOV languages** (Subject – Object – Verb languages) like Japanese.

unacceptable /ˌʌnəkˈseptəbəl/ *adj*
    see under GRAMMATICAL[2]

unaspirated /ʌnˈæspəreɪtəd/ *adj*
    see under ASPIRATION

uncountable noun /ʌnˌkaʊntəbəl ˈnaʊn/ *n*
    see under COUNTABLE NOUN

underlying form /ʌndəˈlaɪ-ɪŋ ˌfɔːm ‖ -dər- ˌfɔrm/ *n*
    see under SYSTEMATIC PHONEMICS

underlying structure /ʌndəˈlaɪ-ɪŋ ˈstrʌktʃər ‖ -dər-/ *n*
    another term for DEEP STRUCTURE

unit-credit system /ˈjuːnət ˈkredət ˌsɪstəm/ *n*
    a language-learning system suggested by the European regional
    organization The Council of Europe in connection with their
    THRESHOLD LEVEL. In this system the OBJECTIVES for a foreign language
    programme are divided into portions or units. Each of these units
    represents a selection of the learner's language needs and is related
    to all the other units in the programme. If after successful
    completion of each unit the learners receive some sort of official
    recognition, the system is known as a unit-credit system.
    [*Further reading*: Van Ek & Alexander 1975; Van Ek 1976]

universal /ˌjuːnəˈvɜːsəl ‖ -ˈvɜr-/ *n*
    see LANGUAGE UNIVERSAL

unmarked /ˌʌnˈmɑːkt ‖ -ɑr-/ *adj*
    see under MARKEDNESS

unrounded vowel /ʌnˈraʊndəd ˈvaʊəl/ *n*
    see under VOWEL

uptake /ˈʌpteɪk/ *n*
    the illocutionary force (see SPEECH ACT) a hearer interprets from an
    utterance. For example in the following exchange:
    Child: *I'm tired.*
    Mother: *You can stop doing your homework now.*
    the uptake or interpretation by the mother is as if the child had said
    "Can I stop doing my homework now?" But sometimes there may be
    a difference between the intended uptake (what the speaker wants
    the hearer to understand) and the actual uptake (what the hearer
    actually understands).
    see also PRAGMATICS
    [*Further reading*: Austin 1962]

usage[1]

usage[1] /ˈjuːzɪdʒ, ˈjuːsɪdʒ/ *n*

the ways people actually speak and write. In this sense, usage is closely related to PERFORMANCE, and can be studied by the analysis of specimens of AUTHENTIC language and by experiments of various kinds. The study of usage can reveal, for example, that the passive voice (see VOICE[1]) is more than ordinarily frequent in scientific writing, or that the spellings *all right* and *alright* both occur.

It is also possible to study reactions to usage, and on this basis to make recommendations when usage is divided. **Usage guides** attempt to do this. They may say, for example, that people write both *all right* and *alright*, but that there are still strong feelings against the spelling *alright*, and that therefore it is better to write *all right* as two words.

[*Further reading*: Haegeman 1982; Ilson 1982, 1984]

usage[2] *n*

a distinction has been proposed by Widdowson between the function of a linguistic item as an element in a linguistic system (**usage**) and its function as part of a system of communication (**use**). For example the PROGRESSIVE ASPECT may be studied as an item of grammar or usage (ie to consider how it compares with other ASPECTS and TENSES in English and the constructions in which it occurs) and in terms of its use (ie how it is used in DISCOURSE for performing such communicative acts as descriptions, plans, commentaries, etc).

The meaning a linguistic item has as an example of usage is called its **signification**, and the meaning it has as an example of use is called its **value**.

see also SPEECH ACT, UPTAKE

[*Further reading*: Widdowson 1978]

use /juːs/ *n*

see under USAGE[2]

utterance /ˈʌtərəns/ *n*

(in DISCOURSE) what is said by any one person before or after another person begins to speak.

For example, an utterance may consist of:

(a) one word, eg B's reply in:
   A: *Have you done your homework?*
   B: *Yeah.*

(b) one sentence, eg A's question and B's answer in:
   A: *What's the time?*
   B: *It's half past five.*

(c) more than one sentence, eg A's complaint in:
   A: *Look, I'm really fed up. I've told you several times to wash your hands before a meal. Why don't you do as you're told?*
   B: *But Mum, listen. . .*

see also MOVE, SEQUENCING[1]
[*Further reading*: Coulthard 1985]

uvula /'juːvjʊlə ‖ -vjə-/ *n*
see under PLACE OF ARTICULATION, UVULAR

uvular /juːvjʊləʳ ‖ -vjə-/ *adj*
describes a speech sound (a CONSONANT) which is produced by the
back of the tongue against the very end of the soft palate (the
uvula), or by a narrowing in the VOCAL TRACT near the uvula.
The /r/ used by some speakers in the northeast of England, and by
some speakers of Scottish English, is an uvular ROLL [ʀ].
see also PLACE OF ARTICULATION, MANNER OF ARTICULATION
[*Further reading*: Gimson 1980]

valency /ˈveɪlənsi/ *n*
see under DEPENDENCY GRAMMAR

validity /vəˈlɪdəti/ *n*
(in testing) the degree to which a test measures what it is supposed
to measure, or can be used successfully for the purposes for which it
is intended. A number of different statistical procedures can be
applied to a test to estimate its validity. Such procedures generally
seek to determine what the test measures, and how well it does so.
see also CONSTRUCT VALIDITY, CONTENT VALIDITY, CRITERION MEASURE,
CRITERION-RELATED VALIDITY, EMPIRICAL VALIDITY, FACE VALIDITY,
PREDICTIVE VALIDITY

value /ˈvæljuː/ *n*
see under USAGE[2]

variable[1] /ˈveərɪəbəl/ *n*
a linguistic item which has various forms (**variants**). The different
forms of the variable may be related to differences in STYLE or to
differences in the socio-economic background, education, age, or sex
of the speakers (see SOCIOLECT). There are variables in the
PHONOLOGY, MORPHOLOGY, SYNTAX, and LEXICON[1] of a language.
Examples in English include:
(a) the *ng* variable as in *coming, working*. In careful formal speech
   it often occurs as [ɪŋ], eg [kʌmɪŋ] *coming*, [wɜːkɪŋ] *working*, but
   in informal or regional speech it often occurs as [kʌmn] *com'n*,
   [wɜːkn] *work'n*
(b) the marker on verb forms for 3rd-person singular present tense
   (as in *He works here*), which is a variable because in some NON-
   STANDARD and some new varieties of English a variant without
   the ending (as in *He work here*) may occur.
   Linguistic rules which try to account for these variables in
   language are referred to as **variable rules**.
[*Further reading*: Labov 1972a, b; Trudgill 1978]

variable[2]
(in testing and statistics) a property whereby the members of a set
or group differ from one another. In comparing teaching methods,
for example, different variables may be (a) the level of interest each
creates, (b) the amount of teaching time each method is used for,
and (c) how difficult each method is to use.
see also DEPENDENT VARIABLE

variable rule /ˈveərɪəbəl ˈruːl/ *n*
see under VARIABLE[1]

variance /'veərɪəns/ *n*

(in testing and statistics) a statistical measure of the DISPERSION of a SAMPLE. The variance of a set of scores on a test, for example, would be based on how much the scores obtained differ from the MEAN, and is the square of the STANDARD DEVIATION.

variant /'veərɪənt/ *n, adj*

see under VARIABLE[1]

variation /ˌveəri'eɪʃən/ *n*
also **language variation**

differences in pronunciation, grammar, or word choice within a language. Variation in a language may be related to region (see DIALECT, REGIONAL VARIATION), to social class and/or educational background (see SOCIOLECT) or to the degree of formality of a situation in which language is used (see STYLE).

see also FREE VARIATION

variety /və'raɪəti/ *n*

see SPEECH VARIETY

velar /'viːlər/ *adj*

describes a speech sound (a CONSONANT) which is produced by the back of the tongue touching the soft palate (the **velum**) at the back of the mouth.

For example, in English the /k/ in /kɪn/ *kin* and the /g/ in /get/ *get* are velars, or, more precisely, velar STOPs.

Because the back of the tongue is called the **dorsum**, these sounds are sometimes called **dorsal**.

see also PLACE OF ARTICULATION, MANNER OF ARTICULATION

[*Further reading*: Gimson 1980]

velum /'viːləm/ *n*
also **soft palate**

see under PLACE OF ARTICULATION, VELAR

verb /vɜːb ‖ vɜrb/ *n*

(in English) a word which, (a) occurs as part of the PREDICATE of a sentence (b) carries markers of grammatical categories such as TENSE, ASPECT, PERSON, NUMBER[1] and MOOD, and (c) refers to an action or state. For example:

He opened the door.
Jane loves Tom.

see also AUXILIARY VERB, FINITE VERB, INCHOATIVE VERB, MODAL, PHRASAL VERB, REGULAR VERB, STATIVE VERB, TRANSITIVE VERB, VERB GROUP, VERB PHRASE

verbal /'vɜːbəl ‖ -ɜr-/ *n*

(in GENERATIVE TRANSFORMATIONAL GRAMMAR) a WORD CLASS including VERBs and ADJECTIVEs.

The reason for considering verbs and adjectives as belonging to one class is that they have many properties in common.

For example, some verbs and adjectives in English can occur in IMPERATIVE SENTENCES: _Throw the ball! Be quiet!_ while other verbs and adjectives normally cannot: *_Resemble me!_ *_Be tall!_

verbal association /ˌvɜːbəl əˌsəʊʃiˈeɪʃən ‖ -ɜr-/ *n*
see under VERBAL LEARNING
see also WORD ASSOCIATION

verbal deficit hypothesis /ˌvɜːbəl ˈdefəsət haɪˈpɒθəsəs ‖ -ɜr- -ˈpɑ-/ *n*
another term for DEFICIT HYPOTHESIS

verbal learning /ˈvɜːbəl ˈlɜːnɪŋ ‖ ˈvɜr- ˈlɜr-/ *n*
(in behaviourist psychology) the learning of language. Also used to refer to studies of the learning and remembering of linguistic items. The forming of associations between words is known as **verbal-association**.
see also ASSOCIATIVE LEARNING, BEHAVIOURISM, WORD ASSOCIATION

verbal repertoire /ˈvɜːbəl ˈrepətwɑːʳ ‖ ˈvɜr- / *n*
the speech varieties (LANGUAGE*s*[2], DIALECT*s*, SOCIOLECT*s*, STYLE*s*, REGISTER*s*) which an individual knows.
Sometimes a language may be part of someone's verbal repertoire although he or she has no chance to use it.
For example, a person who knows English and Welsh and moves from Wales to New Zealand may not be able to continue using Welsh. It would still be part of his or her verbal repertoire but it does not belong to the SPEECH REPERTOIRE of the community, in this case, New Zealand.
[_Further reading_: Platt & Platt 1975]

verb group /ˈvɜːb ˌgruːp ‖ ˈvɜrb/ *n*
A VERB, together with any associated MODAL VERB or AUXILIARY VERB(*s*).
For example:
  He didn't come.
  She can't have been there.

verb phrase /ˈvɜːb ˌfreɪz ‖ ˈvɜrb/ *n*
also **VP**
(in GENERATIVE TRANSFORMATIONAL GRAMMAR) the part of a SENTENCE which contains the main verb and also any OBJECT[2](*s*), COMPLEMENT(*s*) and ADVERBIAL(*s*).
For example, in:
  Tom gave a watch to his son.
all the sentence except _Tom_ is the verb phrase.
see also NOUN PHRASE

vernacular /vəˈnækjʊləʳ ‖ -kjə-/ *n, adj*
a term used of a language or language variety:
(a) when it is contrasted with a classical language, such as Latin, eg:

Church services in the Roman Catholic church used to be conducted in Latin, but now they are in the vernacular. (eg, in English, Italian, Swahili, etc)

(b) when it is contrasted with an internationally used language such as English, eg:

If you want to teach English in that country, it will be useful to know the vernacular.

(c) in BILINGUAL and MULTILINGUAL countries, when it is spoken by some or most of the population but when it is not the official or the NATIONAL LANGUAGE of a country, eg:

In addition to schools that teach in the national language, there are also vernacular schools.

see also BLACK ENGLISH VERNACULAR, DIGLOSSIA, DOMAIN

visual perception /ˈviʒʊəl pəˈsepʃən ‖ pər-/ *n*
see under PERCEPTION

vocabulary /vəˈkæbjʊləri, vəʊ- ‖ -bjəleri/ *n*
a set of LEXEMES, including single words, COMPOUND WORDS and IDIOMS.
see also ACTIVE/PASSIVE LANGUAGE KNOWLEDGE, CONTENT WORD, FREQUENCY², TYPE

vocabulary control /vəˈkæbjʊləri kənˌtrəʊl, vəʊ- ‖ -bjəleri/ *n*
(in the preparation of materials for language teaching, reading, etc) the practice of using a limited vocabulary based on a WORD LIST or other source. GRADED READERS are often written using vocabulary control.

vocal cords /ˈvəʊkəl ˈkɔːdz ‖ -ɔr-/ *n*
also **vocal chords**
the folds of tough, flexible tissue in the LARYNX extending from back to front. The space between the vocal cords is the **glottis**. When the vocal cords are pressed together, the air from the lungs is completely sealed off. During speech, the vocal cords open and close the air passage from the lungs to the mouth.
In the production of vowels and voiced consonants (see VOICE²) the vocal cords vibrate.

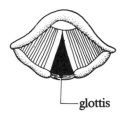

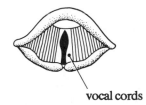

wide open for breathing   *loosely together and vibrating as for a voiced sound*

see also PITCH, PLACE OF ARTICULATION
[*Further reading*: Denes & Pinson 1963; Gimson 1980]

vocal tract /'vəʊkəl 'trækt/ *n*

(in phonetics) the air passages which are above the VOCAL CORDS and which are involved in the production of speech sounds.

The vocal tract can be divided into the **nasal cavity**, which is the air passage within and behind the nose, and the **oral cavity**, which is the air passage within the mouth and the throat.

The shape of the vocal tract can be changed, eg by changing the position of the tongue or the lips. Changes in the shape of the vocal tract cause differences in speech sounds.

vocative /'vɒkətɪv ‖ 'vɑ-/ *n*

a NOUN PHRASE[1] which is an optional part of a sentence, and which names or indicates one being addressed.

For example:

Really dear, do you think so?
That's a pretty dress, Mrs Johnson.

voice[1] /vɔɪs/ *n*

the ways in which a language expresses the relationship between a verb and the noun phrases which are associated with it. Two sentences can differ in voice and yet have the same basic meaning. However, there may be a change in emphasis and one type of sentence may be more appropriate (see APPROPRIATENESS).

For example, in:

The wind damaged the fence.

the wind is the subject of the verb *damaged*, which is in the **active voice**, while in:

The fence was damaged by the wind.

the fence is the subject of the verb *was damaged*, which is in the **passive voice**.

The first sentence would be a suitable answer to the question:

Did the wind damage anything?

while the second sentence would be a suitable answer to the question:

How did the fence get damaged?

The so-called "agentless" passive, eg:

The fence has been damaged.

is used when the speaker or writer does not know or wish to state the cause, or when the cause is too obvious to be stated.

voice[2] *n*

voiced and **voiceless** (speech sounds)

speech sounds which are produced with the VOCAL CORDS vibrating are called "voiced". Such vibration can be felt when touching the neck in the region of the LARYNX.

For example, VOWELS are usually voiced, and, in English:

(a) the /d/ in /den/ *den* is a voiced STOP

(b) the /z/ in /zɪŋk/ *zinc* is a voiced FRICATIVE.

Speech sounds which are produced without vibration of the vocal cords are called "voiceless".

For example, in English:

(a) the /t/ in /tɪn/ *tin* is a voiceless stop

(b) the /s/ in /sæd/ *sad* is a voiceless fricative.

When a speech sound which is normally voiced is pronounced without vibration or only slight vibration, this is called **devoicing**. Devoicing of voiced consonants often occurs in English when they are at the end of a word, eg *lid* is pronounced [lɪd̥] where the mark ₒ under the /d/ means devoicing.

see also INTERNATIONAL PHONETIC ALPHABET, MANNER OF ARTICULATION, PLACE OF ARTICULATION

[*Further reading*: Gimson 1980]

voice quality /'vɔɪs 'kwɒlǝti ‖ 'kwɑ-/ *n*

the overall impression that a listener obtains of a speaker's voice. It is also at times called **timbre**, and refers to those characteristics of a particular voice that enable the listener to distinguish one voice from another, eg when a person is able to identify a telephone caller.

[*Further reading*: Crystal 1969, 1975]

vowel /'vaʊǝl/ *n*

a speech sound in which the airstream from the lungs is not blocked in any way in the mouth or throat, and which is usually pronounced with vibration of the VOCAL CORDS, eg English /iː/ in /siː/ *see* and /uː/ in /tuː/ *too*.

The type of vowel sound which is produced depends largely on the position of the tongue:

(a) which part of the tongue (the front, the middle, or the back) is raised

(b) how far the tongue is raised.

A division of vowels can be made into **front**, **central**, and **back vowels** (according to which part of the tongue is raised) and **close**, **half-close**, **half-open**, and **open vowels** (according to how far the tongue is raised).

For example, /iː/ in /tiː/ *tea* is a close front vowel and /ɑː/ in /fɑːðǝʳ/ *father* is an open back vowel.

Sometimes, instead of the four-way division for tongue height, a

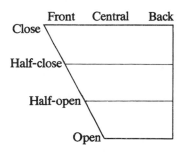

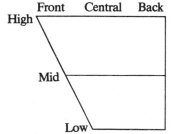

three-way division is made: **high**, **mid**, and **low vowels**. Thus /iː/
would be described as a high front vowel and /ɑː/ as a low back
vowel.

Vowel sounds also depend on the shape of the lips. The lips are
rounded for **rounded vowels**, eg /uː/ in /ʃuː/ *shoe*, and the lips are
spread for **unrounded vowels**, eg /iː/ in /biː/ *bee*.

see also CARDINAL VOWEL, MANNER OF ARTICULATION, NASAL, PLACE OF
ARTICULATION, SEMI-VOWEL

[*Further reading*: Fromkin & Rodman 1983; Gimson 1980]

vowel harmony /'vaʊəl 'hɑːməni ‖ 'hɑr-/ *n*
a modification (ASSIMILATION) of the pronunciation of vowels in a
word so that one agrees or "harmonizes" with another one.

For example, in Turkish the word for the number *1* is *bir* and for
the number *10* is *on*. When suffixes are added to them, the vowel of
the suffix must be either a front vowel or a back vowel, depending
on the vowel that precedes it, eg:

   bir + *de* = *birde* "at one"
   both /i/ and /e/ are front vowels
   on + *da* = *onda* "at ten"
   both /o/ and /a/ are back vowels.

[*Further reading*: Lehmann 1972]

vowel length /'vaʊəl 'leŋθ/ *n*
the duration of a vowel sound.

In phonetic script (see NOTATION), vowel length is often shown by ː
after the vowel.

Many languages have pairs of similar vowels that differ in length
and usually also in VOWEL QUALITY. For example, in English, /iː/ (as
in /siːt/ *seat*) may be longer than /ɪ/ (as in /sɪt/ *sit*), but it is also
higher and tenser, and may have the quality of a DIPHTHONG.

vowel quality /ˌvaʊəl 'kwɒləti ‖ 'kwɑ-/ *n*
features other than length which distinguish one vowel from
another. Vowel quality is determined by the shape of the mouth
when the particular vowel is produced. The shape of the mouth
varies according to the position of the tongue and the degree of lip
rounding (see VOWEL).

VP /ˌviː 'piː/ *n*
an abbreviation for VERB PHRASE

weak form /'wiːk ˌfɔːm ‖ ˌfɔrm/ *n*
    see under STRONG FORM

weak verb /'wiːk 'vɜːb ‖ 'vɜrb/ *n*
    see under STRONG VERB

weighting /'weɪtɪŋ/ *n*
also **weighted scoring** /ˌweɪtəd 'skɔːrɪŋ/
    (in testing) determining the number of points to be given to correct
    responses in a test, when not all of the responses in a test receive
    the same number of points. Such a SCORING procedure is known as
    weighted scoring.

Wernicke's area /'veənɪkəz ˌeərɪə/ *n*
    see under BRAIN

whole-word method /ˌhəʊl 'wɜːd 'meθəd ‖ -ɜr-/ *n*
also **word method, sight method**
    a method for teaching children to read, commonly used in teaching
    reading in the MOTHER TONGUE, in which children are taught to
    recognize whole words rather than letter-names (as in the ALPHABETIC
    METHOD) or SOUNDS (as in PHONICS). It usually leads to the use of a
    SENTENCE METHOD, where whole sentences are used.

Whorfian hypothesis /'wɔːfiən haɪ'pɒθəsəs ‖ 'wɔr- -'pɑ-/ *n*
    see under LINGUISTIC RELATIVITY

wh-question /ˌdʌbəlju: 'eɪtʃ 'kwestʃən/ *n*
    (in English) a question that begins with *what, who(m), when, where,*
    which, why or *how.*
    see also YES-NO QUESTION

word /wɜːd ‖ wɜrd/ *n*
    the smallest of the LINGUISTIC UNITS which can occur on its own in
    speech or writing.
    It is difficult to apply this criterion consistently. For example, can a
    FUNCTION WORD like *the* "occur on its own"? Is a CONTRACTION like
    can't ("can not") one word or two? Nevertheless, there is evidence
    that NATIVE SPEAKERS of a language tend to agree on what are the
    words of their language.
    In writing, word boundaries are usually recognized by spaces
    between the words. In speech, word boundaries may be recognized
    by slight pauses.
    see also BOUNDARIES, CONTENT WORD, LEXEME

word association /'wɜːd əˌsəʊʃieɪʃən, -ˌsəʊsi- ‖ 'wɜrd/ *n*
    ways in which words come to be associated with each other and
    which influence the learning and remembering of words. In a word-

association test, a person is given a word or list of words and asked to respond with another word or words. Word associations have been studied in SEMANTICS, VERBAL LEARNING theory and PSYCHOLINGUISTICS. The following are common associations to words from American college students:

word	response
accident	*car*
airplane	*fly*
American	*flag*
baby	*child*
depression	*recession*

see also ASSOCIATIVE MEANING

[*Further reading*: Deese 1965]

word blindness /'wɜːd 'blaɪndnəs ‖ 'wɜrd/ *n*
another term for DYSLEXIA

word class /'wɜːd ˌklɑːs ‖ 'wɜrd ˌklæs/ *n*
a group of words which are similar in function.
Words are grouped into word classes according to how they combine with other words, how they change their form, etc.
The most common word classes are the PARTS OF SPEECH: NOUN, VERB, ADJECTIVE, ADVERB, PREPOSITION, PRONOUN, ARTICLE, DEMONSTRATIVE, CONJUNCTION, INTERJECTION, etc.
see also FORM CLASS, OPEN CLASS

word formation /'wɜːd fɔː'meɪʃən ‖ 'wɜrd fɔr-/ *n*
the creation of new words. There are several ways of doing this, including:
(a) the addition of an affix in DERIVATION
(b) the removal of an affix: BACK FORMATION
(c) the addition of a COMBINING FORM
(d) the construction of a COMPOUND WORD
(e) the shortening of an old word, as when *influenza* becomes *flu*
(f) the repetition of a word or part of a word: REDUPLICATION
(g) the invention of a completely new word, such as the mathematical term *googal*
In addition, other processes are sometimes regarded as part of word formation. These include:
(h) the addition of an affix in INFLECTION
(i) the use of words as different PARTS OF SPEECH, as when the noun *cap* is used as the verb *to cap*.

word frequency /'wɜːd 'friːkwənsi ‖ 'wɜrd/ *n*
the frequency with which a word is used in a text or corpus.
see also FREQUENCY[2]

word frequency count /'wɜːd 'friːkwənsi 'kaʊnt ‖ 'wɜrd/
also **word frequency list** /'wɜːd 'friːkwənsi lɪst ‖ 'wɜrd/ *n*
see under FREQUENCY COUNT, FREQUENCY[2]

word list /'wɜːd ˌlɪst ‖ 'wɜrd/ *n*

a list of the basic and most important words in a language or in a REGISTER of a language, generally intended for use as a basis for language teaching or for the preparation of teaching materials. Word lists are usually based on FREQUENCY COUNTs, often supplemented by other measures of the importance of words (see COVERAGE).
[*Further reading*: Hindmarsh 1980]

word method /'wɜːd ˌmeθəd ‖ 'wɜrd/ *n*

another term for WHOLE-WORD METHOD

word order /'wɜːd ˌɔːdəʳ ‖ 'wɜrd ˌɔr-/ *n*

the arrangement of words in a sentence. Languages often differ in their word order.
For example, the past participle occurs in German at the end of the main clause rather than after the auxiliary as in English:
Er hat mir   das Buch gegeben.
He has to me the book given
"He has given me the book."
In English, the position of a word in a sentence often signals its function. Thus, in the sentence:
Dogs eat meat.
the position of *dogs* shows that it is the SUBJECT, and the position of *meat* shows that it is the OBJECT. In some languages, including English, a change from the usual word order may often be used to emphasize or contrast, eg:
That cheese I really don't like.
where the object of the sentence is shifted to the beginning.
see also FUNCTIONAL SENTENCE PERSPECTIVE

writing system /'raɪtɪŋ ˌsɪstəm/ *n*

a system of written symbols which represent the sounds, syllables, or words of a language. The three main types of writing system are ALPHABETIC, based on sounds; SYLLABIC, based on syllables; and IDEOGRAPHIC, based on words.
see also GRAPHEME
[*Further reading*: Gelb 1963]

χ² /ˈkaɪ ˈskweəʳ/ *n*
a symbol for CHI-SQUARE

yes-no question /ˌjes ˈnəʊ ˈkwestʃən/ *n*
(in English) a question that can be answered with Yes or No, such as a question formed with a MODAL verb or an AUXILIARY VERB. For example:
  Can you swim?
  Are you hungry?
see also WH-QUESTION

Z

zero article /ˈzɪərəʊ ˈɑːtɪkəl ‖ ˈziːrəʊ ˈɑr-/ *n*
see under ARTICLE

Z score /ˈzed ˌskɔːʳ ‖ ˈziː ˌskɔr/ *n*
(in statistics) a STANDARD SCORE expressed in units of STANDARD DEVIATION.

Further reading

Abercrombie, D. 1965 *Studies in phonetics and linguistics*. London: Oxford University Press.

Abercrombie, D. 1969 "Voice qualities". In N. N. Markel (ed) *Psycholinguistics. An introduction to the study of speech and personality*. London: The Dorsey Press.

Aitchison, J. 1978 *Linguistics*. London: Hodder and Stoughton.

Aitchison, J. 1981 *Language change: progress or decay?* London: Fontana Paperbacks.

Alderson, J. and A. Urquhart 1983 *Reading in a Foreign language*. London: Longman.

Alexander, L. G., W. Stannard Allen, R. A. Close, and R. J. O'Neill 1975 *English grammatical structure*. London: Longman.

Anthony, E. M. 1963 "Approach, method, and technique". *English Language Teaching* 17: 63–67.

Ardener, E. (ed) 1971 *Social anthropology and language*. London: Tavistock Publications.

Asher, J. 1977 *Learning another language through actions: the complete teacher's guidebook*. Los Gatos, CA: Sky Oaks Productions.

Austin, J. L. 1962 *How to do things with words*. Cambridge, Mass: Harvard University Press.

Ausubel, D. P. 1968 *Educational psychology – a cognitive view*. New York: Holt, Rinehart, and Winston.

Ausubel, D. P. 1977 *Developmental psychology*. New York: Grune and Stratton.

Bach, E. 1974 *Syntactic theory*. New York: Holt, Rinehart, and Winston.

Bailey, K. D. 1982 (2nd edition) *Methods of social research*. New York: The Free Press.

Bailey, R. W. and M. Görlach (eds) 1982 *English as a world language*. Ann Arbor: University of Michigan Press.

Baker, C. and D. Cokely 1980 *American sign language: a teacher's resource text on grammar and culture*. Maryland: TJ Publishers.

Bernstein, B. 1971 *Class, codes and control 1: theoretical studies towards a sociology of language*. London: Routledge and Kegan Paul.

Berry, M. 1975 *An introduction to systemic linguistics: structures and systems*. London: Batesford.

Bickerton, D. 1975 *Dynamics of a creole system*. London: Cambridge University Press.

Bloomfield, L. 1933 *Language*. New York: Holt.

Bolinger, D. 1975 (2nd edition) *Aspects of language*. New York: Harcourt, Brace, and World.

Brazil, D. C., M. Coulthard, and C. Johns 1980 *Discourse intonation and language teaching*. London: Longman.

Brown, E. K. and J. E. Miller 1980 *Syntax: a linguistic introduction to sentence structure*. London: Hutchinson.

Brown, H. D. 1980 *Principles of language learning and teaching*. New Jersey: Prentice Hall.

Brown, P. and S. Levinson 1978 Universals in language usage: politeness phenomena. In E. Goody (ed) *Questions and politeness: strategies in social interaction*. Cambridge: Cambridge University Press.

Brown, R. 1973 *A first language: the early stages*. Cambridge, Mass: Harvard University Press.

Brown, R. and A. Gilman 1972 "The pronouns of power and solidarity". In P. P. Giglioli (ed) *Language and social context*. Harmondsworth: Penguin.

Burt, M. K. and C. Kiparsky 1972 *The gooficon: a repair manual for English*. Rowley: Newbury House.

Burt, M. K., H. Dulay, and E. Hernández-Chávez 1975 *Bilingual syntax measure 1*. New York: Harcourt, Brace, Jovanovich.

Carroll, J. B. 1973 "Implications of

aptitude test research and psycholinguistic theory for foreign language teaching". *International Journal of Psycholinguistics* 2: 5–14.

Carroll, J. B. 1981 "Twenty-five years of research of foreign language aptitude". In Karl C. Diller (ed) *Universals in language learning aptitude*. Rowley: Newbury House.

Carton, S. A. 1971 "Inferencing; a process in using and learning language". In P. Pimsleur and T. Quinn (eds) *The psychology of second language learning*. Cambridge: Cambridge University Press.

Cherry, C. 1957 *On human communication*. Cambridge, Mass: The MIT Press.

Chomsky, C. 1969 *Acquisition of syntax in children from 5 to 10*. Cambridge, Mass: The MIT Press.

Chomsky, N. 1957 *Syntactic structures*. The Hague: Mouton.

Chomsky, N. 1965 *Aspects of the theory of syntax*. Cambridge, Mass: The MIT Press.

Chomsky, N. 1968 *Language and mind*. New York: Harcourt, Brace, Jovanovich.

Chomsky, N. 1971 "Deep structure, surface structure and semantic representation". In D. D. Steinberg and L. A. Jakobovits (eds) *Semantics: an interdisciplinary reader in philosophy, linguistics and psychology*. London: Cambridge University Press.

Chomsky, N. and M. Halle 1968 *The sound pattern of English*. New York: Harper and Row.

Clark, H. H. and E. Clark 1977 *Psychology and language*. New York: Harcourt, Brace, Jovanovich.

Close, R. A. 1975 *A reference grammar for students of English*. London: Longman.

Clyne, M. 1972 *Perspectives on language contact*. Melbourne: The Hawthorn Press.

Cohen, A. D. 1980 *Testing language ability in the classroom*. Rowley: Newbury House.

Comrie, B. 1976 *Aspect*. Cambridge: Cambridge University Press.

Comrie, B. 1981 *Language universals and linguistic typology*. Oxford: Basil Blackwell.

Corder, S. P. 1973 *Introducing applied linguistics*. Harmondsworth: Penguin.

Coulmas, F. (ed) 1981 *Conversational routine*. The Hague: Mouton.

Coulthard, M. 1985 (2nd edition) *An introduction to discourse analysis*. London: Longman.

Crystal, D. 1969 *Prosodic systems and intonation in English*. London: Cambridge University Press.

Crystal, D. 1975 *The English tone of voice*. London: Edward Arnold.

Cummins, J. 1979 "Linguistic interdependence and the educational development of bilingual children". *Review of Educational Research* 49: 222–251.

Curran, C. A. 1976 *Counseling-learning in second languages*. Apple River: Apple River Press.

Dakin, J. 1973 *The language laboratory and language learning*. London: Longman.

Dale, P. S. 1975 (2nd edition) *Language development: structure and function*. New York: Holt, Rinehart, Winston.

Dalton, P. and W. J. Hardcastle 1977 *Disorders of fluency*. London: Edward Arnold.

Davies, A., C. Criper, and A. Howatt 1984 *Interlanguage*. Edinburgh: Edinburgh University Press.

Deese, J. 1965 *The structure of associations in language and thought*. Baltimore: The Johns Hopkins Press.

Dehn, N. and R. Schank 1982 "Artificial and human intelligence". In R. J. Sternberg (ed) *Handbook of human intelligence*. Cambridge: Cambridge University Press.

de Joia, A. and A. Stenton 1980 *Terms in systemic linguistics: a guide to Halliday*. London: Batesford.

Denes, P. B. and E. N. Pinson 1963 *The speech chain*. Bell Telephone Laboratories.

Deuchar, M. 1984 *British sign language*. London: Routledge and Kegan Paul.

Further reading

de Villiers, J. G. and P. A. de
Villiers 1978 *Language acquisition.*
Cambridge, Mass: Harvard
University Press.
DeVito, J. 1970 *The psychology of
speech and language.* New York:
Random House.
Disick, R. S. 1975 *Individualization of
instruction: strategies and methods.*
New York: Harcourt, Brace,
Jovanovich.
Downing, J. 1967 *Evaluating the
initial teaching alphabet.* London:
Cassell.
Dulay, H. and M. Burt 1974 "Errors
and strategies in child second
language acquisition". *TESOL
Quarterly* 8: 129–136.
Dulay, H., M. Burt and S. Krashen
1982 *Language two.* New York:
Oxford University Press.
Ebel, R. L. 1972 *Essentials of
educational measurement.* Englewood
Cliffs, NJ: Prentice Hall.
Edwards, J. R. 1979 *Language and
disadvantage.* London: Edward
Arnold.
Elliot, A. J. 1981 *Child language.*
Cambridge: Cambridge University
Press.
Ervin, S. and C. E. Osgood 1954
"Second language learning and
bilingualism". In C. E. Osgood and
T. Sebeok (eds) *Psycholinguistics*
(Supplement). *Journal of Abnormal
and Social Psychology* 49: 139–146.
Ervin-Tripp, S. 1972 "Sociolinguistic
rules of address". In J. B. Pride and
J. Holmes (eds) *Sociolinguistics.*
Harmondsworth: Penguin.
Faerch, C. and G. Kasper 1983
*Strategies of interlanguage
communication.* London: Longman.
Fawcett, R. and M. A. K. Halliday
(eds) 1985 *New developments in
systemic linguistics.* London:
Batesford.
Ferguson, C. A. 1959 "Diglossia".
Word 15: 325–340, also 1972 in P. P.
Giglioli (ed) *Language and social
context.* Harmondsworth: Penguin.
Ferguson, C. A. 1971 "Absence of
copula and the notion of simplicity:
a study of normal speech, baby talk,
foreigner talk, and pidgins." In D.

Hymes (ed) *Pidginization and
creolization of languages.* Cambridge:
Cambridge University Press.
Fillmore, C. J. 1968 "The case for
case". In E. Bach and R. T. Harms
(eds) *Universals in linguistic theory.*
New York: Holt, Rinehart, and
Winston.
Fillmore, C. J. 1971 "Types of lexical
information". In D. D. Steinberg
and L. A. Jakobovits (eds)
*Semantics: an interdisciplinary
reader in philosophy, linguistics and
psychology.* London: Cambridge
University Press.
Fishman, J. A. 1971 *Advances in the
sociology of language I.* The Hague:
Mouton.
Fishman, J. A. 1972 *Advances in the
sociology of language II.* The Hague:
Mouton.
Fishman, J. A. 1974 *Advances in
language planning.* The Hague:
Mouton.
Flanders, N.T. 1970 *Analyzing teacher
behavior.* Reading, Mass: Addison-
Wesley.
Fletcher, P. and M. Garman (eds)
1979 *Language acquisition.*
Cambridge: Cambridge University
Press.
Foss, D. J. and D. T. Hakes 1978
*Psycholinguistics: an introduction to
the psychology of language.* New
Jersey: Prentice Hall.
Fromkin, V. and R. Rodman 1983
(2nd edition) *An introduction to
language.* New York: Holt,
Rinehart, and Winston.
Fry, E. 1965 *Teaching faster reading.*
Cambridge: Cambridge University
Press.
Gagné, R. M. 1970 (2nd edition) *The
conditions of learning.* New York:
Holt, Rinehart, and Winston.
Gardner, R. C. and W. E. Lambert
1972 *Attitudes and motivation in
second-language learning.* Rowley:
Newbury House.
Garfinkel, H. 1967 *Studies in
ethnomethodology.* Englewood Cliffs:
Prentice Hall.
Gattegno, C. 1976 *The common sense
of teaching foreign languages.* New
York: Educational Solutions.

Gelb, J. J. 1963 *A study of writing.* Chicago: The University Press.

Giles, H. and P. F. Powesland 1975 *Speech style and social evaluation.* London: Academic Press.

Giles, H. and R. St Clair 1979 *Language and social psychology.* Oxford: Basil Blackwell.

Gimson, A. C. 1980 *An introduction to the pronunciation of English.* London: The English Language Book Society and Edward Arnold.

Glucksberg, S. and J. H. Danks 1975 *Experimental psycholinguistics: an introduction.* New York: John Wiley and Sons.

Goffman, E. 1959 *The presentation of self in everyday life.* New York: Anchor Books.

Goffman, E. 1967 *Interaction ritual: essays on face to face behaviour.* New York: Anchor Books.

Goldman-Eisler, F. 1968 *Psycholinguistics.* London: Academic Press.

Goodacre, E. J. 1978 "Methods of teaching reading". In J. L. Chapman and P. Czerniewska (eds) *Reading: from process to practice.* London: Routledge and Kegan Paul.

Goodman, K. and Y. M. Goodman 1977 "Learning about psycholinguistic processes by analyzing oral reading behavior". *Harvard Educational Review* 47, 3: 317–333.

Gougenheim, G., R. Michea, and P. Rivenc 1964 *L'élaboration du français fondamental (ler. degré).* Paris: Didier.

Greenberg, J. H 1966 (2nd edition) *Universals of language.* Cambridge Mass: The MIT Press.

Grice, H. P. 1967 William James Lectures, Harvard University 1967. Published in part as "Logic in conversation". In P. Cole and J. L. Morgan (eds) 1975 *Syntax and Semantics* vol. 3 (Speech Acts): 41–58.

Guiora, A. Z., B. Beit-Hallami, R. C. L. Brannon, C. Y. Dull, and T. Scovel 1972 "The effects of experimentally induced changes in ego states on pronunciation ability in second language: an exploratory study". *Comprehensive Psychiatry* 13: 421–428.

Haegeman, L. 1982 "English grammar and the Survey of English Usage". *ELT Journal* 36, 4: 248–255.

Halliday, M. A. K. 1967 "Notes on transitivity and theme in English". *Journal of Linguistics* III: 38–81, 199–244, and IV: 179–215.

Halliday, M. A. K. 1970 *A course in spoken English.* London: Oxford University Press.

Halliday, M. A. K. 1978 *Language as social semiotic.* London: Edward Arnold.

Halliday, M. A. K. 1982 *Functional grammar.* London: Edward Arnold.

Halliday, M. A. K. and R. Hasan 1976 *Cohesion in English.* London: Longman.

Hardyck, C. D. and L. F. Petrinovich 1976 (2nd edition) *Introduction to statistics for the behavioral sciences.* Philadelphia: W. B. Saunders.

Hatch, E. (ed) 1978 *Second language acquisition.* Rowley: Newbury House.

Haugen, E. 1969 *The Norwegian language in America: a study in bilingual behavior.* Bloomington: Indiana University Press. (First published 1953 by University of Pennsylvania Press, Philadelphia.)

Heaton, J. B. 1975 *Writing English language tests. London: Longman.*

Herdan, G. 1964 Quantitative linguistics. London: Butterworths.

Hillerich, R. L. 1978 "Toward an assessable definition of literacy". In L. J. Chapman and P. Czerniewska (eds) *Reading: from process to practice.* London: Routledge and Kegan Paul.

Hindmarsh, R. 1980 *Cambridge English lexicon.* Cambridge: Cambridge University Press.

Howatt, A. 1974 "The background to course design". In J. P. B. Allen and S. P. Corder (eds) *Techniques in applied linguistics: the Edinburgh course in applied linguistics.* Vol. 3. Oxford: Oxford University Press.

Howatt, A. 1983 *A history of English*

language teaching. Oxford: Oxford University Press.

Hudson, R. 1981 *Sociolinguistics*. Cambridge: Cambridge University Press.

Hughes, A. and P. Trudgill 1979 *English accents and dialects: an introduction to the social and regional varieties of British English*. London: Edward Arnold.

Hunt, K. W. 1966 "Recent measures in syntactic development". *Elementary English* 43: 732–739.

Hyltenstam, K. 1977 "Implicational patterns in interlanguage syntax". *Language Learning* 27, 2: 383–411.

Hyman, L. M. 1975 *Phonology: theory and analysis*. New York: Holt, Rinehart, and Winston.

Hymes, D. (ed) 1964 *Language in culture and society*. New York: Harper and Row.

Hymes, D. 1972 "On communicative competence". In J. B. Pride and J. Holmes (eds) *Sociolinguistics*. Harmondsworth: Penguin.

Hymes, D. 1974 *Foundations in sociolinguistics*. Philadelphia: University of Pennsylvania Press.

Ilson, R. F. 1982 "The Survey of English Usage: past, present – and future". *ELT Journal* 36, 4:242–248.

Ilson, R. F. 1984 "The Survey, the language, and the teacher". *World Language English* 3, 1.

Ivic, M. 1965 *Trends in linguistics*. The Hague: Mouton.

Jakobovits, L. A. 1970 *Foreign language learning*. Rowley: Newbury House.

Jakobson. R., G. Fant, and M. Halle 1952 Preliminaries to speech analysis technical report 13, MIT Acoustics Laboratory, MIT Press, reprinted 1963.

James, C. 1980 *Contrastive analysis*. London: Longman.

Johnson, K. 1982 *Communicative syllabus design and methodology*. Oxford: Pergamon.

Johnson-Laird, P. N. and P. C. Wason (eds) 1977 *Thinking: readings in cognitive science*. Cambridge: Cambridge University Press.

Kachru, B. B. 1981 "The pragmatics of non-native varieties of English". In L. E. Smith (ed) *English for cross-cultural communication*. London: MacMillan.

Kaplan, R. B. (ed) 1980 *On the scope of applied linguistics*. Rowley: Newbury House.

Katz, J. J. and J. A. Fodor 1963 "The structure of a semantic theory". *Language* 39: 170–210. Reprinted in J. A. Fodor and J. J. Katz 1964 *The structure of language: readings in the philosophy of language*. Englewood Cliffs: Prentice Hall.

Kelly, L. G. 1969 *Twenty-five centuries of language teaching*. Rowley: Newbury House.

Kiparsky, P. and C. Kiparsky 1971 "Fact". In D. D. Steinberg and L. A. Jakobovits (eds) *Semantics: an interdisciplinary reader in philosophy, linguistics and psychology*. London: Cambridge University Press.

Klare, G. R. 1978 "Assessing readability". In J. L. Chapman and P. Czerniewska (eds) *Reading: from process to practice*. London: Routledge and Kegan Paul.

Krashen, S. D. 1978 "The monitor model for second-language acquisition". In R. Gringras (ed) *Second language acquisition and foreign language teaching*. Washington: Center for Applied Linguistics.

Krashen, S. D. 1981 *Second language acquisition and second language learning*. Oxford: Pergamon.

Krashen, S. D. 1985 *The input hypothesis: issues and implications*. London: Longman.

Kress, G. R. (ed) 1976 *Halliday: system and function in language*. London: Oxford University Press.

Kučera, H. and W. Francis 1967 *Computational analysis of present-day American English*. Providence: Brown University Press.

Labov, W. 1972(a) *Sociolinguistic patterns*. Philadelphia: University of Pennsylvania Press.

Labov, W. 1972(b) *Language in the*

inner city: studies in the Black English vernacular. Philadelphia: University of Pennsylvania Press.

Lado, R. 1957 *Linguistics across cultures*. Ann Arbor: University of Michigan Press.

Lakoff, G. 1971 "On generative semantics". In D. D. Steinberg and L. A. Jakobovits (eds) *Semantics: an interdisciplinary reader in philosophy, linguistics and psychology*. London: Cambridge University Press.

Lambert, E. E. 1967 "The social psychology of bilingualism". *Journal of Social Issues* 23: 91–109.

Lamendella, J. T. 1979 "Neurolinguistics". *Annual Review of Anthropology* 8: 373–391.

Lane, H. 1964 "Programmed learning of a second language". *IRAL* 2, 4: 249–301.

Leech, G. 1971 *Meaning and the English Verb*. London: Longman.

Leech, G. 1981 (2nd edition) *Semantics*. Harmondsworth: Penguin.

Leech, G. 1983 *Principles of pragmatics*. London: Longman.

Leech, G. and J. Svartvik 1975 *A communicative grammar of English*. London: Longman.

Lehmann, W. 1972 *Descriptive linguistics*. New York: Random House.

Lehmann, W. 1973 *Historical linguistics: an introduction*. New York: Holt, Rinehart, and Winston.

Lenneberg, E. 1967 *Biological foundations of language*. New York: Wiley.

Levinson, S. 1983 *Pragmatics*. Cambridge: Cambridge University Press.

Li, C. N. and S. A Thompson 1981 *Mandarin Chinese*. Berkeley: University of California Press.

Littlewood, W. 1981 *Communicative language teaching: an introduction*. Cambridge: Cambridge University Press.

Lockwood, D. G. 1972 *Introduction to stratificational linguistics*. New York: Harcourt, Brace, Jovanovich.

Lozanov, G. 1979 *Suggestology and outlines of suggestopedy*. New York: Gordon and Breach.

Lumsdaine, A. A. and R. Glaser (eds) 1960 *Teaching machines and programmed learning*. Washington, DC: National Education Association.

Lyons, J. 1968 *Introduction to theoretical linguistics*. London: Cambridge University Press.

Lyons, J. 1977 *Semantics I and II*. London: Cambridge University Press.

Lyons, J. 1981 *Language, meaning and context*. London: Fontana.

Mackay, R., R. Barkham, and R. R. Jordan (eds) 1979 *Reading in a second language*. Rowley: Newbury House.

Mackey, W. F. 1965 *Language teaching analysis*. London: Longman.

McDonough, S. 1981 *Psychology in foreign language teaching*. London: George Allen and Unwin.

McNeill, D. 1966 "Developmental psycholinguistics". In F. Smith and G. A. Miller (eds) *The genesis of language: a psycholinguistic approach*. Cambridge, Mass: The MIT Press

McNeill, D. 1970 *The acquisition of language; the study of developmental psycholinguistics*. New York: Harper and Row.

Madsen, H. S. and J. D. Bowen 1978 *Adaptation in language teaching*. Rowley: Newbury House.

Miller, G. A. 1962 *Psychology: the science of mental life*. Harmondsworth: Penguin.

Miller, G. A. and P. N. Johnson-Laird 1976 *Language and perception*. Cambridge: Cambridge University Press.

Milroy, L. 1980 *Language and social networks*. Oxford: Basil Blackwell.

Money, J. (ed) 1962 *Reading disability: progress and research needs in dyslexia*. Baltimore: The Johns Hopkins Press.

Mowrer, O. H. 1960 *Learning theory and behavior*. New York: Wiley.

Munby, J. 1978 *Communicative syllabus design*. Cambridge: Cambridge University Press.

Murray, D. M. 1980 "Writing as process: how writing finds its own meaning". In T. R. Donovan and W. McClelland (eds) *Eight* approaches to the teaching of composition. Illinois: National Council of Teachers of English.

Naiman, N., M. Frohlich, and H. H. Stern 1975 The good language learner. Toronto: Ontario Institute for Studies in Education.

Neisser, U. 1967 Cognitive psychology. New York: Appleton-Century Crofts.

Neustupný, J. V. 1978 Post-structural approaches to language: language theory in a Japanese context. Tokyo: University of Tokyo Press.

Ogden, C. K. 1930 Basic English. London: Routledge and Kegan Paul.

Ogden, C. K. and I. A. Richards. 1923 The meaning of meaning. (8th edition, 1946) London: Routledge.

Oller, J. W., Jr 1979 Language tests at school. London: Longman.

Osgood, C. E. 1957 "A behavioristic analysis of perception and language as cognitive phenomena". In Contemporary approaches to cognition. Cambridge, Mass: Harvard University Press.

Osgood, C. E. 1964 "Semantic differential technique in the comparative study of cultures". American Anthropologist LXVI: 171–200.

Palmer F. R. 1971 Grammar. Harmondsworth: Penguin.

Palmer, F. R. 1981 (2nd edition) Semantics. Cambridge: Cambridge University Press.

Parker, L. L. 1977 Bilingual education: current perspectives. Washington: Center for Applied Linguistics.

Paulston, C. B. 1980 "The sequencing of structural pattern drills". In K. Croft (ed) Readings on English as a second language. Cambridge, Mass: Winthrop.

Penfield, W. and R. Lamar Roberts 1959 Speech and brain mechanisms. Princeton: Princeton University Press.

Piaget, J. 1952 The origins of intelligence in children. New York: Norton.

Piaget, J. 1955 The language and thought of the child. Translated by M. Gabain. Cleveland: Meridian.

Pike, K. L. 1967 Language in relation to a unified theory of the structure of human behavior. The Hague: Mouton.

Platt, J. T. and H. K. Platt 1975 The social significance of speech. Amsterdam: North Holland.

Platt, J. T. and H. Weber 1980 English in Singapore and Malaysia – status: features: functions. Kuala Lumpur: Oxford University Press.

Popham, W. J. 1975 Educational evaluation. Englewood Cliffs: Prentice Hall.

Prabhu, N. S. 1983 "Procedural syllabuses". Paper presented at RELC seminar on new trends on language syllabus design. Singapore: RELC.

Pratt, D. 1980 Curriculum: design and development. New York: Harcourt, Brace, Jovanovich.

Pride, J. B. (ed) 1982 New Englishes. Rowley: Newbury House.

Pride, J. B. and J. Holmes (eds) 1972 Sociolinguistics. Harmondsworth: Penguin.

Quirk, R. and S. Greenbaum 1970 Elicitation experiments in English: linguistic studies in use and attitude. London: Longman.

Quirk, R., S. Greenbaum, G. Leech, and J. Svartvik 1985 A comprehensive grammar of the English language. London: Longman.

Richards, J. C. 1970 "A psycholinguistic measure of vocabulary selection". IRAL VII, 2: 87–102.

Richards, J. C. (ed) 1974 Error analysis: perspectives on second language acquisition. London: Longman.

Richards, J. C. 1982 "Rhetorical and communicative styles in the new varieties of English". In J. B. Pride (ed) New Englishes. Rowley: Newbury House.

Richards, J. C. and T. Rodgers 1982 "Method: approach, design, procedure". TESOL Quarterly 16, 2: 153–168.

Richards, J. C. and T. Rodgers 1986 *Approaches and methods in language teaching*. New York: Cambridge University Press.

Rivers, W. M. 1964 *The psychologist and the foreign language teacher*. Chicago: The University of Chicago Press.

Rivers, W. M. 1972 *Speaking in many tongues*. Rowley: Newbury House.

Rivers, W. M. 1981 (2nd edition) *Teaching foreign language skills*. Chicago: University of Chicago Press.

Rivers, W. M. and M. S. Temperley 1978 *A practical guide to the teaching of English*. New York: Oxford University Press.

Robins, R. H. 1980 (3rd edition) *General linguistics: an introductory survey*. London: Longman.

Robinson, P. 1980 *ESP (English for specific purposes)*. Oxford: Pergamon.

Sacks, H., E. A. Schegloff, and G. Jefferson 1974 "A simplest systematic for the organization of turn-taking for conversation". *Language* 50: 696–735.

Sager, J. C., D. Dungworth, and P. F. McDonald 1980 *English special languages*. Wiesbaden: Brandstetter.

Saussure, F. de (1916) 1966 *Course in general linguistics*. New York: McGraw-Hill.

Savard, J-G. and J. C. Richards 1969 *Les indices d'utilité du vocabulaire fondamental français*. Québec: Les Presses de l'Université Laval.

Saville-Troike, M. 1982 *The ethnography of communication: an introduction*. Oxford: Basil Blackwell.

Schachter, J. 1974 "An error in error analysis". *Language Learning* 24, 2: 73–107.

Schank, R. C. and R. P. Abelson 1977 *Scripts, plans, goals, and understanding*. Hillsdale, NJ: Erlbaum.

Schegloff, E. A. 1972 "Sequencing in conversational openings". In J. J. Gumperz and D. Hymes (eds) *Directions in sociolinguistics*. New York: Holt, Rinehart, and Winston.

Schegloff, E. A., G. Jefferson, and H. Sacks 1977 "The preference for self correction in the organization of repair in conversation". *Language* 53: 361–382.

Schumann, J. H. 1978 *The pidginization process: a model for second language acquisition*. Rowley: Newbury House.

Scriven, M. 1967 "The methodology of evaluation". In R. W. Tyler, R. M. Gagné, and M. Scriven (eds) *Perspectives on curriculum evaluation*. AERA Monograph Series on Curriculum Evaluation No. 1. Chicago: Rand McNally and Co.

Searle, J. R. 1965 "What is a speech act?" In M. Black (ed) *Philosophy in America*. London: Allen and Unwin.

Searle, J. R. 1981 (2nd edition) *Speech acts*. London: Cambridge University Press.

Selinker, L. 1972 "Interlanguage". *IRAL* 10: 201–231.

Shuy, R. W. and R. W. Fasold (eds) 1973 *Language attitudes: current trends and prospects*. Washington: Georgetown University Press.

Sinclair, J. McH. and R. M. Coulthard 1975 *Towards an analysis of discourse*. London: Oxford University Press.

Sinclair, J. McH and D. Brazil 1982 *Teacher talk*. Oxford: Oxford University Press.

Skinner, B. F. 1957 *Verbal behavior*. New York: Appleton Century Crofts.

Skutnabb-Kangas, T. and P. Toukomaa 1976 *Teaching migrant children's mother tongue and learning the language of the host country in the context of the sociocultural situation of the migrant family*. Helsinki: The Finnish National Commission for UNESCO.

Slobin, D. I. 1973 "Cognitive prerequisites for the acquisition of grammar". In C. A. Ferguson and D. I. Slobin (eds) *Studies of child language development*. New York: Holt, Rinehart, and Winston.

Smith, F. 1971 *Understanding reading*. New York: Holt, Rinehart, and Winston.

Smith, L. E. (ed) 1981 *English for*

cross-cultural communication.
London: Macmillan.

Snow, C. E. and C. A. Ferguson
(eds) 1977 *Talking to children:
language input and acquisition.*
Cambridge: Cambridge University
Press.

Spolsky, B. 1978 *Educational
linguistics: an introduction.* Rowley:
Newbury House.

Steinberg, D. 1982 *Psycholinguistics:
language, mind and world.* London:
Longman.

Stenson, N. 1974 "Induced errors".
In J. Schumann and N. Stenson
(eds) *New frontiers in second
language learning.* Rowley: Newbury
House.

Stevick, E. 1980 *A way and ways.*
Rowley: Newbury House.

Svartvik, J. 1973 *Errata: papers in
error analysis.* Lund: CWK Gleerup.

Swain, M. 1978 "Home-school
language switching". In J. C.
Richards (ed) *Understanding second
and foreign language learning.*
Rowley: Newbury House.

Swain, M., G. Dumas, and N.
Naiman 1974 "Alternatives to
spontaneous speech: elicited
translation and imitation as
indicators of second language
competence." *Working Papers in
Bilingualism* 4: 68–79.

Tarone, E. 1977 "Conscious
communication strategies: a progress
report". In H. D. Brown, C. Yorio,
and R. Crymes (eds) *On TESOL
1977.* Washington DC: TESOL

Terrell, T. D. 1977 "A natural
approach to second language
acquisition and learning". *Modern
Language Journal* 61: 325–337.

Titone, R. 1968 *Teaching foreign
languages: an historical sketch.*
Washington: Georgetown University
Press.

Todd, L. 1984 *Modern Englishes:
pidgins and creoles.* Oxford: Basil
Blackwell.

Trudgill, P. 1975 *Accent, dialect and
the school.* London: Edward Arnold.

Trudgill, P. (ed) 1978 *Sociolinguistic
patterns in British English.* London:
Edward Arnold

Trudgill, P. 1980 (2nd edition)
Sociolinguistics. Harmondsworth:
Penguin.

Turner, R. (ed) 1970
Ethnomethodology. Harmondsworth:
Penguin.

Ure, J. 1971 "Lexical density and
register differentiation". In G. E.
Perren and J. L. M. Trim (eds)
Applications of linguistics.
Cambridge: Cambridge University
Press.

Vachek, J. (ed) 1964 *A Prague school
reader in linguistics.* Bloomington,
Indiana: Indiana University Press.

Valette, R. M. 1977 (2nd edition)
Modern language testing. New York:
Harcourt, Brace, Jovanovich.

Van Dijk, T. A. 1977 *Text and
context: explorations in the semantics
and pragmatics of discourse.*
London: Longman.

Van Ek, J. A. 1976 *The threshold
level.* Strasbourg: Council of
Europe.

Van Ek, J. A. and L. G. Alexander
1975 *Threshold level English.*
Oxford: Pergamon.

Vygotsky, L. S. 1962 *Thought and
language.* Translated by E.
Hanfmann and G. Vakar.
Cambridge, Mass: The MIT Press.

Wardhaugh, R. 1969 *Reading: a
psycholinguistic perspective.* New
York: Harcourt, Brace, and World.

Watts, A. F. 1944 *The language and
mental development of children.*
London: Harrap.

Wells, J. C. 1982 *Accents of English.*
Cambridge: Cambridge University
Press.

West, M. 1953 *A general service list
of English words.* London:
Longman.

Widdowson, H. G. 1978 *Teaching
language as communication.* Oxford:
Oxford University Press.

Wilkins, D. 1976 *Notional syllabuses.*
Oxford: Oxford University Press.

Williams, F. 1970 *Language and
poverty.* Chicago: Markham.

Winitz, H. (ed) 1981 *The
comprehension approach to foreign
language instruction.* Rowley:
Newbury House.